COLLECTOR'S ENCYCLOPEDIA OF

DEPRESSION GLASS

SIXTEENTH EDITION

GENE & CATHY FLORENCE

America's #1 Bestselling Glass Book!

COLLECTOR BOOKS
A Division of Schroeder Publishing Co., Inc.

PRICING

All prices in this book are retail prices for mint condition glassware. This book is intended to be only a guide to prices as there are a few regional price differences that cannot reasonably be dealt with herein. You may expect dealers to pay from 30% to 50% less than the prices quoted. Glass that is in less than mint condition, i.e., chipped, cracked, scratched, repaired, or poorly moulded, will bring only a small percentage of the price of glass that is in mint condition — if wanted at all.

Prices have become reasonably well established due to national advertising by dealers, the Depression glass shows held from coast to coast, and the Internet. I have my own web page operated for books and glass (www.geneflorence.com). However, there are still some regional differences in prices due partly to glass being more available in some areas than in others. Companies distributed certain pieces in some areas that they did not in others. Generally speaking, prices are about the same among dealers from coast to coast.

Prices tend to increase swiftly on rare items and they have increased as a whole due to more collectors entering the field and people becoming aware of the worth of Depression glass.

One of the important aspects of this book is the attempt to illustrate as well as realistically price those items that are in demand. All items listed are priced. The desire is to give you the best factual guide to collectible patterns of Depression glass available.

MEASUREMENTS

To illustrate why there are discrepancies in measurements, I offer the following sample from just two years of Hocking's catalog references:

Year	Item	Ounces	Item	Ounces	Item	Ounces
1935	Pitcher	37, 58, 80	Flat Tumbler	5, 9, 13½	Footed Tumbler	10, 13
1935	Pitcher	37, 60, 80	Flat Tumbler	5, 9, 10, 15	Footed Tumbler	10, 13
1936	Pitcher	37, 65, 90	Flat Tumbler	5, 9, 13½	Footed Tumbler	10, 15
1936	Pitcher	37, 60, 90	Flat Tumbler	5, 9, 13½	Footed Tumbler	10, 15

All measurements in this book are exact as to some manufacturer's listing or to actual measurement. You may expect variance of up to ½" or 1 – 5 ounces. This may be due to mould variations or reworking worn moulds or changes by the manufacturer as well as rounding off measurements for catalog listings.

On the Cover:
Front: Green Lotus lamp, $295.00; yellow Iris sugar, $195.00; and pink Mayfair cookie jar, $55.00. Back: Lotus.

Title Page: Courtesy of artist Linda Humphrey

Cover design by Beth Summers
Book design by Terri Hunter

Collector Books
P.O. Box 3009
Paducah, KY 42002-3009
www.collectorbooks.com

Gene and Cathy Florence
P.O. Box 22186   P.O.Box 64
Lexington, KY 40522   or   Astatula, FL 34705

Searching For A Publisher?

We are always looking for people knowledgeable within their fields. If you feel that there is a real need for a book on your collectible subject and have a large comprehensive collection, contact us.

The current values in this book should be used only as a guide. They are not intended to set prices, which vary from one section of the country to another. Auction prices as well as dealer prices vary greatly and are affected by condition as well as demand. Neither the authors nor the publisher assumes responsibility for any losses that might be incurred as a result of consulting this guide.

CONTENTS

ACKNOWLEDGMENTS

I treasure all the information dealers, collectors, and readers have shared with me through writing, e-mailing, calling, and talking to me at shows in various regions of the country. Thanks for transporting those newly encountered pieces to shows for documentation and sending pictures of your discoveries. Thanks for the 1930s coupon advertisements that you've shown me promoting products from seeds to farm equipment with Depression glass "enticements." Thank you for your exceptional knowledge regarding the glassware you collect, what you find and can't find in the region in which you live. All this has been priceless to me and to collectors as a whole. All these efforts combined have greatly added to the body of knowledge regarding Depression glass.

I have appreciated the shows that Depression glass clubs and show promoters have invited me to. I have found them to be an immeasurable source of information about the glass. I hope I helped to promote the glass and shows to all our benefit. I know I certainly tried. However, 32 years of doing this are beginning to take a toll on both my wife, Cathy, and me. I hope you will forgive us for slowing down our scampering about the country and cutting back on many of the shows we've been privileged to be a part of in the past. Cathy's help is inestimable; quite honestly, these books would not exist without her, beginning with her typing my first longhand manuscript. She has worked many years at my side as my chief editor, critic, and proofreader and, most recently, research assistant — all while wearing her other hats of wife and mother. She was always the labor end of unpacking, packing, sorting, and labeling the glass. Unfortunately, as her job descriptions expanded, so did her stress levels, which are not being resolved by our chaotic schedule. We have decided our shows and travel should be dramatically reduced and have taken steps to do so.

Specific thanks regarding this particular book need to go to Dick and Pat Spencer, Dan and Geri Tucker, Glen and Carolyn Robertson, Lorrie Kitchen, Verlon Webb, Barbara Wolfe and Marianne Jackson at Anchor Hocking, and various readers throughout the United States and Canada for glass photos and information provided. There have also been bits and pieces forthcoming from readers out of the United States, in Australia, New Zealand, The Philippines, England, Canada, and Puerto Rico.

I need to thank my children who come to my rescue from time to time. Marc, my youngest, who is trying to oversee my web page while handling a full-time work schedule teaching computer technology all over the country. No, I do not have much time to surf the net myself. These books take more of my time than I care to admit or than you could ever imagine. Chad, my eldest, has tackled the job of helping Cathy organize the storage area recently and has taken time out to help at a show amidst working in construction as much as weather permits. Thanks, too, to Cathy's mom and dad, Sibyl and Charles, who have helped us wash, sort, pack, repack, shelve, measure, and otherwise do whatever was needed to be done for both photography sessions and shows. Any way you slice it, there's an enormous amount of work that must be accomplished by many hands before these books come to you with a wealth of current information systematically prepared between glossy covers.

Richard Walker of New York and Charles R. Lynch of Kentucky creatively achieved photographs herein. They both labored long over hundreds of setups during one 12-day session and several smaller sessions scheduled throughout the two-year period since the last book. Glass arranging, unpacking, sorting, and repacking was accomplished by Jane White, Zibby Walker, Dick and Pat Spencer, and Cathy Florence completed carting and repacking. Billy Schroeder and some other members of the Collector Books' shipping crew simplified loading and unloading vans. In addition, Jane White and many of the crew previously mentioned helped on several other photography sessions for my books done independently of my being there.

Thanks for the expertise of the editorial department at Collector Books, especially Terri Hunter, who knew how to take my often-piecemeal mailings and make them into a book.

If you write me, please enclose a SASE (self-addressed, stamped envelope) that is large enough to return your photos if you wish them back. Writing books from January through May (three this year) leaves precious little time for answering the stacks of letters that arrive each week. I want to thank the thoughtful people who send postcards with the possible answers to their questions for me to check off the correct response. Those are a joy. I want to inform people who forget to include the SASE that they're wasting their time writing; they'll not be answered. I want to encourage you to send pictures of items you hope to have identified, or even pencil rubbings of the pattern, rather than descriptions. I want to explain that my expertise, such as it is, lies in knowledge of the patterns presented in my books. I know quite a bit about the collectible patterns I have researched and will gladly help you any way I can with those when time permits. I don't know the names, manufacturers, line numbers, and worth of every single piece of Depression glassware made nor do I have the time to research them for you. I now have three *Florence's Glassware Pattern Identification Guides* that contain over 1,500 patterns identified for you by names, dates, colors, companies, and how many different pieces were made when known. They should save you searching in over 300 books on your own. No, I don't provide lists or prices for those patterns. The books are for identifying your patterns only. We're trying to document those "wonder who made this" type pieces you see at markets but never in books. Please know these words are not so much sour grapes as self-preservation. I'm suffering from a tidal wave of questions I have no knowledge of and it's a waste and frustration for both of us. I would hate to come to the place where I'd discourage your writing me at all; but these questions on everything other than the glassware in my books is giving me pause to consider that. You wouldn't believe the questions I get on pottery, musical, and metallic objects, let alone those wanting prices for everything the person owns.

This book was written in Florida, sitting before my computer that faces the lake, where I usually can watch my fishing poles on the dock, alligators cruising by, and see the fellow anglers motoring along and occasionally hauling up a fish. Unfortunately, the water levels are down and the fishing is so uncertain that I don't have to worry about missing the fish while confined inside.

As we go to press with this sixteenth edition, thank you once again, my readers, for making this America's #1 bestselling book on glass. I encourage you to enlighten your friends on Depression glass. Point them to, or give them, a book. In the grand scheme of things, it appears that only a few of us realize this glass's inherent, as well as monetary, value. I receive letters nearly every day from people who have just learned about Depression glass — or who just discovered they essentially gave away some family heirlooms at a sale. Also, if you get a chance, educate and delight yourself by taking in a Depression glass show. They're "awesome and wonderful fun" and "well worth the price of admission" — quotes from people passing my table at shows. Collecting is satisfying, stimulating, exasperating fun! I wish you very good luck in your treasure hunting for Depression era glassware!

PREFACE

As I sit down to write this sixteenth book, I have to remind myself that, every day, new people are still discovering this beautiful, old Depression era glassware; and I have to try to somehow acquaint them with all the information I've gathered over 32 years and to do it in a way that the readers who have heard it all before are not totally bored. For those who don't know, these books are completely rewritten every two years to include all the latest facts, finds, prices, and changes noticed by me.

Depression glass as defined in this book is the colored glassware made fundamentally during the Depression years in the colors of amber, blue, black, crystal, green, pink, red, yellow, and white. There are other colors and some glass made before, as well as after, this time; but primarily, the glass within this book was manufactured from the late 1920s through 1940. Further, this publication is mostly concerned with the inexpensively made dinnerware turned out by machine in bulk and sold through smaller stores or given away as publicity or premium items for other products of that time. Depression glass was often packaged in cereal boxes and flour sacks or given as incentive gifts for buying tickets or products at the local movie theaters, gasoline stations, and grocery stores. Merchandise was offered with magazine subscriptions, for buying (or selling) certain amounts of seeds, or in return for amounts of coupons garnered with butter or soap purchases. One collector showed me an ad with a picture of a butter dish that could be had by buying a cream separator, something dairy operators might know more about than I.

We are running out of space in this book for adding more patterns after 11 additional ones this time. If we have to add more pages, the book is going to have to increase in price, something we have tried not to do these many years of color production. (Have you noticed all the new books rolling off the presses with only a few pages of color clustered in the center of the book, and then miles of black and white history filling page after page?)

Foremost, I need to address the economy caused downsizing of pricing that is apparent in some pattern pieces. Remember, I don't make up these prices; I simply record or acknowledge what is happening in the market. As I write this, the war in Iraq is ending and the economy is seemingly headed upward. Therefore, after reflecting some of the market unrest, perhaps we can look forward to glass spheres beginning to recover from their doldrums. The wild, surplus "paper" wealth that people had to toss about on collectibles a few years ago is presently being parsimoniously allocated. This has happened before, so don't panic. Now is the time to pick up some bargains. I remember my publisher being very concerned once before when I reflected lower pricing in a book. Then, as now, I felt my job was to report market prices as accurately as I knew how. This is how it is now as I write and price this book. Do I expect it to continue in this fashion? I doubt it. It didn't before; but I wasn't born with a crystal ball and there are no guarantees with much of anything in this life — except change. I think I can guarantee changes happening in our glass markets. Glass collecting isn't all about money, anyway. The majority collect because of nostalgia or some emotional pull of the glass itself. I very much doubt that appeal is suddenly going away.

Collectors have also been seeking later made patterns encompassing the time from 1940 to the 1960s, which has led to a companion book, entitled *Collectible Glassware from the 40s, 50s, 60s...*, now in its sixth edition. However, to correctly date glassware from this latter period, it was necessary to move some patterns previously exclusive to this Depression glass book into the time frame encompassed by the 50s book. If your pattern is no longer found within this Depression book, you should seek it in the 40s, 50s, 60s.... Also, there were elegant, etched tablewares being manufactured during this 20s through 60s time frame which, today, are highly collectible; so, those have been covered in my *Elegant Glassware of the Depression Era* book.

There have been significant changes in collecting Depression glass since my first book was published in 1972. Prices have increased faster than stocks; seemingly plentiful patterns have been gathered into countless collections throughout the world and removed from the marketplace. Collectors, rather than accumulating complete sets of dishes, have branched into collecting items only from many different patterns, i.e., cups and saucers, pitchers, shakers, tumblers, shot glasses, cruets, sugar and creamer sets, luncheon plates. Smaller Depression patterns and previously ignored crystal and satinized wares have attracted patrons; collecting a rainbow set (many colors) of one or more patterns is now in fashion, rather than the one-color collecting of old. Honestly, anything that is Depression glass, a recognized pattern or not, suddenly has added significance and collectibility. Glass is now sold daily on the Internet, which has had the greatest impact on the collectibles market in the two years since my last book. Well-educated glass collectors are more the norm than the exception, and they are crossing fields and branching into other areas of glass appreciation. This ever-broadening interest has prompted me to research 14 more books in the field of Depression glass (the Elegant and 50s previously mentioned), one on kitchenware items of the Depression, seven others on the very rare glassware of those times, not to mention the latest ones on stemware identification, candlesticks, and three on pattern identification. Regarding these last three, I have had several dealers write or seek me out to express their gratitude in saving them endless hours of searching through their libraries of books to identify some new piece they've acquired. I'll admit to being rather surprised and extremely gratified by those comments. These words of encouragement are certainly appreciated, but truthfully, not as ego swelling as it sounds because I recognize that the books are not just my work anymore. They have evolved into something of a community work at this juncture with me acting as liaison. Be sure and read the acknowledgments for the countless people who contribute to this body of work.

Over 40 previously unknown pieces have been added to the listings since the last edition, as well as some previously unseen colors in several patterns. Those of you who feel nothing new is ever found should look closely at your favorite pattern. Similarly, there have been deletions of a dozen pieces that have never been found. These were due to original catalog misinformation or misinterpretation, entry mistakes, or errors of measurements in the past.

Information for this book comes from over 32 years of research and selling experience, via communication with fellow dealers and collectors throughout the country, and over 1,525,000 miles of traveling the country, hunting and locating glassware. I must say that some of the most interesting (and surprising) enlightenment has come directly from readers, sharing catalogs, magazines, photographs of glass, and the glass itself. (See "Kaleidoscope" for an example.) They may have a family member who worked at a plant, talked with an engraver, heard something at a market, or found something at a garage sale they thought significant. More importantly, they bothered to share it. It is invaluable information and adds to all our knowledge of the glass.

ADAM, JEANNETTE GLASS COMPANY, 1932 – 1934

Colors: pink, green, crystal, some yellow, and Delphite blue (See Reproduction Section.)

Jeannette's Adam pattern continues to be one of the most collected patterns in Depression glass. There is a multitude of new collectors seeking this pattern based upon the number of questions I am receiving about reproductions. Only the butter dish has been reproduced. The rip-off artists reproduced a regular pink butter and lid years ago in Taiwan; but it is no major concern now, because I have regularly explained how to tell old from new in the Reproduction Section at the back of the book. Do not apply that method of telling old from new to any other piece of Adam. It only holds true for the butter top and no other piece. Prices on pink butters dipped temporarily when the reproductions first appeared, but they are back to as normal as can be expected 20 plus years later in a struggling economy. Green butters were never reproduced.

Adam has Deco era shapes including triangles, squares, and linear lines, combined with a kind of Art Nouveau scrolled center motif of fern-like leaves surrounded by a festoon of petite flowers. Add to that the variety of pieces made in the line and the fact that it was only made for a three-year period, and you have several reasons for collecting Adam. Thirty years ago, nearly every booth at markets or shows displayed pieces of Adam. Today, you are fortunate to come across a few pieces. Therefore, new collectors must be aware that it will probably take some time to gather an entire set piece by piece. However, one cool thing about collecting these days is that table settings don't have to match. Any woman's magazine you pick up shows myriad combinations of wares delightfully presented. Accordingly, with imagination, you can effectively use whatever you find.

Specifics to know include that pitchers come with both square and round bases. The square has the motif on the base while the round has only concentric rings. These round-footed pitchers are usually very light in color and are sometimes ignored due to that. They are much rarer than their counterparts. Candy and sugar lids are one and the same. Any round plates or saucers you stumble upon are rare. There are at least five different pieces found in crystal, i.e. pitcher, ashtray, coaster, divided relish, and grill plate, and almost nobody cares at present even though they are truly rare.

Inner rim damage is a plague for bowls, which have been used and stacked in cabinets for about 70 years. Ads say "irr" for inner rim roughness. You do not want to pay mint prices for damaged merchandise. There are skilled people who can smooth these chips out if they aren't too bad. Do not routinely assume everybody grinding glass is competent. Some will do more damage to your piece than if you had left it alone. The good ones fix pieces so you cannot tell there was damage. If you can see where they fixed it, then it isn't fixed properly.

A particularly rare pink butter dish top possesses *both* the Adam (outside) motif and the Sierra (inside) mold design. It's one top having two designs and if you find one, it will bring you big bucks in today's marketplace. The first one found sold for $250.00 in 1974. There is, also, a rare lamp to be found. It's made from a notched sherbet, frosted to hide the cord and covered with a metal cover, which holds a tall bulb. One just sold a few years ago on an Internet auction for over $2,000.00. However, the last one I heard sell was for less than $500.00. Prices are not gospel when quoted from an auction, as rare things will sell cheaply if only one person is interested. Iced tea tumblers and cereal bowls, though not exactly rare, will be hard to come by as they have vanished from the markets into collections.

	Pink	Green			Pink	Green
Ashtray, 4½"	30.00	28.00		**Cup	28.00	25.00
Bowl, 4¾", dessert	25.00	25.00		Lamp	495.00	495.00
Bowl, 5¾", cereal	50.00	55.00		Pitcher, 8", 32 ounce	45.00	45.00
Bowl, 7¾"	30.00	30.00		Pitcher, 32 ounce, round base	75.00	
Bowl, 9", no cover	45.00	45.00		Plate, 6", sherbet	10.00	10.00
Bowl cover, 9"	25.00	45.00		***Plate, 7¾", square salad	18.00	17.00
Bowl, 9", covered	80.00	95.00		Plate, 9", square dinner	35.00	32.00
Bowl, 10", oval	35.00	40.00		Plate, 9", grill	28.00	23.00
Butter dish bottom	30.00	65.00		Platter, 11¾"	33.00	35.00
Butter dish top	80.00	385.00		Relish dish, 8", divided	20.00	25.00
Butter dish & cover	110.00	450.00		Salt & pepper, 4", footed	100.00	125.00
Butter dish combination				****Saucer, 6", square	6.00	6.00
with Sierra pattern	1,650.00			Sherbet, 3"	32.00	38.00
Cake plate, 10", footed	28.00	30.00		Sugar	22.00	35.00
*Candlesticks, 4", pair	95.00	115.00		Sugar/candy cover	25.00	45.00
Candy jar & cover, 2½"	125.00	125.00		Tumbler, 4½"	33.00	30.00
Coaster, 3¼"	22.00	20.00		Tumbler, 5½", iced tea	70.00	70.00
Creamer	25.00	28.00		Vase, 7½"	495.00	95.00

* Delphite $225.00   ** Yellow $100.00   *** Round pink $60.00; yellow $100.00   **** Round pink $75.00; yellow $85.00

"ADAMS RIB," LINE #900, DIAMOND GLASSWARE CO., c. 1925

Colors: amber, blue, green, pink; some marigold; milk and crystal w/marigold iridescence, vaseline; and colors decorated
w/gold, silver, white enamel, florals; and flashed colors of blue and orange w/black trim

A few months before the last book was issued, Cathy and I were buying a blue covered pitcher and four handled lemonades when the mall operator asked me if I knew what the pattern was. I told what it was and that it would be in my new book coming out in July. When I went back last year, there was an "Adams Rib" lemonade priced at more than half again what we had paid for the set previously. Learning about "Adams Rib" was fairly fast. It took a while to gather enough examples for a picture, but now, after its introduction in my book, I am seeing it for sale rather frequently. I doubt that the listing below is complete. You may find other pieces and I would very much appreciate a notice of such. Some of the pieces listed below were shown in a 1928 Sears catalog that peddled six orange and black "ribbed" pieces for $1.32. Indications are that orange was a really big color craze during that time.

There is a pedestal candy made by Fenton that closely resembles the "Adams Rib" one. The knob of the Diamond Company's candy has a tiny protrusion on the top of the knob, whereas the one made by Fenton is smooth.

Many of the flat-bottomed bowls were originally offered on black, three-toed pedestal bases, also a glass vogue of the time. Black, in fact, may be a color possibility, though I could not document or find any. The marigold pieces are valued by carnival glass people; so, you will have competition for those. There are iridized blue and green pitchers that most collectors have not found mugs to accompany. Keep your eye out for those.

Though the company had long been in business, this is one of those ill-fated factories that was destroyed by fire in the early 30s. The #900 line was one of their last big triumphs.

	Non Iridescent	Iridescent		Non Iridescent	Iridescent
Base, black, pedestal, 3 toe (for flat bowls)	15.00		Cup	18.00	
Bowl, vegetable, flared (belled) rim	60.00		Creamer	25.00	45.00
			Mayonnaise, 6", w/ladle	45.00	
Bowl, flat, rolled edge	40.00		Mug (or lemonade)	35.00	85.00
Bowl, console, pedestal foot	55.00	175.00	Pitcher, lemonade, applied handle	225.00	350.00
Bowl, 8", 3-footed, salad	50.00		Plate, dessert	10.00	
Candy, 3-footed bonbon w/lid	45.00		Plate, lunch	18.00	
Candy, oval, flat	65.00		Plate, cracker, w/center rim	30.00	
Candy, footed jar and cover	55.00		Saucer	6.00	
Candle, blown	30.00	50.00	Sandwich, center flat top handle		50.00
Candle, tall	30.00	60.00	Sandwich, center ½ hex handle	30.00	55.00
Cigarette holder, footed	25.00		Sherbet, flat rim	20.00	
Compote, cheese, non-ribbed	25.00		Sugar, open	25.00	45.00
Comport, small	35.00		Tray, oval sugar/creamer (8½x6¼")	20.00	35.00
Comport, 6½" tall	40.00	80.00	Vase, fan	35.00	65.00
Comport, large fruit	60.00	100.00	Vase, 8½", footed, flair rim	75.00	110.00
			Vase, 9¾"	95.00	150.00

8

"ADDIE," "TWELVE POINT," LINE #34, NEW MARTINSVILLE GLASS MFG. CO., c. 1930

Colors: amethyst, black, crystal, cobalt, green, jade green satin, pink, red; and w/Lotus Glass Co. silver decoration

After adding "Addie" to the last book, I asked for your help on additional pieces and colors. I received around 50 e-mails and letters reporting amethyst as a color. Thanks! The name I've mostly heard this called in the marketplace is "Twelve Point," simply because it has that many points. However, when I started doing the research, I found that 20 years ago author William Heacock had christened the pattern in tribute to Addie Miller, a pioneer author for New Martinsville Glass Company wares. The company designated it Line #34.

Notice the lions/heraldry design on the black saucer. Since this decoration turns up on various colors of Line #34 and at least one other New Martinsville blank (see pg. 130, of my *Elegant Glassware, 10th Edition*), is it a Lotus or a New Martinsville decoration?

When I have displayed "Addie" at shows, more people seemed to admire the cobalt blue color. I suspect once people are exposed to the jade green satin, that's going to capture major attention. Anything jadite colored has been snatched up in the last few years. This jade green was marketed with the black, a striking combination — and definitely in keeping with the bi- and tri-colored glass productions of that era.

Once more, it is possible you are going to find other colors or pieces and I'd appreciate notification of what you turn up. In addition, any measurements you could supply would be helpful.

	Black, Cobalt, Jade, Red	All other colors
Bowl, large flare rim, vegetable	50.00	35.00
Candlestick, 3½"	30.00	20.00
Creamer, footed	20.00	10.00
Cup, footed	12.50	8.00
Mayonnaise, 5"	25.00	15.00
Plate, lunch, 8"	12.50	8.00
Sandwich tray, 2-handle	35.00	25.00
Saucer	5.00	2.50
Sherbet, footed	15.00	10.00
Sugar, open, footed	20.00	10.00
Tumbler, footed, 6 oz., juice	15.00	10.00
Tumbler, footed, 9 oz., water	22.50	15.00

AMELIA, "STAR MEDALLION," "BOXED STAR," LINE #671, IMPERIAL GLASS
COMPANY, c. 1920s

Colors: amber, blue, Clambroth, crystal, green, pink, Rubigold iridescent, Smoke; Azalea, Turquoise, and Verde, 1960s; pink carnival, 1980s

Production of Amelia began in the 1920s, but not all pieces are to be found in all colors. The items I see most often at markets are the milk or hotel pitcher and sugar in either crystal or Rubigold, Imperial's name for their marigold carnival color. There are wide varieties of prices on the pitcher, especially the Rubigold.

Another Amelia piece being found is a pink carnival, crimped rim compote that frequently turns up in malls and flea markets. Both the carnival colored custard cup and nut bowl are difficult to find. Actually, only the pitcher is easily spotted in the carnival color.

We've been looking for Amelia for a few years, and as you can see from the photo, we are not finding colored Amelia very easily. We haven't even found the 1960s colors, which seems to indicate a shortage in the market. That could mean owners are keeping it or not much was made by Imperial in the first place.

If your piece comes with an IG mark, it's been made since 1951 when Imperial began so marking their wares.

	Clambroth	Rubigold	Smoke	All other colors
Butter w/cover, round				45.00
Bowl, 5", lily				15.00
Bowl, 5½", square	25.00	30.00	45.00	15.00
Bowl, 5½", deep nut, ftd.		35.00		20.00
Bowl, 6", round nappy	20.00	25.00	40.00	15.00
Bowl, 6¼", oval preserve				25.00
Bowl, 7", oval				25.00
Bowl, 7½", berry, flare (belled) rim		25.00		
Bowl, 8", round berry				35.00
Cup, custard		25.00		12.50
Compote, straight rim				20.00
Compote, crimped rim (late)	35.00	35.00		15.00

	Clambroth	Rubigold	Smoke	All other colors
Creamer				20.00
Celery, 2-handle				30.00
Celery vase, footed	80.00	90.00	150.00	40.00
Goblet, wine		50.00	75.00	20.00
Pitcher, milk or hotel	30.00	37.50	80.00	25.00
Plate, 6½", dessert		35.00		12.00
Plate, 9½", lunch	40.00	50.00	70.00	25.00
Spoon holder (open sugar)				20.00
Sugar w/cover				30.00
Tumbler, 4"		30.00	40.00	20.00
Tumbler, 4½", lemonade, flare rim	30.00	40.00	40.00	

10

AMERICAN PIONEER, LIBERTY WORKS, 1931 – 1934

Colors: pink, green, amber, and crystal

Liberty Works was originally Cut Glass Works, which was then a part of its name. I've been informed by devotees of American Pioneer that this looks like "better glass" than your run of the mill Depression era wares and should be in my *Elegant Glassware* book. It probably should be, but I inherited its acceptance as Depression glass when I started writing in 1972. Once Liberty started manufacturing Depression tableware lines, management was aiming to be ahead of its time, groundbreaking with its products. Unfortunately, the plant experienced fire damage in 1931 and could not recover financially from this blow. This seemed to be an ever-present problem of glassware manufacturing facilities back then.

American Pioneer is suffering from a lack of new caches being discovered which means prices are remaining rather steady. Candy jar lids are identical even though the two candies are fashioned in a different way. One looks like a typical footed candy, the other is taller and has the profile of a footed vase. There are two styles of cups, one being a bit more flared than the other. One has a 4" diameter and is 2½" tall; the other has a 3⅜" diameter and is 2⅜" tall. These discrepancies are very minute and may well be mold differences; but collectors have noticed them enough to say the flared rim cup is the more frequently found.

Covers for the vegetable bowls are rarely seen; and one collector insisted there are three sizes, not the two I have actually seen; but I never received any corroboration of this. Amber cocktails have been discovered in two sizes; but none has surfaced in any other color. One holds three ounces and is 3¹³⁄₁₆" high; the other holds 3½ ounces and is 3¹⁵⁄₁₆" tall. Under liners for the hard-to-get urns, or pitchers in today's terminology, are the regular 6" and 8" plates. That 6" plate in pink is rare. Both sizes of urns have turned up in amber, but not often. Handled candlesticks are in demand by collectors of candles and they do not appear as often as they once did. Dresser sets are desirable pieces in American Pioneer and one has recently surfaced in crystal. Collectors have to fend off collectors of powder jars and colognes to add these to their sets. Thirty years later, and hundreds of thousands of people collecting Depression glass, heretofore unknown items and colors are still being found! This is what makes collecting exciting. There is the possibility that any collector can find something rare in the next shop or market.

You do need to learn the design as it must have those plain banded, horizontal ribbed areas in order to be American Pioneer. Various companies made hobnailed designs that are analogous.

	Crystal, Pink	Green		Crystal, Pink	Green
* Bowl, 5", handled	25.00	25.00	Lamp, 5½", round, ball		
Bowl, 8¾", covered	125.00	165.00	shape, amber $150.00	175.00	
Bowl, 9", handled	30.00	38.00	Lamp, 8½", tall	135.00	165.00
Bowl, 9¼", covered	125.00	165.00	Mayonnaise, 4¼"	60.00	90.00
Bowl, 10¾", console	60.00	70.00	Pilsner, 5¾", 11 ounce	150.00	150.00
Candlesticks, 6½", pair	110.00	135.00	** Pitcher, 5", covered urn	175.00	225.00
Candy jar and cover, 1 pound	95.00	110.00	*** Pitcher, 7", covered urn	195.00	250.00
Candy jar and cover, 1½ pound	100.00	135.00	Plate, 6"	12.50	15.00
Cheese and cracker set (in-			* Plate, 6", handled	12.50	15.00
dented platter and comport)	60.00	70.00	* Plate, 8"	11.00	12.00
Coaster, 3½"	35.00	35.00	* Plate, 11½", handled	30.00	40.00
Creamer, 2¾"	25.00	20.00	* Saucer	4.00	5.00
* Creamer, 3½"	20.00	22.00	Sherbet, 3½"	16.00	20.00
* Cup	12.00	12.00	Sherbet, 4¾"	40.00	45.00
Dresser set (2 colognes, powder			Sugar, 2¾"	20.00	22.00
jar, indented 7½" tray)	495.00	495.00	* Sugar, 3½"	20.00	22.00
Goblet, 3¹³⁄₁₆", 3 oz., cocktail (amber)	40.00		Tumbler, 5 ounce, juice	40.00	45.00
Goblet, 3¹⁵⁄₁₆", 3½ oz., cocktail (amber)	40.00		Tumbler, 4", 8 ounce	40.00	55.00
Goblet, 4", 3 oz., wine	40.00	55.00	Tumbler, 5", 12 ounce	50.00	65.00
Goblet, 6", 8 oz., water	45.00	57.50	Vase, 7", 4 styles	120.00	145.00
Ice bucket, 6"	65.00	75.00	Vase, 9", round		250.00
Lamp, 1¾", w/metal pole 9½"		80.00	Whiskey, 2¼", 2 ounce	50.00	100.00

* Amber — Double the price of pink unless noted   **Amber $300.00   ***Amber $350.00

AMERICAN SWEETHEART, MacBETH-EVANS GLASS COMPANY, 1930 – 1936

Colors: pink, Monax, ruby, and cobalt; some Cremax and color-trimmed Monax

American Sweetheart was an abundantly produced pattern during its seven-year run as is evidenced by the lingering pieces found by the collecting public in these last 30 years. Prices on some of the commonly found pieces, especially cups, saucers, and plates, have softened in the last couple of years. Although the ware is rather delicate looking, it was miraculously long lasting. A Louisville Tin & Stove Company catalog, dated 1937, offered a 32-piece set of Monax American Sweetheart for $2.75 as well as a 42-piece set (including a two-piece sugar) for $4.15. You must also remember that a day's wages in the 1930s were in the range of twenty cents to a dollar a day. That day was sunrise to sunset on the farms of Kentucky. These sets cost three to 20 days work for an average worker.

Both pink and Monax (white with translucent edges) shakers are rarely found. You will find plates in Monax that come in two styles, with and without a center motif. You will also find luncheon pieces in Monax that were trimmed in gold. These were made near the end of production, but are not looked upon as favorably by today's collector. In fact, many people purposely remove the gold with a pencil eraser. Monax pieces are found with colored edgings of yellow, green, pink, and smoky/black, any of which is highly collectible. See the photo below. Additionally, rarely found items include the sugar lid (with two different styles of knobs), and large (18", triple wide, flat rim) and small console bowls that appear in Monax; the larger console was also manufactured in red and blue.

Pitchers and water tumblers came only in pink and there are similar shaped pitchers having no design that were sold with plain, Dogwood shaped tumblers. These pitchers are not deemed to be American Sweetheart, though some people do buy them to go with their sets. If It does not have the pattern, don't pay American Sweetheart prices for it. These plain pitchers usually sell in the $50.00 range.

Ruby, cobalt, and Monax colors were used for tidbit servers (stacked plates with a center rod), 15" sandwich plates, and the aforementioned large console bowl. Creative individuals have made up tidbit servers in recent years; so, you need to check for older hardware; but I know of no way to tell original from newly made other than that.

Sherbets were made in two sizes, with the smaller 3¾" one being harder to find. Sherbets also appear in crystal with metal holders.

Cremax items were made by the company in the mid-30s, ostensibly to compete with the china trade. Cremax is a beige color that does not appeal to today's crowd. Back then, getting people to set their dining tables with glass dishes was a marketing chore; so, they tried to make their glass look more like fine china.

It is still possible to collect this cherished pattern in basic pieces to use and enjoy; and harder items do still turn up, but usually with premium prices. We in the trade tend to feel that everybody knows about Depression glass by now, but they do not. New people to the glass write, call, e-mail, or drop by shows all the time, fascinated by this glass and wanting to know more about it. The sadder ones are those who just gave it away, sold it for pennies at a garage sale, or trashed their aunt or grandmother's dishes because they had no clue they were valuable.

AMERICAN SWEETHEART

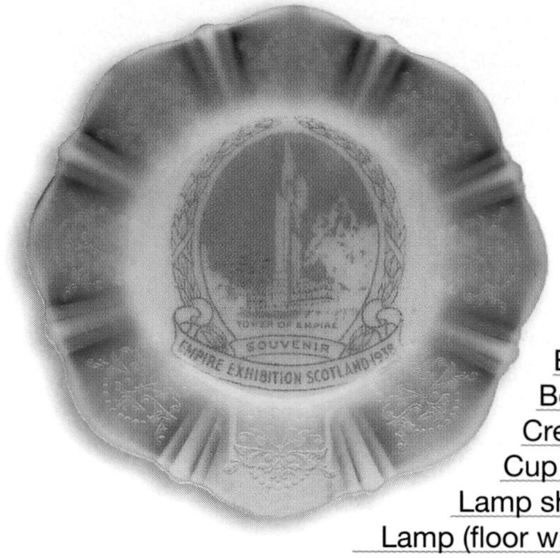

	Ruby	Cobalt	Cremax	Smoke & Other Trims
Bowl, 6", cereal			16.00	50.00
Bowl, 9", round, berry			50.00	250.00
Bowl, 9½", soup				165.00
Bowl, 18", console	1,100.00	1,250.00		
Creamer, footed	185.00	210.00		110.00
Cup	120.00	150.00		110.00
Lamp shade			495.00	
Lamp (floor with brass base)			795.00	
Plate, 6", bread and butter				22.00
Plate, 8", salad	120.00	130.00		30.00
Plate, 9", luncheon				45.00
Plate, 9¾", dinner				100.00
Plate, 12", salver	195.00	265.00		125.00
Plate, 15½", server	325.00	425.00		
Platter, 13", oval				225.00
Saucer	25.00	30.00		17.50
Sherbet, 4¼", footed (design inside or outside)				110.00
Sugar, open footed	185.00	210.00		110.00
Tidbit, 2 tier, 8" & 12"	250.00	335.00		
Tidbit, 3 tier, 8", 12" & 15½"	625.00	750.00		

	Pink	Monax
Bowl, 3¾", flat, berry	85.00	
Bowl, 4½", cream, soup	85.00	120.00
Bowl, 6", cereal	18.00	20.00
Bowl, 9", round, berry	55.00	75.00
Bowl, 9½", flat, soup	75.00	90.00
Bowl, 11", oval, vegetable	70.00	80.00
Bowl, 18", console		495.00
Creamer, footed	15.00	10.00
Cup	16.00	9.00
Lamp shade		495.00
Plate, 6" or 6½", bread & butter	6.00	6.50
Plate, 8", salad	14.00	10.00
Plate, 9", luncheon		12.00
Plate, 9¾", dinner	42.50	30.00
Plate, 10¼", dinner		28.00
Plate, 11", chop plate		22.00
Plate, 12", salver	24.00	22.00
Plate, 15½", server		250.00

	Pink	Monax
Platter, 13", oval	55.00	70.00
Pitcher, 7½", 60 ounce	995.00	
Pitcher, 8", 80 ounce	795.00	
Salt and pepper, footed	595.00	495.00
Saucer	4.00	2.00
Sherbet, 3¾", footed	25.00	
Sherbet, 4¼", footed (design inside or outside)	20.00	20.00
Sherbet in metal holder (crystal only)	3.50	
Sugar, open, footed	15.00	8.00
* Sugar lid		500.00
Tidbit, 2 tier, 8" & 12"	60.00	60.00
Tidbit, 3 tier, 8", 12" & 15½"		325.00
Tumbler, 3½", 5 ounce	95.00	
Tumbler, 4¼", 9 ounce	95.00	
Tumbler, 4¾", 10 ounce	125.00	

*Three styles of knobs.

ARDITH, PADEN CITY GLASS COMPANY, c. 1920s

Colors: amber, black, crystal, cobalt, green, pink, ruby, yellow

Paden City had a number of line blanks on which the pattern Ardith was etched. It appeared on the squared (#412) and round (#890) Crow's Foot blanks, the squared, cropped cornered #411 Mrs. B line, the #211 four Spired line, the #210 Stacked paneled line, the linear lined #215 Glades line, the #555 "Teardrop and Bead" line, etc. You may well find this on others. The flowered, cherry blossom motif seems to have been a popular etching judging from the number of pieces on which it can be found. Don't be mislead into thinking this is commonly found, today, however. It will take searching to come up with pieces of Ardith. For this first listing, I am using only one price for all colors. Realize that red, black, and cobalt blue will fetch 20% – 25% more and crystal 50% less, but prices are rather unpredictable on this pattern now.

	All colors		All colors
Bowl, 5⅝", 2 hdld.	50.00	Cup	50.00
Bowl, 9", ped., ftd., sq.	125.00	Cheese & cracker, 10¼" plate; 5" sq. stand	130.00
Bowl, 9½", sq. ped., ftd.	125.00	Ice bucket w/lid	195.00
Bowl, 10", rolled edge console	75.00	Mayonnaise, w/ladle & liner plate	60.00
Bowl, 10", sq.	80.00	Pitcher, 7¼"	210.00
Bowl, 10", 2 hdld,	100.00	Pitcher, 10"	275.00
Bowl, 10½", sq.	75.00	Plate, 8⅜" sq.	50.00
Bowl, 12", sq.	80.00	Saucer	20.00
Bowl, 12½" 4-toed console	85.00	Sugar, flat	45.00
Candle, 4", rolled edge	125.00	Sugar, ftd.	50.00
Candle, 4⅝", sq. flattened top	45.00	Tray, 7½", 2 hdld.	50.00
Candle, 5¼", keyhole	45.00	Tray, 9", cupped center hdld.	1000.00
Candle, 6", 'wings"	60.00	Tray, 10" sq., center handle,	90.00
Candle, 6", center circle	60.00	Tray, 10¼", sq., center handle	90.00
Candy, w/lid, 2-part	100.00	Tumbler, 3 oz.	45.00
Candy, w/lid, 3-part	100.00	Vase, 3", high	185.00
Candy, w/lid, 8" ftd.	155.00	Vase, 4¼" ivy/rose, ftd.	75.00
Cake stand, 9¼", ped., ftd.	75.00	Vase, 5½", elliptical	150.00
Compote, 6½" high, sq.	65.00	Vase, 7½" bulbous bottom	135.00
Creamer, flat	45.00	Vase, 8½", horizontal ribbed	150.00
Creamer, ftd.	50.00	Vase, 10"	175.00

"ARTURA," PATTERN #608, INDIANA GLASS COMPANY, c. 1930s

Colors: crystal and w/color decoration, green, pink

"Artura" is a relatively small pattern which was marketed in 15-, 21-, and 27-piece sets to use for breakfast, luncheon, or bridge type gatherings. Its characteristic is a double rib at an unusual nine points of its design. It has the wonderful Deco linear look, which is softened by "S" curving handles and a wonderfully ornate double S interwoven on the sandwich tray center handle. It's truly a shame they didn't fashion more items in this delightful pattern. This, too, often sits unrecognized. Collectors seem to notice the crystal decorated pieces before they do other items. If you find crystal undecorated ware, price it about 30% lower than the prices listed.

	Green, Pink, Crystal Decorated		Green, Pink, Crystal Decorated
Cup	8.00	Sugar, open	10.00
Creamer	10.00	Tray, sandwich w/ornate center handle	30.00
Plate, 7½", salad	6.00	Tray, sugar and sugar	12.50
Saucer	2.00	Tumbler, ftd.	15.00

AUNT POLLY, U.S. GLASS COMPANY, Late 1920s

Colors: blue, green, and iridescent

Amazingly, no one wrote to inquire about the ruffled vase pictured. This vase was created from the regular vase mold. I'm sure it was experimental, but there should be more out there awaiting discovery.

So far, the two-handled covered candy pictured in green has never materialized in blue. The footed, double handled open candy shown in blue is a very desirable item. It is on most Aunt Polly collectors' wish lists, along with the oval vegetable, sugar lid, shakers, and butter dish. The Aunt Polly butter bottom is identical to other U.S. Glass patterns of the time, namely Strawberry, Cherryberry, and U.S. Swirl; but none of those patterns were made in blue. Thus, blue Aunt Polly butter bottoms have always been scarce. The canary ("vaseline") colored tumbler pictured represents the yellow, glow-in-the-dark color that factories were then producing. The color was compared to the new petroleum jelly product that had recently hit the market and the term stuck. Green glass will glow, but it is not "vaseline" as some try to call it.

Some Aunt Polly creamers come with a more pronounced lip than others, due to the fact these were made by hand with a wooden paddle while the glass was still hot. Sometimes a delicate touch was not used and varying degrees of spout were obtained.

One problem in collecting Aunt Polly is that there are conspicuously different shades of green and blue to be found. Witness the color variations shown. Aunt Polly, like most U.S. Glass patterns, suffers from excessive mould roughness at the seams. This is off putting to some collectors. However, most accept it as a normal characteristic of the pattern, along with its earlier, turn of the century, appearance.

	Green, Iridescent	Blue
Bowl, 4¾", berry	7.00	16.00
Bowl, 4¾", 2" high	16.00	
Bowl, 5½", one handle	15.00	25.00
Bowl, 7¼", oval, handled, pickle	15.00	45.00
Bowl, 7⅞", large berry	20.00	50.00
Bowl, 8⅜", oval	75.00	150.00
Butter dish and cover	275.00	250.00
Butter dish bottom	100.00	100.00
Butter dish top	175.00	150.00
Candy, cover, 2-handled	70.00	
Candy, footed, 2-handled	30.00	55.00

	Green, Iridescent	Blue
Creamer	35.00	55.00
Pitcher, 8", 48 ounce		225.00
Plate, 6", sherbet	6.00	14.00
Plate, 8", luncheon		20.00
Salt and pepper		250.00
Sherbet	10.00	14.00
Sugar	25.00	35.00
Sugar cover	55.00	150.00
Tumbler, 3⅝", 8 ounce		38.00
Vase, 6½", footed	35.00	60.00

AURORA, HAZEL ATLAS GLASS COMPANY, Late 1930s

Colors: cobalt blue, pink, green, and crystal

A few pieces of Aurora have been found in pink, and these fetch a price comparable to the blue due to their scarcity. The small bowl, creamer, and tumbler have, so far, never been found in pink. Several Canadian readers report pink and green are more readily found there than in the States.

Both green and crystal cereal bowls, cups, and saucers have been found. So far, only collectors of cups and saucers have been very excited over this news. One cup and saucer collector expressed disappointment that there were additional sets to find. That person is probably not going to be happy with my adding all these new patterns to the book since his list was almost complete for having found a cup and saucer for every pattern in my book. He started with one of every pattern and color and soon switched to just the patterns only.

Of course, blue is the color most desired, but that is beginning to be a problem with the lack of 4½" deep bowls being found. Demand and rarity have forced the upward spiraling price, which causes many collectors to buy only one. That is a shame since this is one of the only cobalt blue sets that can be obtained for less than a small fortune. Here, in Florida, many windows display cobalt glassware as a decoration. It does absorb heat, so be careful about putting it in direct sunlight. I've heard a couple of stories about pieces "just exploding."

Several readers have suggested that patterns with a creamer and no sugar, such as this one, should have the creamer listed as a milk pitcher. The reason I didn't list it as such was that milk pitchers usually held at least 16 ounces; this one was a little small for that. However, lending credence to that idea, a collector reported that creamers were given away as premiums for buying a breakfast cereal in her hometown. She remembers boxed displays on the counter from which the proprietor handed you one with your purchase of cereal. Unfortunately, she could not remember the name of the cereal, but thought it might have been Corn Flakes. Her grandmother had several of the creamer/milk pitchers in her attic. Obviously, the deep bowls must never have been premiums.

	Cobalt, Pink		Cobalt, Pink
Bowl, 4½" deep	65.00	Plate, 6½"	12.50
* Bowl, 5⅜", cereal	17.50	***Saucer	4.00
Creamer, 4½"	25.00	Tumbler, 4¾", 10 ounce	27.50
** Cup	16.00		

*Green $8.00 or crystal $5.00   **Green $8.00   ***Green $2.50

"AVOCADO," "SWEET PEAR," NO. 601, INDIANA GLASS COMPANY, 1923 – 1933

Colors: pink, green, crystal; white, 1950s; yellow mist, burnt honey, and water sets in myriad frosted and transparent colors for Tiara Home Products, 1974 – 1998 (See Reproduction Section.)

This #601 line was originally called "Sweet Pear" by authors of pattern glass books. Early Depression glass authors called it "Avocado," though it looks more like a pear to me, too.

"Avocado" is a popular pattern among collectors; there just isn't enough of the older green and pink surfacing these days for new collectors to get truly interested. Prices were rather steady for several years, but recently these have been slipping on all but the rarer pieces. The pitcher and tumblers remain high on "wanted lists" of most collectors. Be aware that reproductions of these two items abound in pink, but the pink repro is usually an orange tinted pink. Do read the Reproduction Section telling about the various "Avocado" items and colors produced by Indiana for their Tiara Home Products line during their 1970 – 1998 life span. You don't want to be caught paying collectible prices for recent wares, although I will admit that the yellow produced in the mid 1980s is a wonderful shade of yellow. They made a plate, three-toed bowl, two-handled pickle, cup, saucer, sugar, and creamer. The burnt honey production, with its amberina look of red rims, also included a footed sherbet and a two-handled nappy; but I'm uncertain that the transparent yellow did. If you know, I'd appreciate your passing that information to me.

I've had several inquiries, recently, regarding crystal "Avocado," heretofore, ignored. If you see those items, perhaps you shouldn't dismiss them out of hand. To date, there are no known cups, saucers, or sherbets in crystal, but a large vegetable, pitcher, and tumblers have surfaced. We know the frosted pitcher and tumblers were made since 1980 for Tiara, as well as myriad other frosted colors not original.

Indiana produced milk glass items in the mid-1950s and collectors for milk glass vie for those.

	Crystal	Pink	Green		Crystal	Pink	Green
Bowl, 5¼", 2-handled	10.00	28.00	30.00	* Pitcher, 64 ounce	350.00	1,000.00	1,500.00
Bowl, 6", footed relish	9.00	28.00	30.00	*** Plate, 6⅜", sherbet	5.00	14.00	16.00
Bowl, 7", 1-handle preserve	8.00	28.00	30.00	** Plate, 8¼", luncheon	7.00	17.00	22.00
Bowl, 7½", salad	12.00	50.00	70.00	Plate, 10¼", 2-handled, cake	14.00	55.00	65.00
Bowl, 8", 2-handled, oval	11.00	30.00	35.00	Saucer, 6⅜",		22.00	24.00
Bowl, 9½", 3¼", deep	22.00	150.00	200.00	*** Sherbet		55.00	65.00
*** Creamer, footed	12.00	35.00	38.00	*** Sugar, footed	12.00	35.00	38.00
Cup, footed, 2 styles		35.00	38.00	* Tumbler	35.00	195.00	325.00

* Caution on pink. The orange-pink is new.
* White: Pitcher $425.00; Tumbler $35.00.

** Apple design $10.00. Amber has been newly made.
*** Remade in dark shade of green.

BEADED BLOCK, #710, IMPERIAL GLASS COMPANY, 1927 – 1930s; Late 1970s – Early 1980s

Colors: pink, green, crystal, ice blue, Canary, iridescent, amber, red, opalescent colors, and milk white

Squared Beaded Block plates are commonly found while round plates are scarce. Most round plates were transformed into bowls and these bowls are sparse in the collecting landscape. There are size variances in this pattern. The sizes listed here were all obtained from actual measurements of the pieces and not those listed in catalogs. The two-handled jelly, so called by Imperial, was called a cream soup by most companies and varies from 4¾" to 5". Neither one seems to be prevalent. Be sure to read the section on measurements on page 2. I have found company catalog size listings were more nearly approximations than precise calculations.

The red lily bowl is considered rare today and was made during that 30s thirst for red. For some reason they were commonly found around Vandalia, Ohio, in the mid-1970s. I ran out of customers for them and ended up keeping one for photography. A couple of years ago a dealer approached me and asked if I were interested in one for $250.00 and I said no as I already owned one. I received an e-mail from him a few weeks later referring me to an Internet auction. I looked and noticed a bidding war between two bidders had raised this piece to over $1,200.00. It only takes two people! To prove this was a fluke, I put mine up for sale and it brought less than a third of the previous price. That is why books using Internet auction prices are so suspect. Prices are not consistent there depending upon who is viewing at any particular time and how much money is available to them at that one moment.

Imperial reissued pink and iridized pink (pink carnival) in the late 1970s and early 1980s. These pieces are clearly marked IG in the bottom. When I visited the factory in 1981, I found out that the white was made in the early 1950s and the IG mark (for Imperial Glass) was first used about that time. Only a few marked pieces of Beaded Block are found, but they include the white covered pear. This two-part candy in the shape of a large pear is found infrequently and dates from the mid-50s. Pears have been found in yellow, green, pink, and amber. Amber seems to be the more easily found color and usually these are seen on the West Coast. They generally are priced in the $300.00 to $400.00 range; but I have seen them for as much as $695.00. The key word is priced, and notice I did not say selling for that amount.

Pink and white Beaded Block pitchers are scarce when compared to green and crystal. Yet, a collecting surge for Beaded Block has even boosted the price for the green pitcher. Beaded Block was one of the patterns that had only sporadic recognition until the Internet came along. For some reason new collectors latched onto it and prices were jumping regularly. That has passed, but the price adjustments were upward and are only beginning to settle down. You should know that true connoisseurs of this pattern make a distinction between the frosted, stippled pieces, referring to them as "Frosted Block."

New collectors should observe that 6" vases sold as Beaded Block usually are not. The true vase has a scalloped top as shown on other pieces. There is a 6" vase/parfait with a straight top and no beading that was called a footed jelly by Imperial. These level edged ones were premium items found with a product inside at grocery stores. Most commonly found are ones with labels and tops from "Frank Tea & Spice Co., Cin., O." Dry mustard and pepper were most often packed in these. Just know they are "go-with" pieces and not truly Beaded Block.

Unknowing dealers like to label Beaded Block as pricey, older Sandwich glass, which is either a compliment to Beaded Block or an insult to Sandwich glass. It was sold at Woolworth's. I have also seen at least one "expert" accrediting the 1930s Sea Foam decoration to about four decades before it was cataloged by Imperial.

	*Crystal, Pink, Green, Amber	Other colors
Bowl, 4⅞"-5", 2-handled jelly	20.00	35.00
** Bowl, 4½", round, lily	20.00	40.00
Bowl, 5½", square	20.00	35.00
Bowl, 5½", 1-handle	20.00	35.00
Bowl, 6", deep, round	25.00	40.00
Bowl, 6¼", round	25.00	40.00
Bowl, 6½", round	25.00	40.00
Bowl, 6½", 2-handled pickle	30.00	42.00
Bowl, 6¾", round, unflared	25.00	40.00
Bowl, 7¼", round, flared	30.00	45.00
Bowl, 7½", round, fluted edges	30.00	45.00
Bowl, 7½", round, plain edge	30.00	45.00
Bowl, 8¼", celery	38.00	60.00
Candy, pear shaped	325.00	425.00
Creamer	22.00	45.00
*** Pitcher, 5¼", pint jug	110.00	
Plate, 7¾", square	20.00	30.00
Plate, 8¾", round	30.00	50.00
Stemmed jelly, 4½"	28.00	42.00
Stemmed jelly, 4½", flared top	28.00	42.00
Sugar	22.00	45.00
Vase, 6", bouquet	22.00	45.00

* All pieces 25% to 40% lower.   ** Red $495.00   *** White $195.00, pink $175.00, crystal $85.00

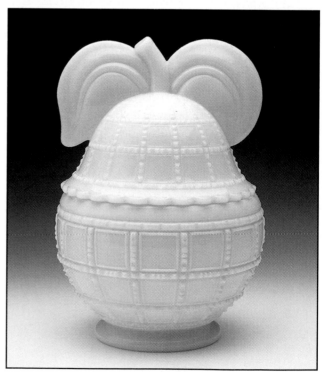

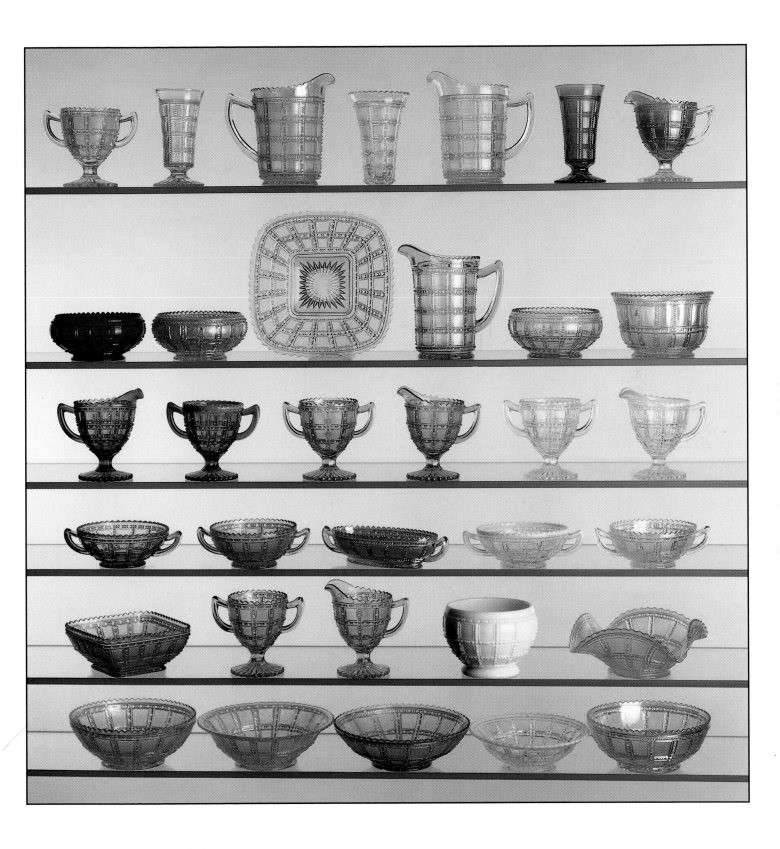

"BEEHIVE," LINE 350S, HAZEL-ATLAS, c. 1940s – 50s

Colors: crystal, pink, and some white

To date, most of what has brought any notice to the "Beehive" pattern in Depression ware circles were the large, footed tea tumblers and pitchers. They have been collectible in their own right for 30 years. This pattern was meant to be placed in the *Collectible Glassware from 40s, 50s, 60s...*, but through some miscommunication, allowances to fit this book were made and it was too late to change when I noticed. I will move it where it belongs in the next edition. There may be other pieces to be found, but these were all to be seen on the catalog pages I viewed.

	Crystal	Pink		Crystal	Pink
Bowl, 4⅞", berry	3.00	5.00	Pitcher, 84 oz. w/ice lip	25.00	35.00
Bowl, 8⅝" berry, 2 hdld.	10.00	14.00	Sherbet, 3¾", flat	4.00	6.00
Bowl, 19¾ oz., utility	12.50	17.50	Sugar, 11½ oz.	5.00	8.00
Butter and cover, 6"	25.00	35.00	Sugar lid	4.00	5.00
Creamer, 9½ oz.	5.00	8.00	Tray 12¼", serving	12.00	15.00
Goblet, 15 oz., ftd. tea	8.00	12.50			

"BERLIN," "REEDED WAFFLE," LINE #124, WESTMORELAND SPECIALTY COMPANY, c. 1924

Colors: blue, crystal, green, pink; ruby, c. 1980s

The names "Berlin" and "Reeded Waffle" for Westmoreland's Line #124 are holdovers from a pattern glass design first produced in the 1870s. The older ware could be found with colored stains of ruby or amber. Westmoreland made at least 15 pieces of this pattern in the prevailing Depression era colors. Thus, its inclusion here.

You should know that there has been some confusion between this pattern and one known as "Plaid" or "Open Plaid," which is similar at first glance. Plaid has an actual basketweave design and was only produced in crystal.

Consulting an assortment of pattern glass books, I found that the older "Berlin" design sported tumblers, wines, cracker jars, cruets, cups, butter dishes, etc. Therefore, an abundance of items occur in this design, but were ascribed to other companies.

I am told Westmoreland made a ruby colored pitcher sometime in the 1980s, just before going out of business, but I have been unable to find one for sale.

	*Crystal		*Crystal
Basket	27.50	Creamer	18.00
Bowl, bonbon, 1 handle	15.00	Mayonnaise	30.00
Bowl, 6½", round	15.00	Pitcher	65.00
Bowl, square	20.00	Plate, 9", lunch	15.00
Bowl, 2-handle cream soup	22.00	Sugar	18.00
Bowl, 7", round	22.00	Tray, 2- handle, celery	30.00
Bowl, 7½", round	25.00	Vase, footed	35.00
Bowl, oval, pickle	22.50	* Double price of crystal for colors.	

BLOCK OPTIC, "BLOCK," HOCKING GLASS COMPANY, 1929 – 1933

Colors: green, pink, yellow, crystal, and some amber, blue, and clambroth green

Block Optic is another Hocking pattern that ranks highly with collectors. This is due to availability through length of production, its charm of form and design, its variety of colors and, somewhat, to its history of being less expensive to collect. There are a few pricey items, but, in general, most collectors can afford to pursue this pattern. Many a beginner started with Block and went on to collect additional patterns when time and money permitted.

Lately, I've run into quite a few collectors looking for crystal Block, something mostly ignored in the past. One of those told me she picked that because she thought it had a wonderful Deco quality about it. In addition, at shows, a few have been asking for the black footed stems, something else glanced over in the past. Around the 1928 – 1932 period, glass companies started in a big way to make bi-colored wares, either by decorating that way, or by actually fusing two (or three) colors and the Deco black was a big part of that; hence, firing the foot of Block stems with black.

Newcomers to collecting should know that Block Optic has five variations of sugars and creamers, due to their variety of handles, their being footed or flat, or their having rayed or non-rayed bottoms. In yellow Block, only the fancy handled sugar and creamer are found. Concerns of collectors of Block Optic that I have tried to address this time are these different styles of pitchers, cups, creamers and sugars. I hope that the individual pictures of these items will help you differentiate.

Pieces of Block come satinized or frosted, also a big push of that era. It was relatively easy to do by using camphoric acid and it gave the items a very different look. In fact, I understand that today's crafters are etching things much the same way. In the early days of collecting, no one wanted anything to do with the satinized wares. However, that, too, is changing.

A majority of collectors look for green Block. Pink has nearly all been swallowed up into collections, even the pieces that were a lighter pink which were disregarded at first. Stems are difficult to find, now. Many people liked their shape and capacity whether they collected much glass or not. Yellow Block, though very striking, comes in far fewer items than the green and is seen much less often. Both yellow and green fluoresce in black light, a display technique being used more and more often. Do not fall for the tale that this guarantees glass to be old, however; it simply means there's uranium oxide among the mix, something being used to produce glassware by some factories today.

Grill plates, those plates with the "T" shaped dividers most often associated with diner and grill eateries, are infrequently found. Note the price increases for those.

	Green	Yellow	Pink
Bowl, 4¼" diam., 1⅜" tall	11.00		12.00
Bowl, 4½" diam., 1½" tall	30.00		45.00
Bowl, 5¼", cereal	13.00		40.00
Bowl, 7¼", salad	195.00		175.00
Bowl, 8½", large berry	40.00		35.00
* Bowl, 11¾", rolled-edge console	85.00		85.00
** Butter dish and cover, 3" x 5"	50.00		
Butter dish bottom	30.00		
Butter dish top	20.00		
*** Candlesticks, 1¾" pr.	120.00		80.00
Candy jar & cover, 2¼" tall	65.00	75.00	60.00
Candy jar & cover, 6¼" tall	65.00		165.00
Comport, 5⅜" wide, mayonnaise	90.00		95.00
Creamer, 3 styles: cone shaped, round, rayed-foot & flat (5 kinds)	13.00	13.00	15.00
Cup, four styles	7.00	8.00	6.00
Goblet, 3½", short wine	525.00		525.00
Goblet, 4", cocktail	40.00		40.00
Goblet, 4½", wine	45.00		45.00
Goblet, 5¾", 9 ounce	30.00		35.00
Goblet, 7¼", 9 ounce thin		40.00	
Ice bucket	45.00		95.00
Ice tub or butter tub, open	65.00		125.00
Mug	40.00		
Pitcher, 7⅝", 54 ounce, bulbous	95.00		495.00
Pitcher, 8½", 54 ounce	65.00		55.00
Pitcher, 8", 80 ounce	110.00		165.00
Plate, 6", sherbet	3.00	3.00	3.00
Plate, 8", luncheon	7.00	8.00	8.00
Plate, 9", dinner	27.50	50.00	38.00

	Green	Yellow	Pink
Plate, 9", grill	125.00	100.00	
Plate, 10¼", sandwich	25.00		25.00
Plate, 12¾"	35.00		
Salt and pepper, footed, pair	45.00	95.00	90.00
Salt and pepper, squatty, pair	130.00		
Sandwich server, center handle	75.00		75.00
Saucer, 5¾", with cup ring	9.00		8.00
Saucer, 6⅛", with cup ring	9.00		8.00
Sherbet, non-stemmed (cone)	3.75		
Sherbet, 3¼", 5½ ounce	6.00	10.00	7.50
Sherbet, 4¾", 6 ounce	18.00	21.00	18.00
Sugar, 3 styles: as creamer	12.50	12.50	12.50
Tumbler, 3 ounce, 2⅝"	25.00		30.00
Tumbler, 5 ounce, 3½", flat	25.00		28.00
Tumbler, 9½ ounce, 3¹³⁄₁₆", flat	15.00		15.00
Tumbler, 10 or 11 oz., 5", flat	20.00		18.00
Tumbler, 12 ounce, 4⅞", flat	30.00		30.00
Tumbler, 15 ounce, 5¼", flat	50.00		50.00
Tumbler, 3 ounce, 3¼", footed	30.00		30.00
Tumbler, 9 ounce, footed	22.00	27.50	17.00
Tumbler, 6", 10 ounce, footed	35.00		38.00
Tumble-up night set	77.50		
Tumbler, 3" only	60.00		
Bottle only	17.50		
Vase, 5¾", blown	365.00		
Whiskey, 1⅝", 1 ounce	45.00		48.00
Whiskey, 2¼", 2 ounce	32.00		35.00

* Amber $45.00

** Green clambroth $275.00, blue $595.00, crystal $175.00

*** Amber $50.00

BLOCK OPTIC

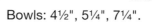

Bowls: 4½", 5¼", 7¼".

Tumblers, left to right: 15 ounce, 5¼"; 12 ounce, 4⅞"; 9½ ounce, 3¹³⁄₁₆"; 5 ounce, 3½"; 3 ounce, 2⅝"; 2 ounce, 2¼"; 1 ounce, 1⅝".

Left, heavy moulded sherbet; right, thin blown sherbet.

Left to right: 9 ounce, 7¼" goblet; 6 ounce, 4¾" sherbet; 9 ounce, 5¾" water; 3 ounce, 3½" short wine; 3½ ounce, 4½" wine; 3 ounce, 4" cocktail.

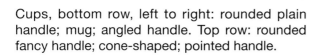

Cups, bottom row, left to right: rounded plain handle; mug; angled handle. Top row: rounded fancy handle; cone-shaped; pointed handle.

Creamers and sugars, left to right: rounded plain handle; cone-shaped pointed handle; flat; cone-shaped plain handle; round fancy handle.

"BOWKNOT," ATTRIBUTED TO BELMONT TUMBLER COMPANY, Probably late 1920s

Color: green

An eight-place setting of Bowknot was offered for sale a few months ago over an Internet site. It has been my experience that most collectors do not start out by buying a complete set. They enjoy the hunt and usually can only afford to buy pieces a few at a time. On the other hand are dealers who will buy full sets for inventory to sell piecemeal, but who will expect discounts. There is no premium value for a large set as it is only equal to the sum of its parts to quote an old math saying. A dealer will not pay retail or above as he has to make a profit to stay in business. The good old days of dealers paying 60% – 70% have disappeared. Fifty percent of book is the more standard price today — but then, prices are generally much higher now per piece than they were in those "olden days" of collecting.

Newcomers to Depression glass should know that most dealers do not display some of these smaller patterns such as "Bowknot" at glass shows because they take up the same valuable space as more costly items. Space is at a premium in a show booth and expenses include gas, food, motel, and booth rent before the first customer even arrives. Therefore, if you have chosen a smaller pattern, you will probably have to inquire if the dealers have any pieces in inventory. I have found that "Bowknot" pieces sell well, when you can find them. Since this ware was heavily used, it is very necessary to check them for inner rim roughness (irr), particularly on the bowls and sherbets. Cereal bowls and tumblers are on many collectors' wish lists; and there are two styles of tumblers, a footed and a flat version (pictured in my *Florence's Glassware Pattern Identification I*).

To date, no saucer has turned up for the cup. However, it was the routine back then to produce custard cups alone. This is perhaps one of those. People don't drink custard much these days, but judging from the pages of these found in older company catalogs, it seems to have been a very popular beverage back then, equivalent to our ice cream consumption, today. I suppose they could make custard without ice, a precious product to obtain in the not so long ago; and milk and eggs were readily available in a largely agricultural society.

Bowl, 4½", berry	28.00	Sherbet, low footed	25.00
Bowl, 5½", cereal	38.00	Tumbler, 5", 10 ounce	28.00
Cup	12.00	Tumbler, 5", 10 ounce, footed	28.00
Plate, 7", salad	15.00		

CAMEO, "BALLERINA," or "DANCING GIRL," HOCKING GLASS COMPANY, 1930 – 1934

Colors: green, yellow, pink, and crystal w/platinum rim (See Reproduction Section.)

Cameo could possibly be called the most adored pattern in Depression glass. Cameo, Cherry Blossom, and Miss America are three of the most collectible patterns and Hocking Glass Company manufactured all of these in the early 1930s. Cameo integrated a pattern design named "Springtime" from Monongah Glass Company (bought by Hocking). Several of Monongah's patterns were altered or continued by Hocking. Monongah's glass was plate etched, made in crystal, and usually was gold trimmed. Hocking took the plate etchings and converted them into their moulds. Collectors now are seeking "Springtime" (see page 214) which is relatively scarce in comparison to Cameo.

I need to emphasize that all miniature pieces with the Cameo design are newly made in the last 20 years by Mosser Glass Company in Cambridge, Ohio. These were never made originally. See the Reproduction Section (p 242) regarding these "Jennifer" sets. I've now seen the miniature comport peddled as rare or as a salt dip on the Internet auctions and commanding fantastic sums from the unaware. While we are discussing what isn't Cameo, I should remind you of the imported, weakly patterned shakers that appeared a few years ago in pink, and a darker green and cobalt blue color that were never made originally. Don't pay more than $12.00 for these fakes.

The Cameo centered-handled sandwich server and short, 3½" wines are choice Cameo collectibles. A few of these shorter pink wines have surfaced in the last three years, but no green ones, lately. I bought a center-handled server that had been purchased 10 years ago for $125.00 at an auction in Lancaster, Ohio, the home of Anchor Hocking. You might want to check out the price that piece commands, today, *if* they can be found. It beats the stock market.

I receive more letters and calls about Cameo saucers than any other piece of Cameo. The rare Cameo saucer has a recessed, 1¾" diameter cup ring. Surprisingly two different batches of these have turned up this year in Florida from collectors selling their sets. Twenty-two of these have recently been on the market. Due to the price, collectors are buying one and not one for each place setting as they have done in the past. Hocking ordinarily made a smooth center, dual-purpose saucer/sherbet plate for their patterns, which will accommodate the foot of a sherbet. No recessed ring, yellow Cameo saucers have ever been confirmed even though I get a dozen or so letters a year from people not understanding what a recessed indentation is. It's kind of like a well in the otherwise smooth surface of the glass to catch drips and firmly seat the cup foot.

Cameo yellow butter dishes and milk pitchers are rare. However, there is more than enough cups, saucer/sherbet plates, footed waters, and dinner and grill plates to supply all the collectors searching for them.

You can still assemble a large set of green Cameo, the most collected color, without investing an enormous amount of money as long as you stay away from buying the rarer pieces and purchase only one or two sizes of stems or tumblers when they can be found.

Cameo has two styles of grill ("T" shape divider bars) plates. One has tab handles and one does not. Both styles are common in yellow. However, the green grill with the tab or closed handles is harder to find and priced accordingly. The 10½" rare, rimmed dinner or flat cake plate is like the heavy edged (no tabs) grill plate without the dividers. The regular dinner plate has a large center as opposed to the small centered sandwich plate. The less expensive sandwich plate is often priced as the more expensive dinner plate. Some collectors are beginning to buy those sandwich plates to use as dinners. They are a little cheaper and also a little larger than the regular dinner.

Darker green bottles with the Cameo design are marked on the bottom "Whitehouse Vinegar." These were sold with vinegar and a cork. Glass stoppers, however, should be found atop water bottles. The glass stoppers do not have a Cameo pattern on them, but are plain, paneled stoppers with hollow centers and are often absent on the bottles. In many cases, these decanters were sold with bath salts and the stopper was used as a measuring device, so many were possibly dropped from wet hands.

	Green	Yellow	Pink	Crystal w/Plat.
Bowl, 4¼", sauce				7.00
Bowl, 4¾", cream soup	205.00			
Bowl, 5½", cereal	40.00	38.00	150.00	7.00
Bowl, 7¼", salad	70.00			
Bowl, 8¼", large berry	45.00		175.00	
Bowl, 9", rimmed soup	75.00		225.00	
Bowl, 10", oval vegetable	35.00	42.00		
Bowl, 11", 3-legged console	90.00	125.00	75.00	
Butter dish and cover	250.00	1,500.00		
Butter dish bottom	140.00	500.00		
Butter dish top	95.00	1,000.00		
Cake plate, 10", 3 legs	30.00			
Cake plate, 10½", flat	125.00		195.00	
Candlesticks, 4", pair	130.00			
Candy jar, 4", low, and cover	95.00	115.00	595.00	
Candy jar, 6½", tall, and cover	205.00			
Cocktail shaker (metal lid) appears in crystal only			1,000.00	
Comport, 5⅜" wide, mayonnaise	45.00		225.00	
Cookie jar and cover	65.00			
Creamer, 3¼"	25.00	25.00		
Creamer, 4¼"	32.00		125.00	
Cup, 2 styles	14.00	8.00	85.00	5.50
Decanter, 10", with stopper	210.00			275.00
Decanter, 10", with stopper, frosted (stopper represents ⅓ value of decanter)	40.00			
Domino tray, 7", with 3" indentation	210.00			
Domino tray, 7", with no indentation			275.00	165.00
Goblet, 3½", wine	1,000.00		750.00	
Goblet, 4", wine	80.00		250.00	
Goblet, 6", water	65.00		195.00	
Ice bowl or open butter, 3" tall x 5½" wide	210.00		750.00	325.00

	Green	Yellow	Pink	Crystal w/Plat.
Jam jar, 2", and cover	265.00			175.00
Pitcher, 5¾", 20 ounce syrup or milk	325.00	2,000.00		
Pitcher, 6", 36 oz., juice	68.00			
Pitcher, 8½", 56 oz., water	70.00		1,500.00	500.00
Plate, 6", sherbet	5.00	3.00	90.00	2.00
Plate, 7", salad				3.50
Plate, 8", luncheon	13.00	10.00	35.00	4.00
Plate, 8½", square	60.00	250.00		
Plate, 9½", dinner	25.00	12.00	85.00	
Plate, 10", sandwich	20.00		55.00	
** Plate, 10½", rimmed, dinner	125.00		195.00	
Plate, 10½", grill	15.00	10.00	50.00	
Plate, 10½", grill with closed handles	75.00	6.00		
Plate, 10½", with closed handles	18.00	14.00		
Platter, 12", closed handles	30.00	40.00		
Relish, 7½", footed, 3 part	35.00			175.00
* Salt and pepper, ftd. pr.	75.00		900.00	
Sandwich server, center handle	7,000.00			
Saucer with cup ring	250.00			
Saucer, 6" (sherbet plate)	5.00	3.00	90.00	
Sherbet, 3⅛", molded	16.00	40.00	75.00	
Sherbet, 3⅛", blown	18.00		75.00	
Sherbet, 4⅞"	33.00	90.00	125.00	
Sugar, 3¼"	23.00	22.00		
Sugar, 4¼"	30.00		125.00	
Tumbler, 3¾", 5 oz., juice	37.50		90.00	
Tumbler, 4", 9 oz., water	30.00		80.00	9.00
Tumbler, 4¾", 10 oz., flat	30.00		95.00	
Tumbler, 5", 11 oz., flat	40.00	90.00	95.00	
Tumbler, 5¼", 15 oz.	80.00		135.00	
Tumbler, 3 oz., footed, juice	70.00		135.00	
Tumbler, 5", 9 oz., footed	33.00	18.00	115.00	
Tumbler, 5¾", 11 oz., ftd.	75.00		135.00	
Tumbler, 6⅜", 15 oz., ftd.	500.00			
Vase, 5¾"	285.00			
Vase, 8"	60.00			
Water bottle (dark green) Whitehouse vinegar	30.00			

* Beware reproductions
** Same as flat cake plate

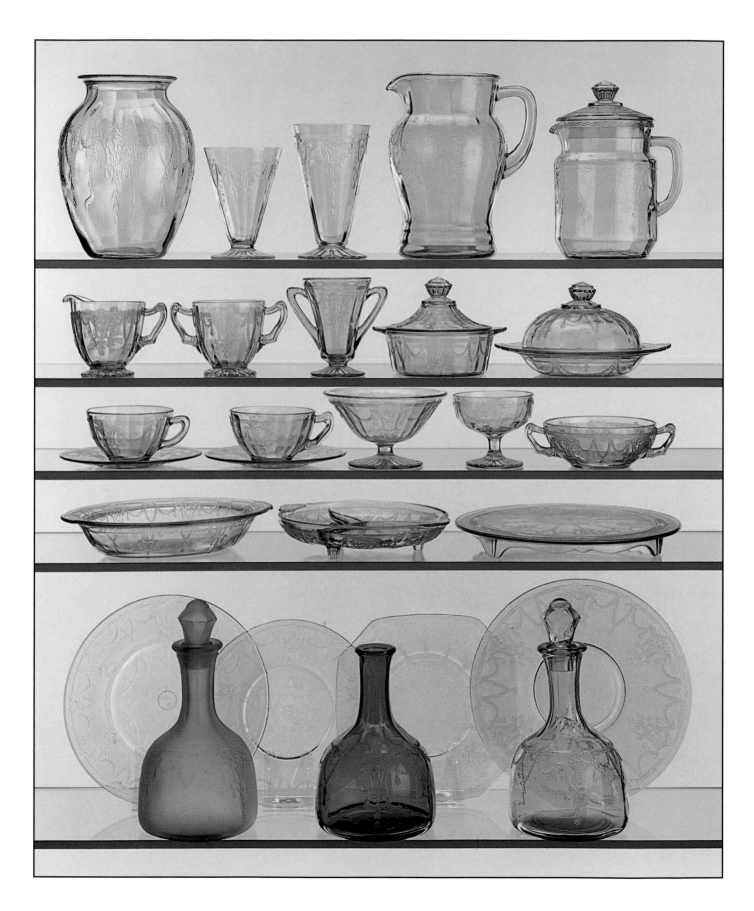

CHERRYBERRY, U.S. GLASS COMPANY, Early 1930s

Colors: pink, green, crystal; some iridized

A small circle of collectors search just for the Cherryberry pattern, first observed by collectors of Strawberry who assumed their pattern was unique until closer examination revealed cherries rather than strawberries. Though U.S. Glass patterns have comparatively few pieces, there are other collectors vying for some of those items, specifically, carnival glass followers looking for the iridized pitchers, tumblers, and butters which are the most precious pieces. Then, there are "item" collectors of butters dishes and pitchers who secure those, too. Therefore, there is quite a bit of rivalry for the few pieces emerging.

Crystal is the rarest "color"; however, only a few try to find it. As with other U.S. Glass Company patterns, many pieces have uneven mould seams. Color discrepancies in green cause a further problem. Green coloration can be found from a very yellow tint to a bluish one. There is not as much color difference with the pink, but there are some pieces that are noticeably lighter than others. If you are a collector who is concerned about matching color hues, this may not be the pattern for you. If you can accept that this old glassware was made under less restricted conditions than is currently used, and that the ensuing burned out and imperfect color matches were part of that glass package, then there is no problem.

Cherryberry is a U.S. Glass pattern that has no cup or saucer and a plain butter base. If all these Depression era U.S. Glass patterns are "sister" patterns, then Strawberry and Cherryberry are twins. You can only differentiate by fruit inspection.

	Crystal, Iridescent	Pink, Green		Crystal, Iridescent	Pink, Green
Bowl, 4", berry	6.50	15.00	Olive dish, 5", one-handled	9.00	20.00
Bowl, 6¼", 2" deep	50.00	150.00	Pickle dish, 8¼", oval	9.00	20.00
Bowl, 6½", deep, salad	20.00	25.00	Pitcher, 7¾"	185.00	195.00
Butter dish and cover	150.00	210.00	Plate, 6", sherbet	6.00	12.00
Butter dish bottom	80.00	100.00	Plate, 7½", salad	7.50	16.00
Butter dish top	70.00	110.00	Sherbet	6.50	10.00
Comport, 5¾"	18.00	28.00	Sugar, small ,open	11.00	22.00
Creamer, small	11.00	22.00	Sugar, large	15.00	20.00
Creamer, 4⅝", large	16.00	40.00	Sugar cover	30.00	50.00
Olive dish, 5", one-handled	9.00	20.00	Tumbler, 3⅝", 9 ounce	20.00	38.00

CHERRY BLOSSOM, JEANNETTE GLASS COMPANY, 1930 – 1939

Colors: pink, green, Delphite (opaque blue), crystal, Jadite (opaque green), and red
(See Reproduction Section.)

On a recent trip to the West Coast, I noticed Cherry Blossom was being sold for prices above those I am asking here in Florida. So prices for some patterns are again being regionalized, as they were in the past. Dealers out west have to pay postage to get glass from the eastern sellers, so cost is higher. Right now, if I were to pack up my booth at a show here and move it 4,000 miles, I would most likely be wiped out by the dealers. That is a slightly puzzling change since the Internet prices are generally pushing more universal standardization. However, the fact that you can *see* exactly what you're buying at a show may be a factor in this equation, also.

The reproduction pessimism does not seem to bother anyone today as educated collectors treat it as just an annoying part of all collecting. If you are a beginner, turn to the Reproduction Section in the back of the book and educate yourself on Cherry Blossom reproductions. (See page 244 – 245.)

Remember that only two pairs of original pink Cherry Blossom shakers were ever documented and as far as I know, these have never resurfaced for sale. Therefore, that price has remained constant. (Original ones are pictured on page 36.) I have lost count, but either 27 or 28 times the third pair materialized. One of these was a single shaker and old, but one other pair sounds promising, though it has not been confirmed. However, the country has been absolutely flooded with reproduction Cherry shakers with their squared, jut wing collars. I continue to get many calls, letters, and e-mails on pink Cherry Blossom shakers. The odds are not on your side for finding genuine pink Cherry shakers today, but I have learned never to say never.

The letters AOP in listings and advertisements stand for "all over pattern" on the footed tumblers and rounded pitcher. The large, footed tumblers and the AOP pitcher come in two styles. One style has a scalloped or indented foot while the other is merely round with no indentations. Sherbets are also found like that. The letters PAT stand for "pattern at the top," illustrated by the flat-bottomed tumblers and pitchers.

I used to list two sizes of flat PAT pitchers in my earlier books, and somehow between third and fourth edition the 36 oz. pitcher was omitted. This time I am presenting them side by side so you can see there really are two different ones available.

That 9" platter is the most difficult piece to find (after genuine shakers). I have only seen one green 9" platter. (Measure this platter outside edge to outside edge.) I have calls for verification if I really mean outside edge. I do. The 11" platter measures 9" from the inside to inside rim and that common piece is not the rare 9" platter. The pink mug is the next rarely found item, but even green ones have disappeared into collections.

Cherry Blossom is susceptible to inner rim chips, nicks, or those famous "chigger bites" as auctioneers like to call chips. Inner rim roughness (irr) resulted as much from stacking glass together as from using it. Of 13 berry bowls in a set bought not long ago, only one was mint. You can safely store dishes (bowls or plates) with paper plates/bowls between them. This is especially true at glass shows where stacks of items are often fingered repeatedly.

Additional Cherry Blossom items that are hard to procure include the flat iced teas, soup or cereal bowls, and the 10" green grill plate. That larger grill plate has never even been found in pink, although there are two sizes found in green. The 9" one can be found without much difficulty. Mint condition grill plates are a prize. You may notice that the price for these has risen considerably over the last few years — mint being the significant word here.

Crystal Cherry Blossom is sometimes spotted. Generally, that two-handled bowl sells in the $20.00 to $25.00 range. Crystal is scarce, but there is apparently not enough found to be collectible as a set.

There are some known experimental pieces of Cherry such as a pink cookie jar, pink five-part relish dishes, orange with green trim slag bowls, and amber children's pieces. A few red (both opaque and transparent) and yellow pieces have surfaced, but the reproduction red wiped out most collectors' desire to own red. The original red was glossy and quite beautiful. You can see most of these pieces pictured in past *Very Rare Glassware of the Depression Era* books and my new *Treasures of Very Rare Glassware*.

Pricing on experimental items or colors is particularly tricky to establish; but do not pass them up if the price is right — for you. The latest rarity being circulated in Cherry Blossom is a green covered casserole dish. I once saw a badly damaged one that had been bought at a neighbor's yard sale for $9.00. Keep looking for another one. Most experimental pieces had a small run of a couple of dozen or more pieces to justify mould costs, if nothing else. Just be sure the piece is old and not a modern day plaything from Taiwan or dupe artists.

CHERRY BLOSSOM

	Pink	Green	Delphite
Bowl, 4¾", berry	18.00	22.00	16.00
Bowl, 5¾", cereal	52.00	47.50	
Bowl, 7¾", flat soup	100.00	90.00	
* Bowl, 8½", round, berry	50.00	50.00	50.00
Bowl, 9", oval vegetable	50.00	50.00	50.00
Bowl, 9", 2-handled	48.00	75.00	28.00
** Bowl, 10½", 3-leg, fruit	100.00	120.00	
Butter dish and cover	90.00	125.00	
Butter dish bottom	20.00	25.00	
Butter dish top	70.00	100.00	
Cake plate (3 legs), 10¼"	35.00	40.00	
Coaster	12.00	12.00	
Creamer	25.00	25.00	22.00
Cup	20.00	20.00	20.00
Mug, 7 oz.	450.00	365.00	
*** Pitcher, 6¾", AOP, 36 ounce scalloped or round bottom	75.00	75.00	80.00
Pitcher, 8", PAT, 42 ounce, flat	75.00	75.00	
Pitcher, 8", PAT, 36 ounce footed	75.00	75.00	
Plate, 6", sherbet	8.00	10.00	10.00
Plate, 7", salad	27.00	25.00	
**** Plate, 9", dinner	22.00	24.00	20.00
***** Plate, 9", grill	35.00	34.00	

	Pink	Green	Delphite
Plate, 10", grill		125.00	
Platter, 9", oval	950.00	1,100.00	
Platter, 11", oval	55.00	60.00	45.00
Platter, 13" and 13" divided	75.00	75.00	
Salt and pepper (scalloped bottom)	1,300.00	1,100.00	
Saucer	4.00	5.00	5.00
Sherbet	20.00	22.00	16.00
Sugar	14.50	17.50	20.00
Sugar cover	20.00	20.00	
Tray, 10½", sandwich	28.00	33.00	22.00
Tumbler, 3¾", 4 ounce, footed, AOP	18.00	20.00	25.00
Tumbler, 4½", 9 ounce, round, footed, AOP	36.00	36.00	25.00
Tumbler, 4½", 8 ounce, scalloped footed, AOP	36.00	36.00	25.00
Tumbler, 3½", 4 ounce, flat, PAT	22.00	33.00	
Tumbler, 4¼", 9 ounce, flat, PAT	17.00	25.00	
Tumbler, 5", 12 ounce, flat, PAT	75.00	85.00	

* Yellow $395.00
** Jadite $325.00
*** Jadite $325.00
**** Translucent green $225.00
***** Jadite $85.00

CHERRY BLOSSOM — CHILD'S JUNIOR DINNER SET

	Pink	Delphite
Creamer	55.00	55.00
Sugar	55.00	55.00
Plate, 6"	12.50	14.00 (design on bottom)
Cup	42.50	50.00
Saucer	7.50	7.25
14 piece set	365.00	390.00

Original box sells for $35.00 extra with pink sets.

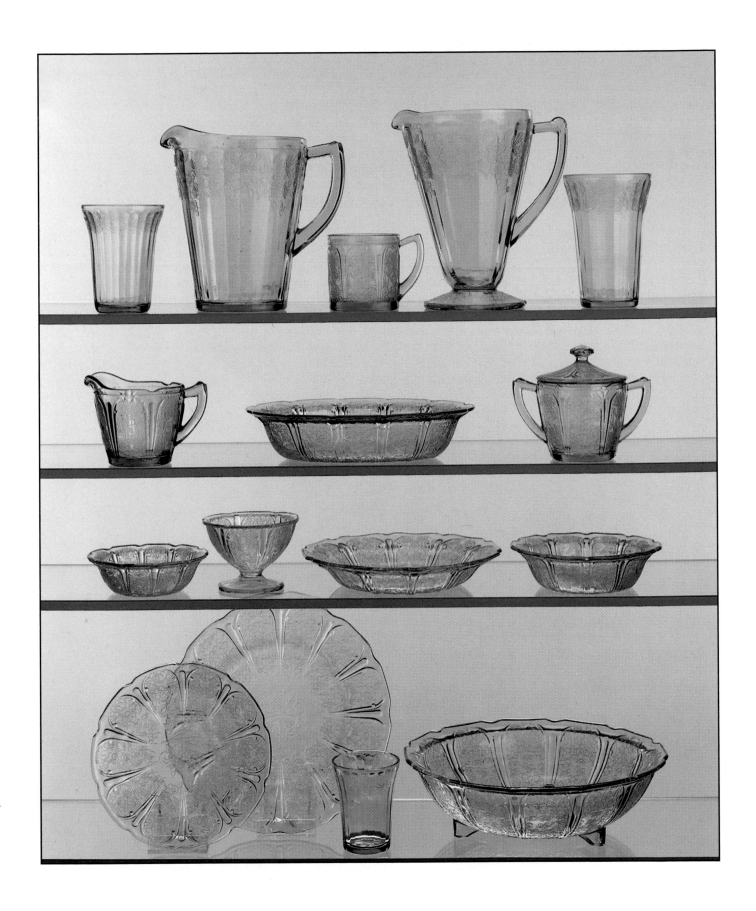

CHINEX CLASSIC, MacBETH-EVANS DIVISION OF CORNING GLASS WORKS, Late 1930s – Early 1940s

Colors: ivory, ivory w/decal decoration

Chinex Classic collectors have an adventure in matching all the different florals found on ivory tint and affiliated Cremax ware. It is bothersome enough to even find the scroll decorated Chinex Classic pattern; but locating a piece you do not have, only to have it decorated with a decal other than the one you seek, is annoying. Those Windsor castle decals are the most captivating decoration to collectors; darker blue trims appear to be more popular than the lighter blue or brown, but they are, also, more difficult to uncover. Notice that the brown Windsor castle comes with or without a brown trim. I see more brown decorated, but that is only a dozen or so pieces displayed at shows each year.

I prefer the dark blue trimmed Windsor castle decal decoration but I have never been lucky enough to find extra to display for sale. Mostly, I see it in the Michigan area when I shop there. I found a butter bottom as you can see in the foreground of the Windsor castle photo. Note the Chinex floral butter top in the bottom photo for which I have been unable to locate a bottom. The floral decal on that top is like those pieces on the right of the lower photograph.

Have you noticed that separate tops and bottoms of butters are becoming scarcer as more collectors are involved in buying glassware?

An additional place to find Chinex is the Pittsburgh area since MacBeth Evans was just down the road. Due to the Internet, recent discoveries have been made in Canada where Corning was a mainstay in glass fabrication. Chinex was promoted as resistant to crazing and chipping which helps explain its comparatively excellent condition, today. It was made to challenge chinaware that did craze and chip. Accordingly, that was an excellent selling point.

Few collect plain, undecorated ivory pieces; but note how they mixed with the floral decorations in our photo. Maybe you could fill in those missing floral decals with this less expensive Chinex.

Notice the butter bottom looks like the Cremax pattern on the edge rather than Chinex. The butter tops have the scroll-like design that distinguishes Chinex, but this scroll design is missing from the butter bottoms. The bottom has a plain "pie crust" edge (like Cremax). The floral or castle designs will be inside the base of the butter, and seemingly surrounding the knob of the top if the top is floral decorated.

	Browntone or Plain Ivory	Decal Decorated	Castle Decal
Bowl, 5¾", cereal	5.50	10.00	18.00
Bowl, 6¾", salad	12.00	20.00	40.00
Bowl, 7", vegetable	14.00	25.00	40.00
Bowl, 7¾", soup	12.50	25.00	40.00
Bowl, 9", vegetable	11.00	25.00	40.00
Bowl, 11"	17.00	35.00	45.00
Butter dish	55.00	75.00	150.00
Butter dish bottom	12.50	27.50	50.00
Butter dish top	42.50	47.50	100.00
Creamer	5.00	10.00	20.00
Cup	4.50	6.50	15.00
Plate, 6¼", sherbet	2.50	4.00	7.50
Plate, 9¾", dinner	4.00	9.00	20.00
Plate, 11½", sandwich or cake	7.50	15.00	30.00
Saucer	2.00	4.00	6.00
Sherbet, low footed	7.00	11.00	27.50
Sugar	5.00	10.00	20.00

CIRCLE, HOCKING GLASS COMPANY, 1930s

Colors: green, pink, and crystal

Green Circle can be collected in sets with time and patience, but one collector informed me that he did not believe it would be possible to buy eight bowls in each style made. Notice that the bowls have jumped in price due to many collectors searching for them. Demand is always the driving factor in prices; rarity only helps. Occasionally a piece is too rare to generate any market interest.

Except for the bowls, Circle is reasonably priced but not so easily found. Pink apparently crops up only in a luncheon set. As you can see by the absence of pink in the picture, I am having no luck getting my hands on it either. Many pieces thought to be common in the early days of collecting are not. If you have a piece of pink not in the listing, please let me know.

Crystal is found only in stems and stems with green. Green stems with crystal tops are more easily found than all green stems. In many Elegant patterns, two-toned stems are often more expensive. This is not the case for Circle. Few currently desire crystal topped items. Thus, you can buy these rather inexpensively.

I have pictured the three different smaller bowls so you can see the differences. They range from 4½" to 5¼" with the flared one measuring 5", but it is clearly a darker shade of green when compared with the other pieces. Different shades of green occur in a few patterns made by Hocking; Cameo comes to mind.

Both the 9⅜" and 5¼" green bowls pictured have ground bottoms. At Hocking, ground bottoms usually suggest early production pieces and generally are a sign of better-made glassware.

The peculiarities of Circle include two different styles of cups. The flat-bottomed style fits a saucer/sherbet plate while the rounded cup takes an indented saucer. I finally found an indented saucer for my round, pink cup, but no saucer/sherbet plate for the flat one.

Collectors of kitchenware (particularly reamer collectors) often buy Circle. They cherish that 80-ounce pitcher with the reamer top. Color dissimilarities on these pitchers make it difficult to obtain a reamer separately that correctly matches the green hue of the pitcher. That 80-ounce pitcher shown here is a darker green (similar to the flared bowl) than the other green items.

	Green	Pink		Green	Pink
Bowl, 4½"	17.50		Plate, 8¼", luncheon	6.00	10.00
Bowl, 5¼"	25.00		Plate, 9½"	12.00	
Bowl, 5", flared, 1¾" deep	30.00		Plate, 10", sandwich	14.00	
Bowl, 8"	35.00		Saucer w/cup ring	2.50	3.00
Bowl, 9⅜"	40.00		Sherbet, 3⅛"	5.00	10.00
Creamer	9.00	25.00	Sherbet, 4¾"	7.00	
Cup (2 styles)	6.00	10.00	Sugar	7.00	25.00
Goblet, 4½", wine	15.00		Tumbler, 3½", 4 ounce, juice	9.00	
Goblet, 8 ounce, water	11.00		Tumbler, 4", 8 ounce, water	10.00	
Pitcher, 60 ounce	75.00		Tumbler, 5", 10 ounce, tea	20.00	
Pitcher, 80 ounce	35.00		Tumbler, 15 ounce, flat	30.00	
Plate, 6", sherbet/saucer	2.00	5.00			

CLOVERLEAF, HAZEL ATLAS GLASS COMPANY, 1930 – 1936

Colors: pink, green, yellow, crystal, and black

Cloverleaf is probably the most recognized pattern of Depression glass. Non-collectors may not know the actual name but they certainly will know it as shamrocks or clover when first seeing it displayed. The "good luck" connected with these little shamrocks may be what you'll need to find some of the pieces in this pattern regardless of the color you choose.

Collectors of green have a wider variety of pieces to gather. It is the color most in demand. The 8" bowl and tumblers sell quickly. All bowls (in any color), as well as grill plates and tumblers are becoming more difficult to gather. Of the three styles of tumblers pictured, it is the flat, straight-sided one, available only in green, which is as shy as a four-leaf clover.

The grill plate (divided in three parts) must suffice as a dinner-sized plate since the luncheon plate will not fill that bill. The candy dish, shakers, and bowls are all difficult to find in yellow. I have seen only one yellow cereal bowl in my travels and none of the other yellow bowls recently. You will be able to find other pieces; but know that many yellow items are getting in short supply and prices are shooting upwards.

There appear to be like numbers of collectors for black or yellow Cloverleaf. Few hunt pink or crystal. Besides luncheon pieces in pink, a berry bowl and a flared, 10 ounce tumbler exist. That pink tumbler was meagerly circulated and has never been found in crystal. How many pink berry bowls have you seen? Prices for these bowls are beginning to wake up.

Black Cloverleaf prices have been relatively stable over the last few years with just a little rise on a few pieces. Small ashtrays are often ignored while the larger ones sell occasionally. I need to point out that the black sherbet plate and saucer are the same size. The saucer has no Cloverleaf design in the center, but the sherbet plate does. Observe the price difference. These sherbet plates still turn up in stacks of saucers occasionally, so keep your eyes open.

I frequently receive questions concerning the Cloverleaf pattern's being moulded on both sides of the pieces, inside or outside. In order for the black to show the pattern, moulds had to be designed with the pattern on the top side of pieces; otherwise, it looked like unadorned black. On transparent pieces, the pattern could be on the bottom or the inside and it would still show. Over the years, transparent pieces were made using the moulds designed for the black; so, you now find these pieces with designs on either top or bottom. This does not make a difference in value or collectibility.

CLOVERLEAF

	Pink	Green	Yellow	Black
Ashtray, 4", match holder in center				60.00
Ashtray, 5¾", match holder in center				95.00
Bowl, 4", dessert	40.00	40.00	40.00	
Bowl, 5", cereal		50.00	60.00	
Bowl, 7", deep salad		80.00	90.00	
Bowl, 8"		100.00		
Candy dish and cover		70.00	125.00	
Creamer, 3⅝", footed		10.00	22.00	16.00
Cup	9.00	9.00	11.00	16.00
Plate, 6", sherbet		10.00	10.00	40.00
Plate, 8", luncheon	11.00	8.00	14.00	15.00
Plate, 10¼", grill		25.00	28.00	
Salt and pepper, pair		40.00	135.00	100.00
Saucer	3.00	3.00	4.00	5.00
Sherbet, 3", footed	10.00	12.00	14.00	20.00
Sugar, 3⅝", footed		10.00	22.00	16.00
Tumbler, 4", 9 ounce, flat		70.00		
Tumbler, 3¾", 10 ounce, flat, flared	30.00	55.00		
Tumbler, 5¾", 10 ounce, footed		30.00	42.50	

COLONIAL, "KNIFE AND FORK," HOCKING GLASS COMPANY, 1934 – 1936

Colors: pink, green, crystal, and Vitrock

Green Colonial is still the color of choice; however all rare and hard to find items are increasing in price regardless of color. Prices for pink are similar to those of green because of rarity more than for any other reason. If pink were as sought as green, there is no telling to what height prices would ascend. Did you notice the white cream soup on the cover of the last book? A white water pitcher was found a couple of years ago and we now have cream soups and liners to add to those already discovered cups, saucers (two styles), luncheon plates, creamers, and sugar bowls. No top has been spotted for that sugar. White has been largely overlooked due to the small number of pieces originally found, but it's beginning to look like a small set might be possible if one wanted to set about that task. There was speculation once that this white was Corning manufactured, but it still looks like Hocking's Vitrock to me.

A crystal Colonial collection can still be started, but it is no longer easy on the pocket. In crystal, Colonial looks incredibly like older pattern glass. Indeed, Cathy found a crystal bowl that is slightly cone shaped that probably is pattern glassware; but it is almost identical to this Colonial design. Perhaps that's where Hocking acquired its "Colonial" name — meaning it had its foundation in an older glass motif.

To date, only one of the beaded top Colonial pitchers in each color has been spotted — though I doubt only one of each was made.

Colonial soup bowls (both cream and flat), cereals, mint shakers, and unmarred dinner plates are still difficult to obtain in each color. The vertical ridges on Colonial pieces have a tendency to chip; when examining a piece, look at those ridges first. Always take the top off any shaker to check for damage. I once bought a shaker with a top I couldn't loosen and when I soaked it free, I found it had been glued on to cover a large chip in the top edge.

Coveted Colonial mugs are seldom seen today. The 11-ounce Colonial tumbler measures 2¾" across the top while the 12 ounce measures exactly 3". These two tumblers are repeatedly confused. It is easier to measure across the top than to measure the contents if you are out shopping. The spooner stands 5½" tall, while the sugar without a lid is only 4½" high. That inch makes a huge difference in price.

The cheese dish consists of a wooden board with an indented groove upon which the glass lid rests. One is pictured below.

The dearth of crystal stemware is now being revealed. Since stems were not made in pink, some collectors mix crystal stems with their pink sets. I have noticed that buyers for both crystal and pink items have picked up recently. The problem with collecting anything other than green is limited availability. I need to point out the pink-footed tumbler next to the pitcher on the bottom of page 44. That is the 3 ounce footed tumbler and not a stem. Because it was brought to my attention at a show, I realize that another book pictures and identifies it as a stem. There are three sizes of footed tumblers and five sizes of stems in Colonial. When collectors ask me why so and so said such and such in their book and they've found out that it is incorrect, I have no answer for why basic glassware knowledge is not present.

COLONIAL

	Pink	Green	Crystal
Bowl, 3¾", berry	65.00		
Bowl, 4½", berry	20.00	20.00	10.00
Bowl, 5½", cereal	65.00	100.00	35.00
Bowl, 4½", cream soup, white $60	75.00	80.00	65.00
Bowl, 7", low soup	75.00	75.00	35.00
Bowl, 9", large berry	30.00	30.00	25.00
Bowl, 10", oval vegetable	40.00	40.00	22.00
Butter dish and cover	750.00	60.00	42.00
Butter dish bottom	475.00	35.00	25.00
Butter dish top	275.00	25.00	17.00
Cheese dish		250.00	
Cream/milk pitcher, 5", 16 oz.	70.00	18.00	20.00
Cup, white $8	10.00	14.00	7.00
Mug, 4½", 12 ounce	600.00	800.00	
+ Pitcher, 7", 54 ounce	50.00	55.00	35.00
*+ Pitcher, 7¾", 68 ounce, white $300	70.00	80.00	45.00
Plate, 6", sherbet	7.00	8.00	3.00
Plate, 8½", luncheon	10.00	11.00	6.00
Plate, 10", dinner	55.00	65.00	30.00
Plate, 10", grill	25.00	25.00	15.00
Platter, 12", oval	35.00	25.00	20.00

	Pink	Green	Crystal
Salt and pepper, pair	150.00	160.00	65.00
Saucer/sherbet plate, white $3	7.00	8.00	3.00
Sherbet, 3"	28.00		
Sherbet, 3⅜"	12.00	14.00	8.00
Spoon holder or celery, 5½"	135.00	130.00	90.00
Stem, 3¾", 1 ounce, cordial		30.00	18.00
Stem, 4", 3 ounce, cocktail		25.00	14.00
Stem, 4½", 2½ ounce, wine		30.00	14.00
Stem, 5¼", 4 ounce, claret		25.00	20.00
Stem, 5¾", 8½ ounce, water		30.00	25.00
Sugar, 4½"	25.00	16.00	8.00
Sugar cover	65.00	27.00	16.00
Tumbler, 3", 5 ounce, juice	22.00	25.00	15.00
** Tumbler, 4", 9 ounce, water	22.00	22.00	15.00
Tumbler, 5⅛" high, 11 ounce	35.00	42.00	22.00
Tumbler, 12 ounce, iced tea	52.00	52.00	24.00
Tumbler, 15 ounce, lemonade	65.00	75.00	45.00
Tumbler, 3¼", 3 ounce, footed	17.00	25.00	10.00
Tumbler, 4", 5 ounce, footed	35.00	45.00	20.00
*** Tumbler, 5¼", 10 ounce, footed	50.00	50.00	27.50
Whiskey, 2½", 1½ ounce	16.00	16.00	12.00

*Beaded top $1,250.00   **Royal ruby $125.00   ***Royal ruby $175.00   +With or without ice lip

COLONIAL BLOCK, HAZEL ATLAS GLASS COMPANY, Early 1930s

Colors: green, crystal, black, pink, and rare in cobalt blue; white in 1950s

Colonial Block is most often found in green and consequently, most collectors buy it rather than pink. Original ads called Colonial Block a modernistic design and "modernism" was the *dernier cri* (latest fashion) of the time. You will find an occasional crystal piece or white creamer and sugar sets. A few black and frosted green Colonial Block powder jars are being found. A cobalt blue Colonial Block creamer is shown in my *Very Rare Glassware of the Depression Years, Second Series.* That creamer can be found with Shirley Temple's image in white. Hazel Atlas also made a different creamer, a mug, and cereal bowl with the same Shirley image. Those have now been reproduced.

Most pieces of Colonial Block are marked HA, but not all. The H is on top of the A, which confuses some people who assume that this is the symbol for Anchor Hocking. The anchor is a symbol used by Anchor Hocking and that was not used until after the 1930s.

U.S. Glass made a pitcher similar in style to Hazel Atlas's Colonial Block. There is little difference in them except most Hazel Atlas pitchers are marked and the one in the photo is not so marked. The handle on the Hazel Atlas pitcher is shaped like those of the creamer and sugar. Collectors today are not as inflexible in their collecting principles as they previously were. Many collectors will buy either pitcher to go with their set. That is why items that are similar to a pattern, but not actually a part of it, are referred to as "go-with" or "look-alike" pieces. In general, these items are more reasonably priced.

Green 4" and 7" bowls, butter tub, sherbets, and the pitcher are the pieces most often lacking in Colonial Block collections. The recently discovered 5-ounce footed juice is the rarest piece in this set. You can check out one of these tumblers in *Very Rare Glassware of the Depression Years, Fifth Series.* How does a small pattern like this have so many hard to find pieces? Colonial Block was most likely limited in distribution; and some of those hard-to-find pieces might have been rewards for some marketed product that did not sell well.

The goblet pictured is Colonial Block and not Block Optic as it is often represented at markets and on the Internet. Some Block Optic collectors use these heavy goblets with their sets because they are more moderately priced than those in Block Optic. Besides, the heavier Colonial Block goblets are probably more durable than the thinner Block Optic. More green sherbets are now finding their way into collections. These were exposed about ten years ago and subsequently, the floodgates released and the market was saturated with these sherbets.

	Crystal	Pink, Green	White		Crystal	Pink, Green	White
Bowl, 4"	4.00	11.00		Goblet	6.00	15.00	
Bowl, 7"	12.00	25.00		Pitcher	25.00	50.00	
Butter dish	30.00	45.00		*Powder jar w/lid	12.00	17.50	
Butter dish bottom	5.00	12.50		Sherbet	4.00	8.00	
Butter dish top	25.00	32.50		Sugar	7.00	10.00	8.00
Butter tub	25.00	45.00		Sugar lid	8.00	15.00	7.50
Candy jar w/cover	25.00	42.00		Tumbler, 5¼", 5 oz., footed		75.00	
Creamer	6.00	12.00	8.00	*Black $22.50			

COLONIAL FLUTED, "ROPE," FEDERAL GLASS COMPANY, 1928 – 1933

Colors: green and crystal

There has not been a new discovery in Colonial Fluted since I started writing 32 years ago. That makes this a difficult pattern to write about for the sixteenth time. The "F" in a shield, usually found in the center of many Colonial Fluted pieces, is the symbol used by the Federal Glass Company. Not all pieces of Federal Glass are marked. No, that "F" does not stand for Fire-King as I am often asked. Many white Federal kitchenware items appear analogous to Fire-King wares. The current Fire-King buying passion has people inspecting these items anyway.

Colonial Fluted was a serviceable pattern that was persistently used; you will find most flat pieces with heavy ware scratches. Knife use erodes the surface of most glassware and Colonial Fluted plates are evidence of that. I rarely see any plates that are not white with wear. When you find Colonial Fluted, it usually is priced moderately enough to use; so, if you like it, do so. Treat this older glass with respect, but enjoy using it.

Colonial Fluted used to be a foundation set for beginning collectors; now, quantities are so limited that new collectors become discouraged looking for it. You will search a long time for bowls. Notice that all bowls have increased in price. Evidently, these were not sold with basic luncheon sets and today their lack is beginning to be recognized.

A few collectors find it an ideal bridge set. Indeed, much of the original advertising for this pattern was centered on bridge parties, which are not as in vogue now as they were in the 1930s. Crystal decorated pieces with hearts, spades, diamonds, and clubs are very collectible.

Colonial Fluted can be mixed with other sets, too, which is a present trend with collectors. There is no dinner plate in the Colonial Fluted pattern. There is a dinner-sized plate made by Federal that goes very well with this which has the roping around the outside of the plate, but not the fluting. There is, also, a grill plate that also goes well with the pattern. It has no roping either. Both of these pieces can expand the number of items in your set and give you larger serving pieces to use. Federal made those items mentioned, so they match in color and most are also Federal marked.

	Green		Green
Bowl, 4", berry	15.00	Plate, 6", sherbet	4.00
Bowl, 6", cereal	18.00	Plate, 8", luncheon	8.00
Bowl, 6½", deep (2½"), salad	35.00	Saucer	2.00
Bowl, 7½", large berry	25.00	Sherbet	7.00
Creamer	10.00	Sugar	10.00
Cup	8.00	Sugar cover	20.00

COLUMBIA, FEDERAL GLASS COMPANY, 1938 – 1942

Colors: crystal, some pink

Crystal Columbia had abundantly distributed butter dishes. Many of these butters were fashioned with flashed colors and floral decal decorations. Some were even satinized (frosted); others were flashed with color after the satin finish was applied. Federal must have fervently promoted these or they came free with some popular product. Other pattern items are less frequently encountered.

Pink Columbia sells particularly well for a pattern that exhibits only four pieces. Prices have calmed down for the moment after some price hikes a few years ago when pink Columbia could not be found fast enough to keep up with demand.

Tumblers have always been in short supply; but, presently, there are other difficulties. Two sizes of Columbia tumblers have now been corroborated, the 2⅞" four-ounce juice and nine-ounce water. A "comparable" tumbler has emerged which is marked "France" on the bottom. Devotees of Columbia need to be aware of this before paying for foreign-made glassware. I might point out that any glassware marked France cannot be considered Depression glass. By definition, Depression glassware is American made.

You might find Columbia water tumblers with advertisements for dairy products printed on them. These were used mostly as containers for cottage cheese. Crystal Columbia bowls continue to increase in value, which may be partly due to non-collectors using them as a "favorite" bowl for company use.

The formerly elusive (except in Colorado) snack tray has begun to turn up more frequently, causing the price to drop. Many collectors have not known what to look for, since it is an unusual piece and shaped differently from most Columbia. The pictures in recent editions have shown the tray so well that collectors are finding these to the point that supply is overrunning demand right now. I have shown a snack tray that has the "winged" tab handles sitting up on the right. These snack plates were found with Columbia cups in a boxed set almost 30 years ago in northern Ohio. Federal Glass Company labeled the box "Snack Sets," with no mention made of Columbia. Snack trays are also being found with Federal cups other than the Columbia pattern, which is probably why so many are being located after all these years. I might mention that there are bowls and a snack set that are designed like the Columbia snack tray. They do not have the center design but do have the "winged" tab handles. These are being found in original Federal boxes labeled "Homestead."

Satinized, pastel-banded, and floral-decaled luncheon sets in Columbia have been seen. These sets are scarce and are selling better now that mixing and matching colors is more popular among collectors.

	Crystal	Pink		Crystal	Pink
Bowl, 5", cereal	18.00		Cup	8.00	25.00
Bowl, 8", low soup	25.00		Plate, 6", bread & butter	4.00	15.00
Bowl, 8½", salad	25.00		Plate, 9½", luncheon	10.00	35.00
Bowl, 10½", ruffled edge	25.00		Plate, 11", chop	18.00	
Butter dish and cover	20.00		Saucer	2.00	10.00
Ruby flashed	22.00		Snack plate	28.00	
Other flashed	21.00		Tumbler, 2⅞", 4 ounce, juice	25.00	
Butter dish bottom	7.50		Tumbler, 9 ounce, water	30.00	
Butter dish top	12.50				

CORONATION, "BANDED RIB," "SAXON," HOCKING GLASS COMPANY, 1936 – 1940

Colors: pink, green, crystal, and Royal Ruby

Coronation was first introduced in 1936 and most likely so designated due to the coronation tribute going on in England at that juncture. It was certainly headline news then. Most collectors first become aware of Coronation because of its tumblers. Coronation's tumblers were perpetually offered for sale as the rarely found Old Colony ("Lace Edge") tumblers. Observe the fine ribs above the middle of the Coronation tumbler. These ribs are missing on the Old Colony footed tumbler. Look at the bottom of page 158 to see the differences with those shown on page 49. Some collectors purposely buy Coronation tumblers to use with Old Colony since they can buy a minimum of three Coronation tumblers for the asking price of one Old Colony. Both are the same shape and color and made by the same manufacturer. Just don't accidentally confuse the two since there is quite a price disparity. Of course, if you see Old Colony tumblers priced as Coronation, which sometimes happen, you smile as you purchase those.

Royal Ruby Coronation cups were sold with crystal saucers. Those crystal saucer/sherbet plates are common crystal pieces found in Coronation. Now, I can report that crystal saucers with an indented cup ring have recently been discovered. I bought a platinum-trimmed cup and saucer set last year in an antique mall in Cincinnati. Not long after that, I had a letter from a collector who had found saucers also. Both lots had platinum decorated rims on the cups and saucers. Cup and saucer collectors, here's another set to seek! A few other crystal pieces are turning up, but there is little demand for them (save for the crescent salads). No Royal Ruby Coronation saucer or sherbet plates have ever been seen. Royal Ruby is the name of the red glass that was made by Hocking beginning in 1938 and only their red glassware can be called Royal Ruby.

Coronation pitchers are rarely seen in person, but I have provided you a photo so you will know what to look for in your explorations. That pitcher is the one piece missing from most collections of Coronation. Most of these were snapped up long ago by collectors of pitchers and tumblers because Coronation collectors themselves thought they were too expensive for this otherwise economically priced pattern. Few pitchers are being advertised for today's collectors to buy.

The handles on Royal Ruby Coronation bowls are open; handles on the pink are closed. Two newly discovered bowls in pink have been without handles. They measure 4¼" and 8", just like the previously discovered green ones. The items in green Coronation at the bottom of page 49 are shown compliments of Anchor Hocking. Additional green pieces now known include the luncheon plate and large or small berry bowls. The larger green tumbler in the lower photograph is 5⁷⁄₁₆" tall and holds 14¼ ounces and, to my knowledge, has never been seen outside the factory. That green crescent salad plate is a rather interesting item for Depression glass. Crescent salads are more prevalent in elegant patterns. A couple of these have also been detected in crystal.

Some dealers often price those commonly found red handled Coronation berry bowls extraordinarily high. I saw one for $22.00 last weekend at a street fair in Florida. They have always been abundant and are rather difficult to sell. Some years ago, a large accumulation was discovered in an old warehouse. They were still in the original boxes. Yet, I regularly see these priced for four to five times their worth. I once saw the large, two-handled berry priced for $75.00. It was marked "rare old pigeon blood." That "pigeon blood" term comes from older collectors who use it to describe dark, red glass (not made from the blood of dead birds). One dealer assured me that his Royal Ruby goblets were rare old pigeon blood pieces, and very valuable. He obviously thought so — since they were priced at $30.00 each two years ago. I recently checked; he still owns them. I suggested an informative book, but he said he has been selling for 30 years and knows all he needs to know. I like to check his booth regularly.

	Pink	Royal Ruby	Green
Bowl, 4¼", berry, handled	8.00	8.00	
Bowl, 4¼", no handles	90.00		55.00
Bowl, 6½", nappy, handled	8.00	20.00	
Bowl, 8", large berry, handled	18.00	20.00	
Bowl, 8", no handles	225.00		195.00
* Cup	5.50	6.50	
Pitcher, 7¾", 68 ounce	650.00		
Plate, 6", sherbet	3.00		
Plate, 8½", luncheon	5.00		60.00
Saucer w/indent (crystal only)	3.00		
Sherbet	11.00		85.00
Tumbler, 5", 10 ounce, footed	33.00		195.00

*Crystal $4.00

CRACKLE, VARIOUS COMPANIES (L.E. SMITH, MCKEE GLASS, MACBETH EVANS, FEDERAL GLASS, U.S. GLASS, ET. AL.), c. 1924

Colors: amber, green, crystal, canary, amethyst, pink, satin (frosted) colors, crystal with color trims

I've had several collectors speak to me from time to time wanting to know why I didn't include crackle in my books. I didn't feel I could afford to spend the hours of research time trying to find out which of the throngs of companies made which pieces. Consequently, I avoided the problem. A couple of years ago, a serious collector appeared at my book table at a show and told me in passionate terms of her love for this type glassware. I asked which company's wares she collected and she said, "Oh, it makes no difference. If it's crackled, that's all I need to know." Captivated, I asked what form of crackle she collected, the genuinely cold water, reheated crackle, or the moulded type. "Oh, I'm only interested in the moulded type. I'm not really into broken looking glass. But," she added, "It would be nice to know what all is available and what kind of prices I should be paying."

I decided that if I were to lump every moulded piece I could find into a listing, then that could serve some objective; and getting it out there would eventually help ascertain what was available to collectors. As a result, here's what I've been able to learn. I'm sure there's more you can contribute and I look forward to hearing what you turn up. Again, we're only dealing with the moulded, crackled appearing wares that were advertised throughout the late twenties and early thirties as making drink liquids "look like cracked ice" or putting you in "refreshing anticipation of a cool summer's drink."

Not everybody had ice available to them at that time, so many companies hopped onto this "suggestion of ice" effect in their glassware lines, particularly in beverage sets; and judging by the available pieces found in markets today, so did the buying public.

There were various finely stippled and crinkled effect wares, too, attempting to mimic the same idea. We're trying not to include them in this list, only the moulded items with the large veins making that cracked ice look. Let me hear what you know about wares with this design. For now, I'm pricing only crystal, using prices I've observed in the market. Colored crackle will fetch 20 – 25% more, except for canary, which will cost up to 50% more.

	*Crystal		*Crystal		*Crystal
Bottle, water	18.00	Cup	10.00	Plate, server, 2-handle	20.00
Butter, small (powder jar style)	25.00	Jar, screw threads	22.00	Sherbet, octagon rim	10.00
Bowl, console	20.00	Pitcher, bulbous middle, water,		Sherbet, round rim	8.00
Bowl, flare rim on black base	35.00	no lid	25.00	Tray, 3-footed, flat	22.50
Bowl, footed, small vegetable	20.00	Pitcher, 64 ounce, bulbous w/lid	40.00	Tumbler, 4¾", footed cone	8.00
Bowl, ruffled, vegetable	20.00	Pitcher, 9", cone, footed	45.00	Tumbler, 5 ounce, bowed middle, juice	10.00
Bowl, hexagon, cereal	12.00	Pitcher, water, slant edge, flat		Tumbler, 9 ounce, bowed middle, water	8.00
Caddy, center handle, 6 holder	12.00	bottom, optic, no lid	30.00	Tumbler, 12 ounce, bowed middle, tea	9.00
Caddy, center handle, 4 holder	10.00	Plate, dessert, round or octagon	8.00	Tumbler, juice, straight side	8.00
Candle, cone	22.00	Plate, salad, round or octagon	9.00	Tumbler, tea, straight side	6.00
Candy box, hexagonal lid	28.00	Plate, 8", round or octagon	10.00	Tumbler, water, straight side	8.00
Candy, footed, round, dome lid	25.00	Plate, cloverleaf snack	13.00	Vase, squat, bulbous with flat rim	12.50
Compote, cheese (for cracker)	12.50	Plate, cracker w/center rim	17.00		

*Colors add 20 – 25%, except canary, add 50%

Cremax, sometimes referred to as "pie crust" design, is a general description for several tableware patterns that were produced in the light ivory glass coloring (called Cremax). These patterns relate to the color itself as well as being part of the pattern name. For instance, there was Cremax Bordette line, with pink, yellow, blue, and green borders; Cremax Rainbow line with pastel pink and green borders; the Cremax Windsor line, with Windsor brown, blue, and green castle decals; and a plain ware simply called Cremax pattern. There was also a six-sided center floral ware called Princess pattern and one with a floral spray known as Flora. The blue or pink-bordered roses have more admirers than do the non-colored border items. The sandwich plate with red flowers on the back right (bottom of page 52) was called "Mountain Flowers." You might recognize it as a Petalware decoration, also. Plain Cremax sets could be acquired very reasonably and were advertised as resistant to chips and guaranteed to be in service for years. Most of what you find today is in good shape, except for worn decaled pieces.

Solid blue glass Cremax has produced the most collectors for this pattern. Even though this blue is commonly seen in Canada and some bordering states, few other collectors realized that there were so many pieces of blue to gather. The Internet has made this blue more available to those wishing to collect it. I have found out that the lighter robin's egg blue was distributed by Corning almost exclusively in Canada. That darker blue shade is not as commonly found in Canada. However, most of what I have found has been in northern states, especially Michigan and New York. At this time, price both shades of blue about the same as the pieces with decals. Assembling a set of the light blue will take time.

Cremax Bordette demitasse sets were advertised in sets of eight. Some sets have been found on a wire rack. The usual make-up of these sets has been two sets each of four colors: pink, yellow, blue, and green. Notice that the interiors of these cups are plain.

The bottom to the butter dish in Chinex is often believed to be Cremax. The scalloped edges of the butter bottom are just like the edges on Cremax plates; however, the only butter tops ever found have the Chinex scroll-like pattern. Thus, if you find only the bottom of butter, it is a Chinex bottom. See page 39 for an example.

The green Windsor castle decal is the most difficult colored decal to find on Cremax. The one piece pictured on page 52 is the only piece I have ever found. This decal is a definite reminder of the infatuation the nation had with the English house of Windsor at this period of Coronation.

	Cremax	*Blue, decal decorated		Cremax	*Blue, decal decorated
Bowl, 5¾", cereal	4.00	12.00	Plate, 6¼", bread and butter	2.00	4.00
Bowl, 7¾", soup	7.50	25.00	Plate, 9¾", dinner	4.50	14.00
Bowl, 9", vegetable	12.00	22.00	Plate, 11½", sandwich	5.50	22.00
Creamer	4.50	10.00	Saucer	1.00	3.50
Cup	4.00	5.00	Saucer, demitasse	4.00	10.00
Cup, demitasse	11.00	25.00	Sugar, open	4.50	10.00
Egg cup, 2¼"	12.00		*Add 50% for castle decal		

"CROW'S FOOT," LINE 412 & LINE 890, PADEN CITY GLASS COMPANY, 1930s

Colors: Ritz blue, Ruby red, amber, amethyst, black, pink, crystal, white, and yellow

"Crow's Foot" is the Paden City mould blank used for most collectible etchings, but the blank itself is sought in Ruby and Ritz blue. The squared mould shape is Line #412, and the round one is Line #890. When "Crow's Foot" is displayed at shows, it never fails to attract new collectors. Price is a significant factor since not everyone can manage to pay for the popular "Cupid," "Orchid," or "Peacock & Wild Rose" etched patterns of Paden City. This new collecting attention has made red and cobalt blue "Crow's Foot" difficult for dealers to keep in stock. New collectors are being shown many Paden City patterns through the Internet; and this publicity seems to be infectious as more and more people are requesting this smaller company's glassware. Frequently, the initial lure is the color rather than the pattern. Some are focused on only round or square items; but a few are mixing them. Fewer collectors are buying amber, crystal, or yellow; but small sets can be found in these colors.

The punch bowl has the telltale "Crow's Foot" pattern rising up from the base. There are similar punch bowls without the "Crow's Foot" on them. Being "just like that, except..." doesn't make it "Crow's Foot!" To command the "Crow's Foot" pattern price, it must have that design.

You may find silver decorated designs on cobalt added by some other company, and even non-"Crow's Foot" collectors often find them attractive. Notice the square-based candles. Black is not ordinarily found, but white is especially limited. You may not admire white glass, but this is one pattern you need to consider purchasing if you find it in white.

Many Paden City red pieces are inclined to run toward an amberina color (especially tumblers). Some collectors will do without before they add a piece showing yellow color. Amberina is a collector's term for the yellowish tint of pieces that were supposed to be red. It was originally an improperly heated glass mistake and not a color that glass manufacturers tried to make. Over the years, amberina has attracted a following of collectors who now seek it for that particular bi-color itself.

	Ruby Red	Black, Ritz Blue	Other colors
Bowl, 4⅞", square	25.00	30.00	12.50
Bowl, 8¾", square	50.00	55.00	25.00
Bowl, 6"	40.00	35.00	15.00
Bowl, 6½", rd., 2½" high, 3½" base	45.00	50.00	22.50
Bowl, 8½", square, 2-handle	50.00	60.00	27.50
Bowl, 10", footed	75.00	75.00	32.50
Bowl, 10", square, 2-handle	75.00	75.00	32.50
Bowl, 11", oval	40.00	45.00	20.00
Bowl, 11", square	60.00	70.00	30.00
Bowl, 11", square, rolled edge	65.00	75.00	32.50
Bowl, 11½", 3 footed, round console	85.00	100.00	42.50
Bowl, 11½", console	75.00	85.00	37.50
Bowl, cream soup, footed/flat	22.00	22.50	10.00
Bowl, Nasturtium, 3 footed	185.00	210.00	90.00
Bowl, whipped cream, 3 footed	55.00	65.00	27.50
Cake plate, square, low pedestal foot	85.00	95.00	42.50
Candle, round base, tall	75.00	85.00	37.50
Candle, square, mushroom	37.50	42.50	20.00
Candlestick, 5¾", sq. based	28.00	30.00	12.50
Candy w/cover, 6½", 3 part (2 styles)	85.00	95.00	40.00
Candy, 3 footed, rd., 6⅛" wide, 3¼" high	150.00	185.00	75.00
Cheese stand, 5"	35.00	30.00	12.50
Comport, 3¼" tall, 6¼" wide	27.50	32.50	15.00
Comport 4¾" tall, 7⅜" wide	50.00	60.00	35.00
Comport, 6⅝" tall, 7" wide	60.00	75.00	30.00
Creamer, flat	14.00	16.00	8.00
Creamer, footed	14.00	16.00	8.00
Cup, footed or flat	12.00	15.00	8.00
Gravy boat, flat, 2 spout	95.00	100.00	50.00
Gravy boat, pedestal	135.00	150.00	65.00
Mayonnaise, 3 footed	55.00	65.00	30.00
Plate, 5¾"	2.25	3.50	1.25
Plate, 8", round	11.00	13.00	4.50
Plate, 8½", square	12.00	14.00	3.50
Plate, 9¼", round, small dinner	35.00	40.00	15.00

	Ruby Red	Black, Ritz Blue	Other colors
Plate, 9½", round, 2-handle	65.00	75.00	32.50
Plate, 10⅜", round, 2-handle	50.00	60.00	25.00
Plate, 10⅜", square, 2-handle	40.00	50.00	20.00
Plate, 10½", dinner	90.00	100.00	40.00
Plate, 11", cracker	45.00	50.00	22.50
Platter, 12"	55.00	60.00	15.00
Relish, 11", 3 part	95.00	100.00	45.00
Sandwich server, round, center-handle	65.00	75.00	32.50
Sandwich server, square, center-handle	45.00	50.00	17.50
Saucer, 6", round	2.50	3.00	1.00
Saucer, 6", square	3.00	3.50	1.50
Sugar, flat	12.00	15.00	5.50
Sugar, footed	12.00	15.00	5.50
Tumbler, 4¼"	75.00	85.00	37.50
Vase, 4⅝" tall, 4⅛" wide	75.00	80.00	40.00
Vase, 10¼", cupped	110.00	129.00	45.00
Vase, 10¼", flared	100.00	115.00	32.50
Vase, 11¾", flared	165.00	195.00	65.00

CUBE, "CUBIST," JEANNETTE GLASS COMPANY, 1929 – 1933

Colors: pink, green, crystal, amber, white, Ultra Marine, canary yellow, and blue

Cube was Jeannettes's geometric pattern made in colors to compete with Fostoria American, a crystal "cubed" design so popular at the time. Novices often confuse the patterns, especially the crystal Cube 2⅝" creamer and 2⁹⁄₁₆" sugar on the 7½" round tray. Only those three Cube pieces were produced in crystal and very little Fostoria American was made in green and is rarely found. The very scarce original pink Fostoria American was a lavender/pink color and not this pretty pink pictured here. Cube is less bright or sparkling in appearance when compared to the brilliant, clearer quality of Fostoria's American pattern.

Any colored Cube-like pitchers shaped differently than the ones pictured here, are almost certainly Indiana's White-hall pattern that was produced in the 1980s and 1990s. I constantly get e-mail photos about these pitchers thought to be Cube or rare Fostoria. Unfortunately, these have been advertised and auctioned on the Internet as "rare" Cube. They are neither Cube nor rare. On Internet auctions, notice whether the seller will guarantee his merchandise. That is usually a strong indication as to whether he is legitimate or not. Other pieces of pink Whitehall, as well as a darker shade of green than Cube's original green, were also made. Cube tumblers are flat, and were made in only one size, as pictured. If you see colored, footed tumblers, they are Whitehall, not Jeannette or Fostoria.

Green Cube is more troublesome to find than the pink, but more collectors search for pink. The quandary in collecting pink (after finding it) is acquiring it in the right hue. Pink Cube varies from a light pink to an orange pink. Pitchers generally look darker due to thickness, but you can find other color discrepancies. This is an example of how difficult it was for glass factories in the Depression to generate consistent quality glassware. As glass tanks got hotter, the pink color got lighter. However, as supplies of this historic glassware diminish, off shades are becoming more acceptable than they once were. There are at least two shades of green. At present, the darker shade of green is not as desirable as the ordinarily found green. Both pink and green Cube cause matching difficulties when ordering through the mail or via the Internet. That it why it is advisable to attend Depression glass shows and examine what you are buying. You might actually be willing to pay a little more for that satisfaction.

Prices for Cube tumblers continue to rise. Almost all collectors are looking for four, six, or eight tumblers; as a result, it takes longer to find tumblers than the pitcher. Inspect the pointed sides of the tumblers and pitchers since they frequently chipped before the heavy rims did.

The Cube powder jar is three footed. A few experimental colors have turned up such as canary yellow and two shades of blue. Occasionally, these jars are found with celluloid or plastic lids. Powder jars came with glass lids from the factory. These may have been sold as replacements when tops were broken. Another possibility is that left-over powder bottoms were sold to someone who made celluloid lids to match brush, mirror, or comb handles for sets they sold. In any case, prices below are for intact, original glass lids. The powder jars with other types of lids sell for half or less. A celluloid lid is better than no lid at all — and for collectors of celluloid items, it's probably better than a glass one!

	Pink	Green
Bowl, 4½", dessert, pointed edge	13.00	13.00
*Bowl, 4½", deep	8.00	
**Bowl, 6½", salad	14.00	15.00
Bowl, 7¼", pointed edge	20.00	22.00
Butter dish and cover	70.00	65.00
Butter dish bottom	20.00	20.00
Butter dish top	45.00	45.00
Candy jar and cover, 6½"	33.00	33.00
Coaster, 3¼"	10.00	10.00
***Creamer, 2⅝"	3.00	
Creamer, 3⁹⁄₁₆"	12.00	14.00
Cup	6.00	7.00
Pitcher, 8¾", 45 ounce	225.00	250.00
Plate, 6", sherbet	3.00	3.00
Plate, 8", luncheon	8.00	9.00
Powder jar and cover, 3 legs	33.00	35.00
Salt and pepper, pair	35.00	35.00
Saucer	2.50	2.50
Sherbet, footed	8.00	9.00
***Sugar, 2⅜"	3.00	
Sugar, 3"	7.00	8.00
Sugar/candy cover	15.00	15.00
Tray for 3⁹⁄₁₆" creamer and sugar, 7½" (crystal only)	4.00	
Tumbler, 4", 9 ounce	80.00	85.00

*Ultra Marine $50.00   **Ultra Marine $90.00
***Amber or white $3.00; crystal $1.00

55

"CUPID," PADEN CITY GLASS COMPANY, 1930s

Colors: pink, green, light blue, peacock blue, black, canary yellow, amber, and crystal

"Cupid" prices have slipped from their upward movement, due to supply finally meeting demand. "Cupid" was introduced to an entirely new group of buyers with the advent of the Internet. Many people found it as exciting as we collectors did when we started buying it almost 30 years ago. With so many people seeing the prices it was bringing, there were many eyes finding it and an equal number of long-time collectors cashing in on the wave of new money. As a result, prices really spiraled and buying was brisk. Then came the economic downturn and more pieces were available than were being bought. Prices run in cycles and demand will cause prices to rise again, but not in a weak economy. Most Paden City etchings have increased at least 20% to 30% in the last few years. Have you seen the stock market in that time?

On my recent trip to Seattle, I counted 23 pieces during the show set-up; and at the end, I counted 23 pieces left. Seven years ago, there were only five pieces and four sold including one to me. Some wild prices are being asked but there seem to be few buyers for now. These prices may well seem very tame in the future, but not at present.

Prices are the most difficult part of writing this book. Even with all the help from other dealers around the country, prices never please everyone. If you own a piece, you want it to be highly priced; if you want to buy the same piece, you want the price to be low. Keep in mind that one sale at a high price does not mean that everyone would be willing to pay that. That is especially true of rare glass and any outrageous sums obtained on Internet auctions. If two people want something and have the money (or if one person simply does not want the other to get the item cheaply), then there may be any price paid. That does not mean that that identical item will sell for that price the next time — or ever again. Only you can determine what a piece of glass is worth to you.

Cupid cups and saucers are still in hiding. They have only been spotted in pink. I once bought six cups but that was an aberration.

A bottom to a tumble-up has been spotted, but there have been no reports of a tumbler surfacing. Several pink and green casseroles have been found, but only two casseroles in black with silver overlay that I pictured in earlier books.

Samovars are found occasionally and are a magnet of attention when they are displayed. Big prices were being asked for the last ones seen. One has been making the show circuit for three years, which has permitted many to see it that might not otherwise have. I might point out that to be a "Cupid" samovar, the "Cupid" pattern has to be etched on it. Mould shape alone does not make the pattern. I once had a beautiful, but plain, samovar shipped to me as "Cupid;" so I speak of this from familiarity. Yes, the etch does makes a difference!

Other information has been added regarding the "Cupid" design found on silver overlay vases marked "Made in Germany." These vases have been found in cobalt, orange, and lavender in Arizona, California, Pennsylvania, and Florida. The newest report concerns a silver overlay vase marked "Made in Czechoslovakia," which may help date these, at least.

"CUPID"

	Green, Pink		Green, Pink
Bowl, 8½", oval footed	275.00	Ice bucket, 6"	325.00
Bowl, 9¼", footed fruit	295.00	Ice tub, 4¾"	325.00
Bowl, 9¼", center-handled	275.00	**** Lamp, silver overlay	495.00
Bowl, 10¼", fruit	215.00	***** Mayonnaise, 6" diameter,	
Bowl, 10½", rolled edge	200.00	fits on 8" plate, spoon, 3 piece	210.00
Bowl, 11", console	200.00	******Plate, 10½"	150.00
Cake plate, 11¾"	200.00	Samovar	1,100.00
Cake stand, 2" high, footed	200.00	Saucer	35.00
* Candlestick, 5" wide, pair	225.00	Sugar, flat	195.00
Candy w/lid, footed, 5¼" high	395.00	Sugar, 4¼", footed	150.00
Candy w/lid, 3 part	295.00	Sugar, 5", footed	150.00
** Casserole, covered	695.00	Tray, 10¾", center-handled	200.00
*** Comport, 6¼"	195.00	Tray, 10⅞", oval-footed	250.00
Creamer, flat	195.00	Vase, 8¼", elliptical	695.00
Creamer, 4½", footed	150.00	Vase, fan-shaped	525.00
Creamer, 5", footed	150.00	Vase, 10"	335.00
Cup	195.00	Water bottle w/tumbler	750.00

*Blue $395.00   *** Blue $250.00   *****Blue $295.00

Black (silver overlay) $750.00   ** Possibly German   ****** Blue $225.00

DAISY AND BUTTON W/NARCISSUS, LINE 124, INDIANA GLASS COMPANY, c. 1920s

Color: crystal and with colored stains; Sunset (amberina) and Ruby for Tiara Exclusives

Early pattern glass books attribute this pattern to the 1890s, so I never gave it much thought. However, in doing research for the *Pattern ID* books, I ran across a *Glass Review* article written in 1980 by Barbara Shaeffer and Vel Hinchliffe that intrigued me. They stated they found this pattern in a 1932 Indiana Glass catalog. That would certainly make the pattern Depression era. Hence, we are including the pattern here. Another author is said to have found a piece of this advertised in a 1918 Sears catalogue. I'm certain there are more items to be found than those listed here and I would appreciate your letting me know what you uncover.

You should know that Indiana reintroduced a decanter and tray with six wines in crystal and their amberina (Sunset) and Ruby color for Tiara Exclusives home partyware division after their opening in the 1970s. The tray was scalloped in the original. The newer version had paneled edging and a flat rim. So, colored wares were made in the last 30 years. I've seen a wine set with faint amethyst staining and that would've been done originally. Staining techniques were used in the early part of the twentieth century to enhance plain crystal wares.

	*Crystal		*Crystal
Bowl, 4⅛", salad (their call)	8.00	Creamer	12.50
Bowl, 4⅛" 3-toed, fruit	12.50	Decanter w/stop, 12½"	35.00
Bowl, 5½", ftd. bonbon	15.00	Goblet, water	12.50
Bowl, round, vegetable	22.50	Goblet, 4⅝", wine	12.50
Bowl, 9½" oval, ftd.	25.00	Pitcher	65.00
Butter w/cover	35.00	Tumbler, 4⅜", water	12.50
Compote, 4½", ftd. jelly	15.00	Sugar	12.50
Cup, custard	8.00	Tray, 10⅜"	22.50

* Add 25% for items with colored stains

DELLA ROBBIA, #1058, WESTMORELAND GLASS COMPANY, Late 1920s – 1940s

Colors: crystal, crystal w/applied lustre colors, milk glass, pink, purple slag, and opaque blue

Note that Della Robbia is pattern #1058. I previously have shown catalog pages that had some other lines shown along with Della Robbia items. If not shown as #1058, then it is not Della Robbia.

Della Robbia is another pattern spurred on by Internet buying. Maybe you noticed the purple slag candy jar on the cover. It was made in Westmoreland's declining years, and not in abundance. I am not sure how much demand there is for it, but the Collector Books' cover designer obviously liked it. No, I do not design the covers. An unusually talented individual who makes this glass look its best does them.

In addition to the purple slag, you will find Della Robbia in crystal, pink, opaque blue, milk glass, and crystal with applied lustre colors. Notice that the fruits on each piece consist of apples, pears, and grapes. Two distinct color variations in the fruit decorations occur on crystal. All apples are red; pears, yellow; and grapes, purple; but the luster of the colors applied is diverse. The darker colored fruits are most in demand. The dilemma with this darker color is that the applied lustre scrapes easily. Scratches are conspicuous on the darker hue. However, most collectors prefer not to mix the two. I have never seen a punch set in the darker stain although I've had a recent report of one.

My listing is just a start from the meager catalog information that I own. Let me know if you have further information. Della Robbia is captivating new collectors and supplies of many pieces are beginning to be strictly limited.

There are a couple of other patterns similar to Della Robbia, but both include a banana in the design. If there is a banana in the design, it probably is an Indiana pattern.

If you have ever tried to carry around an 18" plate for that punch set, you will understand why you see so few of them for sale at shows. Special boxes have to be adapted to hold it.

Dinner plates now fetch $165.00, if you can find one at any price. All serving pieces need to be carefully examined for wear. Remember the prices listed are for mint condition pieces and not ones that are worn or scuffed. One of the reasons prices for mint condition pieces are high is that there are so many worn pieces offered and few perfect ones.

Della Robbia pitcher and tumbler moulds were used to make some carnival colored water sets. These were made for Levay just as were pieces of red English Hobnail. They appear in light blue and amethyst carnival. I am told that Westmoreland collectors seek them, but no collector of Della Robbia has ever questioned me about them.

	Crystal w/ lustre colors		Crystal w/ lustre colors
Basket, 9"	225.00	Plate, 6", finger liner	12.00
Basket, 12"	325.00	Plate, 6⅛", bread & butter	15.00
Bowl, 4½", nappy	30.00	Plate, 7¼", salad	25.00
Bowl, 5", finger	35.00	Plate, 9", luncheon	45.00
Bowl, 6", nappy, bell	35.00	Plate, 10½", dinner	165.00
Bowl, 6½", one handle nappy	35.00	*Plate, 14", torte	150.00
Bowl, 7½", nappy	45.00	Plate, 18"	235.00
Bowl, 8", nappy, bell	65.00	Plate, 18", upturned edge, punch bowl liner	210.00
Bowl, 8", bell, handle	85.00	Platter, 14", oval	215.00
Bowl, 8", heart, handle	125.00	Punch bowl set, 15 piece	995.00
Bowl, 9", nappy	115.00	Salt and pepper, pair	80.00
Bowl, 12", footed	165.00	Salver, 14", footed, cake	160.00
Bowl, 13", rolled edge	160.00	Saucer	10.00
Bowl, 14", oval, flange	275.00	Stem, 3 ounce, wine	30.00
Bowl, 14", punch	335.00	Stem, 3¼ ounce, cocktail	28.00
Bowl, 15", bell	225.00	Stem, 5 ounce, 4¾", sherbet, high foot	25.00
Candle, 4"	35.00	Stem, 5 ounce, sherbet, low foot	22.00
Candle, 4", 2-lite	150.00	Stem, 6 ounce, champagne	28.00
Candy jar w/cover, scalloped edge	125.00	Stem, 8 ounce, 6", water	35.00
Candy, round, flat, chocolate	110.00	Sugar, footed	25.00
Comport, 6½", 3⅝" high, mint, footed	40.00	Tumbler, 5 ounce, ginger ale	28.00
Comport, 8", sweetmeat, bell	115.00	Tumbler, 8 ounce, footed	30.00
Comport, 12", footed, bell	135.00	Tumbler, 8 ounce, water	25.00
Comport, 13", flanged	135.00	Tumbler 11 ounce, iced tea, footed	35.00
Creamer, footed	25.00	Tumbler 12 ounce, iced tea, bell	40.00
Cup, coffee	20.00	Tumbler 12 ounce, iced tea, bell, footed	40.00
Cup, punch	15.00	Tumbler 12 ounce, 5⅜₁₆", iced tea, straight	42.00
Pitcher, 32 ounce	275.00	*Pink $150.00	

DIAMOND QUILTED, "FLAT DIAMOND," IMPERIAL GLASS COMPANY, Late 1920s – Early 1930s

Colors: pink, blue, green, crystal, black; some red and amber

Diamond Quilted can be collected in sets of pink or green with time and patience. Some pieces are discovered in the other colors such as red and amber. Red is purchased more by collectors of red glass than by Diamond Quilted collectors since only a few pieces were made in red. Black Diamond Quilted will take a long time to accumulate the luncheon set. Flat black pieces have the design on the bottom. Thus, the design on the plate can only be seen if it is turned over. Intermittently, items in blue can be located, but it will take more than a little luck to get your hands on very much. There is a similar Fenton pattern found more frequently in both blue and black. If you are willing to blend these, you might serve your guests more quickly. Some of these Fenton pieces were pictured in earlier editions.

Punch bowl sets remain difficult to find. I have only seen one for sale in the last few years and it was missing some cups. Those punch bowls in green are a different shade of green than most other pieces. Therefore finding cups to match is a major predicament. Since the regular cup mold was also used to make the punch cup that creates some havoc in finding green cups and saucers in matching hues. I saw some cups at a recent show that cried out for a punch bowl; they were the wrong color for the saucers on which they were displayed.

There is no dinner-sized plate in Diamond Quilted. Lack of a dinner plate used to be a detriment. I've noticed lately, however, that some actually prefer the smaller luncheon plates. Perhaps that's due to the diet craze in this country.

Hazel Atlas made a quilted diamond pitcher and tumbler set in crystal, pink, green, cobalt blue, and a light blue similar to the one shown here. They are often confused with Imperial's Diamond Quilted. The quilting on Hazel Atlas pieces ends in a straight line around the top of each piece. Notice Imperial's Diamond Quilted pattern ends unevenly in points. You may also notice that the diamond designs on Hazel Atlas pieces are flat as opposed to those Imperial ones that are curved. The Hazel Atlas pitcher is flat and shaped like the straight-sided pitcher so commonly seen in Royal Lace.

Note the original sales catalog depiction below. Console sets at 65¢ and a dozen candy dishes in assorted colors for $6.95 would be quite a bargain today. No, I do not have any for sale at that price. This ad is from a 1930s catalog.

	Pink, Green	Blue, Black		Pink, Green	Blue, Black
Bowl, 4¾", cream soup	15.00	25.00	Cup	9.50	17.50
Bowl, 5", cereal	10.00	15.00	Goblet, 1 ounce, cordial	12.00	
Bowl, 5½", one handle	9.00	22.00	Goblet, 2 ounce, wine	12.00	
Bowl, 7", crimped edge	12.00	25.00	Goblet, 3 ounce, wine	12.00	
Bowl, 7", straight	16.00	22.00	Goblet, 6", 9 ounce, champagne	11.00	
Bowl, 10½", rolled edge console	20.00	60.00	Ice bucket	55.00	85.00
Cake salver, tall, 10" diameter	95.00		Mayonnaise set:		
Candlesticks (2 styles), pair	28.00	40.00	ladle, plate, comport	36.00	56.00
Candy jar and cover, footed	75.00		Pitcher, 64 ounce	55.00	
Compote, 6" tall, 7¼" wide	45.00		Plate, 6", sherbet	4.00	8.00
Compote and cover, 11½"	95.00		Plate, 7", salad	6.00	11.00
Creamer	12.00	15.00	Plate, 8", luncheon	10.00	15.00
			Punch bowl and stand	595.00	
			Plate, 14", sandwich	15.00	
			Sandwich server, center handle	25.00	50.00
			Saucer	4.00	6.00
			Sherbet	10.00	16.00
			Sugar	12.00	15.00
			Tumbler, 9 ounce, water	9.00	
			Tumbler, 12 ounce, iced tea	9.00	
			Tumbler, 6 ounce, footed	8.50	
			Tumbler, 9 ounce, footed	12.50	
			Tumbler, 12 ounce, footed	15.00	
			Vase, fan, dolphin handles	55.00	75.00
			Whiskey, 1½ ounce	10.00	

Covered Bowl—6⅜ in. diam., deep round shape with 3 artistic feet, dome cover, fine quality brilliant finish **pot glass**, allover block diamond design, transparent Rose Marie and emerald green.
1C5603—Asstd. ½ doz. in carton, 20 lbs. **Doz $6.95**

1C989—3 piece set, 2 transparent colors (rose and green), good quality, 10½ in. rolled rim bowl. TWO 3½ in. wide base candlesticks. Asstd. 6 sets in case, 30 lbs. .... **SET (3 pcs) 65c**

DIANA, FEDERAL GLASS COMPANY, 1937 – 1941

Colors: pink, amber, and crystal

Pink Diana remains the color to collect; but that crystal with color enhanced trims, pictured here, created quite a stir when first shown in the last book. Many have searched, but few have found items decorated like this. Price advances are not as frenzied as they were five or six years ago, but prices for candy jars, shakers, and tumblers have increased in each color. For a couple of years the prices doubled on some items, but that is no longer true. Now, in this economic uncertainty, there has been a price correction for many Depression glass patterns on the market, although not as bad as stocks of late.

Crystal Diana is not as available as it once was, and collectors have been paying more to finish sets. Those crystal tumblers may be as rare as their pink counterparts, though not as many collectors are searching for them. Amber and crystal Diana are not as sought by collectors as the pink, a good thing since there is a paucity of these colors. I have seen pictures of one collector's rainbow Diana collection, which was charming as she'd displayed it. Creativity is always a plus. This fusion of colors appears to be the collecting path of the future.

Demitasse sets, sherbets, and even platters are seldom found in any Diana color. There are fewer demitasse sets being marketed than in the past. Sets in crystal are more plentiful, as are the sprayed cranberry pink or red sets. Flashed red demitasses are selling for $10.00 to $12.00 each. Pink demitasse cup and saucer sets are being found occasionally, but the demand for these has slowed. This has caused prices to slip some. I have encountered at least one demitasse collector who told me the Diana pattern is what got her started on those.

Prices listed are actual selling prices for Diana and not advertised or wished-for prices. There is a major difference between an advertised price and the price being accepted by both buyer and seller. Rarely have I heard of something selling for more than advertised, but often I have heard of less. Today, dealers coast to coast are sharing information on prices. That's been a tremendous help to me as I work to keep pricing current in these books. The Internet, though a new tool for pricing, has to be approached carefully and not taken too literally. I attend as many Depression glass shows as possible and spend many hours checking prices and talking to dealers about what is, and what is not selling — and for what price.

Frosted or satinized pieces of Diana that have shown up in crystal and pink have a few admirers. Some of the larger bowls were frosted and drilled for ceiling globes. Some crystal-frosted pieces have been trimmed in colors, predominantly red, but you might spot green, yellow, or blue. A set of crystal-frosted items with different colored trims is not as bizarre looking as you might surmise. However, achieving any of these specialty sets is a major undertaking unless you spy a complete set to start.

There is a propensity for new collectors to mistake Diana with other swirled patterns such as Swirl and Twisted Optic. The centers of Diana pieces are swirled where the centers of other swirled patterns are plain. That elusive and somewhat odd Diana sherbet is shown in amber and in pink. The spirals on this sherbet are often mistaken for Hocking's Spiral and there is understandable debate as to its validity since it hardly resembles the finer lines of the remaining pieces of the pattern. It is shown in an original Federal advertisement for Diana. Pieces advertised by the company with a particular pattern are often accepted as that pattern even though they clearly are not. Another brilliant example of this is the Moderntone tumbler.

	Crystal	Pink	Amber
* Ashtray, 3½"	2.50	3.50	
Bowl, 5", cereal	6.00	10.00	14.00
Bowl, 5½", cream soup	12.00	30.00	20.00
Bowl, 9", salad	12.00	20.00	18.00
Bowl, 11", console fruit	16.00	35.00	15.00
Bowl, 12", scalloped edge	16.00	30.00	20.00
Candy jar and cover, round	16.00	60.00	50.00
Coaster, 3½"	2.50	8.00	10.00
Creamer, oval	9.00	16.00	9.00
Cup	6.00	20.00	9.00
Cup, 2 ounce demitasse and 4½" saucer set	13.00	40.00	
Plate, 6", bread & butter	2.00	5.00	2.00
Plate, 9½"	6.00	20.00	9.00
Plate, 11¾", sandwich	9.00	25.00	10.00
Platter, 12", oval	12.00	33.00	15.00
Salt and pepper, pair	35.00	90.00	115.00
Saucer	1.50	5.00	2.00
Sherbet	3.00	10.00	10.00
Sugar, open oval	9.00	16.00	8.00
Tumbler, 4⅛", 9 ounce	35.00	55.00	30.00
Junior set: 6 demitasse cups & saucers with round rack	100.00	275.00	

* Green $3.00

DOGWOOD, "APPLE BLOSSOM," "WILD ROSE," MacBETH-EVANS GLASS COMPANY, 1929 – 1932

Colors: pink, green, some crystal, Monax, Cremax, and yellow

Dogwood is one of the top ten collectible Depression patterns. Pink is the color most wanted, which is fortunate since pink is most often found. Green is available only in small quantities. Pink luncheon plates are bountiful and anyone who likes this pattern will probably find these first. The larger dinner plates are hard to find without scratches or scuffs; and the large fruit bowl and platter are almost non-existent for today's collectors. They were infrequently found over the years and usually enter the market now only through collections being sold or split among family members.

Large fruit bowls are so scarce because they were marketed to some company that satinized the bowls, bored a hole in the center, and made ceiling fixtures out of them. These sell in the $125.00 range whether pink or green. Notice this is considerably less than prices for normal bowls. There is a growing inclination among collectors to own Depression glass shades and vintage light fixtures. Many use these today.

Pink pitchers and water tumblers are seldom found and are costly. Ice teas are scarce and the pink juice tumbler is truly rare; that price has escalated so that few collectors buy more than one. All green tumblers are difficult to find, but no juice has yet been discovered.

Tumblers and pitchers that have the same shape as those of Dogwood, but do not have the Dogwood silk screening, are not Dogwood. They are merely the mould blanks made by MacBeth-Evans to go with the plain, no design tumblers that they sold separately with various pink sets such as "S" pattern and even American Sweetheart. The Dogwood design has to be silk screened onto the tumbler or pitcher for it to be considered Dogwood and to command those prices shown below. Some collectors buy these plain blanks to use with their sets, and that's perfectly fine as long as they understand that they are not the costly Dogwood.

A few pieces of yellow (cereal bowl or luncheon plate) are found. It is a rarely seen color in Dogwood, and there is not much demand for it. Cremax (beige as shown in center of top photo) and Monax (white) are also unusual colors of Dogwood, but do not thrill many collectors. The Monax salver (12" plate pictured in rear) was once considered rare; but, over the years, it has turned out to be more of a novelty with collectors than a desired item. You can buy them for less now than you could 25 years ago.

There is a rolled edge cereal bowl being found that is different from the regular cereal. The flattened edge turns outward making it not as tall, nor would it hold as much as the normally found cereal (shown as insert on page 67). These are being valued in a broad range, but will sell for $20.00 to $25.00 more than the regular cereal. How rare these are is uncertain right now.

The thick, footed-style Dogwood sugar and creamer are illustrated in pink. There is a thin, flat style creamer and sugar, also. Pink sugar/creamer sets are found in both styles, but green is only found in the thin version. Thin creamers were produced by adding a spout to thin cups while still hot, and some of these have very indistinct spouts. There are thick and thin pink cups, but saucers for both styles are the same. Green cups were only made in thin.

Pink grill plates occur in two styles. Some have the Dogwood pattern all over the plate as the pink one pictured does, and others have the pattern only around the rim. Sherbets, grill plates (rim pattern only), and the large fruit bowls are difficult to acquire in green Dogwood.

Dogwood sherbets are found with a Dogwood blossom etched on the bottom or plain. It makes no difference in price since they are only from different moulds.

Very Rare Glassware of the Depression Years, Second Series pictures the only known Dogwood coaster. A Dogwood-like Tiffin pattern called Sylvan came with stems, unlike Dogwood.

	Pink	Green	Monax, Cremax		Pink	Green	Monax, Cremax
* Bowl, 5½", cereal	33.00	35.00	15.00	Plate, 9¼", dinner	34.00		
Bowl, 8½", berry	62.00	135.00	40.00	Plate, 10½", grill, AOP or			
** Bowl, 10¼", fruit	565.00	295.00	125.00	border design only	25.00	28.00	
Cake plate, 11", heavy				Plate, 12", salver	35.00		15.00
solid foot	1,250.00			Platter, 12", oval	750.00		
Cake plate, 13", heavy				Saucer	4.00	7.00	20.00
solid foot	150.00	135.00	225.00	Sherbet, low footed	33.00	125.00	
Coaster, 3¼"	625.00			Sugar, 2½", thin, flat	18.00	45.00	
Creamer, 2½", thin, flat	18.00	47.50		Sugar, 3¼", thick, footed	16.00		
Creamer, 3¼", thick, footed	23.00			Tumbler, 3½", 5 ounce,			
Cup, thick	16.00		45.00	decorated	235.00		
Cup, thin	14.00	42.00		Tumbler, 4", 10 ounce, decorated	50.00	105.00	
Pitcher, 8", 80 ounce, decorated	265.00	575.00		Tumbler, 4¾", 11 ounce,			
Pitcher, 8", 80 ounce (American				decorated	50.00	110.00	
Sweetheart Style)	650.00			Tumbler, 5", 12 ounce, decorated	80.00	135.00	
Plate, 6", bread and butter	9.00	12.00	22.00	Tumbler, moulded band	25.00		
* Plate, 8", luncheon	7.00	10.00					

* Yellow $75.00
** Lampshade $150.00

DORIC, JEANNETTE GLASS COMPANY, 1935 – 1938

Colors: pink, green, some Delphite, Ultra Marine, and yellow

Doric has become an enjoyable challenge to collectors, and may require years to finish a set. A woman came to me recently to report she had bought the last piece that completed her set after seeking it for over 20 years. She was trying to decide "Which pattern to start next?" She liked the heavy Doric shapes so she was considering green. That might take more than 20 years! Collectors tell me they do not care how difficult a pattern is to acquire because the chase fascinates them almost as much as the glass itself. In addition, some collectors aren't even trying for complete sets in today's market. They're blending patterns and colors they like into rainbow settings.

Collectors of green Doric are distraught by the dearth of pitchers and cream soups. The green 48-ounce pitcher, with or without ice lip, is nearly imaginary for everyone today. Cereal bowls and all tumblers are only being spotted infrequently. Those pieces in pink are not commonly seen either, but they can all be located with determined searching, save for the cream soup, never yet seen in pink. Cream soups, or consommés as some companies called them, are two handled. Cereal bowls have no handles but are often misidentified as cream soups.

There is mould seam roughness on most pieces of Doric, especially on those elusive footed tumblers and cereals. This discourages meticulous collectors who look for flawlessness. I, personally, would not let a little irregularity stop me from owning these pieces if I saw them for sale. Remember that Depression glass was reasonably priced, give-away glass. Mint condition, though desirable in glass collecting, can be carried to ridiculous extremes. Magnifying glasses to look for flaws and black (ultraviolet) lights to check for repairs are seen at shows today. The light shows items that fluoresce, too, a property in some glass that is becoming a collectible factor. This does not mean an item is old just because it fluoresces. That is an erroneous declaration I often hear in malls.

Green Doric is found in Florida, but is often cloudy ("sick") glass. Apparently, well water created mineral deposits that react with the glass. You could make a fortune if you could figure out a way to remove these deposits easily. I know I have heard of everything from Zud® to Efferdent® tablets. As far as I know, this cloudiness cannot be expunged short of polishing it out over a span of time. People with the proper equipment are now doing that, but it is expensive. Do not be hoodwinked into buying cloudy glass unless it is inexpensive, you plan to use and wash it in your dishwasher regularly, or you have that magic cure.

Only one yellow Doric pitcher is known to exist; but it is improbable that the factory made only one. Former workers have advised me that even experimental color runs commonly consisted of 30 to 50 items. Large, footed Doric pitchers come with or without an ice lip. Strangely, candy and sugar lids in this Jeannette pattern are not interchangeable as is true for most of their wares. The candy lid is taller and more domed.

Sherbet and cloverleaf candies are commonly found in Delphite. All other Delphite pieces are rare in Doric and the price is still inexpensive for so rare a color. Only the Delphite pitcher creates much of a pricing stir. Jeannette made mostly kitchenware items in Delphite, rather than dinnerware.

An iridescent, three-part candy was made in the 1970s and sold for 79¢ in our local dish barn. Sometimes an Ultra Marine candy is found within a piece of hammered aluminum. I recently saw a 1950s ad showing that the company Everlast Metal Products Corp. made that 12" piece of aluminum.

	Pink	Green	Delphite		Pink	Green	Delphite
Bowl, 4½", berry	12.00	14.00	55.00	Plate, 6", sherbet	6.00	7.00	
Bowl, 5", cream soup		450.00		Plate, 7", salad	20.00	25.00	
Bowl, 5½", cereal	80.00	95.00		Plate, 9", dinner,			
Bowl, 8¼", large berry	32.00	38.00	150.00	serrated 195.00	18.00	20.00	
Bowl, 9", 2-handled	35.00	40.00		Plate, 9", grill	25.00	25.00	
Bowl, 9", oval vegetable	45.00	55.00		Platter, 12", oval	35.00	40.00	
Butter dish and cover	80.00	100.00		Relish tray, 4" x 4"	15.00	12.00	
Butter dish bottom	25.00	30.00		Relish tray, 4" x 8"	25.00	20.00	
Butter dish top	55.00	70.00		Salt and pepper, pair	32.00	37.50	
Cake plate, 10", 3 legs	30.00	35.00		Saucer	3.50	4.50	
Candy dish and cover, 8"	40.00	45.00		Sherbet, footed	16.00	20.00	10.00
*Candy dish, 3-part	10.00	10.00	12.00	Sugar	15.00	15.00	
Coaster, 3"	17.50	20.00		Sugar cover	20.00	30.00	
Creamer, 4"	20.00	14.00		Tray, 10", handled	28.00	32.00	
Cup	11.00	14.00		Tray, 8" x 8", serving	40.00	45.00	
Pitcher, 5½", 32 ounce, flat	50.00	60.00	1,500.00	Tumbler, 4½", 9 ounce	80.00	125.00	
Pitcher, 7½", 48 ounce,				Tumbler, 4", 10 ounce, footed	75.00	110.00	
footed, yellow at $2,000.00	750.00	1,350.00		Tumbler, 5", 12 ounce, footed	90.00	140.00	

*Candy in metal holder $40.00, Iridescent made in the 70s, Ultra Marine $18.00

DORIC AND PANSY, JEANNETTE GLASS COMPANY, 1937 – 1938

Colors: Ultra Marine; some crystal and pink

Rarely found items of yesteryear in Ultra Marine Doric and Pansy are no longer rare today. They keep coming into America from England and Canada from container importers and via sales on the Internet. We have a booth in an antique mall where the owner regularly imports from England and I cannot compete with his prices on Doric and Pansy as well as some other patterns he receives on a regular basis such as Royal Lace and Floral. Today, a set can be acquired more easily and inexpensively than 20 years ago. No wonder we thought the teal butter, sugar, creamer, salt, and pepper were rare in the early collecting days. They were, but apparently only within the continental United States. We were not looking outside our boundaries for our homemade glassware. We now know that much Depression era glassware was sold overseas. (I just talked to a collector from Australia who informed me there's quite a bit of Depression ware to be found there, but most of it is being sold on the Internet.) He still can find rare colors and elegant glassware, as that has not caught on as well as our Depression era glass has.

The price of the Doric and Pansy butter dish, shaker, creamer, and sugar remains steady, although you cannot presently visit a glass show without seeing at least some of these for sale. Years ago, you could visit several shows without seeing these offered at any price.

Neither tumblers nor berry bowls are being found in the hoards abroad. There are two tumblers pictured. The common one (shaped like the flat Doric tumbler) has a flared out top. Only two of the straight sided, heavy and darker in color, 4¼", ten-ounce tumblers have been unearthed. Both turned up on the West Coast. Beware of weakly patterned shakers. These should be priced less (25% to 40%). If color and shape are the only indications to the shaker's pattern, then leave it alone unless it is seriously under priced. Weak patterns and cloudiness ensnare many shakers. Cloudy shakers are not worth mint prices. Fogginess was caused by a chemical reaction between the glass and its contents either salt or pepper. Salt often corroded original metal shaker tops and while those are desirable, new lids are adequate and available to collectors.

Color variations face every collector buying Jeannette's Ultra Marine. Some pieces have a distinctly green hue instead of blue. Notice differences in my picture. Few collectors currently buy the green shade of Ultra Marine, but it is rarer and who knows how it may be treasured down the collecting road.

Berry bowls and children's sets are found in pink. Strangely, there have been no reports of children's sets or pink Doric and Pansy found in England or Canada.

Luncheon sets in crystal can be gathered, although, with difficulty. Collectors of sugar and creamers, rather than Doric and Pansy collectors usually buy sets of sugars and creamer in crystal.

	Green, Ultra Marine	Pink, Crystal
Bowl, 4½", berry	25.00	15.00
Bowl, 8", large berry	100.00	35.00
Bowl, 9", handled	45.00	25.00
Butter dish and cover	450.00	
Butter dish bottom	50.00	
Butter dish top	400.00	
Cup	16.00	15.00
Creamer	100.00	95.00
Plate, 6", sherbet	11.00	7.50

	Green, Ultra Marine	Pink, Crystal
Plate, 7", salad	40.00	
Plate, 9", dinner	40.00	20.00
Salt and pepper, pr.	425.00	
Saucer	5.00	5.00
Sugar, open	100.00	95.00
Tray, 10", handled	38.00	
Tumbler, 4½", 9 ounce	110.00	
Tumbler, 4¼", 10 ounce	595.00	

DORIC AND PANSY
"PRETTY POLLY PARTY DISHES"

	Teal	Pink
Cup	50.00	35.00
Saucer	9.00	7.00
Plate	11.00	8.00

	Teal	Pink
Creamer	55.00	35.00
Sugar	55.00	35.00
14-piece set	390.00	275.00

"ELLIPSE," "SHERATON," "TWITCH," LINE NO. 92, BARTLETT-COLLINS, c. Late 1930s

Colors: crystal, and with applied primary colors (yellow, red, blue, and green) and patterns; green

I mostly find this pattern when I travel to Midwestern cities near its maker. Since the catalog information didn't list some items or colors I've already found, I'm assuming you can help add to these listings. I got all excited over finding a larger pitcher; but when I got home, it wasn't exactly like the pattern after all. There were panels around the ellipses, which nothing else has.

	All colors		All colors
Bowl, vegetable, hdld.	30.00	Saucer	2.00
Creamer	12.50	Sherbet	10.00
Cup	10.00	Sugar, open	12.50
Goblet, 14 oz,. ftd. tea	20.00	Tumbler, 5 oz., juice	8.00
Jug, 24 oz.	40.00	Tumbler, 9 oz., water	10.00
Plate, 8½"	8.00	Tumbler, 12 oz., Tea	12.50

ENGLISH HOBNAIL, LINE #555, WESTMORELAND GLASS COMPANY, 1917 – 1940s; few
items through 1980s

Colors: pink, turquoise/ice blue, cobalt blue, green, lilac, red, opal trimmed blue, red flashed, black, blue, amber, and milk

Some items of Line #555, English Hobnail, in numerous colors and trims were manufactured intermittently by Westmoreland for over 70 years. It was initially called Early American and was by far Westmoreland's most inexhaustible line. The foremost production years extended from 1926 through the early 1940s; somewhere along the way, it became advertised as English Hobnail. Two separate shapes transpire in the pattern, round and square based items. Black footed (c.1929), flashed red, and gold-trimmed items are occasionally found today, but are mostly thought of as novelties by collectors.

New collectors need to learn to distinguish English Hobnail from Hocking's Miss America, which was a competitive design. English Hobnail pieces have rays of varying distances in the center of the piece. Notice the standing pieces in the photographs for this six-point star effect. In Miss America, shown on page 134, the center rays all end equidistant from the center. The hobs on English Hobnail are more rounded and feel smoother to the touch; goblets flare and the hobs go directly into a plain rim area. Miss America's hobs are sharper to touch and the goblets do not flare at the rim. All goblets and tumblers of Miss America have three sets of rings above the hobs before entering a plain glass rim. If you have a candy jar that measures more or less than Miss America's 11½" including the cover, then it is most likely English Hobnail which is found in several sizes.

Due to space limitations, I have subjectively grouped crystal, amber, Westmoreland's 1960s "Golden Sunset" color, and others into the *Collectible Glassware of the 40s, 50s, 60s...* and am pricing only the most collected colors in this book. I am conscious that crystal was made from the early teens and some amber in the late 1920s; but crystal was a major impetus by the company in the WWII years, when chemicals for color production were unavailable in quantity. There are a number of catalog pages from Westmoreland's later years shown in the fifth edition of the 40s, 50s, 60s book. Refer to those for individual identification of pieces.

Two price assortments are given. Pink and green make up one column and turquoise/ice blue makes up the other. A piece in the very sparse cobalt blue or black will bring 40% to 50% more than the turquoise blue prices listed. Very little cobalt English Hobnail is being unveiled and even fewer pieces in black. More English Hobnail color collectors seek turquoise/ice blue by virtue of its exceptional beauty. I have been able to gather enough items for a decent photo on page 75. Bear in mind, that it took four years to accumulate what is shown. Milk glass items have little following to date, although some of the rarer pieces are found in that 40s, 50s, 60s color; and only a few collectors are found for red items, made in the 1970s for LeVay.

Some turquoise was produced in the 1970s. These later items appear to be an inferior quality and have a deeper color when put side by side with the older pieces. Years ago, some of us were treated to the sight of a large collection of turquoise/ice blue English Hobnail being marketed at a show. It was entrancing to see so much at one time. Several new collections were started with that set. I am positive those that started collections then wish they had bought the entire set, instead of trying to complete it now.

Note the flat, pink shaker in the photograph below. This is also a late discovery as were flat turquoise shakers found in Washington. Surprises still happen in patterns that have been collected for years. That is part of the collecting fascination.

Sets of pink or green English Hobnail can be put together with time and determination. This pattern does have major color inconsistencies, doubtless due to its various times of manufacture. Pink is the simplest color to find, but it is found in two distinct shades. There are three different greens, from a light, yellow-green to a deep, dark green. Some collectors mix shades of color, but others aren't so inclined. This assimilation of colors is being designated as "rainbow" collecting and is presently in fashion and often very artfully done!

ENGLISH HOBNAIL

	Pink, Green	Turquoise, *Ice Blue		Pink, Green	Turquoise, *Ice Blue
Ashtray, 3"	20.00		Bowl, 8", footed	60.00	
Ashtray, 4½"		22.50	Bowl, 8", hexagonal footed, 2-handled	95.00	165.00
Ashtray, 4½", square	25.00		Bowl, 8", pickle	30.00	
Bonbon, 6½", handled	25.00	40.00	Bowl, 8", round nappy	35.00	
Bottle, toilet, 5 ounce	35.00	50.00	Bowl, 9", celery	32.00	
Bowl, 3", cranberry	20.00		Bowl, 10", flared	40.00	
Bowl, 4", rose	50.00		Bowl, 11", rolled edge	50.00	80.00
Bowl, 4½", finger	15.00		Bowl, 12", celery	40.00	
Bowl, 4½", round nappy	13.00	30.00	Bowl, 12", flange or console	50.00	
Bowl, 4½", square footed, finger	15.00	35.00	Candlestick, 3½", round base	25.00	35.00
Bowl, 5", round nappy	15.00	40.00	Candlestick, 9", round base	40.00	50.00
Bowl, 6", crimped dish	18.00		Candy dish, 3 footed	60.00	
Bowl, 6", round nappy	16.00		Candy, ½ lb. and cover, cone shaped	55.00	100.00
Bowl, 6", square nappy	16.00		Cigarette box and cover, 4½" x 2½"	35.00	55.00
Bowl, 6½", grapefruit	22.00		Cigarette jar w/cover, round	50.00	60.00
Bowl, 6½", round nappy	20.00		Compote, 5", round, footed	25.00	
Bowl, 7", round nappy	22.00		Compote, 6", honey, round footed	30.00	
Bowl, 8", cupped, nappy	30.00		Compote, 8", ball stem, sweetmeat	60.00	

*Cobalt blue 40 to 50 percent higher

	Pink, Green	Turquoise, *Ice Blue
Creamer, hexagonal, footed	22.50	45.00
Creamer, square footed	42.50	
Cup	18.00	25.00
Cup, demitasse	55.00	
Ice tub, 4"	50.00	100.00
Ice tub, 5½"	75.00	135.00
Lamp, 6¼", electric	75.00	
Lamp, 9¼", electric	150.00	
Marmalade w/cover	60.00	85.00
Mayonnaise, 6"	20.00	
Nut, individual, footed	20.00	
Pitcher, 23 ounce, rounded	150.00	
Pitcher, 32 ounce, straight side	185.00	
Pitcher, 38 ounce, rounded	225.00	
Pitcher, 60 ounce, rounded	295.00	
Pitcher, 64 ounce, straight side	300.00	
Plate, 5½", round	9.50	
Plate, 6", square finger bowl liner	9.00	
Plate, 6½", round	10.00	
Plate, 6½, round finger bowl liner	9.50	
Plate, 8", round	12.50	
Plate, 8½", round	15.00	25.00
Plate, 10", round	45.00	85.00
Plate, 14", round, torte	60.00	
Puff box, w/ cover, 6", round	50.00	77.50

*Cobalt blue 40 to 50% higher

	Pink, Green	Turquoise, *Ice Blue
Saucer, demitasse, round	15.00	
Saucer, round	4.00	5.00
Shaker, pair, flat	150.00	250.00
Shaker, pair, round footed	77.50	
Stem, 2 ounce, square footed, wine	30.00	60.00
Stem, 3 ounce, round footed, cocktail	20.00	40.00
Stem, 5 oz., sq. footed, oyster cocktail	16.00	
Stem, 8 oz., sq. footed, water goblet	30.00	50.00
Stem, sherbet, round foot, low		12.00
Stem, sherbet, square footed, low	12.00	
Stem, sherbet, round high, foot	1500	
Stem, sherbet, square footed, high	15.00	35.00
Sugar, hexagonal, footed	22.50	45.00
Sugar, square footed	45.00	
Tidbit, 2 tier	45.00	85.00
Tumbler, 5 ounce, ginger ale	18.00	
Tumbler, 8 ounce, water	22.00	
Tumbler, 10 ounce, ice tea	25.00	
Tumbler, 12 ounce, ice tea	30.00	
Urn, 11", w/cover (15")	395.00	
Vase, 7½", flip	90.00	
Vase, 7½", flip jar w/cover	135.00	
Vase, 8½", flared top	135.00	250.00
Vase, 10" (straw jar)	125.00	

Westmoreland's Handmade "English Hobnail" Crystal
Catalog No. 555

WESTMORELAND GLASS COMPANY Handmade Glassware of Quality

GRAPEVILLE, PENNSYLVANIA

Since 1889

FANCY COLONIAL, #582, IMPERIAL GLASS COMPANY, c. 1914

Colors: crystal, pink, green, teal, some iridized Rubigold and Ice (rainbow washed crystal)

I sold many pieces of Fancy Colonial in my shop over the years, never considering I would want to include it in a book. I could have had four or five times the number of pieces shown here. Fancy Colonial was one of the most bountiful, open stock patterns that Imperial ever made. When I first began looking for glass over 30 years ago, this pattern was all over the place, probably due to some reintroduction of it at the time. My wife kept asking me if I wanted to gather this line, which people in the field were calling "Button and Flute" and "Pillar & Optic" and I told her, "No way. People aren't paying attention to stuff they're still making." Well, they weren't, then; but now that Imperial is out of business, I'm being asked for it at shows. Consequently, I'm being forced to catch up. Again, it was in production, off and on, throughout the company's history, a few items being made in whatever colors and for whatever promotions they were running at the time. Moulds were expensive to make. Sheer economics mandated companies use them for as long as they possibly could. I met four brothers from a mould company whose sole job was to rework Hocking's worn molds into reusable forms. Reissues by the company themselves have always been a problem for collectors. Sometimes they create a short run in an odd color, which turns out to be collectible, and other times they deflate the market with the same colors made originally.

In doing my research, I saw information bandied about saying there were "more than 80," "around 100," "over 150" pieces purportedly made in Fancy Colonial. The list below comprises what we could document. I'm very certain this isn't all there was; let me hear from you regarding what you see or have that is not included.

	All colors*		All colors*		All colors*
Bonbon, 5½", handle	25.00	Cup, custard, flare edge	17.50	Stem, 4½ ounce, cocktail, shallow	20.00
Bottle, water, no stop	75.00	Cup, punch, straight edge	15.00	Stem, 4 ounce, burgundy, deep	30.00
Bowl, 3½", nappy	12.00	Goblet, egg cup, low foot deep	30.00	Stem, 5 ounce, claret, deep	30.00
Bowl, 4½", nappy	15.00	Goblet, low foot, café parfait	28.00	Stem, 6 ounce, champagne, deep	21.00
Bowl, 4½", rim foot berry	15.00	Mayo w/liner, flat	55.00	Stem, 6 ounce, saucer/champagne, shallow	20.00
Bowl, 5", nappy or olive	15.00	Oil bottle w/stopper, 6¼ ounce	65.00		
Bowl, 5", footed, 2 handle	20.00	Oil bottle, 5½ ounce, bulbous, w/stopper	75.00	Stem, 8 ounce, goblet, deep	25.00
Bowl, 5", nut or lily (cupped rim)	22.00	Pickle, 8", oval	30.00	Stem, 10 ounce, goblet, deep	25.00
Bowl, 5", rim foot berry	20.00	Pitcher, 3 pint	150.00	Sugar w/lid	32.50
Bowl, 6", nappy	20.00	Plate, 5¾"	12.00	Tumbler, 2 ounce, whiskey	20.00
Bowl, 7", nappy or rim foot berry	35.00	Plate, 7½", salad	22.00	Tumbler, 4 ounce	15.00
Bowl, 7", lily	42.00	Plate, 10½", cake	45.00	Tumbler, 5 ounce, belled rim or not	15.00
Bowl, 8", 2-handle berry	65.00	Plate, mayonnaise liner	15.00	Tumbler, 6 ounce	15.00
Bowl, 8", nappy or salad	38.00	Salt & Pepper, pair	75.00	Tumbler, 8 ounce	18.00
Bowl, 8", spoon tray (hump edge)	38.00	Salt, table or footed almond, handled	22.00	Tumbler, 10 ounce	18.00
Bowl, 8", lily (cupped)	45.00	Saucer	8.00	Tumbler, 12 ounce, iced tea	20.00
Bowl, 8", rim foot berry	38.00	Sherbet, 3¼", low ft., flare rim or not	22.50	Tumbler, 14 ounce, iced tea	25.00
Bowl, 9", rim foot berry	40.00	Sherbet, 4¼", low foot	22.50	Vase, 8", low foot, flare	65.00
Butter & cover	80.00	Sherbet, 4¾", footed Jelly	25.00	Vase, 10" flat, bead base, ruffled rim	85.00
Celery,12", oval	50.00	Spoon (flat open sugar)	20.00		
Comport, 4", footed	25.00	Stem, 1 ounce, cordial, deep	40.00	Vase, 12" flat, bead base, rufffled rim	110.00
Comport, 5½", footed	30.00	Stem, 2 ounce, wine, deep	30.00		
Comport, 6¼", footed	35.00	Stem, 3 ounce, cocktail, shallow	20.00	* Crystal subtract 25%; teal add 25%	
Creamer, footed	22.00	Stem, 3 ounce, port, deep	30.00		

77

FIRE-KING DINNERWARE "PHILBE," HOCKING GLASS COMPANY, 1937 – 1938

Colors: blue, green, pink, and crystal

Fire-King Dinnerware is a pattern that would have collectors begging for more if there were available supplies. As it is, most collectors would settle for a piece of this elusive pattern — any piece. After its inclusion in my *Anchor Hocking's Fire-King & More,* collectors who had never seen my Depression glass book were entranced by it. The most frequently asked question is, "Where do I find a piece?" Finding it is like mining gold with pick and shovel. If you're very lucky, you might see a piece. If more were available, prices would be even higher than they are due to the number of collectors wanting "just one piece." Why put it in the book? People need to recognize it should they find a piece. Everybody gets lucky sometime. You wouldn't want to miss your opportunity.

In 1972, on my first trip to Anchor Hocking there was a large set of blue in this pattern displayed in an outer office window. I didn't know what it was and neither did anyone else I talked to then. All they knew was it was from the morgue and a pattern they made in the 1930s. When I was in the morgue in the mid 1980s, I found that only a few pieces were left, and I have often wondered where it all went.

A high sherbet/champagne is now in the listing, along with a non-stemmed sherbet, which are pictured below. Usually, Fire-King Dinnerware is found on Cameo shaped blanks; but some pieces, including footed tumblers, nine-ounce water goblets, and the high sherbets are on a Mayfair shaped blank. Additional stems could be found.

Somebody turned up a complete green candy. I have owned two green candy bottoms and one complete blue, but I have never found the green top. I once had a lid brought to me that was supposed to fit the candy, but it turned out to be the lid for the cookie. The cookie lid is a tad larger.

The blue of Fire-King Dinnerware is very comparable to Mayfair's blue. Many pieces have that platinum trim that can be seen in the photograph, but I have never seen any blue Mayfair trimmed in platinum. This seems strange since these patterns were made about the same time. Mayfair was finishing up as Fire-King was being introduced. Was this a special order production, which would account for its scarcity? As many different pieces as were made, there should be a supply just waiting to be rescued.

The easiest to find blue items are the footed tumblers that are rare in other colors. The tea seems twice as available as the water.

Usually found pieces of pink include oval vegetable bowls and the 10½" salver. That oval bowl is also available in green and crystal. Next easiest to obtain would be the green grill or luncheon plate. Any color 6" saucer/sherbet plate is rarer than larger plates. Why should you care if you don't collect this pattern? If you actually find a piece, it's guaranteed someone wants it. Sell or trade it for something you want.

	Crystal	Pink, Green	Blue
Bowl, 5½", cereal	30.00	45.00	75.00
Bowl, 7¼", salad	50.00	80.00	115.00
Bowl, 10", oval vegetable	85.00	95.00	175.00
Candy jar, 4", low, with cover	300.00	750.00	850.00
Cookie jar with cover	600.00	995.00	1,500.00
Creamer, 3¼", footed	75.00	135.00	150.00
Cup	60.00		195.00
Goblet, 7¼", 9 ounce, thin	115.00	185.00	235.00
Pitcher, 6", 36 ounce, juice	495.00	695.00	895.00
Pitcher, 8½", 56 ounce	495.00	995.00	1,250.00
Plate, 6", sherbet	40.00	65.00	95.00
Plate, 8", luncheon	20.00	37.50	47.50
Plate, 10", heavy sandwich	40.00	95.00	125.00

	Crystal	Pink, Green	Blue
Plate, 10½", salver	65.00	95.00	110.00
Plate, 10½", grill	40.00	75.00	95.00
Plate, 11⅝", salver	50.00	62.50	95.00
Platter, 12", closed handles	75.00	150.00	195.00
Saucer, 6" (same as sherbet plate)	40.00	65.00	95.00
Sherbet, 3¾", no stem	75.00		550.00
Sherbet, 4¾", stemmed		350.00	400.00
Sugar, 3¼", footed	75.00	135.00	150.00
Tumbler, 4", 9 ounce, flat water	40.00	105.00	130.00
Tumbler, 3½", footed, juice	40.00	150.00	175.00
Tumbler, 5¼", 10 ounce, footed	40.00	80.00	110.00
Tumbler, 6½", 15 ounce, footed, iced tea	50.00	85.00	95.00

FLORAL, "POINSETTIA," JEANNETTE GLASS COMPANY, 1931 – 1935

Colors: pink, green, Delphite, Jadite, crystal, amber, red, black, custard, and yellow

After more than 30 years of collectors calling this pattern "Floral," the name most likely isn't going to change at this point; however; a botanist wrote me that this is a Passion Flower (Passiflora), not a Poinsettia. Drawings were sent lending credence to the supposition that this was not a hemp plant as another reader thought it to be.

Notice on page 81 the rare, straight top, pink Floral comport. These comports also are found with a ruffled top. Both are rarely discovered. Pink comports are harder to find than green, but there are more collectors seeking green ones.

Several green Floral pieces, rarely found in the United States, are being uncovered in England and Canada. These include the vases, rose bowls, flat pitcher, and flat tumblers. Slight variations of color and design exist in these items. They are frequently a lighter green color, slightly paneled, and have ground bottoms. A ground bottom often indicates an earlier production run of the pattern. The green cups found in England have ground bottoms and are slightly footed. The base of the cup is larger than the normally found saucer indentation.

Today, some dealers have buyers in England hunting for American-made glassware along with those fine European antiques. I ship more and more books to England as well as Australia and New Zealand. Prices remain steady on green Floral, flat-bottomed pitchers and tumblers. Northwestern (Washington, Oregon) dealers tell me that lemonade pitchers are disappearing from that market. Pink lemonade pitchers substantially outnumber green.

Two types of pink Floral platters exist. One has a normal flat edge; the other, higher priced and more rarely seen, has a sharp, inner rim just as that of the platter in Cherry Blossom. This price has some Floral collectors settling for the more inexpensive one. Be sure to read about the similarly made Floral lamp in Adam pattern on page 6.

On a bitter note, the smaller, footed Floral shakers have now been reproduced in pink, cobalt blue, red, and a very dark green color, the last four colors of little concern since they originally were never made. The darker green will not glow under a black (ultraviolet) light, as will the old. The new pink shakers, however, are a convincingly good copy of pattern and color. The best way to tell the Floral reproduction is to look at the threads where the lid screws onto the shaker. On the old, two parallel threads end right before the side mould seams. The new Floral has one continuous line thread that starts on one side and continues around the shaker until it ends above the beginning line on the other side. There is approximately one inch of overlapped thread making two lines for that inch; but the whole thread is one continuous line and not two separate ones as on the old. To my knowledge, no other Floral reproductions have been made as of May 2003.

Floral sugar and candy lids are interchangeable, as are most such Jeannette lids. Floral designs can be found on the under side of lids and on the bottom of square Jadite kitchenware/refrigerator storage containers made by Jeannette in the mid-1930s. As with other Jadite items, these have rapidly increased in value recently.

Note the rarely encountered crimp edges found on the bowl and sherbet below.

FLORAL

	Pink	Green	Delphite	Jadite
Bowl, 4", berry, ruffled $75.00	20.00	22.00	50.00	
Bowl, 5½", cream soup	750.00	750.00		
* Bowl, 7½", salad, ruffled $150.00	32.00	32.00	60.00	
Bowl, 8", covered vegetable	55.00	70.00	75.00 (no cover)	
Bowl, 9", oval vegetable	25.00	30.00		
Butter dish and cover	105.00	105.00		
Butter dish bottom	30.00	30.00		
Butter dish top	75.00	75.00		
Canister set: coffee, tea, cereal, sugar, 5¼" tall, each				95.00
Candlesticks, 4", pair	85.00	90.00		
Candy jar and cover	42.00	45.00		
Creamer, flat, Cremax $160.00	18.00	20.00	77.50	
Coaster, 3¼"	12.00	12.50		
Comport, 9", ruffled or plain rim	1,000.00	1,025.00		
*** Cup	15.00	15.00		
Dresser set		1,250.00		
Frog for vase, also crystal $500.00		725.00		
Ice tub, 3½", high, oval	925.00	995.00		
Lamp	325.00	325.00		
Pitcher, 5½", 23 or 24 ounce		500.00		
Pitcher, 8", 32 ounce, footed, cone	40.00	48.00		
Pitcher, 10¼", 48 ounce, lemonade	265.00	295.00		
Plate, 6", sherbet	7.00	8.00		
Plate, 8", salad	14.00	15.00		
** Plate, 9", dinner	20.00	22.00	150.00	
Plate, 9", grill		325.00		
Platter, 10¾", oval	25.00	27.50	150.00	
Platter, 11" (like Cherry Blossom)	95.00			
Refrigerator dish and cover, 5" square		75.00	95.00	50.00
*** Relish dish, 2-part oval	20.00	22.00	160.00	
**** Salt and pepper, 4", footed, pair	50.00	55.00		
Salt and pepper, 6", flat	55.00			
*** Saucer	10.00	10.00		
Sherbet	18.00	20.00	85.00	
Sugar, Cremax $160.00	12.00	14.00	72.50 (open)	
Sugar/candy cover	17.50	20.00		
Tray, 6", square, closed handles	20.00	25.00		
Tray, 9¼", oval for dresser set		195.00		
Tumbler, 3½", 3 ounce, footed		175.00		
Tumbler, 4", 5 ounce, footed, juice	20.00	25.00		
Tumbler, 4½", 9 ounce, flat		185.00		
Tumbler, 4¾", 7 ounce, footed, water	25.00	25.00	195.00	
Tumbler, 5¼", 9 ounce, footed, lemonade	50.00	58.00		
Vase, 3 legged rose bowl		500.00		
Vase, 3 legged flared (also in crystal)		495.00		
Vase, 6⅞" tall (8 sided)		*****425.00		

* Cremax $125.00

** These have now been found in amber and red.

*** This has been found in yellow.

**** Beware reproductions.

***** Crystal $275.00

FLORAL AND DIAMOND BAND, U.S. GLASS COMPANY, Late 1920s

Colors: pink, green; some iridescent, black, and crystal

The ads below are from Sear's catalogs of the late 1920s. In a 1928 catalog, you could buy a Floral and Diamond Band jelly compote for 35 cents. Notice that half the ad for the berry set says diamond and floral and not vice versa.

Rough mould seams on many Floral and Diamond Band pieces are emblematic of all U.S. Glass Company patterns of this era. This heavy, seamed pattern was not finished as well as many of the later patterns. This is customary for Floral and Diamond Band and not considered a detriment by long-time collectors who have come to disregard some roughness. Another difficulty in gathering Floral and Diamond Band is finding varying hues of green. Some green has a distinctive blue tint. You need to decide how flexible you are about color matching.

Floral and Diamond Band luncheon plates, sugar lids, pitchers, and iced tea tumblers (in both pink and green) are hard to acquire. Six tumblers were advertised in that '28 catalog mentioned above for 85 cents. The pitcher and six tumblers were $1.15 so the pitcher added only 30 cents to your bill. Many Floral and Diamond Band butter bottoms have been "borrowed" over the years to be used with tops from more expensive U.S. Glass patterns such as Strawberry and Cherryberry. This has taken place because these U.S. Glass butter bottoms are plain and, thus, compatible, since the patterns are located on the top only. The small Floral and Diamond Band creamer and sugar have been found in black with ground bottoms; but no other pieces have been spotted in that color. That same sugar and creamer, in various colors, is often found with a cut flower over the top of the customary moulded flower.

Floral and Diamond Band pitchers with exceptional iridescent color bring premium prices from carnival glass collectors as a pattern called "Mayflower." Unfortunately, most of these iridescent pitchers are generally weakly colored and unacceptable to carnival buyers. Several of these types have surfaced lately at shows. Sometimes glassware overlaps categories of collecting, as does Floral and Diamond Band; and, occasionally, it receives more respect from one group of collectors than it does the other.

	Pink	Green		Pink	Green
Bowl, 4½", berry	10.00	12.00	* Pitcher, 8", 42 ounce	115.00	125.00
Bowl, 5¾", handled, nappy	15.00	15.00	Plate, 8" luncheon	40.00	40.00
Bowl, 8", large berry	20.00	20.00	Sherbet	7.00	8.00
* Butter dish and cover	135.00	125.00	Sugar, small	10.00	12.00
Butter dish bottom	100.00	100.00	Sugar, 5¼"	18.00	18.00
Butter dish top	35.00	25.00	Sugar lid	55.00	65.00
Compote, 5½", tall	20.00	25.00	Tumbler, 4", water	22.00	22.00
Creamer, small	10.00	12.00	Tumbler, 5", iced tea	45.00	50.00
Creamer, 4¾"	18.00	20.00	* Iridescent $275.00; Crystal $125.00		

FLORENTINE NO. 1, OLD FLORENTINE, "POPPY NO. 1,"
HAZEL ATLAS GLASS COMPANY, 1932 – 1935

Colors: pink, green, crystal, yellow, and cobalt blue (See Reproduction Section.)

Collectors often confuse Florentine No. 1 and Florentine No. 2 and they need to learn how to distinguish between them. Study the shapes. The jagged edged pieces are hexagonal (six sided); this edging occurs on all flat pieces of Florentine No. 1. All footed pieces (such as tumblers, shakers, or pitchers) also have that serrated edge on the foot. In Florentine No. 2, all pieces have plain edges as can be seen in the photographs on page 87. Florentine No. 1 was once promoted as hexagonal and Florentine No. 2 was promoted as round. However, both patterns were advertised and put up for sale in mixed sets. Today, some collectors follow that lead. Mingled sets display very well.

The 48 ounce, flat-bottomed pitcher was offered with both Florentine No. 1 and No. 2 sets. It was listed as 54 ounces in catalogs, but usually measures six ounces less. It depends upon the shape of the lip as to how many ounces it will hold before liquid runs out. My penchant is to list this pitcher only with Florentine No. 1 using the handle shape as the decisive factor. However, this pitcher is repeatedly found with flat-bottomed Florentine No. 2 tumblers, forcing me to list it with both.

Flat tumblers with paneled interiors are being found in sets with Florentine No. 1 pitchers. These paneled tumblers should be accepted as Florentine No. 1 rather than Florentine No. 2. That recommendation is for dyed-in-the-wool collectors only. Paneled flat tumblers are tough to find; but only a few collectors seem concerned.

Pink Florentine No. 1 is the most difficult color to find. Pink footed tumblers, covered oval vegetable bowls, and ruffled creamers and sugars are practically unavailable at any price in mint condition. Chipped and damaged pieces can be found, but most collectors search for mint items only. Those irregular edges are easily spoiled; look there, beneath, and on the top, when you pick up a piece to buy. Sets can be obtained in green, crystal, or yellow with time and effort.

Fired-on colors have appeared in luncheon sets, but there is little collector zeal for these now. You can find all sorts of colors and colored bands on crystal. A disadvantage to these banded colors is finding enough to put a set together; however, if you should run into a large set, do not pass it by.

Most 5½" yellow ashtrays have VFW (Veterans of Foreign Wars) embossed in the bottom. I have seen more with this imprint than without it. I have not seen VFW designs on any color other than yellow.

A genuine, second cobalt blue Florentine No. 1 pitcher has appeared on the West Coast. Do not mix up one of these for the cone shaped, reproduction cobalt No. 2 pitcher found all over the place.

Florentine No. 1 shakers have been replicated in pink and cobalt blue. Other colors could follow. No real cobalt blue Florentine No. 1 shakers have ever been discovered, so those are easy to disregard. The reproduction pink shaker is somewhat trickier to discern from old. When comparing a reproduction shaker to several old pairs from my inventory, the old shakers have a major open flower on each side. There is a top circle on this blossom with three smaller circles down each side. The seven circles form the outside of the blossom. The reproduction blossom looks more like a strawberry with no circles forming the outside of the blossom. Do not use the threading test mentioned under Floral for the Florentine No. 1 shakers, however. It will not work for Florentine although the same importing company out of Georgia makes these. The threads are correct on this reproduction pattern. The reproductions I have seen as of May 2003 have been badly formed, but that is not to say it will not be rectified.

	* Green	Yellow	Pink	Cobalt blue		* Green	Yellow	Pink	Cobalt blue
Ashtray, 5½"	22.00	30.00	30.00		Plate, 8½", salad	10.00	14.00	12.00	
Bowl, 5", berry	14.00	18.00	18.00	25.00	Plate, 10", dinner	22.00	28.00	30.00	
Bowl, 5", cream					Plate, 10", grill	14.00	20.00	22.00	
soup or ruffled nut	28.00		20.00	65.00	Platter, 11½", oval	28.00	28.00	28.00	
Bowl, 6", cereal	25.00	32.00	38.00		**Salt and pepper, footed	37.50	55.00	55.00	
Bowl, 8½", large berry	30.00	35.00	40.00		Saucer	3.00	4.00	4.00	17.00
Bowl, 9½", oval vegetable					Sherbet, 3 ounce, footed	12.00	15.00	15.00	
and cover	65.00	85.00	85.00		Sugar	9.50	12.00	12.00	
Butter dish and cover	125.00	180.00	160.00		Sugar cover	18.00	30.00	30.00	
Butter dish bottom	50.00	85.00	85.00		Sugar, ruffled	40.00		45.00	70.00
Butter dish top	75.00	95.00	75.00		Tumbler, 3¼", 4 oz., footed	16.00			
Coaster/ashtray, 3¾"	20.00	22.00	30.00		Tumbler, 3¾", 5 ounce,				
Comport, 3½", ruffled	40.00		18.00	65.00	footed, juice	16.00	28.00	28.00	
Creamer	10.00	22.00	20.00		Tumbler, 4", 9 oz., ribbed	16.00		22.00	
Creamer, ruffled	45.00		50.00	70.00	Tumbler, 4¾", 10 ounce,				
Cup	9.00	13.00	12.00	85.00	footed, water	22.00	26.00	26.00	
Pitcher, 6½", 36 oz., footed	40.00	50.00	50.00	895.00	Tumbler, 5¼", 12 ounce,				
Pitcher, 7½", 48 ounce,					footed, iced tea	28.00	33.00	33.00	
flat, ice lip or none	75.00	135.00	265.00		Tumbler, 5¼", 9 ounce,				
Plate, 6", sherbet	6.00	7.00	7.00		lemonade (like Floral)			150.00	

*Crystal 20 to 30% less   **Beware reproductions

FLORENTINE NO. 2, "POPPY NO. 2," HAZEL ATLAS GLASS COMPANY, 1932 – 1935

Colors: pink, green, yellow, crystal, some cobalt, amber, and ice blue (See Reproduction Section.)

Peruse the dissimilarities mentioned between the two Florentines in the first paragraph of the preceding Florentine No. 1 pattern. If you are a new or advanced collector running out of pieces to find, try mixing the Florentines together, a practice the company itself engaged in since boxed sets have turned up over the years including both patterns.

A mystery in this pattern is illustrated by the green ruffled nut/cream soup, left of the regularly found cream soup. This piece meets the criteria as Florentine No. 1 because it matches the other ruffled pieces (comport, creamer, and sugar) in that pattern. The frustration here is the shape of the handles on the bowl, which only match items in Florentine No. 2. Thus, we have common characteristics on a piece that can be used with either pattern. A pink one is pictured with Florentine No. 1. This shows that no strict rule will apply with Florentine.

The more costly, seldom seen, footed, 6¼", 24-ounce cone-shaped pitcher is shown on the right in the top photograph. The more frequently found footed pitcher that stands 7½" tall is pictured on the left. Measure the height perpendicular from the base to the top of the spout. There is over an inch difference and this will not vary as greatly as ounce capacities often do in pitchers with handmade spouts.

That 7½" pitcher and footed water tumbler have been reproduced in an extremely dark cobalt blue, amber, pink, and a dark green. This pitcher was never originally made in those colors; therefore, no one should presume these reproductions to be old, although you would not believe the letters and e-mails I receive about those colors. I see these misrepresented as old in antique malls and flea markets often. Just because a place says antique mall does not mean everything in it is antique. In fact, many of the ones I enter, the clerk at the desk is older than most of the items displayed for sale.

Custard cups remain the most elusive piece in Florentine No. 2; a crystal one is pictured on a yellow, 6¼" indented plate. The saucer curves up on the edges while the custard plate is flat with a larger indentation than the bottom of a regular cup.

The 10" relish dish comes in three styles. The most commonly found "Y" style is pictured in green and yellow. The unusual style has two curved, separate divisions, one on each side. The undivided is the most difficult to acquire. Grill plates with a round indent for the cream soup have been found in green, crystal and, now, yellow.

Green Florentine is more requested than crystal, but crystal is scarce; hence, prices are analogous. Some amber, shown in earlier editions, is the rarest Florentine color; but only a few items have been discovered. Most sizes of flat tumblers have been found in amber, but no old pitcher.

Both lids to the butter dishes and the oval vegetables are interchangeable in the two Florentine patterns. Candy lids and butter lids are similar in size. The candy lid measures 4¾" in diameter, but the butter dish lid measures 5" exactly. Those measurements are from outside edge to outside edge.

Luncheon set mixtures of red, orange, green, and blue have been seen, with the fired-on colors sprayed over crystal. That orange does stand out! Orange seems to have been a favorite decorator color in the late 1920s.

	Green	Pink	Yellow	Blue
Bowl, 4½", berry	*16.00	17.00	22.00	
Bowl, 4¾", cream soup	18.00	16.00	22.00	
Bowl, 5½"	33.00		40.00	
Bowl, 6", cereal	33.00		40.00	
Bowl, 7½", shallow			100.00	
Bowl, 8", large berry	28.00	32.00	40.00	
Bowl, 9", oval vegetable				
and cover	65.00		95.00	
Bowl, 9", flat	27.50			
Butter dish and cover	110.00		155.00	
Butter dish bottom	25.00		70.00	
Butter dish top	75.00		85.00	
Candlesticks, 2¾", pair	50.00		70.00	
Candy dish and cover	100.00	145.00	155.00	
Coaster, 3¼"	13.00	16.00	22.00	
Coaster/ashtray, 3¾"	17.50		30.00	
Coaster/ashtray, 5½"	20.00		38.00	
Comport, 3½", ruffled	40.00	45.00		65.00
Creamer	9.00		12.00	
Cup, amber 50.00	9.00		10.00	
Custard cup or jello	60.00		85.00	
Gravy boat			65.00	
Pitcher, 6¼", 24 ounce,				
cone-footed			165.00	
** Pitcher, 7½", 28 ounce,				
cone-footed	38.00		35.00	
Pitcher, 7½", 48 ounce	75.00	135.00	265.00	
Pitcher, 8¼", 76 ounce	110.00	225.00	450.00	

	Green	Pink	Yellow	Blue
Plate, 6", sherbet	4.00		6.00	
Plate, 6¼", with indent	22.00		30.00	
Plate, 8½", salad	8.50	8.50	10.00	
Plate, 10", dinner	16.00		15.00	
Plate, 10¼", grill	14.00		18.00	
Plate, 10¼", grill				
w/cream soup ring	45.00			
Platter, 11", oval	16.00	16.00	25.00	
Platter, 11½", for				
gravy boat			55.00	
Relish dish, 10", 3-part				
or plain	28.00	30.00	35.00	
*** Salt and pepper, pair	42.50		50.00	
Saucer, amber $15.00	3.00		4.00	
Sherbet, ftd., amber $40.00	10.00		10.00	
Sugar	10.00		12.00	
Sugar cover	15.00		28.00	
Tray, round, condiment for				
shakers, creamer/sugar			80.00	
Tumbler, 3⅜", 5 oz., juice	14.00	12.00	22.00	
Tumbler, 3⁹⁄₁₆", 6 oz., blown	18.00			
**** Tumbler, 4", 9 oz., water	14.00	16.00	20.00	70.00
Tumbler, 5", 12 oz., blown	20.00			
**** Tumbler, 5", 12 oz., tea	35.00		55.00	
Tumbler, 3¼", 5 oz., footed	15.00		16.00	
Tumbler, 4", 5 oz., footed	15.00		16.00	
Tumbler, 5", 9 oz., footed	30.00		35.00	
Vase or parfait, 6"	30.00		60.00	

*Crystal – 20 to 30% less   **Ice Blue – $595.00 ***   Fired-on Red, Orange, or Blue, Pr. – $42.50 ****   Amber – $75.00

FLOWER GARDEN WITH BUTTERFLIES, "BUTTERFLIES AND ROSES,"
U.S. GLASS COMPANY, FACTORY "R," TIFFIN PLANT, c. 1924

Colors: pink, green, blue-green, canary yellow, crystal, amber, blue, and black

Old catalog pages continue to be exhumed from all over the country, so we are fortunate to learn things about our glassware that our pioneer authors didn't know when they identified patterns. The original designation for this was Brocade, after the wonderful brocade etching decorating the exterior. It is assumed to have been in production for roughly speaking, a 10-year period, though evidently not constantly judging from the absence of items available. Flower Garden with Butterflies was one pattern we enjoyed collecting for 20 years. After selling it, I have had a taxing time buying enough to illustrate the book. I should have kept more pieces; but hindsight is always 20-20. Earlier editions will show a much larger exhibit. This pattern is found so rarely that few new collectors are attempting it. Over the years, Brocade collections have been assembled and today, only materialize on the market when sets are sold. Yet, this is one pattern that lends itself extremely well for a one-piece display. Note the desirable, heart-shaped, green candy shown.

Brocade has three styles of powder jars, which probably explains why so many oval and rectangular dresser trays are found. Dresser trays and luncheon plates are the only consistently found items in the pattern. Two different footed powders exist with the smaller, 6¼", shown in amber and green. The taller, not shown, stands 7½" high. Thankfully, the lids for these footed powders are the same. The flat powder jar has a 3½" diameter. We never found a blue, flat powder while we were collecting, though I feel certain there must be one out there.

I owned a black candlestick that only had the end of a butterfly antenna on it. You really had to search to find that little piece of butterfly. The other candlestick of the pair had half a butterfly. Perhaps some item will turn up where the butterfly flew away entirely.

A crystal cologne with black stopper turned up after I had previously photographed a black cologne sans stopper. I missed my opportunity to photograph them both whole. Be sure to check out the dauber in the perfumes. Many of them are broken off or ground down to hide the broken end. Daubers are much harder to find than the bottles themselves; take that into consideration if buying only the bottle. That goes for any perfume/cologne in any pattern. The piece handled most often usually suffered the damage and was tossed away.

I have already talked about the so-called "Shari" perfume or cologne set in earlier books, but I frequently get letters and e-mails about it as an unknown piece of Flower Garden. A semi-circular, footed glass dresser box holds five wedge (pie shaped) bottles. This container is often confused with Flower Garden because it has flower designs on it. Labels found intact on bottles promoted the New York/Paris affiliation of "Charme Volupte" but nowhere was the word "Shari" mentioned on the labels. One bottle contained cold cream, another vanishing cream, and three others once held parfumes. There are dancing girls at either end of the box, and flowers abound on the semi-circle. There are no dancing girls on Flower Garden. Other not-to-be-mistaken-for Flower Garden pieces include the 7" and 10" trivets with flowers all over them made by U.S. Glass. They were also used for mixing bowl covers and they do not have butterflies.

	Amber, Crystal	Pink, Green, Blue-Green	Blue, Canary		Amber, Crystal	Pink, Green, Blue-Green	Blue, Canary
Ashtray, match-pack holders	160.00	175.00	225.00	Mayonnaise, footed, 4¾" h. x 6¼" w., w/7" plate & spoon	75.00	95.00	135.00
Candlesticks, 4", pair	42.50	55.00	95.00	Plate, 7"	15.00	20.00	30.00
Candlesticks, 8", pair	77.50	135.00	150.00	Plate, 8", two styles	15.00	16.00	22.00
Candy w/cover, 6", flat	130.00	155.00		Plate, 10"		42.50	48.00
Candy w/cover, 7½", cone-shaped	80.00	130.00	175.00	Plate, 10", indent for 3" comport	32.00	40.00	45.00
Candy w/cover, heart-shaped		1,250.00	1,400.00	Powder jar, 3½", flat		80.00	
* Cologne bottle w/stopper, 7½"		210.00	350.00	Powder jar, footed, 6¼" h.	80.00	145.00	185.00
Comport, 2⅞" h.		23.00	28.00	Powder jar, footed, 7½" h.	80.00	145.00	195.00
Comport, 3" h., fits 10" plate	20.00	23.00	28.00	Sandwich server, center handle	55.00	70.00	100.00
Comport, 4¼" h. x 4¾" w.			50.00	Saucer		25.00	
Comport, 4¾" h. x 10¼" w.	48.00	65.00	85.00	Sugar		75.00	
Comport, 5⅞" h. x 11" w.	55.00		95.00	Tray, 5½" x 10", oval	55.00	60.00	
Comport, 7¼" h. x 8¼" w.	60.00	80.00		Tray, 11¾" x 7¾", rectangular	60.00	75.00	90.00
Creamer		75.00		Tumbler, 7½"	175.00		
Cup		75.00		Vase, 6¼"	75.00	100.00	175.00
				Vase, 10½"		135.00	235.00

* Stopper, if not broken off, ½ price of bottle

PRICE LIST FOR BLACK ITEMS ONLY

Bonbon w/cover, 6⅝" diameter	250.00
Bowl, 7¼", w/cover, "flying saucer"	395.00
Bowl, 8½", console, w/base	150.00
Bowl, 9", rolled edge, w/base	200.00
Bowl, 11", footed orange	200.00
Bowl, 12", rolled edge console w/base	195.00
Candlestick 6" w/6½" candle, pair	495.00
Candlestick, 8", pair	300.00
Cheese and cracker, footed, 5⅜" h. x 10" w.	250.00
Comport and cover, 2¾" h. (fits 10" indented plate)	200.00
Cigarette box & cover, 4⅜" long	150.00
Comport, tureen, 4¼" h. x 10" w.	225.00
Comport, footed, 5⅝" h. x 10" w.	225.00
Comport, footed, 7" h.	175.00
Plate, 10", indented	100.00
Sandwich server, center-handled	120.00
Vase, 6¼", Dahlia, cupped	155.00
Vase, 8", Dahlia, cupped	210.00
Vase, 9", wallhanging	350.00
Vase, 10", 2-handled	225.00
Vase, 10½", Dahlia, cupped	265.00

"FLUTE & CANE," "SUNBURST & CANE," "CANE," "HUCKABEE," SEMI-COLONIAL,
NO. 666 & 666½, IMPERIAL GLASS COMPANY, c. 1921

Colors: crystal, pink, green, Rubigold (marigold), Caramel slag

Since the last book came out, I have not had one communication on this pattern, so I will repeat from the last book how this pattern came to be listed. My wife talked me into including this pattern with the unfortunate "Devil's" line number. She finds the cane look intriguing. In an aside, we were standing in line at a license bureau in officialdom once, when a lady came in and pitched a license at the clerk and said very loudly, "I'm not having this Devil's number on my car." Sure enough, she'd been issued "666" something. Bible belt people know this association. It appears whoever assigned the numbers at Imperial did not. (Neither did the state.) I was told that the half number beside Imperial's line numbers indicated the less expensively made glassware sold in places like F.W. Woolworth, Sears, Montgomery Wards, et. al.

I suspect there are additional pieces and had hoped for confirmation from collectors, but that has not happened. I imagine there are even pieces out there in blue, which was being run in this period; but I can't confirm that right now. I am certain I've seen some; but since I wasn't paying specific attention to this pattern until recent years, I can't be one hundred percent sure of it. I do remember seeing a sugar and creamer in slag when I was at the factory in the 80s, though it is not in any of the catalogs they presented me then. As was Imperial's (and other) glass companies' want, they launched a few items from older moulds into their wares from time to time, and in whatever colors they were running at that time. Since my catalog information doesn't encompass Imperial's entire history, I can't be positive what other colors you'll find in "Flute and Cane." If you'll be kind enough to let me know what you turn up, I'd be most appreciative and will make an effort to pass it along to collectors.

Many of the marigold pieces are quite rare and highly prized by carnival glass collectors. The tall, slender pitcher, tumblers, cups, 6" plates, and goblets are considered very desirable items to own. However, various bowls are what are usually seen, today. The 6" plate was marketed with the sherbet as an ice cream set, with the molasses as an underliner, and with the custard cup as a saucer. There ought to be quite a few of those available; but, alas, not so. Sorry, but there is a very cane-appearing candle in the picture that officially belongs with the Amelia #671 line, shown on page 10. You cannot always trust what you see in an author's photo, so one does actually need to read the text from time to time.

	Crystal*		Crystal*		Crystal*
Bowl, 4½", fruit	10.00	Compote, 6½", oval, ftd., 2-handle	30.00	Salt & pepper	45.00
Bowl, 6½", oval, pickle	16.00	Compote, 7½", stem w/bowl	25.00	Sherbet, 3½", stem	10.00
Bowl, 6½", square	15.00	Compote, 7½", stem, flat	25.00	Spooner (open sm. sug)	15.00
Bowl, 7½", salad	25.00	Creamer	15.00	Stem, 1 ounce, cordial	25.00
Bowl, 8½", large. fruit	30.00	Cup, custard	12.00	Stem, 3 ounce, wine	18.00
Bowl, crème soup, 5½"	20.00	Molasses, nickel top	65.00	Stem, 6 ounce, champagne	15.00
Butter w/lid, small		Oil bottle w/stopper, 6 ounce	45.00	Stem, 9 ounce, water	18.00
(powder box look)	35.00	Pitcher, 22 ounce, 5¼"	45.00	Sugar w/lid	20.00
Butter, dome lid	55.00	Pitcher, 51 ounce	65.00	Tumbler, 9 ounce	25.00
Celery, 8½", oval	22.00	Pitcher, tall/slender	75.00	Vase, 6"	37.50
Celery, tall, 2 handle	40.00	Plate, 6"	20.00	*Add 50% for colors	

FORTUNE, HOCKING GLASS COMPANY, 1937 – 1938

Colors: pink and crystal

An outlay of time and a little stroke of luck can help assemble a set of Fortune, a small pattern where luncheon plates are valuable and you normally find them only one at a time. Over the years, both Fortune tumblers have been gathered by collectors of Queen Mary and Old Colony to use with those sets because they were inexpensive and looked satisfactory. Since Hocking made all three patterns, the colors do match very well. Now the prices of Fortune tumblers have come into their own and it is not as reasonable to use them with other sets. I generally see tumblers and small berry bowls when I stumble upon Fortune. Other items are not as widely dispersed.

There is a pitcher whose pattern is similar to Fortune that is turning up occasionally and some collectors are buying them for use with their sets. These "go-with" pitchers are selling in the $30.00 to $40.00 range. So far, no actual Fortune pitcher has turned up; but never say never.

The covered candy is a useful display item. They make wonderful gifts for beginning collectors and are one of **the** most economically priced pink candy dishes in Depression glass.

	Pink, Crystal		Pink, Crystal
Bowl, 4", berry	10.00	Cup	12.00
Bowl, 4½", dessert	10.00	Plate, 6", sherbet	8.00
Bowl, 4½", handled	10.00	Plate, 8", luncheon	30.00
Bowl, 5¼", rolled edge	22.00	Saucer	5.00
Bowl, 7¾", salad or large berry	28.00	Tumbler, 3½", 5 ounce, juice	12.50
Candy dish and cover, flat	30.00	Tumbler, 4", 9 ounce, water	15.00

FRUITS, HAZEL ATLAS AND OTHER GLASS COMPANIES, 1931 – 1935

Colors: pink, green, some crystal, and iridized

Fruits patterned water tumblers (4") in all colors are the pieces regularly found. Iridescent "Pears" tumblers are plentiful. Federal Glass Company probably made these carnival-colored tumblers while they were making iridescent Normandie and a few pieces in Madrid in the late 1930s. Water tumblers with cherries or other fruits are found in pink, but locating any green tumbler is a dilemma.

Fruits collectors have several pieces, now, that are almost unattainable in this scarce 1930s pattern. The 3½" (5 ounce) juice and 5" (12 ounce) ice tea tumblers have joined the large and small berry bowls as the pieces of green to possess. Few of the berry bowls are being found but even fewer tumblers. I have only owned one iced tea; but two juice tumblers promised to me turned out to be Cherry Blossom. Fruits tumblers have only cherries and no blossoms as do Cherry Blossom.

Given that so many collectors are pursuing green iced teas, juice tumblers, and bowls, their prices continue escalating and may never stop. I have never found pink juice or tea tumblers, though I inadvertently listed them — as did a come-lately competitor. In the beginning, I only scheduled one price for all Fruits colors. As more collectors bought the green, the price of green rose faster than pink; so, I split prices into two listings, not realizing until later the absence of *pink* juice or tea tumblers, which had been shrouded under that "all colors" label. Most collectors pursue accessible green water tumblers to go with the pitcher and ignore the two rarely found sizes. Some collectors settle for buying only one of each. Pink water tumblers have no pitcher.

Fruits berry bowls in both sizes are among the hardest to obtain in all Depression glass patterns. Since this is not one of the most collected patterns and does not have thousands of admirers, the scantiness of both sizes of bowls has only been perceived in recent years.

Fruits pitchers have only cherries in the pattern. Sometimes they are mislabeled as Cherry Blossom, flat-bottomed pitchers. Notice that the handle is shaped like that of flat Florentine pitchers (Hazel Atlas Company) and not like Cherry Blossom (Jeannette Glass Company) flat pitchers. Crystal Fruits pitchers sell for less than half the price of green and other crystal pieces are hardly noticed. They are obtainable should you want an economically priced beverage set.

	Green	Pink		Green	Pink
Bowl, 4½", berry	38.00	30.00	Sherbet	12.00	12.00
Bowl, 8", berry	95.00	55.00	Tumbler, 3½", juice	75.00	
Cup	8.00	9.00	* Tumbler, 4" (1 fruit)	20.00	18.00
Pitcher, 7", flat bottom	100.00		Tumbler, 4" (combination of fruits)	30.00	22.00
Plate, 8", luncheon	12.00	12.00	Tumbler, 5", 12 ounce	175.00	
Saucer	5.50	4.00	* Iridized $8.00		

92

GEORGIAN, "LOVEBIRDS," FEDERAL GLASS COMPANY, 1931 – 1936

Colors: green, crystal, and amber

Federal Glass Company's Georgian pattern shows two lovebirds (or parakeets, as one reader admonished) perched side by side. This pattern is easily identified by most. However, there are a few pieces to the pattern without the birds. These include both sizes of tumblers, the hot plate, and a few dinner plates. Few collectors seek dinner plates without birds; that style plate sells for less. Baskets alternate with birds in the design on all other pieces. The tumblers and hot plates only have baskets; you can sometimes find a good deal on tumblers if the owner does not know about those missing birds.

In the mid-1970s, the Peach State Depression Glass Club in the name of President Jimmy Carter donated a set to the Smithsonian. Those pieces were engraved and numbered. Some extras were sold or given as prizes. Thus, if you run into such an item, it is now a double part of our history.

Basic pieces in Georgian are easily found. Berry bowls, cups, saucers, sherbets, sherbet plates, and luncheon plates can be accumulated. Georgian tumblers, however, are difficult to find. Several boxed sets of 36 water tumblers were found in the Chicago area, where a newspaper gave the tumblers away to subscribers in the 1930s. I've even been told that these were found stored in Al Capone's vault, albeit by a notorious leg puller. Prices for iced teas have more than doubled the price of water tumblers. I have owned at least a dozen Georgian waters for every iced tea to give you an idea of how difficult teas are to find.

Lack of new collectors seeking this pattern has caused a little softening on the prices of items offered for more than $50.00. Many of the Georgian serving pieces were greatly utilized; be cautious of mint pricing for pieces that are scratched and worn from use. You pay a premium for mint condition. Keep in mind that all prices listed in this book are for mint condition pieces. Damaged or scratched and worn pieces should go for less depending upon the degree of damage and deterioration. If you are gathering this glass to use, some defects may not make as much difference as collecting for eventual marketing. Mint condition glass will sell without difficulty and for a much better price if you ever decide to part with your collection.

Georgian Lazy Susans (cold cuts servers) are more rarely seen than the Madrid ones that turn up, infrequently, at best. You can see one pictured below. A walnut tray turned up in Ohio with an original decal label that read "Kalter Aufschain Cold Cuts Server Schirmer Cincy." Most of these servers have been found in Kentucky and southern Ohio. These wooden Lazy Susans made of walnut are 18½" across with seven 5" openings for holding the so-called hot plates. Somehow, I believe these 5" hot plates are misidentified since they are found on a cold cuts server. These cold/hot plates have only the center motif design and can be found in crystal.

The so-called Georgian mug was a creamer that missed getting a spout — making it different, but not really a mug. There are other patterns known that have creamers or pitchers without a spout. One other Federal pattern, Sharon, has at least one two-spouted creamer known. There is a Holiday milk pitcher without a spout, which also looks like a large mug. Spouts were applied by hand at most glass factories using a wooden tool. Quality control of this glass was not as demanding as today. Most actual mugs from the period have flat bottoms or are larger in capacity or decidedly taller than creamers.

There is a round, thin plate made by Indiana Glass having two large parakeets as its center design, covering nearly the whole plate. This is not Georgian, but can be found in green as well as amber and canary.

GEORGIAN

	Green			Green
Bowl, 4½", berry	9.00	* Hot plate, 5", center design		80.00
Bowl, 5¾", cereal	22.00	** Plate, 6", sherbet		7.00
Bowl, 6½", deep	65.00	Plate, 8", luncheon		11.00
Bowl, 7½", large berry	60.00	Plate, 9¼", dinner		25.00
Bowl, 9", oval vegetable	60.00	Plate, 9¼", center design only		20.00
Butter dish and cover	85.00	Platter, 11½", closed-handled		65.00
Butter dish bottom	50.00	Saucer		3.00
Butter dish top	35.00	Sherbet		11.00
Cold cuts server, 18½", wood with		Sugar, 3", footed		10.00
seven 5" openings for 5" coasters	950.00	Sugar, 4", footed		18.00
Creamer, 3", footed	12.00	Sugar cover for 3"		50.00
Creamer, 4", footed	18.00	Tumbler, 4", 9 ounce, flat		65.00
Cup	10.00	Tumbler, 5¼", 12 ounce, flat		125.00

* Crystal $30.00   ** Amber $40.00

94

GLADES, LINE #215, NEW MARTINSVILLE, c. 1930s

Colors: amethyst, crystal and w/etches, cobalt, ruby

Glades line shows that wonderful linear influence that was so strong in the early to mid-1930s and you cannot get more "Deco" than the double cone shaped cocktail often found with the cocktail shaker. You will find pieces of this in crystal with the "Bird & Blossom" etching more often than not. The amethyst items pictured have ground bottoms, which is indicative of earlier, hand-finished glassware. Canton Glass was still making Glades as late as 1954 from Paden City moulds.

	*Crystal		*Crystal
Bowl, 4½", tab hdld., fruit	10.00	Plate, 8"	7.50
Bowl, 4¾" cream soup	12.50	Plate. 10"	15.00
Bowl, 5", tab hdld, flare rim, cereal	12.50	Plate, 11½" serving	20.00
Bowl, 6" tab. hdld, shallow	15.00	Relish, 4 pt., tab hdld	32.50
Bowl, 6", tab hdld, bonbon	15.00	Relish tray, 12¾", 2 hdld., 2 part	40.00
Bowl, 7"	12.50	Server, center-handle w /round, lined center knob	35.00
Bowl, 7¼", gravy	27.50	Saucer	2.50
Bowl, 10", tab hdld, oval	50.00	Shaker, 2⅛", round, pr.	30.00
Bowl, 3 toe, 12½", flat rim, console	45.00	Sugar, 7 oz.	12.50
Candle, 5", double light	35.00	Tray, 11", oval celery	20.00
Cocktail, 8", 30 oz.; w/metal lid, 11"	45.00	Tumbler, 3 oz., flat whiskey	12.50
Cocktail, double cone shape, 3 oz.	12.50	Tumbler, 3½ oz.	17.50
Comport, 3½", high	27.50	Tumbler, 4", 8 oz.	17.50
Comport, 7⅝", high, indented top	37.50	Tumbler, 5¼", 12 oz. tea	20.00
Creamer, 7 oz.	12.50		
Cup	12.50	* Double price for	
Decanter, 6½", 12 oz., tilt w/handle, cordial	50.00	color; add 10 –	
Ice tub, 4" high x 6⅜" diameter	75.00	15% with etching	
Plate, 6½", tab hdld.	5.00		
Plate, 7"	6.00		

GOTHIC GARDEN, PADEN CITY GLASS COMPANY, 1930s

Colors: pink, green, black, yellow, and crystal

Gothic Garden does have a creamer and sugar that lends credence to the thought that there may be a luncheon set available; lack of cups and saucers has not hurt the collecting of other Paden City patterns. Cups and saucers are rare in all etched patterns of this company. Did the etching department not like to work on smaller pieces? For the present, I am only listing one price; add 25% for black and subtract 25% for crystal. What little crystal I have seen has been gold trimmed which, with good gold, will fetch nearly the price of colored ware. I see quite a bit of this at formal shows, some pieces with astronomical prices. However, since I keep seeing those same pieces, I think for some reason Gothic Garden has not caught on with collectors to that extent just yet.

All the favorite elements of 1930s ware, birds, flowers, scrolls, garlands, and urns are found on Paden City's etch, Gothic Garden. It should be the most desirable etch ever made in that period. The bird's body faces outward on either side of the design medallion, but their heads turn backward toward the center floral motif. It is reminiscent of a Phoenix bird, which was a mythological bird that rose from the ashes. Gothic Garden is found mostly on Paden City's Line #411 (square shapes with the corners cut off), but you may find it on other Paden City blanks. Other colors than those I have listed may occur; let me know what you find, so I can add to the listings. Measurements may vary up to an inch due to the turned up edges on bowls; do not take listings as absolute gospel.

I bought a black bowl like the one pictured in pink and saw a flat, yellow candy like the one pictured in "Peacock Reverse" on page 172. Since it was prized more highly by the seller than by me, he still owns it.

	All colors			All colors
Bowl, 9", tab handle	65.00		Creamer	40.00
Bowl, 10", footed	85.00		Plate, 11", tab handle	60.00
Bowl, 10⅛", handle	95.00		Server, 9¾", center handled	85.00
Bowl, 10½", oval, handle	110.00		Sugar	40.00
Cake plate, 10½", footed	85.00		Vase, 6½"	130.00
Candy, flat	130.00		Vase, 8"	175.00
Comport, tall, deep top	65.00		Vase, 9½"	120.00

HEX OPTIC, "HONEYCOMB," JEANNETTE GLASS COMPANY, 1928 – 1932

Colors: pink, green, Ultra Marine (late 1930s), and iridescent in 1950s

Jeannette's Hex Optic was one of the first Depression glass patterns made in those new brilliant green and wild rose colors that were making an impact on the buying public. It was introduced in 1928 and was a historic glass design, manufactured in one of the first fully automated systems of the time. Hex Optic was heavily used and few pieces found today are without scratches or nicks. It arrived as tableware and kitchenware items so that a homemaker's total glass needs could be assembled in matching ware. It was innovative and impressive in a trade just moving from making glass by hand into an age of mechanization.

Now, Hex Optic is more observed by kitchenware collectors than any other pattern of Depression glass because of the numerous kitchenware pieces available. Sugar shakers, bucket reamers, mixing bowls, stacking sets, and butter dishes were planned in green and pink. In fact, were it not for kitchenware collectors becoming passionate about Hex Optic, it might still be overlooked in the glass-collecting domain.

There are two styles of pitchers in Hexagon Optic, one being footed and having the Deco age cone shape (pictured below) and the other, a flat bottomed, cylindrical shape. This 8" tall, 70-ounce, flat-bottomed version is being found in both colors, although green is not as abundant. Five or six people have written to say they find them in Minnesota and Wisconsin. The footed pitcher is hard to find now, having quietly disappeared into collections. Note that Jeannette's Hex Optic pitcher is thick. Other companies' honeycomb pitchers are thin.

Iridescent oil lamps, both style pitchers, and tumblers were all made during Jeannette's iridized craze of the late 1950s. The Ultra Marine tumblers were possibly a product of the late 1930s when the company was making Doric and Pansy.

Cups, sugars, and creamers in this pattern have innovative ear-shaped, solid handles which make them easily dumped if not picked up properly. You might note that the green creamer and sugar have a floral cutting. Someone outside of Jeannette would have cut that. Early pieces of Jeannette's glass carried a J in a triangle trademark.

	Pink, Green		Pink, Green
Bowl, 4¼", ruffled berry	9.00	Plate, 8", luncheon	5.50
Bowl, 7½", large berry	16.00	Platter, 11", round	15.00
Bowl, 7¼", mixing	18.00	Refrigerator dish, 4" x 4"	18.00
Bowl, 8¼", mixing	25.00	Refrigerator stack set, 4 piece	85.00
Bowl, 9", mixing	28.00	Salt and pepper, pair	30.00
Bowl, 10", mixing	30.00	Saucer	3.00
Bucket reamer	70.00	Sugar, 2 styles of handles	7.00
Butter dish and cover, rectangular 1 pound size	95.00	Sugar shaker	250.00
Creamer, 2 style handles	7.00	Sherbet, 5 ounce, footed	7.00
Cup, 2 style handles	10.00	Tumbler, 3¾", 9 ounce	4.50
Ice bucket, metal handle	32.00	Tumbler, 5", 12 ounce	7.00
Pitcher, 5", 32 ounce, sunflower motif in bottom	25.00	Tumbler, 4¾", 7 ounce, footed	7.50
Pitcher, 9", 48 ounce, footed	45.00	Tumbler, 5¾" footed	9.00
Pitcher, 8", 70 ounce, flat	175.00	Tumbler, 7", footed	10.00
Plate, 6", sherbet	2.50	Whiskey, 2", 1 ounce	9.00

HOBNAIL, HOCKING GLASS COMPANY, 1934 – 1936

Colors: crystal, crystal w/red trim, and pink

Most Depression-era glass companies made some variety of hobnailed patterns, but Hocking's Hobnail is promptly recognized by experienced collectors due to its pieces being moulded like those found in Miss America or Moonstone. If truth were told, the 1940s Moonstone pattern is essentially Hocking's Hobnail design with an added white emphasis to the hobs and edges. Crystal Hobnail serving pieces are not easy to find, but beverage and decanter sets are plentiful.

The light amethyst color pictured below was named Lilac according to Anchor Hocking labels on most of the pieces shown. The other color is Ivory that was made regularly for ovenware usage. I believe the Lilac would have been a hit with the public, but it appears to have never been offered for sale. The three items shown are compliments of Anchor Hocking who have been helpful in allowing me to photograph pieces that you would never get a chance see otherwise.

The red-trimmed crystal Hobnail on page 99 displays and photographs beautifully. Collectors have been captivated by the red trim that is found predominantly on the West Coast. The decanter and footed juices/wines are the only red-trimmed pieces I see in my travels in the eastern half of the country. When we find any, it always sells at the first show.

Hocking made only four pieces in pink. Another pink Hobnail pattern, such as one made by MacBeth-Evans, can coexist with this Hocking pattern; that way, you can add a pitcher and tumblers, something unavailable in Hocking's ware. Many other companies' Hobnail patterns will mingle with Hocking's Hobnail.

Footed juice tumblers were sold to complement the decanter as a wine set; thus, it was also a wine glass unless the preacher stopped by. Timing had a lot to do with tumblers and stems during this era. During Prohibition, wine glasses were sold as juices and the champagnes as high sherbets. Wine glasses during that era routinely held approximately three ounces. Today, people consider the eight- to ten-ounce water goblets from the Depression era as wine goblets; twenty-first century wine connoisseurs want larger glasses. Dealers should verify size with customers when they ask for wines since they may really be wanting water goblets.

	Pink	*Crystal		Pink	*Crystal
Bowl, 5½", cereal		4.00	Plate, 8½", luncheon	8.00	4.00
Bowl, 7", salad		4.50	Saucer/sherbet plate	4.00	1.50
Cup	6.00	4.50	Sherbet	6.00	3.00
Creamer, footed		6.00	Sugar, footed		6.00
Decanter and stopper, 32 ounce		30.00	Tumbler, 5 ounce, juice		4.00
Goblet, 10 ounce, water		8.00	Tumbler, 9 ounce, 10 ounce, water		5.00
Goblet, 13 ounce, iced tea		10.00	Tumbler, 5¼",15 ounce, iced tea		14.00
Pitcher, 18 ounce, milk		20.00	Tumbler, 3 ounce, footed, wine/juice		5.00
Pitcher, 67 ounce		25.00	Tumbler, 5 ounce, footed, cordial		6.00
Plate, 6", sherbet	5.00	1.50	Whiskey, 1½ ounce		6.00

*Add 20 – 25% for red trimmed pieces

HOMESPUN, "FINE RIB," JEANNETTE GLASS COMPANY, 1939 – 1949

Colors: pink and crystal, fired-on colors

Homespun has nine tumblers, which is surprising for a pattern so small that it does not include a pitcher. A large Fine Rib pitcher, made by Hazel-Atlas was originally packaged by some unknown company for use with Homespun tumblers with 13½ ounce, band-at-top iced teas. The pitcher has similar narrow bands around the neck and matches in color, but has no waffling design. Band-at-top tumblers are harder to find; but most collectors seek the ribbed.

Pictured on the right are the flat, 13½ ounce (band at top) tea and the 12½ ounce (no band) tea. In front of them is the 9 ounce (band above ribs, waffle bottomed) tumbler. Confusion reigns with the three tumblers on the left in front of the footed teas. There is little difference in height; but the 7 ounce (ribs to top, straight, concentric ring bottom) and 9 ounce (ribs to top, straight, waffle bottomed) are often confused Although there is a two ounce difference in capacity, there is only ³⁄₁₆" difference in height. Notice the small 8 ounce (ribs to top, flared, plain bottomed) tumbler on the right of those. This style is challenging to find. The two footed teas are often confused because they both hold 15 ounces and there is only ⅛" difference in height. Collectors sometimes refer to them as skinny and fat bottomed. There is a slight stem on the taller one and no stem on the other. It only makes a difference when ordering by mail or off the Internet. You need to specify no stem or slight stem and hope the seller knows enough to distinguish them.

There is no Homespun sugar lid. The lid occasionally exhibited on the sugar is a Fine Rib powder jar top.

Homespun bowls have tab handles. Sherbets suffer from inner rim roughness (irr), but are elusive. Buy them when you see them. The sherbet is pictured in front of the sugar on the right.

There is no child's teapot in crystal and there are no sugars and creamers in this child's tea set.

	Pink, Crystal
Bowl, 4½", closed handles	20.00
Bowl, 5", cereal, closed handles	32.00
Bowl, 8¼", large berry	32.00
Butter dish and cover	60.00
Coaster/ashtray	6.50
Creamer, footed	12.50
Cup	13.00
Plate, 6", sherbet	7.00
Plate, 9¼", dinner	22.00
Platter, 13", closed handles	20.00
Saucer	4.00

	Pink, Crystal
Sherbet, low flat	18.00
Sugar, footed	12.50
Tumbler, 3⅞", 7 ounce, straight	22.00
Tumbler, 4⅛", 8 ounce, water, flared top	22.00
Tumbler, 4¼", 9 ounce, band at top	22.00
Tumbler, 4⁵⁄₁₆", 9 ounce, no band	22.00
Tumbler, 5⅜", 12½ ounce, iced tea	33.00
Tumbler, 5⅞", 13½ ounce, iced tea, banded at top	33.00
Tumbler, 4", 5 ounce, footed	8.00
Tumbler, 6¼", 15 ounce, footed	33.00
Tumbler, 6⅜", 15 ounce, footed	33.00

HOMESPUN CHILD'S TEA SET

	Pink	Crystal
Cup	35.00	25.00
Saucer	11.00	8.00
Plate	14.00	10.00
Teapot	60.00	

	Pink	Crystal
Teapot cover	100.00	
Set: 14-pieces	400.00	
Set: 12-pieces		175.00

INDIANA CUSTARD, "FLOWER AND LEAF BAND," INDIANA GLASS COMPANY, 1930s; 1950s

Colors: ivory or custard, early 1930s; white, 1950s

Indiana Custard attracts a few new admirers every year, but most cannot find sufficient pieces unless they live in central Indiana. On the other hand, at a recent antique show, a dealer from Chicago had a significant set displayed. There were no sherbets, but most everything else was there. Shading on the cups and saucers varied, which is a small problem with Indiana Custard. Some of the pieces are more yellow and translucent than the beige of others.

This set was being marketed as a whole, with an extra premium for its being a set — something that seldom works with glass. Sets are not worth more than the sum of the pieces. Few people buy complete sets unless they are dealers buying wholesale. Collectors generally buy a piece or two at a time. Granted, obtaining an entire set a piece or two at a time is a formidable task. However, most people enjoy chasing glass patterns. They tell me repeatedly at shows how much fun they've had doing it — often for years. In my experience, individual pricing of items will often see an entire set sell in a much smaller amount of time than trying to market the entire set.

Indiana Custard is the only Depression-era pattern where cups and sherbets are the most elusive items to find. Some collectors consider the sherbet overrated; but those who have searched for years without owning one, would contradict that. In all honesty, they are likely a good acquisition at today's price. Cups have been more difficult for me to find than the sherbets, but I usually have found the sherbets in groups of six or eight and the cups one or two at a time. Both sell, even at these prices.

Indiana made this pattern in white in the 1950s under the name Orange Blossom. So far, there is only minor demand for this color, though it is a lovely, pristine white. Orange Blossom can now be found in my *Collectible Glassware from the 40s, 50s, 60s....*

I have been unable to establish if there is a full set of yellow floral decorated pieces available. I have seen a set of Indiana Custard decorated like the saucer with the colored flowers in the center. After 60 years, a problem with collecting the florals might be that the decorations flake.

	French Ivory		French Ivory
Bowl, 5½", berry	11.00	Plate, 7½", salad	16.00
Bowl, 6½", cereal	28.00	Plate, 8⅞", luncheon	18.00
Bowl, 7½", flat soup	32.00	Plate, 9¾", dinner	30.00
Bowl, 9", 1¾" deep, large berry	32.00	Platter, 11½", oval	35.00
Bowl, 9½", oval vegetable	32.00	Saucer	7.00
Butter dish and cover	65.00	Sherbet	100.00
Cup	33.00	Sugar	10.00
Creamer	15.00	Sugar cover	25.00
Plate, 5¾", bread and butter	7.00		

INDIANA SILVER, INDIANA GLASS COMPANY, c. 1918

Colors: crystal w/sterling silver overlay

The catalog I have before me lists two assortments being presented to dealers of the time, a 130-pound 13 dozen-piece "Sensation" assortment and a 100-pound "Sterling dining assortment." The dining assortment selling prices were to be $1.25 – $1.50 each — which was costly at that time, considering most wares in their other lines were designed to be sold for 10¢ to 25¢.

Somehow, this ware managed to encompass both the look of the past Art Nouveau (flowered scrolls) era and the simple, linear lined Deco era that was about to emerge. Firing silver onto it fitted it perfectly with the silver craze of that particular period. Much of what you find now is missing good silver; but the wonderful design is still present. If you choose to collect this, worry about good silver after you find the pieces, and then replace them with good silver ones you run across. Please note that the plate was designated as a calling card tray — elegantly gracing the foyer table, no doubt. Of all pieces, those footed vases seem the most elusive.

Bowl, 4½" dessert	10.00	Goblet, wine	15.00
Bowl, 5½", ftd., bonbon	15.00	Plate, 7½", card tray	10.00
Bowl, 8½", berry	25.00	Pitcher, ½ gal.	45.00
Butter w/cover	35.00	Sherbet, ftd.	12.50
Cup, custard	12.50	Spoon	10.00
Compote, ftd., jelly	15.00	Sugar w/cover, large	20.00
Creamer, small, berry	10.00	Sugar, open small, berry	10.00
Creamer, large	15.00	Tumbler	18.00
Goblet, water	25.00	Vase, 6½", ftd.	40.00

IRIS, "IRIS AND HERRINGBONE," JEANNETTE GLASS COMPANY, 1928 – 1932; 1950s; 1970s

Colors: crystal, iridescent; some pink and green; recently bi-colored red/yellow and blue/green combinations, and white
(See Reproduction Section.)

The reproduction shysters are thumping our much-loved Iris. Do not panic; as has happened with other patterns, this, too, shall pass. Reproduced dinner plates and iced teas from Taiwan hit the market two years ago. Since then, coasters and flat tumblers have been remade and there are constant reports, right now, of cereal and soup bowls turning up. I have not been able to confirm either of these last items being remade, but it wouldn't surprise me. All the new crystal is exceedingly clear. If you place old crystal Iris on a white tablecloth or paper, it will look gray or even slightly yellow. The new is very crystal without a tinge of color of any sort. The flat tumblers have no herringbone on the bottom — just Iris. The coaster is more than half-full of glass when you look from the side. Turn to page 247 for details.

Would you believe a bright yellow Iris sugar bowl to go with the pink and green that are found occasionally? One was found and brought into a Texas show recently. I first thought it was sprayed on yellow, but it is not. Most interesting is where it was found — Australia! I wasn't fond of the price, but I had to own it.

Prices for crystal Iris have stabilized or even softened a bit, especially for iced teas and dinner plates. Prices for coasters and flat water tumblers have been harder hit. We have been through this with other patterns over the years and it will take a while for collectors to adjust. Prices plateau or drop for a while, and then they start an upward march again. As prices increase, collectors who have sets observe these higher prices and begin to sell their wares and rare items once again appear for sale. Original crystal production for Iris began in 1928. Some was made in the late 1940s and 1950s; candy bottoms and vases appeared as late as the 1970s.

The Internet has opened up a world that has both good and bad aspects to collecting. Bad news is that there are people selling who misrepresent their wares. Reproduced items get on there first as "old" and people pay high prices before word gets out in the collecting world. The other side of that coin is that once known, word is flashed worldwide. An Internet address where reputable dealers furnish merchandise is www.glassshow.com.

Iridescent candy bottoms are a product of the 1970s when Jeannette made crystal bottoms and flashed them with two-tone colors such as red/yellow or blue/green. Many of these were sold as vases; and, over time, the colors have peeled off or been purposely stripped to make them, again, crystal candy bottoms. These later pieces can be distinguished by the lack of rays on the foot. Similarly, white vases were made and sprayed outside with green, red, and blue. White vases sell in the area of $15.00 – 18.00. These are not rare. I have seen a pink painted over white vase in a local antique mall for $90.00 marked rare pink Iris. I hope that no one believes that. The rare vase is transparent pink.

The decorated red and gold Iris that keeps turning up was called Corsage and styled by Century in 1946. This information was on a card attached to a 1946 wedding gift.
A number of collectors are seeking this.

103

IRIS

	Crystal	Iridescent	Transparent Green, Pink
Bowl, 4½", berry, beaded edge	40.00	8.00	
Bowl, 5", ruffled, sauce	10.00	22.00	
Bowl, 5", cereal	110.00		
Bowl, 7½", soup	155.00	60.00	
Bowl, 8", berry, beaded edge	80.00	25.00	
Bowl, 9½", ruffled, salad	14.00	13.00	200.00
Bowl, 11½", ruffled, fruit	15.00	14.00	
Bowl, 11", fruit, straight edge	60.00		
Butter dish and cover	47.50	45.00	
Butter dish bottom	12.50	12.50	
Butter dish top	35.00	32.50	
Candlesticks, pair	42.50	45.00	
Candy jar and cover	185.00		
***Coaster	90.00		
Creamer, footed	12.00	12.00	150.00
Cup	15.00	14.00	
*Demitasse cup	45.00	150.00	
*Demitasse saucer	145.00	250.00	
Fruit or nut set	110.00	150.00	
Goblet, 4", wine		25.00	

	Crystal	Iridescent	Transparent Green, Pink
Goblet, 4½", 4 ounce, cocktail	22.00		
Goblet, 4½", 3 ounce, wine	15.00		
Goblet, 5½", 4 ounce	24.00	495.00	
Goblet, 5½", 8 ounce	24.00	295.00	
**Lamp shade, 11½"	90.00		
Pitcher, 9½", footed	40.00	42.50	
Plate, 5½", sherbet	13.00	11.00	
Plate, 8", luncheon	100.00		
***Plate, 9", dinner	48.00	45.00	
Plate, 11¾", sandwich	35.00	30.00	
Saucer	8.00	9.00	
Sherbet, 2½", footed	26.00	15.00	
Sherbet, 4", footed	24.00	295.00	
****Sugar	11.00	11.00	150.00
Sugar cover	12.00	12.00	
***Tumbler, 4", flat	110.00		
Tumbler, 6", footed	18.00	18.00	
***Tumbler, 6½", footed	26.00		
Vase, 9"	30.00	25.00	225.00

* Ruby, Blue, Amethyst priced as iridescent
** Colors, $85.00

*** Has been reproduced
**** Yellow, $195.00

JUBILEE, LANCASTER GLASS COMPANY, Early 1930s

Colors: yellow, crystal, and pink

I decided to try to unravel the Jubilee knot we've been in over the years in the last book and since many collectors buy every other book, I will repeat from the previous book. The accepted cut (#1200) considered the Jubilee pattern is a piece having a 12 petal, open centered flower. (I clarify that for readers who wrote thinking any ware with an open center, 12-petal flower is Jubilee. No, it is not. I also need to point out that the cut design has to be on the piece. Plain, uncut blanks are not Jubilee.) The confusion with Jubilee occurs when you find Standard Glass Company's paneled blanks with a #1200 cut. A pioneer author gave these the name "Tat"; but people finding these pieces over the years said, "Ah! Jubilee!" and placed them with their pattern. This practice became so common that the Standard items are now accepted as "Jubilee" pattern. Further confusion arises when people find Standard Glass Company's closed center, 12-petal flower cut (#89) on paneled blanks, which Standard sold as Martha Washington pattern. Basic pieces of Lancaster's Jubilee were presented on smooth blanks (no optic panels). Standard's #1200 was presented on optic paneled blanks. Martha Washington came on optic paneled blanks, with rayed foot tumblers and fancy handled cups. Both of these sister companies showed companion-serving wares for these patterns using the same petal edged, fancy handled blanks. To further confuse things, Standard had a #200 and a #28 cut, very like #1200, which had the same flower with more cut branches, which were presented on those same type serving pieces, with some petal blank, three-toed bowls and trays thrown in for good measure. Other like cuts include a mayo bowl with 16 petals and a cutting with 12 petals, but having a smaller petal in between the larger ones. Frankly, most collectors are happy to buy any of these pieces as Jubilee pattern to enhance their sets.

Notice the four pink pieces pictured. The petal blank, three-toed bowl is Standard's #200 cut. The cup, saucer, and plate are Lancaster #1200. Probably all the pulled (no ball) stems are Standard lines; but there are ball-stemmed, optic panel goblets like the smooth ones found in Jubilee. Therefore, these ball types cannot only belong to Lancaster.

After all the detailed information above, I must point out that two pieces of Jubilee only have 11 petals, the 3", 8 ounce, non-stemmed sherbet and the three-footed covered candy. You can see that sherbet and the oyster cocktail in the *Very Rare Glassware of the Depression Years, Fourth Series.* Having only 11 petals on the candy and sherbet apparently came from cutting problems experienced when using the typical 6" cutting wheel. The foot of the sherbet and the knob on the candy were in the way when a petal of the design was cut directly up and down. The glasscutter had to move over to the side in order to cut a petal. Because of this placement, only an 11-petal flower resulted on these pieces. Yes, those two 11 petal pieces are Jubilee and both are hard to find. The 12" vase has a 4" top, 3½" base, and a bulbous 6" middle. This massive vase is one piece of Jubilee that not all collectors desire.

The #889 liner plate for the #890 mayo does have a raised rim, making that liner plate even rarer than the mayo. I have been wrong about that in the past. When I got my magnifying glass out to read the catalog numbers, the plates do not have the same number as I first believed. Sorry. Some mayonnaise sets have 16 petals on bowl and plate.

New collectors can be assured that Jubilee luncheon sets are plentiful. However, there is a decided lack of serving pieces for #1200 Jubilee. Prices on these seldom-found items are high.

JUBILEE

	Pink	Yellow
Bowl, 8", 3-footed, 5⅛" high	250.00	200.00
Bowl, 9", handled fruit		125.00
Bowl, 11½", flat fruit	195.00	160.00
Bowl, 11½", 3-footed	250.00	250.00
Bowl, 11½", 3-footed, curved in		225.00
Bowl, 13", 3-footed	250.00	225.00
Candlestick, pair	185.00	185.00
Candy jar, w/lid, 3-footed	325.00	325.00
Cheese & cracker set	225.00	225.00
Creamer	35.00	17.00
Cup	35.00	12.00
Mayonnaise & plate	250.00	225.00
w/original ladle	320.00	270.00
Plate, 7", salad	20.00	12.00
Plate, 8¾", luncheon	25.00	12.00
Plate, 13½", sandwich, handled	75.00	50.00
Plate, 14", 3-footed		190.00
Saucer, two styles	10.00	4.00
Sherbet, 3", 8 ounce		70.00
Stem, 4", 1 ounce, cordial		300.00
Stem, 4¾", 4 ounce, oyster cocktail		75.00
Stem, 4⅞", 3 ounce, cocktail		125.00
Stem, 5½", 7 ounce, sherbet/champagne		75.00
Stem, 7½", 11 ounce		160.00
Sugar	35.00	16.00
Tray, 11", 2-handled cake	65.00	45.00
Tumbler, 5", 6 ounce, footed, juice		95.00

	Pink	Yellow
Tumbler, 6", 10 ounce, water	65.00	35.00
Tumbler, 6⅛", 12½ ounce, iced tea		135.00
Tray, 11", center-handled sandwich	165.00	175.00
Vase, 12"	250.00	295.00

"KALEIDOSCOPE," GEM, HOCKING GLASS COMPANY, c. 1933

Colors: "Mayfair" blue, crystal, green, and pink

"Kaleidoscope" was our given name for this ware, but my new year started out with an e-mail about this pattern. A former Anchor Hocking employee's wife gave him my book for Christmas. He found my new listing for "Kaleidoscope" and sent me documentation that this was indeed a Hocking pattern and he had a labeled piece designating it Gem. It is not a plentiful pattern, but there are enough basic pieces to gather a nice table setting if you wish.

Blue seems to be the most plentiful color; but pieces in pink, green, and even crystal can be unearthed. Crystal does exist since I have bought a crystal celery and a divided relish recently. I did not originally put crystal in the color listing because I was relying on memory thinking I had seen a sugar and creamer at one time. As a younger man, I would have known. Now, memory is not as reliably photographic as it once was. I saw several sets of blue years ago when I wasn't looking for photography items. Some items were made for Woolworth's, which should make those more available. Let me know what you find.

	Blue	*Green, Pink		Blue	*Green, Pink
Bowl, 5", berry	20.00	15.00	Plate, 9½", dinner	35.00	25.00
Bowl, flat soup	50.00	35.00	Plate, 9½", grill	30.00	20.00
Bowl, oval vegetable w/tab handles	65.00	55.00	Platter, oval w/tab handles	75.00	60.00
Celery, tab handles	60.00	50.00	Relish, 11½", divided, tab handles		45.00
Creamer	50.00	35.00	Saucer	20.00	15.00
Cup	75.00	60.00	Stem, 6 ounce, sherbet	25.00	20.00
Plate, 6", bread	12.00	10.00	Stem, 10 ounce, water	40.00	30.00

* Price crystal 20% less

LACED EDGE, "KATY BLUE," IMPERIAL GLASS COMPANY, Early 1930s

Colors: blue w/opalescent edge and green w/opalescent edge, et al.

Imperial's Laced Edge pattern was produced piecemeal in an array of colors, although only the large opalescent blue and green dinnerware offerings are being dealt with in this book since that is where collector interest lies. Many of the colors without the white edge were made into the 1950s and later; so they slip out of the time restriction (pre-1940) for this book. Imperial called this white edging "Sea Foam." Sea Foam treatment varies from scarcely encasing the edge of pieces to others having a ½" of prominent, opalescent edging.

Long-time collectors commonly call opalescent blue "Katy Blue." I believe there was an old 30s tune about Katy with the blue eyes. Some have called the green, "Katy Green," but I still get a chuckle remembering the display of green at a show in Michigan labeled "Katy Blue." Blue and green pieces without the white edge sell for about half of the prices listed, but there are few collectors actively seeking those. There does not appear to be much demand for crystal pieces, which are often spotted in malls. I have never seen crystal pieces with Sea Foam edging.

Creamers have several different appearances on the spouts because their lips were individually formed using a wooden tool. Cereal bowls vary from 4⅞" to 5⅝", soup bowls from 6⅞" to 7¼", and berry bowls from 4⅜" to 4¾". Turning out the edge of the bowl while still hot caused size differences. Some edges go straight up while others are flattened. Collectors will accept these minor discrepancies in order to have enough bowls.

Some collectors do not accept the 12" cake plate (luncheon plate in Imperial catalog) or the 9" vegetable bowl (salad in ad) as Laced Edge because the edges are more open than those of the other items. Thanks go to a Laced Edge collector from Illinois for sharing an original ad (page 109) showing an inflated retail price along with the cost in coupons for Laced Edge pieces. Notice the bowl and cake plate are both shown with this pattern. Originally, you could obtain six tumblers for fewer coupons than the platter or divided, oval bowl. Maybe that is why they are so difficult to find today. Not many would exchange their costly coupons for them. Enjoy this ad, as I will need the space for glass next time.

The rarely discovered, undivided, oval vegetable bowl is absent from this ad and most collections today. Notice the divided bowl was the most expensive piece in this pattern to obtain with coupons.

	Opalescent
Basket bowl	225.00
Bowl, 4⅜"– 4¾", fruit	28.00
Bowl, 5"	35.00
Bowl, 5½"	35.00
Bowl, 5⅞"	35.00
Bowl, 7", soup	85.00
Bowl, 9", vegetable	110.00
Bowl, 11", divided oval	125.00
Bowl, 11", oval	160.00
Candlestick, double, pair	175.00
Cup	32.00
Creamer	38.00

	Opalescent
Mayonnaise, 3-piece	135.00
Plate, 6½", bread & butter	15.00
Plate, 8", salad	30.00
Plate, 10", dinner	75.00
Plate, 12", luncheon (per catalog description)	80.00
Platter, 13"	185.00
Saucer	12.00
Sugar	38.00
Tidbit, 2-tiered, 8" & 10" plates	110.00
Tumbler, 9 ounce	50.00

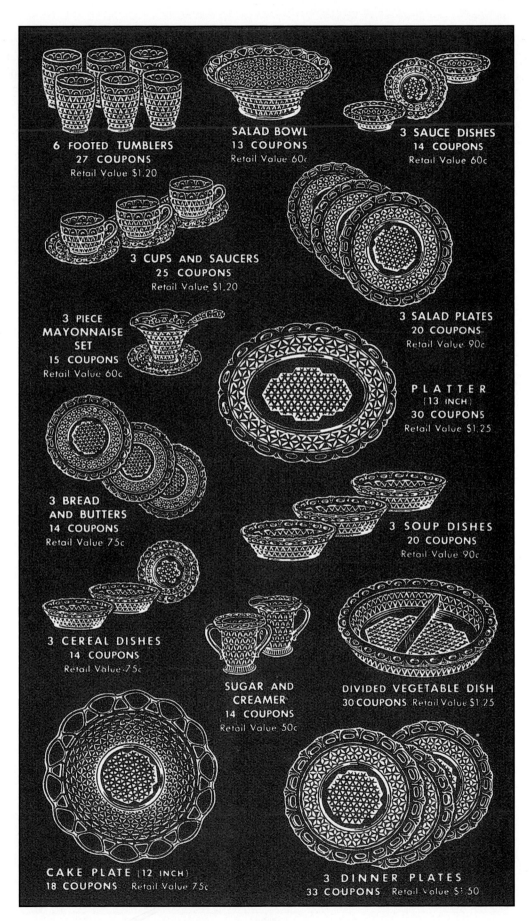

6 FOOTED TUMBLERS
27 COUPONS
Retail Value $1.20

SALAD BOWL
13 COUPONS
Retail Value 60c

3 SAUCE DISHES
14 COUPONS
Retail Value 60c

3 CUPS AND SAUCERS
25 COUPONS
Retail Value $1.20

3 SALAD PLATES
20 COUPONS
Retail Value 90c

3 PIECE
MAYONNAISE
SET
15 COUPONS
Retail Value 60c

PLATTER
(13 INCH)
30 COUPONS
Retail Value $1.25

3 BREAD
AND BUTTERS
14 COUPONS
Retail Value 75c

3 SOUP DISHES
20 COUPONS
Retail Value 90c

3 CEREAL DISHES
14 COUPONS
Retail Value 75c

SUGAR AND
CREAMER
14 COUPONS
Retail Value 50c

DIVIDED VEGETABLE DISH
30 COUPONS Retail Value $1.25

CAKE PLATE (12 INCH)
18 COUPONS Retail Value 75c

3 DINNER PLATES
33 COUPONS Retail Value $1.50

109

LAKE COMO, HOCKING GLASS COMPANY, 1934 – 1937

Color: white with blue scene; some with red scene

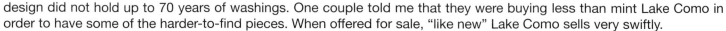

I pictured the red Lake Como creamer and sugar in the last book without any writing emphasis, hoping to elicit some comment from readers. Alas, that did not happen. I was excited to see them and the owners knew they were rare; so I hope some of you, at least, noticed them. These are the only red decorated pieces I have seen.

Lake Como is so obscure that some collectors tell me they never see it. I find it now and then, but usually pieces are worn. Apparently, this design did not hold up to 70 years of washings. One couple told me that they were buying less than mint Lake Como in order to have some of the harder-to-find pieces. When offered for sale, "like new" Lake Como sells very swiftly.

There are only 13 different pieces of Lake Como and all but the large vegetable bowl are seldom seen. Prices below are for mint condition Lake Como (full bright pattern). You should be able to buy worn Lake Como at 40% to 80% of the prices listed depending upon the amount of wear.

The cereal bowl has been tilted so it does not look so much like a plate in the photo as it once did. The camera loses the depth.

The flat soup is directly in the middle. The floral decoration on the edge is embossed (like the normally found Vitrock soup) instead of painted in blue. Only the center of the soup has the design and if ever used, the design is usually missing. You will find platters almost as difficult to find as soup bowls; but most collectors are looking for only one platter, which is a smaller problem than finding several soups. A small supply of vegetable bowls have been found in the last few years; thus, the price has softened on them somewhat. Finding either style cup in mint condition will be a headache.

Bowl, 6", cereal	25.00	Plate, 9¼", dinner	35.00
Bowl, 9¾", vegetable	48.00	Platter, 11"	75.00
Bowl, flat soup	105.00	Salt & pepper, pair	45.00
Creamer, footed	30.00	Saucer	10.00
Cup, regular	30.00	Saucer, St. Denis	10.00
Cup, St. Denis	30.00	Sugar, footed	30.00
Plate, 7¼", salad	20.00		

LARGO, LINE #220, PADEN CITY GLASS COMPANY, Late 1937 – 1951; CANTON GLASS COMPANY, 1950s

Colors: amber, crystal, crystal w/ruby flash, light blue, red

Splitting Paden City's Largo (#220) and Maya (#221) into separate patterns in the last book had more collectors noticing the differences in these two patterns.

Collectors for Cambridge's Caprice may be more aware of this pattern since there is a tendency of dealers to misidentify the light blue Largo as Caprice. Largo was not as widely distributed as was Cambridge glass; hence our looking high and low for it today. Our experience of searching leads us to believe that the flat candy dish and the two-lipped comport are relatively scarce. We have found several divided candy bottoms in our travels, but never a top in Largo. That 5" bowl in the foreground on the bottom of the page may possibly take a lid of some kind.

Collectors find the delightful, four-footed sugar and creamer appealing. Item collectors for those help to put a dent in the sparse supply. Paden City etchings occur on both light blue and crystal. I have never yet found etched designs on red.

We found blue cups on several occasions but always with the non-indented 6⅝" plates. I was beginning to think there was no indented saucer until we found one in amber; alas, no amber cup though.

Please note that Largo pieces can be distinguished from Maya by the thistle (ball) design found on Maya. You have to be observant to notice the Largo pattern line on the candle.

	Amber, Crystal	Blue, Red
Ashtray, 3", rectangle	16.00	30.00
Bowl, 5"	15.00	25.00
Bowl, 6", deep	18.00	35.00
Bowl, 7½"	20.00	37.50
Bowl, 7½", crimped	22.50	45.00
Bowl, 9", tab-handled	30.00	70.00
Bowl, 11⅝", 3½" deep, tri-footed, flared rim	35.00	80.00
Bowl, 12¾", 4¾" deep, tri-footed, flat rim	35.00	80.00
Cake plate, pedestal	35.00	95.00
Candleholder	30.00	55.00
Candy, flat w/lid, 3-part	35.00	95.00
Cigarette box, 4" x 3¼" x 1½"	30.00	65.00
Comport, cracker	15.00	25.00

	Amber, Crystal	Blue, Red
Comport, double spout, pedestal	35.00	75.00
Comport, fluted rim, pedestal	35.00	75.00
Comport, 6½" x 10", plain rim, pedestal	32.50	70.00
Creamer, footed	25.00	45.00
Cup	15.00	30.00
Mayonnaise, toed	25.00	55.00
Plate, 6⅝"	8.00	15.00
Plate, 8"	10.00	20.00
Plate, 10¾", cheese w/indent	20.00	40.00
Saucer	5.00	10.00
Sugar, footed	25.00	45.00
Tray, 13¾", tri-footed, serving	25.00	75.00
Tray, 14", five-part, relish	40.00	100.00

LAUREL, McKEE GLASS COMPANY, 1930s

Colors: French Ivory, Jade Green, White Opal, Poudre Blue, and various colors of decorated rims

Poudre Blue Laurel has customarily been the color most wanted by collectors. The flood in demand for Jadite colored glassware has created a splurge into McKee's Jade Green Laurel ware, raising prices in that color. Luckily, Jade Laurel is the color most often seen, followed closely by French Ivory (beige) and then Poudre Blue, inaccurately called Delphite blue by some collectors. French Ivory stimulates few collectors at this time; prices there have remained stable. I have moved the White Opal pricing into the same column as French Ivory since those prices are more typical of its worth, now, than that of the Jade.

Soup bowls measuring 7⅞" in any color are rarely seen, but demand for Jade ones has prices rising even though few are being found. Laurel shakers are hard to find with vivid patterns. Many Laurel shaker designs are blurry. Jade Green Laurel shakers are relatively rare, as some of those searching for them have found and Poudre Blue have never been found.

Serving pieces in all colors are scanty. That tendency is increasingly rearing its head in many patterns from this era. Evidently, serving pieces were considered too expensive and were not purchased to go with basic sets.

Beloved children's Laurel tea sets are concealed in long-time collections. The Scottie dog decal sets were produced in Jade Green or French Ivory colors. Collectors of Scottie items have spurred the prices on these sets to levels where few collectors try to buy full sets. They are thrilled just to acquire one piece. Laurel children's sets are also found with border trims of red, green, or orange. Orange borders appear to be the most difficult to locate, though all trims are scarce. Watch for wear on these colored trims; it appears many children did, in fact, play with these dishes.

I have included a pattern shot of a dinnerware piece trimmed in black, a heretofore unheard of trim. Cathy ran into four black trimmed pieces of Laurel, a plate, dessert, saucer, and berry bowl. There was no cup. Upon questioning the owner, she was told there were six sets found in a Pennsylvania farmhouse. These are the only black-trimmed Laurel confirmed to date.

	Jade or Decorated Rims	White Opal, French Ivory	Poudre Blue		Jade or Decorated Rims	White Opal, French Ivory	Poudre Blue
Bowl, 4¾", berry	15.00	10.00	15.00	Plate, 6", sherbet	16.00	10.00	10.00
Bowl, 6", cereal	28.00	12.00	28.00	Plate, 7½", salad	20.00	10.00	16.00
Bowl, 6", three legs	28.00	15.00		Plate, 9⅛", dinner	25.00	15.00	30.00
Bowl, 7⅞", soup	45.00	35.00	85.00	Plate, 9⅛", grill, round or scalloped	25.00	15.00	
Bowl, 9", large berry	45.00	30.00	55.00	Platter, 10¾", oval	55.00	30.00	60.00
Bowl, 9¾", oval vegetable	55.00	30.00	55.00	Salt and pepper	90.00	50.00	
Bowl, 10½", three legs	60.00	40.00	70.00	Saucer	4.50	3.00	7.50
Bowl, 11"	60.00	40.00	85.00	Sherbet	20.00	12.00	
Candlestick, 4", pair	65.00	35.00		Sherbet/champagne, 5"	80.00	50.00	
Candlestick, 3 footed	150.00			Sugar, short	25.00	10.00	
Cheese dish and cover	110.00	60.00		Sugar, tall	25.00	11.00	35.00
Creamer, short	25.00	12.00		Tumbler, 4½", 9 ounce, flat	75.00	40.00	
Creamer, tall	25.00	15.00	40.00	Tumbler, 5", 12 ounce, flat		55.00	
Cup	15.00	9.00	22.50				

CHILDREN'S LAUREL TEA SET

	French Ivory	Jade or Decorated Rims	Scottie Dog Jade	Scottie Dog Ivory
Creamer	30.00	100.00	260.00	130.00
Cup	25.00	50.00	100.00	50.00
Plate	10.00	20.00	80.00	40.00
Saucer	8.00	12.50	75.00	37.50
Sugar	30.00	100.00	260.00	130.00
14-piece set	235.00	530.00	1,550.00	775.00

LINCOLN INN, FENTON GLASS COMPANY, Late 1920s

Colors: red, cobalt, light blue, amethyst, black, green, green opalescent, pink, crystal, amber, and jade (opaque)

If you are into collecting stems, Lincoln Inn is for you. Champagne/sherbets in every color are bountiful. A small collection could be made of just these pieces. Stems appear to be the only pieces of the pattern you spot with regularity. If someone asks me for Lincoln Inn, it is usually prefaced with, "I don't need stems, but…." Stemware was sold to accompany china. With so many colors, Lincoln Inn filled color demands quite well. Now, you might possibly collect a setting in crystal, but other colors are less certain, even using the Internet. In spite of the fact that tableware was advertised in at least eight of the above listed colors in 1929, little color other than red and the several shades of blue are sought today. By chance, those colors are occasionally stumbled upon, though not serving pieces. Illustrated on page 115 are some of the sundry colors you may collect if you are willing to buy a piece or two at a time. This pattern absolutely fits rainbow-collecting trends beginning to flourish in the Depression world.

Tumblers are a little more difficult to find than stems, but acquiring an old pitcher in any color is a chore. Fenton remade an iridized, dark carnival colored pitcher and tumblers in the 1980s. Any other iridescent piece you might see in this pattern is of recent production. All light blue pitchers have turned up in the south, so look there for them.

A 1930s catalog shows Lincoln Inn plates with a fruit design (intaglio) in the center. I have a shown some crystal ones in the bottom row on page 115. I have seen a 9" crystal bowl with the fruit center, but it was highly valued by the owner.

Lincoln Inn shakers are scarce. Even crystal shakers are proficient at hiding. Collectors gathering only shakers tell me these Lincoln Inn ones may not be the highest priced in the book, but they are among the most difficult to find. Red and black shakers are favored colors; but do not bypass any in your travels. I once found a red pair sitting with Royal Ruby in a dark corner of a shop. They were priced as red shakers. You need to check in every nook and cranny in shops that do not appreciate Depression glass as we do.

Most red Lincoln Inn pieces are amberina in color. For novices, amberina is red glass that has some yellow hues in it. Reheating yellow glass made it change to red; irregular heating caused some parts to continue being yellow. Some dealers have told collectors this is a rare color in order to sell it. In a certain sense, that may have a trace of truth. Actually, it was an error; and the unpredictable amounts of yellow on each piece make it hard to match colors. Some old timers in glass collecting reject amberina pieces for their collections as unfit to own. However, there are some devotees actually searching for amberina glass. There is a growing fascination for all two-toned glassware; and amberina color certainly fits that bill.

	Cobalt Blue, Red	**All other colors		Cobalt Blue, Red	**All other colors
Ashtray	17.50	12.00	Plate, 6"	9.00	4.50
Bonbon, handled, square	15.00	12.00	Plate, 8"	15.00	10.00
Bonbon, handled, oval	16.00	12.00	Plate, 9¼"	45.00	11.50
Bowl, 5", fruit	11.50	8.50	Plate, 12"	65.00	15.50
Bowl, 6", cereal	18.00	9.00	* Salt/pepper, pair	275.00	175.00
Bowl, 6", crimped	18.00	8.50	Sandwich server, center handle	175.00	110.00
Bowl, handled olive	18.00	9.50	Saucer	5.00	3.50
Bowl, finger	22.00	12.50	Sherbet, 4½", cone shape	17.00	11.50
Bowl, 9", shallow		23.00	Sherbet, 4¾"	20.00	12.50
Bowl, 9¼", footed	80.00	30.00	Sugar	20.00	14.00
Bowl, 10½", footed	80.00	35.00	Tumbler, 4 ounce, flat, juice	30.00	9.50
Candy dish, footed, oval	45.00	20.00	Tumbler, 9 ounce, flat, water		19.50
Comport	30.00	14.50	Tumbler, 5 ounce, footed	30.00	11.00
Creamer	20.00	14.50	Tumbler, 9 ounce, footed	30.00	14.00
Cup	12.00	12.00	Tumbler, 12 ounce, footed	50.00	19.00
Goblet, water	30.00	15.50	Vase, 9¾"	165.00	85.00
Goblet, wine	30.00	16.50	Vase, 12", footed	250.00	125.00
Nut dish, footed	25.00	12.00	* Black $300.00		
Pitcher, 7¼", 46 ounce	800.00	700.00	** w/fruits, add 20 – 25%		

LINE #555, PADEN CITY GLASS COMPANY, Late 1930s – 1951; CANTON GLASS COMPANY, 1950s

Colors: crystal, light blue, red

Line #555 blank was used for several different Paden City etches and cuttings. Most notable is the Gazebo pattern illustrated in my *Elegant Glassware of the Depression Era*. Additional pieces of Line #555 are pictured there. The heart-shaped candy bottoms, pictured in front, are divided into three sections and the lids were placed along the back for height in the photo. There is a tulip etch on the right side and a Floral etch on left. There is a single candle here. You can see the double version pictured with the Gazebo pattern.

The tray on the left was for the creamer and sugar, but was also listed separately. Canton Glass bought Paden City moulds and continued many of the pieces of Line #555 during the early 1950s. They mostly made crystal, but color could be specially ordered.

	*Crystal		*Crystal
Bowl, 6", 2-part nappy	12.00	Plate, 8"	10.00
Bowl, 6", nappy	13.00	Plate, 12½", 2-handled	22.50
Bowl, 9", 2-handled	22.00	Plate, 16", salad or punch liner	45.00
Bowl, 14", shallow	28.00	Punch bowl	70.00
Cake stand, pedestal foot	30.00	Punch cup	8.00
Candlestick, 1-light	17.50	Relish, 11", round, 3-part	25.00
Candlestick, 2-light	25.00	Relish, 7½", square, 2-part	14.00
Candy, w/lid, "heart"	50.00	Relish, 9¾", rectangular, 3-part	20.00
Candy, w/lid, 10¼", pedestal foot	35.00	Saucer	3.00
Candy, w/lid, 11", pedestal foot	40.00	Relish, 10½", round, 5-part	26.00
Creamer	10.00	Sugar	10.00
Cup	8.00	Tray, 9"	14.00
Mayonnaise liner	7.50	Tray, 11", center handle	28.00
Mayonnaise	15.00	* Double price for colors	
Plate, 6"	5.00		

"LITTLE JEWEL" DIAMOND BLOCK, LINE #330, IMPERIAL GLASS COMPANY, Late 1920s – Early 1930s

Colors: black, crystal, green, iridescent, pink, red, white, yellow

After photography last October, we priced most of the items pictured here to sell. After two shows, collectors wiped out our supply of "Little Jewel." "Little Jewel" is a diminutive Imperial pattern that is attracting people. Seldom do these customers recognize it as Depression-era glass. They are only buying it because it appeals to them. This appreciation for the pattern makes owning a piece or two desirable rather than collecting it as a set.

Several pieces of Diamond Block were advertised for sale in a 1920s catalog under the "Little Jewel" moniker. This name stuck rather than the Diamond Block one given by Imperial. Colored items are the most popular, but not a lot of color is being found. Yet, even crystal with this delightful design can make an excellent display. This "Little Jewel" will not cause you sticker shock, another enhancing aspect.

Blue and black items sold the fastest when we displayed them. Keep that in mind when you see them for sale.

	Crystal	Colors*		Crystal	Colors*
Bowl, 5½", square, honey dish	10.00	16.00	Jelly, 4½", handle	8.00	14.00
Bowl, 5", lily	10.00	15.00	Jelly, 5", footed	10.00	15.00
Bowl, 6½"	10.00	15.00	Jug, pint tankard	22.50	45.00
Bowl, 7½", berry	15.00	20.00	Pickle dish, 6½"	12.50	20.00
Celery, 8½", tray	18.00	22.50	Sugar	8.00	15.00
Creamer	8.00	15.00	Vase, 6", bouquet	12.00	18.00

* Add 20% for black or red

"LOIS," LINE #345 et al., UNITED STATES GLASS COMPANY, c. 1920s

Colors: crystal, green, and pink

"Lois" was a line that I kept getting pictures and questions about regularly, so it seemed time to add it to my book. "Lois" was etched predominantly on Line #345, which is made-up of octagonal shapes. As was the practice with early factory lines, these pieces were offered to merchants as a variety package. "Assortments," as they were labeled, normally consisted of six to 15 items, and in the case of etchings, they could be on several numbered line wares. It may have been a way of getting rid of remaining product, a gathering of "all those pink items left and put thus and so etch on all of them and offer them as assortment #12." Sometimes assortment packages were assembled around a theme, such as table settings or bridge sets or serving items; but, often as not, they were just various wares put in a grouping. Sometimes assortments came as numbers 1, 2, or 3, so that to get a complete line, the merchant had to buy all the various assortments. These were early marketing ploys used by companies to sell their wares; and we know this ware was thus marketed.

I am very certain you will find other items than those in the listing and some of them will be on other than octagon shape #345. Thanks for the additional information sent, and may it keep coming.

	All colors		All colors
Bowl, 10", fruit, pedestal foot	50.00	Mayo or whipped cream w/ladle	45.00
Bowl, 10", salad, flat rim	40.00	Pitcher, milk	50.00
Bowl, 12", console, rolled edge	50.00	Plate, cheese liner	25.00
Cake, salver, pedestal foot	55.00	Plate, dinner	35.00
Candle, short, single	30.00	Server, center handled	50.00
Candy box, octagonal lid	70.00	Stem, cocktail	25.00
Candy jar w/lid, cone shape	55.00	Stem wine	30.00
Comport, cheese	22.00	Sugar, footed	25.00
Creamer, footed	25.00	Tumbler, footed	35.00
		Vase, 10"	75.00

LORAIN, "BASKET," NO. 615, INDIANA GLASS COMPANY, 1929 – 1932

Colors: green, yellow, and some crystal

Indiana's yellow Lorain, acclaimed by early collectors, is scarce today. When you do locate it, you probably will have to settle for mould roughness on the seams of the pieces. If you are resolved about totally mint condition glassware, then you should concentrate on some other pattern.

After buying and selling various collections of Lorain and discussing diverse ideas with collectors who have pursued Lorain for years, certain conclusions arise. First, you should buy any cereal bowls you can find. Inspect inner rims closely; they damage. The 8" deep berry is the most difficult piece to locate. Most collectors only want one, but they often wait years to find it. Dinner plates are almost as scarce as cereals, but scratches are the rule for these. There are a few people who know how to polish these scratches away, now; so, if the plates are reasonable enough, you might speculate that in the future this service will be more accessible. Oval vegetable bowls are uncommon in both colors. Saucers are harder to locate because of mould roughness and wear and tear on them over the years. Collecting has turned upside-down. Dealers used to decline to buy saucers unless there were cups with them. Today, many of these once ignored saucers are enthusiastically bought even if there are no cups available. There are more than a dozen patterns of Depression glass where saucers are more difficult to find than cups, and this is one of them. Since Lorain is limited, you might be tempted to buy pieces that are less than mint when you come across them; remember to pay less than the mint prices listed.

Periodically, rarer pieces of Lorain soar in price. Usually that means several collectors are searching for the same piece at about the same time. Collectors are starting to buy green Lorain because of price and availability. Green is less expensive and more easily found. A few pieces are found in crystal, but I am not sure a set is feasible. A few items could enhance your colored wares, however.

Some crystal is found with fired-on colored borders of red, yellow, green, and blue. For those who have written to ask about the snack tray, one with yellow trim is pictured below. It was made from the platter mould that had an indented ring added for a cup. In talking to several collectors recently, I have been informed that the snack plates trimmed in yellow or green do not seem to be offered at any price. Collectors of yellow or green used to find these for inclusion into their sets. Crystal cups are found trimmed in the four colors to match the snack trays; but sometimes, they were just crystal, lacking the trim.

New collectors, please note that the white and green avocado-colored sherbets (which have an open lace border) are a mid-1950s (or later) issue made by Anchor Hocking. They were sold to florists for small floral arrangements and many are found with a tacky, clay-like substance in the bottom that was used to secure flowers. Not long ago, they were also recognized as an Indiana product, which is possible. The more research I do, the more I find out about wares starting with one company and being subsequently made by others. We know it was a custom to lend moulds out from one company to another for special product runs. However, several of these have been found with Anchor Hocking paper stickers, a practice of theirs in the late 1950s and early 1960s.

I have had a couple of letters regarding goblets with a basket design like that of Lorain. These are probably an early Tiffin product. If you want to use them with Lorain, do so. There is also a heavy Hazel-Atlas green goblet similar in shape to Colonial Block that has a basket etching. Basket designs were prolific in the 1920s and 1930s. These are known in the trade as "go-with" items.

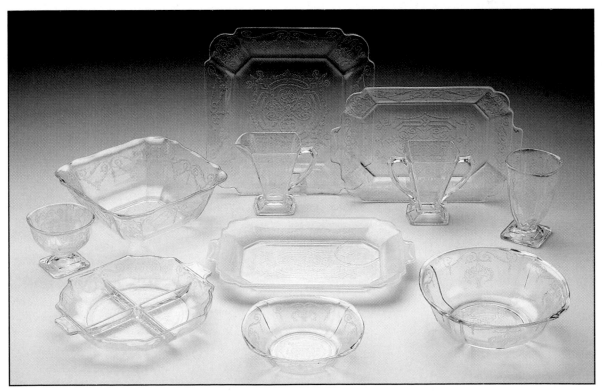

	Crystal, Green	Yellow
Bowl, 6", cereal	50.00	70.00
Bowl, 7¼", salad	65.00	95.00
Bowl, 8", deep berry	135.00	210.00
Bowl, 9¾", oval vegetable	57.50	67.50
Creamer, footed	20.00	25.00
Cup	12.00	14.00
Plate, 5½", sherbet	9.00	11.00
Plate, 7¾", salad	13.00	14.00
Plate, 8⅜", luncheon	20.00	25.00
Plate, 10¼", dinner	58.00	60.00
Platter, 11½"	30.00	45.00
Relish, 8", 4-part	25.00	38.00
Saucer	4.50	6.00
Sherbet, footed	25.00	28.00
Snack tray, crystal/trim	35.00	
Sugar, footed	20.00	25.00
Tumbler, 4¾", 9 ounce, footed	26.00	32.00

LOTUS, PATTERN #1921, WESTMORELAND GLASS COMPANY, 1921 – 1980

Colors: amber, amethyst, black, blue, crystal, green, milk, pink, red, and various applied color trims; satinized colors

Lotus, pattern #1921, was in production over 60 years, off and on; and thanks to Chas West Wilson's *Westmoreland Glass,* we know it to have been designed by Gustav Horn in the early 1920s.

We bought almost every different piece and color of Lotus we found in the last ten years as you can see by our photos. We decided to weed out items not decorating our house after our photo session last October and had almost three boxes of Lotus to sell and barely half a box left at first show's end. Many pieces were purchased by customers who had to ask what it was after picking out several pieces to buy. I now know that more people are charmed with this intriguing flower shaped pattern than just my wife — something that should have been apparent from the longevity of the design for the company!

Supposedly, candles with a domed foot are more recently made than those with the foot flattened which is an indication of an earlier mould. Red is a newer color and most of it tends to be amberina (yellow tint in the red) which is just fine with collectors of amberina glass.

There are several rare pieces of Lotus including a lamp, tumbler, cologne bottle, and puff box, although most colognes found are of later manufacture. They are still desirable. The elusive tumbler is crystal with a green petal foot. All opalescent-edged Lotus was made near the end of Westmoreland's production in the 1970s and 1980s. Numerous companies had their own versions of Lotus designs on their glassware during this early era.

	Satinized Colors, Amber, Crystal, White	Blue, Green, Pink	Cased colors		Satinized Colors, Amber, Crystal, White	Blue, Green, Pink	Cased colors
Bowl, 6", lily (flat mayonnaise)	15.00	25.00	40.00	Lamp	195.00	295.00	
Bowl, 9", cupped	50.00	85.00	110.00	Mayonnaise, 4", ftd., flared rim	15.00	25.00	30.00
Bowl, 11", belled	60.00	95.00	125.00	Mayonnaise, 5", footed, bell rim	27.50	52.50	72.50
Bowl, oval vegetable	45.00	85.00	110.00	Plate, 6", mayonnaise	8.00	12.00	15.00
Candle, 4", single	18.00	35.00	40.00	Plate, 8½", salad	10.00	35.00	40.00
Candle, 9" high, twist stem	50.00	75.00	100.00	Plate, 8¾", mayonnaise	12.50	17.50	22.50
Candy jar w/lid, ½ pound	65.00	100.00	135.00	Plate, 13", flared	35.00	50.00	65.00
Coaster	12.00	15.00	20.00	Puff box, 5", w/cover	110.00	145.00	
Cologne, ½ ounce	85.00	110.00	145.00	Salt, individual	14.00	22.00	25.00
Comport, 2½", mint, twist stem	30.00			Shaker	30.00	45.00	
Comport, 6½", honey	18.00	25.00	45.00	Sherbet, tulip bell	22.00	35.00	40.00
Comport, 5" high	30.00	40.00	50.00	Sugar	22.00	30.00	40.00
Comport, 8½" high, twist stem	55.00	85.00	110.00	Tray, lemon, 6", handle	30.00	40.00	50.00
Creamer	22.00	30.00	40.00	Tumbler, 10 ounce		50.00	

121

MADRID, FEDERAL GLASS COMPANY, 1932 – 1939; INDIANA GLASS COMPANY, 1980s

Colors: green, pink, amber, crystal, and "Madonna" blue (See Reproduction Section.)

In early collecting days, blue Madrid was one of those Depression glass patterns that you loved. You could not visit a show without seeing it on dealers' tables. Today, you never see a piece of the old, soft "Madonna" blue Madrid. It has all vanished into collections. What you see outside of shows from malls to the Internet are blue reproductions. New collectors are avoiding the blue today since so little of the old is available. Amber, however, is still very available in today's marketplace, and is still being collected even though there have been tons of the new amber Madrid dumped on the market since 1976.

Madrid has been subject of discussion since 1976 when the Federal Glass Company remanufactured this pattern for the Bicentennial under a new name, "Recollection" glassware. Many companies resurrected wares from past lines during this period, not just Federal. Each piece of this reissued Federal ware was embossed '76 in the design. The flaw, here, was that it was remade in an amber color comparable to the original which caused concern with collectors of the older amber Madrid. Collectors were informed about the products, and many purchased these sets presuming they would someday be collectible as Bicentennial products. Unfortunately, Indiana Glass bought the Madrid moulds when Federal went out of business, removed the '76 date and made crystal and amber without the '76 mark. The older crystal butter was selling for several hundred dollars and the new one sold for $2.99. Prices nose-dived! Next, they made pink; and even though it was a lighter pink than the original, prices dipped in the collectibles market for the old pink. Later, Indiana made blue; it was a brighter, harsher blue than the beautiful, soft blue of the original Madrid; still, it had a detrimental effect on the prices of the 1930s blue. All pieces made in pink have now been made in blue. Any blue piece found without a price in the listings is new. After blue came teal, finally, a color not made in the 1930s. Today, that is all water under the bridge and learned collectors are now buying the beautiful older Madrid with confidence at Depression glass shows.

I keep noticing the later-made, lightly colored pink Madrid sugar and creamers with high prices at flea markets and antique malls. Originally, there were no pink sugars and creamers made. Check my list for pieces made in pink. If no price is listed, then it was not made in the 1930s. (See the new pink in the Reproduction Section in the back.)

The rarely seen Madrid gravy boats and platters have usually been found in Iowa. The most recently found set was for $12.00 at a yard sale. The platter was nicked. These two pieces are listed separately, but reflect a decided increase in price. Rare Depression glass is beginning to command higher and higher prices. I do not expect this trend to stop as more and more collectors enter the field and the rare pieces become even scarcer than they already are.

Mint condition sugar lids in any color Madrid are a treasure. Footed tumblers are harder to find than flat ones, with juice tumblers making a surge in price. Amber footed shakers are harder to find than flat ones. Footed shakers are the only style you can find in blue. Any heavy, flat shakers you spot are new.

Collectors of green Madrid have turned out to be almost as sparse as the pattern. Green is possibly as rare as blue, but with fewer collectors.

A wooden Lazy Susan is pictured in *Very Rare Glassware of the Depression Years, Second Series.* It is like the Georgian one pictured on page 93 only with Madrid inserts. Those Madrid inserts have seen a big jump in price in the last two years.

MADRID

	Amber	Pink	Green	Blue
Ashtray, 6", square	450.00		450.00	
Bowl, 4¾", cream soup	16.00			
Bowl, 5", sauce	7.00	8.00	7.00	30.00
Bowl, 7", soup	16.00		16.00	
Bowl, 8", salad	14.00		17.50	50.00
Bowl, 9⅜", large berry	20.00	20.00		
Bowl, 9½", deep salad	35.00			
Bowl, 10", oval veg.	18.00	15.00	22.50	40.00
* Bowl, 11", low console	14.00	11.00		
Butter dish w/lid	70.00		90.00	
Butter dish bottom	27.50		40.00	
Butter dish top	37.50		50.00	
* Candlesticks, pr., 2¼"	22.00	20.00		
Cookie jar w/lid	45.00	30.00		
Creamer, footed	9.00		12.50	20.00
Cup	7.00	7.50	9.00	16.00
Gravy boat	1,000.00			
Gravy platter	1,000.00			
Hot dish coaster	95.00		95.00	
Hot dish coaster w/indent	95.00		95.00	
Jam dish, 7"	27.50		20.00	40.00
Jello mold, 2⅛", tall	9.00			
Pitcher, 5½", 36 ounce juice	40.00			
** Pitcher, 8", sq., 60 oz.	50.00	35.00	125.00	175.00

	Amber	Pink	Green	Blue
Pitcher, 8½", 80 ounce	60.00		200.00	
Pitcher, 8½", 80 ounce, ice lip	60.00		225.00	
Plate, 6", sherbet	4.00	3.50	4.00	8.00
Plate, 7½", salad	9.00	9.00	9.00	22.00
Plate, 8⅞", luncheon	8.00	7.00	9.00	18.00
Plate, 10½", dinner	63.00		55.00	75.00
Plate, 10½", grill	9.50		20.00	
Plate, 10¼", relish	15.00	12.50	16.00	
Plate, 11¼", round cake	20.00	10.00		
Platter, 11½", oval	17.00	14.00	16.00	24.00
Salt/pepper, 3½", footed, pair	130.00		110.00	165.00
Salt/pepper, 3½", flat, pair	50.00		65.00	
Saucer	3.00	5.00	5.00	10.00
Sherbet, two styles	7.00		10.00	17.50
Sugar	7.00		14.00	15.00
Sugar cover	55.00		60.00	225.00
Tumbler, 3⅞", 5 ounce	13.00		32.00	40.00
Tumbler, 4¼", 9 ounce	15.00	15.00	20.00	35.00
Tumbler, 5½", 12 ounce, 2 styles	20.00		30.00	50.00
Tumbler, 4", 5 oz., footed	40.00		40.00	
Tumbler, 5½", 10 ounce, footed	35.00		45.00	
Wooden Lazy Susan, cold cuts coasters	1,195.00			

* Iridescent priced slightly higher   ** Crystal $150.00

125

If you find a piece of Manhattan that does not match the measurements in the list below, then you may have a piece of Anchor Hocking's newer line, Park Avenue. You can see this recent pattern and listings for it in my book *Anchor Hocking's Fire-King & More, Second Edition.*

Park Avenue was introduced by Anchor Hocking in 1987 to "re-create the Glamour Era of 1938 when Anchor Hocking first introduced a classic" according to the Inspiration '87 catalog issued by the company. Anchor Hocking went to the trouble to preserve the integrity of their older glassware, however. None of the pieces in this line is precisely like the old Manhattan. They are only similar and Manhattan was never made in blue as this line has been. Some collectors of Manhattan have bought this new pattern to augment Manhattan or for use. Manhattan's collectibility has not been affected by the making of Park Avenue; however, the new line has caused some chaos with Manhattan cereal bowls. The older 5¼" cereals are rarely seen, particularly in mint condition; Park Avenue line lists a small bowl at 6". All the original Manhattan bowls measure 1¹⁵⁄₁₆" high. If the bowl you have measures more than two inches in depth, then you have a piece of Park Avenue. Be especially vigilant if the bowl is mint. Manhattan cereals do not have handles. The handled berry measures 5⅜". I mention the measurements because there is an immense price difference. In fact, the reason the 5⅜" handled berry has increased in price so much is from dealers selling them as cereals to uninformed customers.

Manhattan comport price hikes can be directly attributed to margarita and/or martini drinkers. These were intended for candy or mints at inception, but you cannot persuade an avid drinker that these were not designed for mixed drinks. Now we get a Park Avenue piece that is creating a problem. A Park Avenue martini glass has been designed for the beverage market which is so similar to the old comport that it took me a while to figure out a difference that can easily be seen. The old comport has four wafers on the stem while the new one has five. That is not much difference, but luckily, it has only been made in crystal.

It's fairly certain that manufacturers outside the factory made metal accessories. Anchor Hocking sold their wares to other companies who made these appendages with tongs or spoons hanging or otherwise attached to them. There is a remote possibility that metal pieces were sold to Hocking; but years ago employees told me that they never made anything but glass at the factory.

Pink Manhattan cups, saucers, and dinner plates do exist, but are rarely found. The saucer/sherbet plates of Manhattan are like many of Hocking's saucers; they have no cup ring. Both sizes of Manhattan Royal Ruby pitchers turn up occasionally. The real mind blower was the Jade-ite large Manhattan pitcher that has now been found. Actually, there are four or five known and I am sure that number will increase.

Manhattan sherbets have a beaded bottom like the tumblers, but the center insert to the relish tray does not have these beads. These are often confused. Relish tray inserts can be found in crystal, pink, and Royal Ruby. The center insert is always crystal on these relish trays although a pink sherbet was placed in the center of the pink relish at the photo session. Sorry. My help is great, but they slip some things past me in the photo sessions while I am laying out future photos.

Manhattan is one pattern that is bolstered by the many look-alike pieces that can be added to it. Some collectors buy Hazel-Atlas shakers to use with Manhattan since they are round rather than the original squared ones that Hocking made. However, I have deliberately left out all the other look-alike Manhattan pieces we used to show except for the L.E. Smith double candle, which was a way to get it noticed by the burgeoning candle collectors. Manhattan candles are squared as you can see by the one placed directly in front of the Smith one in the photo.

MANHATTAN

	Crystal	Pink			Crystal	Pink
* Ashtray, 4", round	10.00			Relish tray, 14", 5-part	30.00	
Ashtray, 4½", square	14.00			Relish tray, 14", with inserts	85.00	85.00
Bowl, 4½", sauce, handles	11.00		***	Relish tray insert	5.50	8.00
Bowl, 5⅜", berry w/handles	18.00	24.00	****	Pitcher, 24 ounce	40.00	75.00
Bowl, 5¼", cereal, no handles	110.00	195.00		Pitcher, 80 ounce, tilted	50.00	75.00
Bowl, 7½", large berry	22.00			Plate, 6", sherbet or saucer	5.00	75.00
Bowl, 8", closed handles	25.00	28.00		Plate, 8½", salad	15.00	
Bowl, 9", salad	30.00			Plate, 10¼", dinner	225.00	195.00
Bowl, 9½", fruit, open handle	35.00	45.00		Plate, 14", sandwich	28.00	
Candlesticks, 4½", square, pair	22.00			Salt & pepper, 2", square, pair	30.00	50.00
Candy dish, 3 legs, 6¼"		15.00		Saucer/sherbet plate	5.00	75.00
** Candy dish and cover	37.50			Sherbet	12.00	18.00
Coaster, 3½"	14.00			Sugar, oval	12.00	15.00
Comport, 5¾"	33.00	42.00	*****	Tumbler, 10 ounce, footed	20.00	24.00
Creamer, oval	12.00	15.00		Vase, 8"	25.00	
Cup	15.00	275.00	**	Wine, 3½"	6.00	

*Add for Hocking $15.00; add for others $12.50   **Look-Alike   ***Ruby $4.00   ****Ruby $650.00   *****Green or iridized $20.00

MAYA, LINE #221, PADEN CITY GLASS COMPANY, Late 1930s – 1951; CANTON GLASS COMPANY, 1950s

Colors: crystal, light blue, red

Splitting Paden City's Largo (#220) and Maya (#221) into separate patterns helped collectors differentiate between these two similar patterns. I hope that we can get the listings separated appropriately, it should be entertaining; so if you find a listing under the wrong pattern, or one missing, just let me know. The cheese dish seems to be the most desirable piece of Maya to own.

The sugar and creamer in Maya appear to be rarer than those of Largo. Sugar and creamer collectors also prize them, but they are flat and not footed. I have a pair, but they didn't make it into the Maya photography box by the time we needed them. We buy glass for two years for each of the major books and then have to sort all those purchases into the separate patterns. A major difficulty in that is living in Florida and photographing in Kentucky. You cannot drive 800 miles to rectify mistakes in omission. I have driven from Paducah to Lexington overnight to fetch glassware forgotten more than once when we lived there. Sometimes, even two van loads of glass are not enough to show you everything needed for the books.

Etched patterns can be found on both light blue and crystal. Please note that Maya pieces can be distinguished from Largo by the thistle (ball) design.

	Crystal	Colors		Crystal	Colors
Bowl, 7", flared rim	18.00	35.00	Comport, 6½" x 10", plain rim,		
Bowl, 9½", non-flared	30.00	60.00	pedestal	32.50	70.00
Bowl, 11⅝", 3½" deep, tri-footed,			Creamer, flat.	20.00	50.00
flared rim	35.00	80.00	Mayonnaise, tri-footed	15.00	40.00
Bowl, 12¾", 4¾" deep, tri-footed,			Mayonnaise, tri-footed, crimped	20.00	45.00
flat rim	35.00	80.00	Plate, 6⅝"	8.00	15.00
Cake plate, pedestal	35.00	75.00	Plate, 7", mayonnaise	10.00	20.00
Candleholder	30.00	55.00	Sugar, flat	20.00	50.00
Candy, footed w/lid, 3-part	42.50	97.50	Tray, 13¾", tri-footed, serving	25.00	70.00
Cheese dish w/lid	75.00	175.00	Tray, tab-handled	25.00	60.00
Comport, fluted rim, pedestal	35.00	75.00			

MAYFAIR, FEDERAL GLASS COMPANY, 1934

Colors: crystal, amber, and green

Federal redesigned their Mayfair glass moulds into what finally became known as the Rosemary pattern because Hocking had copyrighted the name Mayfair first. I have shown only the old Federal Mayfair pattern before it was altered.

Federal's Mayfair was a very limited production (before limited productions were the mode of selling merchandise). Maybe that is a hint that you ought to start looking at it as another possible set to collect. Amber and crystal are the colors that can be collected (in the true pattern form). Amber cream soups have been found in small numbers and platters in even fewer numbers. Federal's crystal Mayfair can be collected as a set. I had a letter about transitional crystal cream soups, but no confirming picture. Green can only be bought in transitional form.

You will have to refer to a previous book to see the transitional period glassware made between the old Federal Mayfair pattern and what was to become known as the Rosemary pattern. These transitional pieces have arching in the bottom of each piece rather than the waffle design, and there is no waffling between the top arches. If you turn to the Rosemary (page 199) for reference, you will see that the design under the arches is entirely plain. Collectors regard the transitional pieces a part of Federal Mayfair rather than Rosemary and that is why they are priced here.

Generally, you will find several pieces of Mayfair together, rather than a piece here and there. You can get a quick start to a collection that way.

	Amber	Crystal	Green
Bowl, 5", sauce	9.00	6.50	15.00
Bowl, 5", cream soup	25.00	15.00	25.00
Bowl, 6", cereal	20.00	10.00	30.00
Bowl, 10", oval vegetable	35.00	18.00	45.00
Creamer, footed	13.00	10.50	25.00
Cup	12.00	5.00	15.00
Plate, 6¾", salad	7.00	4.50	9.00

	Amber	Crystal	Green
Plate, 9½", dinner	17.50	12.00	15.00
Plate, 9½", grill	17.50	8.50	15.00
Platter, 12", oval	30.00	20.00	45.00
Saucer	4.00	2.50	4.00
Sugar, footed	13.00	11.00	25.00
Tumbler, 4½", 9 ounce	38.00	18.00	50.00

MAYFAIR, "OPEN ROSE," LINE NO. 2000, HOCKING GLASS COMPANY, 1931 – 1937

Colors: Ice blue, pink; some green, yellow, and crystal (See Reproduction Section.)

This is probably *the* pattern in Depression glass. Mayfair was the most popular Depression glass pattern in the country, due in part to its major distribution throughout the states. Many families still have pieces left in their possession. The cookie jar pictured on the cover is one piece recognized as Depression glass by millions of today's generation.

In a 1937 distributor's catalog, ten items of No. 2000 line pink Mayfair "exquisitely etched with rose floral design" (painted) could be bought by the dozen for under $1.75. The least expensive item was the cereal bowls for 37¢ a dozen. The most expensive was the 80-ounce pitcher for $1.75. This illustrates how inexpensively a shop owner could obtain this ware to help sell his product or lure people to his store. This particular ware advertised above was satinized using camphoric acid and hand painted. Few collectors cared about these satin pieces in the past; but that has changed today. Collectors seek mint examples of this hand-painted pattern.

Rare colors found in Mayfair include yellow and green. Sets are possible in both colors but today it would take a lot of money, patience, and pure unadulterated luck. There are a few sets in those colors in collections I have been privileged to view, but they were assembled 20 to 25 years ago. Pieces in these colors are rarely seen and very expensive in mint condition. Be sure to note the blue cup with a pink trim. There were several of these rarities found, the first bi-colored Mayfair pieces known.

The crystal creamer and covered sugar are rarely seen, but I have only met a few collectors searching for crystal Mayfair. Though these items are rare, with little demand, they do not yet command big prices. The juice pitcher, shakers, butter bottom (only), and the divided platter are commonly seen pieces in crystal. A reader wrote that the divided platter was given as a premium with the purchase of coffee or spices in late 1930s. This platter is often found in a decorative metal holder.

Blue Mayfair is strikingly beautiful and regrettably, nearly all gone from the market today. In the early days of collecting, the supply for this seemed similar to the pink. Unfortunately, that was not so. It commands goodly sums when found; however, its lack of availability is preventing its rise in price at this time. One new collector asked me if I had a piece available to show her. "I've been doing this for two years, and I've never seen a piece of blue!" she confided. The blue has always been my favorite since the first time I saw it in the late 1960s.

Pink Mayfair has a large variety of pieces and an equally large following. Various stems and tumblers facilitate collecting from several perspectives. A setting for four with all the accessory pieces is expensive. However, if you try not to buy everything made, you can put a small set together for about the same money as most other patterns. It depends upon how many different stems or tumblers you wish as well as whether you want a sugar lid or the elusive three-footed bowl. Check out the prices for those items!

There are a few details about Mayfair that need to be stated. Some stems have a plain foot while others are rayed. The 10" celery measures 11½" handle to handle and the 9" one measures 10½" handle to handle. (The measurements in this book normally do not include handles unless so noted.) Footed iced teas vary in height. Some teas have a short stem above the foot and others have almost none. This causes the heights to vary to some extent. It is just a mould variation, which may account for capacity differences, too. Note under measurements on page 2 the listings of tumblers that I have taken from old Hocking catalogs. In two catalogs from 1935, these were listed as 13 ounce; but in 1936, both catalogs listed the tumbler as 15 ounces. I have never found a 13-ounce tumbler.

I spend hours answering questions and calls about rare and reproduction pieces in Mayfair. There was an inquiry on the Internet about reproduction shot glasses. It is uncomplicated. The originals have a split stem on the flower design while the reproductions have a single stem. That has never changed since they were first made at Mosser. I have updated the Reproduction Section in the back to take care of the odd colors of cookie jars and shakers now being found. Please read pages 249 and 250 if you are having problems.

If given the chance, I would recommend you attend at least one glass show in your life. You will be glad you did. At a recent show, two women said it was the most "fantastic, fun experience" they'd ever had. In Florida, a person told me he hadn't known there was this much beautiful old glass left in the world, let alone one show!

	*Pink	Blue	Green	Yellow
Bowl, 5", cream soup	65.00			
Bowl, 5½", cereal	35.00	55.00	85.00	85.00
Bowl, 7", vegetable	30.00	60.00	175.00	175.00
Bowl, 9", 3⅛ high, 3-leg console	5,995.00		5,500.00	
Bowl, 9½", oval vegetable	38.00	80.00	125.00	135.00
Bowl, 10", vegetable	35.00	80.00		135.00

*Frosted or satin finish items slightly lower if paint is worn or missing

MAYFAIR

	*Pink	Blue	Green	Yellow
Bowl, 10", same covered	140.00	150.00		995.00
Bowl, 11¾", low flat	65.00	72.50	50.00	225.00
Bowl, 12", deep, scalloped fruit	65.00	105.00	50.00	255.00
Butter dish and cover or 7", covered vegetable	85.00	325.00	1,300.00	1,300.00
Butter bottom with indent				300.00
Butter dish top	45.00	265.00	1,150.00	1,150.00
Cake plate, 10", footed	35.00	75.00	150.00	
Candy dish and cover	65.00	325.00	595.00	495.00
Celery dish, 9", divided			195.00	195.00
Celery dish, 10"	50.00	75.00	125.00	125.00
Celery dish, 10", divided	295.00	80.00		
Cookie jar and lid	55.00	295.00	595.00	895.00
Creamer, footed	30.00	85.00	225.00	225.00
Cup	20.00	55.00	155.00	155.00
Cup, round	350.00			
Decanter and stopper, 32 ounce	235.00			
Goblet, 3¾", 1 ounce cordial	1,200.00		995.00	
Goblet, 4⅛", 2½ ounce	995.00		950.00	
Goblet, 4", 3 ounce cocktail	115.00		395.00	
Goblet, 4½", 3 ounce, wine	120.00		450.00	
Goblet, 5¼", 4½ ounce, claret	1,000.00		950.00	
Goblet, 5¾", 9 ounce, water	75.00		495.00	
Goblet, 7¼", 9 ounce, thin	325.00	250.00		
** Pitcher, 6", 37 ounce	70.00	165.00	600.00	600.00
Pitcher, 8", 60 ounce	85.00	195.00	650.00	500.00
Pitcher, 8½", 80 ounce	125.00	250.00	800.00	850.00
Plate, 5¾" (often substituted as saucer)	15.00	25.00	90.00	90.00
Plate, 6½", round sherbet	18.00			
Plate, 6½", round, off-center indent	25.00	30.00	135.00	135.00
Plate, 8½", luncheon	28.00	55.00	85.00	85.00
Plate, 9½", dinner	55.00	80.00	150.00	150.00
Plate, 9½", grill	50.00	55.00	85.00	125.00
Plate, 11½", handled grill				125.00
Plate, 12", cake w/handles	55.00	75.00	40.00	
*** Platter, 12", oval, open handles	35.00	75.00		
Platter, 12½", oval, 8" wide, closed handles			235.00	235.00
Relish, 8⅜", 4-part	35.00	75.00	165.00	165.00
Relish, 8⅜", non-partitioned	225.00		295.00	295.00
**** Salt and pepper, flat, pair	65.00	325.00	1,100.00	875.00
Salt and pepper, footed	10,000.00			
Sandwich server, center handle	55.00	85.00	40.00	135.00
Saucer (cup ring)	35.00			150.00
Saucer (same as 5¾"plate)	15.00	25.00	90.00	90.00
Sherbet, 2¼", flat	165.00	165.00		
Sherbet, 3", footed	17.50			
Sherbet, 4¾", footed	85.00	90.00	165.00	165.00
Sugar, footed	30.00	85.00	210.00	210.00
Sugar lid	1,995.00		1,500.00	1,500.00
Tumbler, 3½", 5 ounce, juice	50.00	125.00		
Tumbler, 4¼", 9 ounce, water	40.00	115.00		
Tumbler, 4¾", 11 ounce, water	225.00	150.00	225.00	225.00
Tumbler, 5¼", 13½ ounce, iced tea	67.50	275.00		
Tumbler, 3¼", 3 ounce, footed, juice	95.00			
Tumbler, 5¼", 10 ounce, footed	50.00	160.00		225.00
Tumbler, 6½", 15 ounce, footed, iced tea	45.00	300.00	300.00	
Vase (sweet pea)	195.00	145.00	325.00	
Whiskey, 2¼", 1½ ounce	110.00			

*Frosted or satin finish items slightly lower if paint is worn or missing
***Divided Crystal $12.50

** Crystal $15.00
**** Crystal $17.50 pair — Beware reproductions.

132

MISS AMERICA (DIAMOND PATTERN), LINE #2500, HOCKING GLASS COMPANY, 1935 – 1938

Colors: crystal, pink; some green, ice blue, Jade-ite, and Royal Ruby (See Reproduction Section.)

The name Miss America brings the word beauty to mind, which is definitely apropos when referring to this beloved 1930s Depression pattern. Popular Miss America continues to be sought at shows and often is seen at flea markets. In fact, our last major purchase of it was at a flea market in Georgia. A dealer had a stack of Miss America in amongst the imported swords, car accessories, and assorted wallpapers. It was moderately priced and hardly used (without scratches or chips) and I couldn't believe it was still there after weekend buyers had been there! Novices need to know to check the points carefully on the design, particularly the plate edges. Often parts of these points are missing, particularly underneath. You need also to peruse candy jar knobs to make certain they have not been glued back on.

All Miss America tumblers and stems have three parallel lines before leading into a plain glass rim. Westmoreland's English Hobnail pattern, which was made earlier and continued production past that of Miss America, is often incorrectly labeled as Miss America. Check the differences by reading the comparison of the two under that pattern on page 73. Because of wonderful marketing schemes promoting Hocking's wares, Miss America eventually exceeded English Hobnail's popularity with the public. I expect it was offered to merchants more inexpensively.

A set of rare Royal Ruby (c. 1938) Miss America is pictured below. A former employee of the company originally owned it. There were two styles of water goblets, footed juices, and sherbets in this group. Notice how one of the water goblets and one of the footed juices flare at the top. The sherbets do the same; but only one style was photographed. This set contained the first Miss America cups, sherbets, footed and flat juices I had seen in Royal Ruby. It was originally a basic set for eight. A few other pieces turn up occasionally in the market. An individual reproduced butter dish surfaced in several colors in the late 1970s; but the red ones were an amberina red. No original red butter has been discovered. Reproductions have appeared in a few other pieces of Miss America pattern since the early 1970s. Please refer to page 251 for a listing and facts regarding these annoyances.

Some pieces of Miss America are found with metal lids. The relish (four-part dish) and cereal bowl are often found that way. These glass pieces were sold to some company who made lids to fit. They are not original factory lids.

Any time a glass pattern was made for several years, it will be possible to find pieces that deviate in size. In talking to former mould makers, I learned that moulds were "cut down" when they wore. Therefore, some pieces deviated a little each time the moulds were reworked and cut away to sharpen the design.

Shakers that are fatter toward the foot are the best ones to buy, since that style has not been reproduced. Narrow, thinner bottomed reproduction shakers are like flies at stockyards now, everywhere.

A few odd-colored or flashed pieces of Miss America surface infrequently. I have shown some of these in previous editions. Flashed-on red, green, or amethyst are not plentiful enough to collect a set. However, there may be more interest in odd colors now that rainbow collections are in fashion.

	Crystal	Pink	Green	Royal Ruby
Bowl, 4½", berry			15.00	
Bowl, 6¼", cereal	10.00	30.00	20.00	
Bowl, 8", curved in at top	40.00	100.00		695.00
Bowl, 8¾", straight, deep fruit	35.00	90.00		
Bowl, 10", oval vegetable	15.00	45.00		
Bowl, 11", shallow				950.00
*Butter dish and cover	210.00	625.00		
Butter dish bottom	10.00	30.00		
Butter dish top	200.00	595.00		
Cake plate, 12", footed	26.00	67.00		
Candy jar and cover, 11½"	65.00	160.00		
***Celery dish, 10½", oblong	16.00	42.00		
Coaster, 5¾"	16.00	35.00		
Comport, 5"	17.50	32.00		
Creamer, footed	11.00	25.00		250.00
Cup	9.00	25.00	15.00	325.00
Goblet, 3¾", 3 oz., wine	20.00	120.00		325.00

	Crystal	Pink	Green	Royal Ruby
Goblet, 4¾", 5 oz., juice	25.00	110.00		325.00
Goblet, 5½", 10 oz., water	18.00	55.00		295.00
Pitcher, 8", 65 ounce	50.00	170.00		
Pitcher, 8½", 65 ounce, w/ice lip	70.00	225.00		
**Plate, 5¾", sherbet	6.00	13.00	8.00	60.00
Plate, 6¾"			14.00	
Plate, 8½", salad	7.50	27.00		175.00
***Plate, 10¼", dinner	16.00	40.00		
Plate, 10¼", grill	10.00	30.00		
Platter, 12¼", oval	15.00	42.00		
Relish, 8¾", 4-part	10.00	25.00		
Relish, 11¾", round, divided	25.00	6,000.00		
Salt and pepper, pair	33.00	67.50		
Saucer	3.00	8.00		75.00
**Sherbet	7.00	18.00		165.00
Sugar	9.00	25.00		250.00
***Tumbler, 4", 5 oz., juice	16.00	70.00		235.00
Tumbler, 4½", 10 oz., water	14.00	40.00	22.00	
Tumbler, 5¾", 14 ounce, iced tea	25.00	115.00		

*Absolute mint price   **Also in Ice Blue $50.00   ***Also in Ice Blue $150.00

MODERNTONE, HAZEL ATLAS GLASS COMPANY, 1934 – 1942; Late 1940s – Early 1950s

Colors: amethyst, cobalt blue; some crystal, pink, and Platonite fired-on colors

Platonite Moderntone has been moved into the *Collectible Glassware from the 40s, 50s, 60s...* since it better fits the era covered by that book. Moderntone is popular first for its rich colorings and for its uncomplicated style. It is more reasonably priced today than many of its counterpart patterns made in cobalt blue or amethyst. It originally cost about the same as those other patterns.

Originally a 36-piece set of cobalt blue Moderntone could be bought for $1.69 plus freight costs for 24 pounds. You had to send two or four coupons from flour, no hardship since baking was an everyday thing then. However, $1.69 was more than a day's wages for laborers.

There is no Moderntone tumbler as such. Tumblers sold, today, as Moderntone were just marketed together with this pattern, but they were never sold as a part of the set. There are two unlike style tumblers that have been accepted for this set. Some water tumbler and juice tumblers are paneled and have a rayed bottom, while another juice is not paneled and has a plain bottom and

is marked H over top A which is the Hazel Atlas trademark. Either tumbler is acceptable, but most collectors choose the circled, paneled one. All sizes of these tumblers are hard to find except for the water. Green, pink, or crystal tumblers were produced, but there is little demand for these except for the tiny shot glass that is hunted by a growing horde of those collectors.

The butter bottom and sugar were seemingly sold to some company who made metal tops. Lids come with black, red, or blue knobs, but red materializes most often. By adding a notched lid and spoon, mustards were made from the handle-less custard. Speaking of that custard, there is a punch set being sold as Moderntone, which uses a Hazel Atlas mixing bowl and either the plain, cobalt, roly-poly cups found with the Royal Lace toddy set or Moderntone custard cups. This was not Hazel Atlas assembled; but some embrace it to go with Moderntone. I would think that you should at least have one with the handle-less cups rather than roly-poly cups.

In past editions, I have shown a boxed set with crystal Moderntone shot glasses in a metal holder that came with a Colonial Block creamer. The box was marked "Little Deb" Lemonade Server Set. That crystal pitcher has turned up in cobalt and several have been found with Shirley Temple's picture. These boxed children's sets sell in the $100.00 range. There are a few collectors chasing crystal Moderntone. It brings about half the price of amethyst. Flat soups are rare in any color except crystal. Today's collectors combine colors; so, crystal soups may become desirable in place of the rarer and pricey colored ones.

Ruffled cream soups have surpassed the sandwich plates in price. Sandwich plates can be located, but nearly all are heavily chafed or worn, a basis for collectors to reject them. When you pick up a blue plate that looks white in the center from years of use, that is not a good sign. A collector gleefully related that she bought nearly a dozen of these sandwich trays on a table in a used furniture store for $18 not so long ago.

The cheese dish remains the highest priced piece of Moderntone. This cheese dish is fundamentally a salad plate with a metal cover and wooden cutting board inside the lid.

Green, crystal, and pink ashtrays are around, but there is restricted demand for them by Moderntone collectors themselves. However, I am encountering ever more collectors of ashtrays themselves; so, that could change. Blue ashtrays still command a hefty price for an ashtray. Finding any Moderntone bowls without inner rim roughness (irr) is a difficult assignment. Prices are for mint condition pieces. That is why bowls are so highly priced. Used, nicked, and bruised bowls are the norm and should be priced accordingly. Bowls, themselves, are not rare; mint condition bowls are.

MODERNTONE

	Cobalt	Amethyst
* Ashtray, 7¾", match holder in center	175.00	
Bowl, 4¾", cream soup	24.00	20.00
Bowl, 5", berry	30.00	25.00
Bowl, 5", cream soup, ruffled	65.00	33.00
Bowl, 6½", cereal	75.00	75.00
Bowl, 7½", soup	165.00	100.00
Bowl, 8¾", large berry	50.00	40.00
Butter dish with metal cover	110.00	
Cheese dish, 7", with metal lid	350.00	
Creamer	12.50	11.00
Cup	10.00	11.00
Cup (handle-less) or custard	20.00	15.00
Plate, 5⅞", sherbet	6.00	5.00
Plate, 6¾", salad	12.00	10.00

* Pink $75.00; green $95.00
** Pink or green $17.50

	Cobalt	Amethyst
Plate, 7¾", luncheon	13.00	9.00
Plate, 8⅞", dinner	18.00	13.00
Plate, 10½", sandwich	50.00	40.00
Platter, 11", oval	50.00	37.50
Platter, 12", oval	90.00	45.00
Salt and pepper, pair	40.00	35.00
Saucer	4.00	3.00
Sherbet	12.50	12.00
Sugar	13.00	12.00
Sugar lid (metal)	37.50	
Tumbler, 5 ounce	75.00	40.00
Tumbler, 9 ounce	40.00	30.00
Tumbler, 12 ounce	135.00	90.00
** Whiskey, 1½ ounce	45.00	

MONTICELLO, Later WAFFLE, #698, IMPERIAL GLASS COMPANY, c. 1920 – 1960s

Colors: crystal, Rubigold, milk, clambroth, teal

Monticello was introduced in the early 1920s in colors of crystal and Rubigold, Imperial's name for their marigold colored carnival glass. Evidently, carnival collectors gather up their part of this pattern as I have had difficulty finding a single piece to photograph with the crystal. Given the number of pieces made and the forty plus years they were manufactured, Monticello was a successful pattern for Imperial. Most crystal pieces I see out are valued very sensibly. Years later, Monticello was renamed by Imperial as Waffle, which is what it was being called at markets in the late 1960s and 1970s when I first become aware of it.

As with their other wares, Imperial reissued an assortment of items from this line throughout their production years in whatever colors were prime at that moment. So, it's to be expected you will find other, later colors than those listed above. I am pricing crystal only for now. Colors will add to the prices listed, with teal and clambroth bringing the most. Forgive the older, pattern glass, footed mug pictured in the bottom row, not a part of Imperial's workmanship.

	Crystal		Crystal		Crystal		Crystal
Basket, 10"	22.00	Bowl, 8½", belled	17.50	Compote, 5¾", belled		Punch cup	8.00
Bonbon, 5½", 1 handle	12.00	Bowl, 8", lily (cupped)	40.00	rim	15.00	Relish, 8¼", divided	18.00
Bowl, 4½", finger	10.00	Bowl, 8", round veg	25.00	Creamer	12.50	Salt & pepper w/glass	
Bowl, 4½", fruit, 2 styles	8.00	Bowl, 8", round	17.00	Cup	10.00	tops	20.00
Bowl, 5½", crème soup	12.50	Bowl, 8", shallow	17.00	Cuspidor	60.00	Saucer	3.00
Bowl, 5", lily	20.00	Bowl, 9", round	20.00	Mayo set, 3-piece	30.00	Sherbet	9.00
Bowl, 5", fruit	10.00	Bowl, 9", shallow	17.50	Pickle, 6", oval	17.00	Stem, cocktail	12.50
Bowl, 6½", belled	12.50	Bowl, 10", belled	25.00	Pitcher, 52 oz., ice lip	60.00	Stem, water	15.00
Bowl, 6", lily	22.50	Bowl, 10", shallow	25.00	Plate, 6", bread	5.00	Sugar, open	12.50
Bowl, 6", round	10.00	Bowl, 12", deep	30.00	Plate, 8", salad	9.00	Tidbit, 2-tier	
Bowl, 7½", square	17.50	Buffet set, 3-pc. (mayo,		Plate, 9", dinner	20.00	(7½" & 10½")	45.00
Bowl, 7½", belled	15.00	spoon, 16½" rnd. plate)	75.00	Plate, 10½", square	25.00	Tumbler, 9 oz., water	15.00
Bowl, 7", flower		Butter tub, 5½"	35.00	Plate, 12", round	35.00	Tumbler, 12 oz., tea	18.00
(w/flower grid)	40.00	Celery, 9", oval	20.00	Plate, 16", cupped	55.00	Vase, 6"	20.00
Bowl, 7", lily	30.00	Cheese dish and cover	75.00	Plate, 16½", round	55.00	Vase, 10½", flat	38.00
Bowl, 7", nappy	12.50	Coaster, 3¼"	8.00	Plate, 17", flat	55.00		
Bowl, 7", round	12.50	Compote, 5¼"	12.50	Punch bowl, belled rim	65.00		

MOONDROPS, NEW MARTINSVILLE GLASS COMPANY, 1932 – 1940

Colors: amber, pink, green, cobalt, ice blue, red, amethyst, crystal, dark green, light green, Jadite, smoke, and black

Moondrops collectors find red and cobalt blue the irresistible colors; and these are selling briskly on Internet auctions, though red is dominant. Every antique dealer knows that red and cobalt blue glass are expensive colors; consequently, prices are generally high even if they are not acquainted with Moondrops. On the other hand, other colors escape unappreciated; you might find a deal if you know what to look for. Pink and light green cordial prices have amazed me on Internet auctions. So, other colors of Moondrops are being accredited in collecting circles but only in rarely found items. Amber was the least chosen color for a while, but even that is changing, not only in Moondrops, but in other patterns as well. Perfume bottles, powder jars, mugs, gravy boats, and triple candlesticks are symbols of more elegant glassware than most of its contemporaries, so those items are swept off the market quickly. Bud vases, decanters, and popular "rocket style" stems present an arcade of unusual pieces. A number of "rocket style" decanters are pictured in my *Very Rare Glassware* series.

Apparently, New Martinsville or one of their glass distributors mismatched some of their Moondrops colors. I have found two powder jars with crystal bottoms and cobalt blue tops in antique malls in Ohio and Florida, so they were probably marketed that way. I have seen one complete cobalt perfume. They can be found that way, too.

The butter has to have a matching glass top to obtain the prices listed below. The metal top with a bird finial found on some butter bottoms sells for about $35.00. However, a metal top with a fan finial sells for approximately $65.00. Those fan finials are not easily found. Collectors have a propensity to want glass tops on their butter dishes.

	Blue, Red	Other colors		Blue, Red	Other colors
Ashtray	30.00	17.00	Goblet, 5¾" 8 ounce	40.00	20.00
Bowl, 4¼", cream soup	100.00	40.00	Goblet, 5⅛", 3 ounce, metal stem wine	16.00	11.00
Bowl, 5¼", berry	25.00	12.00	Goblet, 5½", 4 ounce, metal stem wine	20.00	11.00
Bowl, 5⅜", 3-footed, tab handle	75.00	40.00	Goblet, 6¼", 9 ounce, metal stem water	23.00	16.00
Bowl, 6¾", soup	90.00		Gravy boat	195.00	100.00
Bowl, 7½", pickle	35.00	20.00	Mayonnaise, 5¼"	65.00	40.00
Bowl, 8⅜", footed, concave top	45.00	25.00	Mug, 5⅛", 12 ounce	40.00	23.00
Bowl, 8½", 3-footed divided relish	40.00	20.00	Perfume bottle, "rocket"	295.00	195.00
Bowl, 9½", 3-legged, ruffled	70.00		Pitcher, 6⅞", 22 ounce, small	165.00	90.00
Bowl, 9¾", oval vegetable	75.00	45.00	Pitcher, 8⅛", 32 ounce, medium	185.00	115.00
Bowl, 9¾", covered casserole	250.00	145.00	Pitcher, 8", 50 ounce, large, with lip	195.00	115.00
Bowl, 9¾", handled, oval	52.50	36.00	Pitcher, 8⅛", 53 ounce, large, no lip	185.00	125.00
Bowl, 11", boat-shaped celery	32.00	23.00	Plate, 5⅞"	11.00	8.00
Bowl, 12", round, 3-footed console	85.00	32.00	Plate, 6⅛", sherbet	8.00	5.00
Bowl, 13", console with "wings"	120.00	42.00	Plate, 6", round, off-center sherbet indent	12.00	9.00
Butter dish and cover	475.00	250.00	Plate, 7⅛", salad	14.00	10.00
Butter dish bottom	60.00	40.00	Plate, 8½", luncheon	17.00	12.00
Butter dish top (glass)	415.00	210.00	Plate, 9½", dinner	30.00	20.00
Candles, 2", ruffled, pair	45.00	25.00	Plate, 14", round, sandwich	45.00	20.00
Candles, 4½", sherbet style, pair	30.00	20.00	Plate, 14", 2-handled, sandwich	60.00	25.00
Candlesticks, 5", ruffled, pair	40.00	25.00	Platter, 12", oval	45.00	25.00
Candlesticks, 5", "wings," pair	110.00	60.00	Powder jar, 3-footed	295.00	160.00
Candlesticks, 5¼", triple light, pair	150.00	95.00	Saucer	4.00	3.00
Candlesticks, 8½", metal stem, pair	50.00	33.00	Sherbet, 2⅝"	16.00	11.00
Candy dish, 8", ruffled	40.00	20.00	Sherbet, 4½"	28.00	16.00
Cocktail shaker with or without handle,			Sugar, 2¾"	15.00	10.00
metal top	60.00	35.00	Sugar, 3½"	16.00	11.00
Comport, 4"	27.50	18.00	Tumbler, 2¾", 2 ounce, shot	22.00	10.00
Comport, 11½"	95.00	55.00	Tumbler, 2¾", 2 ounce, handled shot	16.00	11.00
Creamer, 2¾", miniature	18.00	11.00	Tumbler, 3¼", 3 ounce, footed juice	20.00	11.00
Creamer, 3¾", regular	16.00	10.00	Tumbler, 3⅝", 5 ounce	18.00	10.00
Cup	16.00	8.00	Tumbler, 4⅜", 7 ounce	16.00	10.00
Decanter, 7¾", small	67.50	38.00	Tumbler, 4⅜", 8 ounce	20.00	11.00
Decanter, 8½", medium	70.00	42.00	Tumbler, 4⅞", 9 ounce, handled	30.00	16.00
Decanter, 11¼", large	100.00	50.00	Tumbler, 4⅞", 9 ounce	20.00	15.00
Decanter, 10¼", "rocket"	595.00	425.00	Tumbler, 5⅛", 12 ounce	30.00	14.00
Goblet, 2⅞, ¾ ounce, cordial	40.00	27.50	Tray, 7½", for mini sugar/creamer	37.50	19.00
Goblet, 4", 4 ounce, wine	22.00	12.00	Vase, 7¾" flat, ruffled top	60.00	57.00
Goblet, 4¾", "rocket", wine	65.00	35.00	Vase, 8½", "rocket" bud	295.00	195.00
Goblet, 4¾", 5 ounce	24.00	15.00	Vase, 9¼", "rocket" style	295.00	165.00

MT. PLEASANT, "DOUBLE SHIELD," L. E. SMITH GLASS COMPANY, 1920s – 1934

Colors: black amethyst, amethyst, cobalt blue, crystal, pink, green, and white

Prices for Mt. Pleasant are slowly rising unlike some other patterns. Many people are stirred by colored glassware for the color alone. Mt. Pleasant is often acquired for its cobalt blue and black colors rather than for it being Depression glass.

I had to point out the "double shield" to a neophyte collector recently, because you cannot really see that moulded design element in the opaque pieces pictured here. Sorry!

The picture on page 141 illustrates but a few of many adornments found on Mt. Pleasant. A few undecorated pieces of white Mt. Pleasant are known, but the black stripes and handles dress it up from plain white. Few pieces of color-striped crystal are being found; I purchased these few for you to enjoy another variety of this ware. I have had occasional reports of pink and green items, as a rule, sugars and creamers. A few pink plates pop up occasionally, suggesting a luncheon set might be attainable in pastel colors.

Most cobalt blue Mt. Pleasant is discovered in the Midwest and in northern New York. We know that Mt. Pleasant was exhibited and utilized for premiums in hardware stores in those areas. Black dominates in other areas of the country, but I have not found anyone who can document that color used as premiums. Many pieces of both colors are found with a platinum (silver) band encircling them, a kind of trademark with Smith black glassware. This decorated band washes out with use. Price should be less for worn decorations. This brings to mind the fact that gold and silver trims deteriorate quickly with dishwasher/lemon soap exposure; so, you should hand wash items with those trims if you care to preserve them. In that same vein, I should warn that one person was horrified to learn her decal disappeared when she put one such decorated item in the dishwasher. In the 40s and 50s you could buy hand-applied decals at the five and dime. You could wet the backing and apply the decal to whatever you wanted to decorate. However, getting the piece wet again would cause the decal to flake and peel. That is what occurred with the canister jar this woman had put in her dishwasher. You can generally see the edges of this type of temporary decal. Wash it with care to preserve it.

	Pink, Green	Amethyst, Black, Cobalt		Pink, Green	Amethyst, Black, Cobalt
Bonbon, 7", rolled-up, handle	16.00	23.00	Leaf, 11¼"		30.00
Bowl, 4" opening, rose	18.00	27.50	Mayonnaise, 5½", 3-footed	18.00	30.00
Bowl, 4⅞", square, footed, fruit	13.00	20.00	Mint, 6", center handle	16.00	25.00
Bowl, 6", 2-handle, square	13.00	18.00	Plate, 7", 2-handle, scalloped	9.00	16.00
Bowl, 7", 3-footed, rolled out edge	16.00	25.00	Plate, 8", scalloped or square	10.00	20.00
Bowl, 8", scalloped, 2-handle	19.00	35.00	Plate, 8", 2-handle	11.00	20.00
Bowl, 8", square, 2-handle	19.00	35.00	Plate 8¼", square w/indent for cup		16.00
Bowl, 9", scalloped, 1¾" deep, ftd.		35.00	Plate, 9", grill		20.00
Bowl, 9¼", square, footed, fruit	19.00	35.00	Plate, 10½", cake, 2-handle	16.00	38.00
Bowl, 10", scalloped fruit		45.00	Plate, 10½", 1¼" high, cake		45.00
Bowl, 10", 2-handle turned-up edge		35.00	Plate, 12", 2-handle	20.00	35.00
Cake plate, 10½", footed, 1¼" high		37.50	Salt and pepper, 2 styles	25.00	45.00
Candlestick, single, pair	20.00	30.00	Sandwich server, center-handle		45.00
Candlestick, double, pair	35.00	50.00	Saucer	2.50	4.00
Creamer	18.00	20.00	Sherbet, 2 styles	10.00	16.00
Cup (waffle-like crystal)	4.50		Sugar	18.00	20.00
Cup	9.50	14.00	Tumbler, footed		28.00
Leaf, 8"		15.00	Vase, 7¼"		35.00

MT. VERNON, Later WASHINGTON, #699, IMPERIAL GLASS COMPANY, Late 1920s – 1970s

Colors: crystal, red, green, yellow, milk, iridized, red flash

Mt. Vernon was a popular, prismatic design, attuned to its modernistic roots, which is obtainable in markets today. The design embraced square, round, triangle, cubist forms, along with innovative handle points and knob stems. Even its name celebrated the George Washington bicentennial event that was a big hoopla then. Mt. Vernon appears mostly in crystal; limited pieces in color surface from time to time, as is usual with Imperial moulds that were occasionally resurrected throughout production. Cobalt and emerald items were made by another company entirely in a last ditch effort to raise money to "save Imperial Glass." You should be able to gather a large set right now without breaking the bank. The tall celery becomes a pickle by adding a lid; both sugar bowls, the 5¾" two-handled bowl, and the 69-ounce pitcher were sold with or without lids. I just encountered a tall, round, stemmed compote with lid, having the distinctive tri-stemmed knob that you see in the butter top. I hope that you will enjoy the additional pieces pictured.

Tiffin made a similar looking pattern called Williamsburg in the late 20s in crystal and in the 50s in colors. Williamsburg has a rayed star bottom design; Mt. Vernon's pattern shows a waffle type design in the bottom and extended tip handle protrusions.

	Crystal		Crystal
Bonbon, 5¾", one-handle	10.00	Pitcher, 54 ounce	35.00
Bowl, 5", finger	12.00	Pitcher, 69 ounce, straight edge	40.00
Bowl, 5¾", two-handle	10.00	Plate, 6", bread and butter	5.00
Bowl, 5¾", two-handle, w/cover	22.00	Plate, 8", round	10.00
Bowl, 6", lily	15.00	Plate, 8", square	10.00
Bowl, 7", lily	18.00	Plate, 11", cake	20.00
Bowl, 8", lily	20.00	Plate, 12½", sandwich	25.00
Bowl, 10", console	25.00	Plate, 13¼", torte	27.00
Bowl, 10", 3-footed	25.00	Plate, 18", liner for punch	28.00
Bowl, punch	35.00	Saucer	2.00
Butter dish, 5"	30.00	Shaker, pair	22.00
Butter dish, dome top	35.00	Spooner	22.00
Butter tub, 5"	15.00	Stem, 2 ounce, wine	12.00
Candlestick, 9"	30.00	Stem, 3 ounce, cocktail	8.00
Celery, 10½"	22.00	Stem, 5 ounce, sherbet	6.00
Compote, tri-stem knob	30.00	Stem, 9 ounce, water goblet	10.00
Creamer, individual	8.00	Sugar lid, for individual	8.00
Creamer, large	12.00	Sugar lid, for large	12.00
Cup, coffee	8.00	Sugar, individual	8.00
Cup, custard or punch	5.00	Sugar, large	12.00
Decanter	38.00	Syrup, 8½ ounce, w/cover	45.00
Oil bottle, 6 ounce	30.00	Tidbit, two-tier	30.00
Pickle jar, w/cover	35.00	Tumbler, 7 ounce, old fashioned	10.00
Pickle, tall, two-handle	22.00	Tumbler, 9 ounce, water	8.00
Pickle, 6", two-handle	15.00	Tumbler, 12 ounce, iced tea	12.50
Pitcher top, for 69 ounce	35.00	Vase, 10", orange bowl	50.00

NEW CENTURY, HAZEL ATLAS GLASS COMPANY, 1930 – 1935

Colors: green; some crystal, pink, amethyst, and cobalt

New Century is a Hazel Atlas pattern that has attracted collectors for years. Green is the chosen color since sets can only be amassed in that color. A few pieces are found in crystal, but not enough to assemble a set, according to some that tried to do so. Crystal prices are on par with green, even with little demand. This classic "pillow optic" design, as it was promoted in a Butler Brothers catalog, has definitely withstood the test of time.

You can find crystal powder jars made from a sugar lid set atop a sherbet. The knob of the sherbet usually has decorative glass marbles or beads attached by a wire. One of these is pictured on the next page. I believe these were a legitimate product of the 30s. Unfortunately, a lady sent me a picture of a Cherry Blossom one she'd paid $250.00 as a "rare unlisted," powder jar, which no doubt was put together last week. A $20.00 outlay in a good book could save you much more than that.

Thirty years into collecting Depression glass, New Century bowls are all but impossible to find. I haven't owned a 4½" berry bowl in years. That Butler Brothers ad mentioned above sold them for 37¢ a dozen, and they were packed three dozen to a carton. So, where are they today? Cream soups, casseroles, whiskeys, wines, decanters, grill plates, and cocktails are rarely seen. As in Adam, the casserole bottom is harder to find than the top. I saw a chunked casserole lid for $10.00. When I set it down, I was told any lid was worth way more than that. Well, no, not yet, and particularly not a badly damaged one.

Pink, cobalt blue, and amethyst New Century have only been encountered in water sets and an occasional cup or saucer. Only flat tumblers have been found in these colors. By the way, in doing some other research, I found that most beverage sets in the 30s were priced around a $1.00 and were often used as a sales advertisement. If you visited the sales at a certain store, you could buy a seven-piece beverage set for a $1.00. One store opening promotion once sold Cameo pitcher sets for 79¢ per set.

	Green, Crystal	Pink, Cobalt, Amethyst
Ashtray/coaster, 5⅜"	30.00	
Bowl, 4½", berry	30.00	
Bowl, 4¾", cream soup	22.00	
Bowl, 8", large berry	28.00	
Bowl, 9", covered casserole	95.00	
Butter dish and cover	65.00	
Cup	10.00	20.00
Creamer	15.00	
Decanter and stopper	75.00	

	Green, Crystal	Pink, Cobalt, Amethyst
Goblet, 2½ ounce, wine	33.00	
Goblet, 3¼ ounce, cocktail	33.00	
Pitcher, 7¾", 60 ounce, with or without ice lip	35.00	35.00
Pitcher, 8", 80 ounce, with or without ice lip	40.00	42.00
Plate, 6", sherbet	8.00	
Plate, 7⅛", breakfast	10.00	
Plate, 8½", salad	14.00	
Plate, 10", dinner	18.00	
Plate, 10", grill	20.00	
Platter, 11", oval	25.00	
Salt and pepper, pair	40.00	
Saucer	3.00	7.50
Sherbet, 3"	12.00	
Sugar	10.00	
Sugar cover	18.00	
Tumbler, 3½", 5 ounce	18.00	12.00
Tumbler, 3½", 8 ounce	28.00	
Tumbler, 4¼", 9 ounce	22.00	20.00
Tumbler, 5", 10 ounce	22.00	22.00
Tumbler, 5¼", 12 ounce	33.00	30.00
Tumbler, 4", 5 ounce, footed	22.00	
Tumbler, 4⅞", 9 ounce, footed	25.00	
Whiskey, 2½", 1½ ounce	22.00	

NEWPORT, "HAIRPIN," HAZEL ATLAS GLASS COMPANY, 1936 – 1940

Colors: cobalt blue, amethyst; some pink, Platonite white, and fired-on colors

Platonite Newport from the 1950s can be found in my book *Collectible Glassware from the 40s, 50s, 60s...* as it was made mostly during that period.

There is a ⁵⁄₁₆" difference between a so-called "larger" dinner and a luncheon plate. In discussions with a mould worker, it's plausible that the larger plates were made in the later, reworked moulds which had to be cut down, resulting in slightly larger sized items. As moulds wore out, they were revitalized by a process called "cutting down" by mould makers. At any rate, the larger dinner plate measures 8¹³⁄₁₆" while the luncheon plate measures 8½"; and, truthfully, after that first flurry over the difference, few collectors really seem to care. I originally mentioned the quandary because of problems mail order and Internet dealers were having. ("The plates you sent me were smaller than the ones I have!") The only official listing I have states plates of 6", 8½", and 11½". However, after obtaining these plates, I found actual measurements quite different as you can see by the size listings in the price guide below. One of the problems with catalog measurements is that they are not always accurate.

Collectors favor cobalt blue in this pattern. Not much pink Newport is found today; so the set pictured below which was free with collect shipping, upon ordering a $4.00 packet of seeds may not have increased seed sales much. I usually see berry bowls and little else in pink. Price pink ⅓ of amethyst due to less demand. Cereal bowls, sandwich plates, large berry bowls, and tumblers are nowhere to be found unless an old collection is sold into the market. I finally bought a large amethyst berry bowl; but I have not replaced the large cobalt berry bowl that was shattered. I have seen two since, but not at a justifiable price for me.

Newport and Moderntone are among the few Depression ware sets you can assemble in amethyst. Moroccan Amethyst came much later.

	Cobalt	Amethyst		Cobalt	Amethyst
Bowl, 4¾", berry	20.00	17.00	Plate, 8¹³⁄₁₆", dinner	22.00	22.00
Bowl, 4¾", cream soup	25.00	24.00	Plate, 11¾", sandwich	45.00	40.00
Bowl, 5¼", cereal	40.00	35.00	Platter, 11¾", oval	50.00	43.00
Bowl, 8¼", large berry	45.00	45.00	Salt and pepper	50.00	40.00
Cup	14.00	12.00	Saucer	5.00	5.00
Creamer	16.00	14.00	Sherbet	15.00	15.00
Plate, 5⅞", sherbet	8.00	8.00	Sugar	16.00	16.00
Plate, 8½", luncheon	15.00	14.00	Tumbler, 4½", 9 ounce	45.00	40.00

No. 200. LADIES! Here's a gorgeous Dinner Set in that new shade Rose Crystal. It consists of 6 large plates, 6 small plates, 6 cups, 6 saucers, 6 cereal dishes, vegetable dish and large meat platter. This sparkling set, more beautiful than you can imagine, is given for one $4.00 order of Seeds Weight 22 lbs. Sent Express collect.

32-Piece Rose Crystal Dinner Set

NEWPORT, NEW MARTINSVILLE, c. 1930s

Colors: cobalt, red, green

Red seems to be the color sold in Florida as that is the only color I have ever found there. You see Newport priced highly for the colors and not necessarily for the knowledge of the pattern or manufacturer.

	All colors
Creamer	20.00
Cup	20.00
Plate, 8"	15.00
Saucer	5.00
Sugar	20.00
Tray, 13½" round, torte	45.00

NORMANDIE, "BOUQUET AND LATTICE," FEDERAL GLASS COMPANY, 1933 – 1940

Colors: iridescent, amber, pink, and crystal

Normandie was nicknamed "Bouquet and Lattice" by early collectors before the real designation was found. Pink is the most desired color; but it was also made in amber and iridescent, which you will have a better chance of finding. Buy any hard-to-find items first or whenever you find them. That admonition goes for collecting almost anything. Rarer, harder-to-find items have always increased in price faster than frequently found ones. If you spot pieces of pink, snap them up; someone wants them.

Pink Normandie has been very obscure for several years; but amber tumblers, sugar lids, and dinner-sized plates have become sparse also. Pink Normandie tumblers, should you discover any, rival prices of American Sweetheart; and Normandie collectors are vastly outnumbered by those buying American Sweetheart. Pink pitchers could be bought reasonably when compared to those in American Sweetheart were they obtainable; but most are already tucked away in collections. I did spot one at a mall in Ohio last year. It was labeled "pink depression pitcher," so I bought it. It does have a slight crack near the handle, but it will photograph perfectly. I might add that all rare pieces of pink continue to rise in value. I have not seen a pink dinner plate for sale in over three years.

Some iridescent Normandie is being displayed at Depression glass shows, although lack of demand had almost made it disappear. There are people asking for it since rumors got around that it was getting hard to find. There were enough buyers to raise the prices. Iridescent is still reasonably priced in comparison to pink and amber.

That console bowl and candlesticks (frequently found with sets of iridized Normandie) are Madrid pattern. These were sold about the same time as Normandie. That does not make them Normandie; they are still Madrid. The design on the glass determines pattern, not the color. I had two letters recently asking why I did not list Normandie candles as the writer had found a pair in sets of Normandie. See Madrid for pricing of these console sets.

I should mention that there is a *new* pink glassware set based on the design shapes of Normandie, but having a *heart* as its center design, that is being sold through the Cracker Barrel chain of restaurants. It is no threat to Depression ware and is actually rather attractive and fitting to those surroundings. The pitcher I saw was a brighter pink color, also.

	Amber	Pink	Iridescent
Bowl, 5", berry	10.00	10.00	6.00
* Bowl, 6½", cereal	25.00	60.00	10.00
Bowl, 8½", large berry	27.50	40.00	15.00
Bowl, 10", oval vegetable	20.00	45.00	18.00
Creamer, footed	9.00	14.00	10.00
Cup	7.50	10.00	6.00
Pitcher, 8", 80 ounce	85.00	210.00	
Plate, 6", sherbet	4.50	7.00	3.00
Plate, 7¾", salad	10.00	20.00	
Plate, 9¼", luncheon	8.50	20.00	15.00
Plate, 11", dinner	33.00	135.00	11.50

	Amber	Pink	Iridescent
Plate, 11", grill	15.00	25.00	9.00
Platter, 11¾"	22.00	45.00	12.00
Salt and pepper, pair	55.00	100.00	
Saucer	2.00	3.00	2.00
Sherbet	6.50	10.00	7.00
Sugar	9.00	12.00	6.00
Sugar lid	110.00	200.00	
Tumbler, 4", 5 ounce, juice	33.00	95.00	
Tumbler, 4¼", 9 ounce, water	22.00	65.00	
Tumbler, 5", 12 ounce, iced tea	40.00	120.00	

* Mistaken by many as butter bottom.

No. 610, "PYRAMID," INDIANA GLASS COMPANY, 1926 – 1932

Colors: green, pink, yellow, white, crystal, blue, or black in 1974 – 1975 by Tiara

Indiana's pattern No. 610, "Pyramid" as it is called by collectors, is being welcomed by Art Deco devotees as well as Depression glass collectors. Prices have advanced due to increased demand from both segments. Little is being offered for sale, and mint condition "Pyramid" is bringing premium prices. I did buy a beverage set recently simply because I asked how the two tumblers displayed were priced and was informed they belonged with a set. The pitcher was still under the table and the price on the tumblers said set, which scared everyone from picking them up. I asked the best price and was told that the price was firm for the five pieces. I asked to see the others and lo and behold, out came the pitcher and two more tumblers. Tough price for set of two, but okay for a set of five.

Crystal pitchers and tumblers in "Pyramid" are very inadequate for the demand. Crystal pitchers are priced higher than all but yellow, even though yellow ones are seen more often. There are so many collectors of yellow No. 610 that prices continue to increase. Ice buckets turn up often, even in yellow. However, the yellow lid to the ice bucket is nearly unattainable. No lids have yet been found for any other colors. I received a call from someone who wanted to sell me a yellow ice bucket lid with a chip on it for book (mint) price. Chips do downgrade the price — even more on rare items. The prices below are for mint condition glassware; any with a "ding" or two should market for less.

Indiana made blue and black pieces of "Pyramid" for Tiara during the 1970s. You will see two sizes of black tumblers, blue and black berry bowls, small and large, and the four-part center-handled relish in either color. It was advertised as their Art Deco collection. If you like these colors, it is fine to buy them as a reissue from the original company. Just realize that they are not Depression era. Do not pay antique glass prices for them. That handled, four-part relish is sometimes mistaken for Tea Room, but it is not.

The authentic sugar/creamer stand has squared indentations on each side to fit the bottoms of the sugar and creamer. Stands were common in various patterns, but it takes one with square indentations for No. 610.

Oval bowls and pickle dishes are intermittently mixed up because both measure 9½". The oval bowl has pointed edges, shown by bowls in the bottom row below. The pickle dish has rounded edges and is handled and pictured on the right end of the top row below.

Eight-ounce tumblers are found with two different sized bases. One has a 2¼" square foot while the other has a 2½" square foot, only noticeable when placed side by side.

No. 610 was, and still is, easily damaged on its points. Be sure to examine all the ridged panels and all the corners on each piece. You will be amazed how often a chipped or cracked piece of "Pyramid" is offered as mint.

No. 610, "PYRAMID"

	Crystal	Pink	Green	Yellow
Bowl, 4¾", berry	20.00	40.00	40.00	60.00
Bowl, 8½", master berry	30.00	60.00	60.00	90.00
Bowl, 9½", oval	30.00	40.00	45.00	65.00
Bowl, 9½", pickle, 5¾" wide, handle	30.00	35.00	35.00	55.00
Creamer	20.00	35.00	30.00	40.00
Ice tub	110.00	135.00	125.00	225.00
Ice tub lid				700.00
Pitcher	395.00	395.00	265.00	550.00
Relish tray, 4-part, handle	25.00	60.00	65.00	67.50
Sugar	17.50	35.00	30.00	40.00
Tray for creamer and sugar	25.00	30.00	30.00	55.00
Tumbler, 8 ounce, footed, 2 styles	55.00	55.00	55.00	80.00
Tumbler, 11 ounce, footed	80.00	70.00	90.00	100.00

No. 612, "HORSESHOE," INDIANA GLASS COMPANY, 1930 – 1933

Colors: green, yellow, pink, and crystal

The sanctioned name for this Indiana pattern is No. 612, but collectors have nicknamed it "Horseshoe." In reality, that design does not fit any form of horseshoe ever made, but I guess that would be considered nitpicking. Neophytes tend to retreat from this lovely pattern due to its prices, which is a shame, really. If you honestly like something, even a piece or two can give you pleasure. Life is too short to deny yourself the small pleasures. You don't have to buy it all, just buy what you can afford.

The absent piece from many collections is a green "Horseshoe" butter dish, although tumblers, both flat and footed tea, grill plates (which not all collectors want), and pitchers are limited. The only "Horseshoe" butter I have seen at a show recently was priced about $500.00 above the selling price of the last one I saw purchased. That butter has made the show tour for a while, but at least everyone gets to see it even if the price is prohibitive. The "Horseshoe" butter dish has always been highly priced. If you can find a first edition of my book, the butter dish was $90.00 in 1972. That was big money for a butter back then. Actually, putting rare pieces out for "show" is a time-honored tradition in the antique trade. It dresses a booth and speaks to the quality of your merchandise. Some items dealers really don't want to sell and those are easily spotted when the price is observed.

Yellow pitchers, grill plates, and footed iced teas also create problems for collectors of that color. I have never pictured a yellow grill plate, but I have found one to show eventually. Amazingly, this yellow grill and a crystal one I found do not have the inner rim roughness (irr) that was on the six green grill plates I previously owned.

There are two styles of plates and platters. Some are plain in the center, while others have a pattern. Be wary of scuffs on these. They were used.

Candy dishes only have the pattern on the top. The bottom is plain. A few pink candy dishes have been found, but that candy is the only piece of "Horseshoe" to appear in pink.

	Green	Yellow
Bowl, 4½", berry	30.00	25.00
Bowl, 6½", cereal	32.00	40.00
Bowl, 8½", vegetable	40.00	35.00
Bowl, 9½", large berry	50.00	50.00
Bowl, 10½", oval vegetable	30.00	33.00
Butter dish and cover	850.00	
Butter dish bottom	200.00	
Butter dish top	650.00	
Candy in metal holder motif on lid	225.00	
also, pink	195.00	
Creamer, footed	18.00	20.00
Cup	12.00	13.00
Pitcher, 8½", 64 ounce	335.00	375.00
Plate, 6", sherbet	8.00	9.00

	Green	Yellow
Plate, 8⅜", salad	14.00	14.00
Plate, 9⅜", luncheon	14.00	16.00
Plate, 10⅜", grill	135.00	150.00
Plate, 11½", sandwich	25.00	28.00
Platter, 10¾", oval	32.00	35.00
Relish, 3-part, footed	35.00	45.00
Saucer	5.00	5.00
Sherbet	16.00	18.00
Sugar, open	18.00	20.00
Tumbler, 4¼", 9 ounce	185.00	
Tumbler, 4¾", 12 ounce	195.00	
Tumbler, 9 ounce, footed	32.00	32.00
Tumbler, 12 ounce, footed	175.00	195.00

No. 616, "VERNON," INDIANA GLASS COMPANY, 1930 – 1932

Colors: green, crystal, yellow

No. 616 has a delicate appeal in spite of its masculine appellation. This numbered Indiana pattern was designated "Vernon" in tribute to another glass author's spouse. Photographing this pattern is a major complication. Light passes through it without picking up the design well. This one pattern is definitely better seen "in person" than viewed through a photographer's lens.

Nothing new has been found since we once used crystal No. 616 as everyday dishes. It was attractive; but I warn you from experience that there are rough mould lines protruding from the seams of the tumblers. After a cut lip or two from using the tumblers, this set was retired to the sale box. Today, a glass grinder could quickly take care of those prickly problems.

What "Vernon" is being found today is mostly crystal. Some pieces are found trimmed in platinum (silver). Decorated pieces seldom have worn platinum. Evidently, Indiana's process for applying this trim was superior to other companies whose platinum wore easily.

The 11½" sandwich plate is great as a dinner or barbecue plate when grilling out. They are certainly lighter than the Fiesta chop plates that are used for grilled steaks and pizza. I also warn you that this is softer glass than some company's and sharp knives will damage it rather easily. Sets of yellow and green "Vernon" are not easy to finish, but there is even less green than yellow available. I continue to have difficulty locating a green tumbler and creamer even though I have been looking.

	Green	Crystal	Yellow		Green	Crystal	Yellow
Creamer, footed	28.00	12.00	28.00	Saucer	4.00	2.00	4.00
Cup	16.00	10.00	16.00	Sugar, footed	28.00	11.00	20.00
Plate, 8", luncheon	9.00	6.00	9.00	Tumbler, 5", footed	45.00	20.00	45.00
Plate, 11½", sandwich	25.00	12.00	25.00				

No. 618, "PINEAPPLE & FLORAL," INDIANA GLASS COMPANY, 1932 – 1937

Colors: crystal, amber; some fired-on red, green, milk white; late 1960s, avocado; 1980s pink, cobalt blue, etc.

Indiana reissued diamond-shaped comports and 7" salad bowls in "Pineapple and Floral" in a multitude of colors in addition to the original crystal in the late 1980s and early 1990s. Most had sprayed-on colors, although the light pink was an excellent transparent color. ("Pineapple and Floral" was never originally made in pink.) Unfortunately, prices for these two older crystal pieces plummeted as result. Amber and fired-on red are safe colors to collect to avoid reissued ware.

"Pineapple and Floral" is a collector name. To the factory, it was simply one of the many numbered (No. 618) Indiana lines. Crystal sets are not easily assembled; but it is not impossible. Tumblers, cream soups, and sherbets are the most bothersome pieces to find. As with most of Indiana's patterns, there is frequent mould roughness on the seams, an obstacle for some collectors. This is specifically true on both sizes of tumblers as was the case on its sister pattern No. 616. Most times this roughness comes from surplus and not missing glass. Seek out the harder-to-find pieces first. The set is surprisingly attractive due to the design refracting light brilliantly.

There are two sizes of plates that have an indented center ring. No one has stumbled upon a top or anything to fit that ring yet. A cheese dish is the idea most often proposed for this; but no top has turned up. The usual one seen is 11½" in diameter. You may see these advertised as a servitor — defined in my dictionary as a human servant. I am not sure who designated that name, but you can call it what you wish for now.

Amber No. 618 is not collected as often as the crystal because there is so little of it available. Only plates have been found in light green. These are old and will glow under ultraviolet light.

The two-tier tidbit with a metal handle is not priced in my listings although they sell in the $25.00 to $30.00 range. Glass companies themselves seldom made tidbits. They can easily be assembled today if you can find the metal hardware. Many tidbits are a product of the early 1970s when a dealer in St. Louis would make one from any pattern for $10.00 if you furnished the plates. He did a great job!

There are a few items, especially tumblers, found in milk glass that should please the rapidly increasing group of collectors for white.

	Crystal	Amber, Red		Crystal	Amber, Red
Ashtray, 4½"	15.00	18.00	Plate, 11½", w/indentation	25.00	
Bowl, 4¾", berry	22.00	18.00	Plate, 11½", sandwich	20.00	17.50
Bowl, 6", cereal	25.00	22.00	Platter, 11", closed handle	15.00	18.00
* Bowl, 7", salad	2.00	10.00	Platter, relish, 11½", divided	18.00	
Bowl, 10", oval vegetable	22.00	18.00	Saucer	4.00	4.00
* Comport, diamond-shaped	1.00	8.00	Sherbet, footed	15.00	18.00
Creamer, diamond-shaped	9.00	10.00	Sugar, diamond-shaped	9.00	10.00
Cream soup	22.00	22.00	Tumbler, 4¼", 8 ounce	30.00	25.00
Cup	10.00	10.00	Tumbler, 5", 12 ounce	45.00	
Plate, 6", sherbet	4.00	5.00	Vase, cone-shaped	60.00	
Plate, 8⅜", salad	8.50	8.50	Vase holder, metal $35.00		
** Plate, 9⅜", dinner	14.00	14.00			

* Reproduced in several colors   **Green $45.00

OLD CAFE, HOCKING GLASS COMPANY, 1936 – 1940

Colors: pink, crystal, and Royal Ruby

Collectors admire Old Cafe even though it is a relatively small pattern. It was well distributed in a few pieces over 60 years ago and surprisingly, you seldom go to a market without finding a piece (usually the low candy or two-handled bowl). Old Cafe lamps, pitchers, and dinner plates are very sparse and they are high-priced compared to the rest of the pattern. Pitchers, pictured in earlier editions, have alternating large panels with two small panels that constitute the make-up of all Old Cafe pieces. The pitcher that is often mislabeled Old Cafe can be seen on pages 181 under Hocking's Pillar Optic. Some collectors are mistakenly buying Pillar Optic (evenly spaced panels) for Old Cafe because some dealers are tagging them as such. I recommend some time spent in a good book to learn these differences before you spend your hard-earned money. The juice pitcher is shaped like the Mayfair juice pitcher, but with a large panel alternating with two smaller panels.

Lamps are found in pink and Royal Ruby colors. Lamps were sometimes made by drilling through a vase, but I've seen a pink one that has ball feet to raise it enough to allow the cord to pass under the edge. The 5" bowl has an open handle while the 4½" bowl has tab handles, as does the 3¾" berry. The footed sherbet (pictured in row 2) also measures 3¾".

Royal Ruby Old Cafe cups are found on crystal saucers (shown). No Old Cafe Royal Ruby saucers have ever been seen. A 5½" crystal candy with a Royal Ruby lid is also pictured. No Royal Ruby bottom has been reported.

The low candy (or footed tray) is 8⅜" including handles, and 6½" without. You can see a pink and crystal one on either side of the pink dinner plate.

Hocking made a cookie jar (a numbered line) which is an excellent "go-with" piece. It is ribbed up the sides similar to Old Cafe but has a crosshatched lid that does not match Old Cafe.

	Crystal, Pink	Royal Ruby		Crystal, Pink	Royal Ruby
Bowl, 3¾", berry, tab handles	14.00	9.00	Pitcher, 6", 36 oz.	150.00	
Bowl, 5½", cereal, no handles	35.00		Pitcher, 80 ounce	175.00	
Bowl, 6½", open handles	15.00		Plate, 6", sherbet	5.00	
Bowl, 9", closed handles	30.00		Plate, 10", dinner	65.00	
Candy dish, 8", low, tab handles	16.00	20.00	Saucer	5.00	
Candy jar, 5½", crystal with ruby cover		25.00	Sherbet, 3¾", low ftd.	16.00	16.00
Cup	12.00	12.00	Tumbler, 3", juice	18.00	22.00
Lamp	100.00	150.00	Tumbler, 4", water	25.00	35.00
Olive dish, 6", oblong	10.00		Vase, 7¼"	50.00	55.00

OLD COLONY "LACE EDGE," "OPEN LACE," HOCKING GLASS COMPANY, 1935 – 1938
Colors: pink and some crystal and green

In December 1990, I spent a day at Anchor Hocking going through old files and catalogs. I encountered some old store display photographs (page 157 and 158) promoting the name of this glass as Old Colony. I was thrilled to find an authentic name for the pattern which Hocking workers called "Lace." Don't you wish our ancestors had stocked up on those dime sherbets and under liners? No Old Colony sherbet plate has been seen. Regardless, one engineer wrote that he had tried to gauge the size of those plates with his instruments and his supposition was they were saucer size. Oh, to know definitely! I have used these photos for about five books, so I will be looking to retire them to make room for additional patterns.

If you search for this well-liked Old Colony, always inspect the "lace" around the edge and particularly underneath. It damaged easily and still does. Plates and bowls should be stored carefully. A paper plate between each piece is necessary when stacking or packing delicate glassware. Candlesticks, console bowls, and vases are hard to find in mint condition, but are available with chips, nicks, and cracks.

Ribs on the footed tumbler reach roughly half way up the side as they do on the cup. This tumbler is often confused with the Coronation tumbler that has a comparable profile and design. See the Coronation photograph (page 48 – 49) and read there. Notice the fine ribbed effect from the middle up on the Coronation tumbler. This upper ribbing is absent on Old Colony tumblers.

Satinized or frosted pieces currently sell for a fraction of the cost of their unfrosted counterparts. Lack of demand is one reason. Possibly vases and candlesticks are rare because so many candles and vases were satinized. If satinized pieces still have the original painted floral decorations, they will fetch up to 25% more than the prices listed for them. So far, only a few collectors think frosted Old Colony is beautiful; but I have noticed lately that more are noticing it because of price — or perhaps because "blending" has become more fashionable.

The flower bowl with crystal frog becomes a candy jar with a cover added in place of the frog. It was advertised both ways. That cover is the same as fits the butter dish or bonbon as Hocking actually listed it. The 7" comport becomes a footed candy with a cookie lid added. This piece was listed as a covered comport; but today, many dealers call it a footed candy jar. Since both these lids fit two items, it does not take a brainchild to figure why there is a lid shortage today. There are two styles of 7¾" and 9½" bowls. Some are ribbed up the side and some are not. The smaller, non-ribbed salad bowl doubles as the butter bottom. Both sizes of ribbed bowls are harder to find than their non-ribbed counterparts. Moulds were expensive. It was a frequent practice for as many pieces as possible to be obtained from as few moulds as possible.

The correct 9" comport in Old Colony has a rayed base. There is a similar comport that also measures 9". This "aspirant" has a plain foot and was probably made by Standard or Lancaster Glass. Both have been pictured in earlier editions. Both Lancaster and Standard had very similar designs, but their glass generally was better quality and rings when gently tapped on the edge with your finger. Hocking's Old Colony makes a thud sound. If the piece is not shown in my listing, or is in any color other than pink or crystal, the likelihood of your having an unknown Old Colony piece is doubtful.

	Pink		Pink
* Bowl, 6⅜", cereal	30.00	Flower bowl, crystal frog	30.00
Bowl, 7¾", plain	30.00	Plate, 7¼", salad	30.00
Bowl, 7¾", ribbed, salad	67.50	Plate, 8¼", luncheon	24.00
Bowl, 8¼", crystal	12.00	Plate, 10½", dinner	37.50
Bowl, 9½", plain	30.00	Plate, 10½", grill	25.00
Bowl, 9½", ribbed	32.00	Plate, 10½", 3-part relish	25.00
** Bowl, 10½", 3 legs, frosted $65.00	265.00	Plate, 13", solid lace	65.00
Butter dish or bonbon with cover	70.00	Plate, 13", 4-part, solid lace	65.00
Butter dish bottom, 7¾"	30.00	Platter, 12¾"	42.00
Butter dish top	40.00	Platter, 12¾", 5-part	40.00
** Candlesticks, pair, frosted $95.00	365.00	Relish dish, 7½", 3-part, deep	80.00
Candy jar and cover, ribbed	50.00	Saucer	12.00
Comport, 7"	30.00	** Sherbet, footed	120.00
Comport, 7", and cover, footed	65.00	Sugar	30.00
Comport, 9"	995.00	Tumbler, 3½", 5 ounce, flat	195.00
Cookie jar and cover, frosted $60.00	80.00	Tumbler, 4½", 9 ounce, flat	25.00
Creamer	30.00	Tumbler, 5", 10½ ounce, footed	100.00
Cup	28.00	Vase, 7", frosted $90.00	795.00
Fish bowl, 1 gallon, 8 ounce (crystal only)	35.00		

* Officially listed as cereal or cream soup, green $75.00   ** Price is for absolute mint condition

OLD ENGLISH, "THREADING," INDIANA GLASS COMPANY, Late 1920s

Colors: green, amber, pink, crystal, crystal with flashed colors, and forest green

Old English can be assembled in sets of green and possibly amber. Unfortunately, luncheon sets cannot be gathered, as there are no cups, saucers, or plates available. All pieces listed are found in green. Some pieces have never been found in amber. That does not mean they were never created. Amber Old English is a deep color more indicative of Cambridge or New Martinsville products which collectors find so enticing. Most of the amber pieces I have owned over the years have found enthusiastic buyers, but green is simpler to buy or sell.

Pink Old English is scarce with only the center-handled server, cheese and cracker, and sherbets found occasionally. Additional pieces in pink exist, but infrequently surface. I did find a pink pitcher and tumbler (below); it was only the second pink pitcher I had ever seen. Crystal Old English is found with artistic deco adornments; undecorated crystal is rarely seen.

Old English footed pieces are more obtainable than flat items. I have not seen a green center-handled server in almost 25 years. We shipped one to Georgia and it arrived with tire tracks on the box and several hundred pieces inside. I told the customer that I'd find him another one and I hope he isn't holding his breath, as I have not seen another.

There are two styles of sherbets. One is pictured in green (cone shaped) and the other in pink (straight sided). Both large and small berry bowls and the flat candy dish are insufficient in supply. Sugar and candy jar lids have the same cloverleaf-type knob as the pitcher. The flat candy lid is comparable in size to the pitcher lid; but that pitcher lid is notched in the bottom rim to allow for pouring. You cannot co-mingle the two lids since the candy lid is not notched. That flat candy is often found in a metal holder.

A fan vase is the only piece I have ever seen in dark green. A flashed-lavender footed candy bottom is pictured. Does anyone have a lid to match? We have recently discovered that the crystal egg cup is a Hazel Atlas look-alike!

	Pink, Green, Amber
Bowl, 4", flat	25.00
Bowl, 9", footed fruit	40.00
Bowl, 9½", flat	38.00
Candlesticks, 4", pair	40.00
Candy dish and cover, flat	60.00
Candy jar with lid	65.00
Compote, 3½" tall, 6⅜" across, 2-handle	22.50
Compote, 3½" tall, 7" across	25.00
Compote, 3½", cheese for plate	20.00
Creamer	20.00
Fruit stand, 11", footed	45.00
Goblet, 5¾", 8 ounce	35.00
Pitcher	95.00
Pitcher and cover	155.00
Plate, indent for compote	20.00
Sandwich server, center handle	55.00
Sherbet, 2 styles	20.00
Sugar	17.50
Sugar cover	37.50
Tumbler, 4½", footed	28.00

	Pink, Green, Amber
Tumbler, 5½", footed	45.00
Vase, 5⅜", fan type, 7" wide	75.00
Vase, 8", footed, 4½" wide	55.00
Vase, 8¼", footed, 4¼" wide	55.00
Vase, 12", footed	95.00

OLIVE, LINE #134, IMPERIAL GLASS COMPANY, Late 1930s

Colors: red, light blue, emerald, pink

Imperial's Olive Line #134 is a smaller pattern whose major claim to fame is its confusion with Imperial's Old English Line #166. Think round olives and that should help. Olive also has circles in its motif near the bottom of the pieces and grooved feet. Old English Line #166 has elongated indentations reaching upward from its base with olive type balls. The plates in Old English, however, do have a kind of ribbed flower center design. You will notice that the plates in Olive Line #134 have plain centers. Confusing? It is! Actually, they are so compatible that should you care to collect both lines as one pattern, few will notice and you can get some tumblers from Old English that you will not have with Olive. Olive has handled mugs. I will try to show a piece of Old English next time for comparison sake.

	Emerald, Pink	Blue, Red
Bowl, 6½", flared, footed	16.00	22.00
Bowl, 7", rose (cupped)	22.00	32.00
Bowl, 7", shallow	15.00	25.00
Bowl, 9", fruit, pedestal foot	20.00	35.00
Bowl, 9", bun or fruit tray	20.00	35.00
Bowl, 9", shallow	25.00	35.00
Bowl, 10¼", salad	30.00	45.00
Candle, 2½"	15.00	22.00
Candy jar w/lid	30.00	40.00
Compote, 6"	10.00	20.00

	Emerald, Pink	Blue, Red
Compote, 6½"	12.50	22.50
Creamer	10.00	15.00
Cup	9.00	12.00
Mayonnaise	15.00	18.00
Plate, 6"	4.00	5.50
Plate, 8"	8.00	10.00
Plate, 12"	18.00	25.00
Saucer	3.00	4.00
Sugar	10.00	15.00

161

"ORCHID," PADEN CITY GLASS COMPANY, Early 1930s

Colors: yellow, cobalt blue, crystal, green, amber, pink, red, and black

"Orchid," as well as most other patterns produced by Paden City, recently spawned vast price increases. A book with astonishing prices and a few strong buyers on Internet auctions aided this. Things have settled down and those prices haven't held up well. For instance, I was trying to sell items for $15.00 that listed for $90.00 and no one was interested. That's when you begin to recognize that the pricing is askew. I have always stated that the worst person to price a book is a collector or owner of the items pictured. That is one of the reasons I have dealers input in pricing, as they are more aware of what they can get for a piece they've sold repeatedly and are not as personally involved. In any case, prices are settling back into reality, but some of the pieces sold during the rush to enhance collections may well take years to recoup the prices paid.

There are at least three distinct "Orchid" arrangements found on Paden City blanks. Collectors do not mind blending these varieties because so little of any one is found.

All Paden City patterns were more restricted in production runs than those of some of the larger glass companies. Orchid growers may have sparked the interest for this one pattern, but the Internet has unveiled many pieces of these smaller patterns (like Orchid) that few previously had a chance to discover. Instead of dozens buying at shows, there are now thousands eyeing pieces. This "Orchid" pattern was not produced in hundreds of thousands of pieces, as was Heisey's Orchid. Every piece of Paden's "Orchid" we have displayed at shows has sold not long after the show opened — if not before.

Many believed that "Orchid" etched pieces turned up only on #412 Line, the square, Crow's Foot blank made by Paden City. However, "Orchid" has turned up on the #890 rounded blank as well. "Orchid" may well be possible on any Paden City blank. The pattern displays better on the transparent pastel colors, but they do not seem to be as popular with the buying public. A few pieces of "Orchid" are being found on black. Red and cobalt blue seem to be the preferred colors.

New reports of etched Paden City patterns are the norm because most pieces were listed in catalogs with no etchings; and until a piece shows up with a particular etching, there is little way to know if it exists in that pattern.

	All other colors	Red, Black, Cobalt Blue
Bowl, 4⅞", square	30.00	55.00
Bowl, 8½", 2-handle	75.00	135.00
Bowl, 8¾", square	75.00	125.00
Bowl, 10", footed, square	95.00	195.00
Bowl, 11", square	85.00	195.00
Cake stand, square, 2" high	75.00	150.00
Candlesticks, 5¾", pair	125.00	210.00
Candy with lid, 6½", square, 3-part	110.00	195.00
Candy with lid, cloverleaf, 3-part	95.00	195.00
Comport, 3¼" tall, 6¼" wide	25.00	55.00
Comport, 6⅝" tall, 7" wide	65.00	135.00
Creamer	55.00	100.00
Ice bucket, 6"	110.00	225.00
Mayonnaise, 3-piece	85.00	165.00
Plate, 8½", square		125.00
Sandwich server, center handle	75.00	125.00
Sugar	50.00	100.00
Vase, 8"	110.00	275.00
Vase, 10"	135.00	295.00

OVIDE, "NEW CENTURY," HAZEL ATLAS GLASS COMPANY, 1930 – 1935

Colors: green, black, white Platonite trimmed with fired-on colors in 1950s

Varieties of decorated Ovide sets are available if you wish to start an economical collection to use. Finding any specific decoration may prove to be a chore, but possibly less so with the Internet. I had a collector in Texas tell me he had over 40 different patterns on Ovide; he promised further enlightenment. Separating these decorations into time eras for my books has been a task. Call the decorated white one "Dutch Windmills" due to our lack of an actual name. This is priced below under the decorated white heading. I am showing the "Art Deco" design here for the first time in years, so that all those who have never seen it can — in a creamer and sugar set.

Hazel Atlas used a flock of different patterns on this popular Platonite, including one of flying geese. One of the more popular, judging from the amount found today, was the black floral design with red and yellow edge trim. That set encompassed kitchenware items (stacking sets and mixing bowls) as well as a dinnerware line. You can see later made patterns in *Collectible Glassware from the 40s, 50s, 60s....* For some of these I have found documentation for factory names. By the 40s, companies had consistently latched onto the selling value of giving glassware a name rather than merely a number.

Very little black, transparent green, or plain yellow Ovide are ever seen, but there are a few collectors asking for it. A luncheon set should be possible; but it would be simpler to put together an Ovide set in black or yellow Cloverleaf, which would be admittedly more costly but more easily found. Depression glass dealers are prone to bring the Cloverleaf pattern to shows, but leave the plain Ovide home.

	Black	Green	Decorated White	Art Deco		Black	Green	Decorated White	Art Deco
Bowl, 4¾", berry			8.00		Plate, 8", luncheon		3.00	14.00	75.00
Bowl, 5½", cereal			13.00		Plate, 9", dinner			20.00	
Bowl, 8", large berry			22.50		Platter, 11"			22.50	
Candy dish and cover	45.00	22.00	35.00		Salt and pepper, pair	27.50	27.50	24.00	
Cocktail, footed, fruit	5.00	4.00			Saucer	3.50	2.50	6.00	25.00
Creamer	6.50	4.50	17.50	125.00	Sherbet	6.50	3.00	14.00	100.00
Cup	7.50	3.50	12.50	100.00	Sugar, open	6.50	6.00	17.50	125.00
Plate, 6", sherbet		2.50	6.00		Tumbler			17.50	125.00

OYSTER AND PEARL, ANCHOR HOCKING GLASS CORPORATION, 1938 – 1940

Colors: pink, crystal, Royal Ruby, Vitrock, and Vitrock with fired-on pink, blue, and green

In the 32 years I have been writing, not one new discovery of Oyster and Pearl has appeared since my first book in 1972. So, with fanfare, let me introduce you to the newly unearthed large ruffled bowl pictured on the right. Admittedly, I would have preferred pink, Royal Ruby, or even a fired-on Vitrock, but its crystal for now! Know that the colored varieties may exist. It was a rather boring day of shopping in Ohio until Cathy spotted this bowl. She knew that crystal was not commonly found, but had no idea that the ruffled top was the exciting part. You don't have to know everything to spot something rare or different! Be on the lookout for your own discovery.

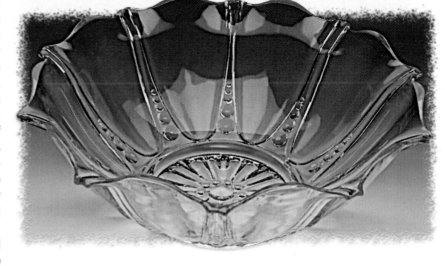

Royal Ruby Oyster and Pearl is pictured under the Royal Ruby pattern shown on page 205, but prices are also listed here. Pink Oyster and Pearl has regularly been used as harmonizing pieces for other Depression glass patterns. That pink relish dish and candlesticks sell well since they are reasonably priced in comparison to other patterns. Though not as true as it once was, Oyster and Pearl prices are generally cheaper than most patterns in this book.

Note: The Oyster and Pearl relish dish measures 11½" when the handles are included. I mention that because of letters I receive saying someone's dish is 11½" and all I list is a 10½" relish. All measurements in this book are specified without handles unless otherwise mentioned. Glass companies rarely measured the handles or included them in their measurements. I have begun to make a point to talk about measurements with handles in my commentary since I have been getting so many letters about measurements on pieces that I have already listed. There is no divided bowl in Oyster and Pearl; it was (and is) listed as a relish.

Pink coloration fired over Vitrock was called Dusty Rose; the fired green was called Springtime Green by Hocking. Most collectors love these shades; but I've met a few who abhor them. The undecorated Vitrock is occasionally seen, and is not as enthralling. A few pieces have been located with fired blue, but this is very scarce.

I have seen a few crystal pieces decorated, and most of them were trimmed in red. They sell faster than undecorated crystal. The 10½" fruit bowl is a great salad bowl and the 13½" plate makes a great server; several collectors have used these for a small punch bowl and liner. You will have to decide what punch cups to use.

The spouted, 5½" bowl is often referred to as "heart" shaped. It might serve as a gravy or sauce boat although most people use them for candy dishes. The same bowl is found without the spout in Royal Ruby, although I mistakenly listed it in the past with a spout. It was enlightening to find that later authors have made that same mistake. This bowl always has a spout in Dusty Rose and Springtime Green when you can find them.

I had a report of a "lamp" made from candleholders; it turned out to be two candles glued together at their bases to form a ball. Obviously, someone had more time to play around recently than I do. It was an entertaining and innovative idea. I once saw another self-produced "lamp" that had been cut down from an obviously damaged Miss America tall candy, leaving enough to make a nice lamp. I remember thinking that at least the item had been salvaged and made useful and attractive again. Evidently, the foot had been broken off because that end had been carefully ground to accommodate lamp parts. So, before you pitch away glass as useless, reconsider. It may yet have a function — if no more than becoming a beautiful work of art as seen in the glass window shown at the front of this book!

	Crystal, Pink	Royal Ruby	White and Fired-On Green or Pink
Bowl, 5¼", heart-shaped, 1-handled	15.00		15.00
Bowl, 5½", 1-handled		22.00	
Bowl, 6½", deep-handled	20.00	30.00	
Bowl, 10½", deep fruit	25.00	60.00	28.00
Bowl, 10½", ruffled edge	35.00		
Candle holder, 3½", pair	40.00	65.00	30.00
Plate, 13½", sandwich	20.00	55.00	
Relish dish, 10½", oblong, divided	20.00		

"PARROT," SYLVAN, FEDERAL GLASS COMPANY, 1931 – 1932

Colors: green, amber; some crystal and blue

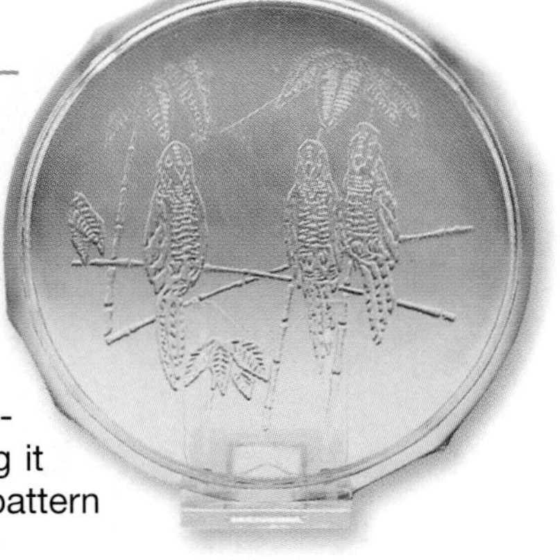

"Parrot" is one of those Depression glass patterns having numerous rare pieces, which has a record of rapid price increases and then plateaus before prices take off again. When several collectors want "Parrot" at the same time, prices increase very rapidly. I have watched these cyclical trends for over 30 years in several patterns.

Parrot pitchers have disappeared from the market at any price. Prices for the few sold in the last few years have reached a ballpark figure of $3,000.00. A few consumers were willing to pay that price and did. Originally, a cache of 37 was found in the basement of an old hardware store in central Ohio. Today, there are still more than 30 in existence. At least a couple of those original ones broke. One cracked from a dealer dusting it out and bumping a diamond ring in a thin spot. The whole pitcher is thin, but where the pattern is designed, it gets even thinner.

There are two types of "Parrot" hot plates. One, pictured as a pattern shot, is created like the pointed edged Madrid; the other, round, is moulded like the one in Georgian. One of these round ones has materialized in amber.

The amber butter dish, creamer, and sugar lid are all more difficult to find than those in green; and even fewer mint butter dish tops or sugar lids have surfaced. Those non-mint ones are available. (Damaged glassware should not bring mint prices.) Frequently found butter bottoms have an indented ledge for the top. The jam dish is the same size as the butter bottom, but without that ledge. The jam dish has never been viewed in green, but is somewhat widespread in amber. There are fewer collectors of amber "Parrot"; so, prices are not as precarious and affected by demand, as are those for green.

Notice that "Parrot" tumblers are moulded on Madrid-like shapes except for the heavy-footed tumbler, whose pointy edges easily chip. The supply of those heavy, footed tumblers (in both colors), green water tumblers, and thin, flat iced teas in amber has met present demand. A woman approached me in Texas and showed me a picture of six heavy, footed tumblers she had recently purchased at an estate sale for a very small price. She made a huge profit on a pattern that she had never bought before. Apparently, the thin, moulded, footed tumbler did not accept the "Parrot" design favorably and the heavier version was made. The thin, 10 ounce footed tumbler has only been found in amber. Prices for both those last two tumblers have stayed stable during other "Parrot" price increases.

Yes, I know the shaker pictured is cracked. It's my way to give worthless old glass a function. You still get to see size, shape, and color, and a collector gets to enjoy a good piece. Actually, many dealers now offer me their damaged, hard-to-find pieces, at reasonable prices so I can photograph them for my books. Several artisans I've talked with conserve, too, using damaged Depression glass in jewelry, ceramic decoration, glass window art, and the like. There's great appreciation for this glassware and some find a way to reclaim even the damaged.

Blue "Parrot" sherbets turn up occasionally, but no other pieces of blue have been found. The blue is the same shade as the Madonna blue of Madrid.

In talking to another dealer about things I see sitting that were there five years ago and remarking that there is no way any profit is made, he chimed in with a tale about someone putting for sale a large set of green three years ago. A week or two later, a serious buyer came in and offered "book" price for all of it. He declined since he had priced some of the harder to find pieces for 20% to 30% more than book. Today, all of the harder to find pieces are gone; but stacks of flatware remain. Perhaps he's gotten all his money out of the good pieces and all that other stuff is "free." More likely, he's still got money tied up in what isn't selling. I believe you can well afford to take a lesser profit fast, turn that profit into four or five more profits in several years time, and come out way ahead.

	Green	Amber		Green	Amber
Bowl, 5", berry	30.00	25.00	Plate, 9", dinner	60.00	50.00
Bowl, 7", soup	55.00	40.00	Plate, 10½", round, grill	35.00	
Bowl, 8", large berry	100.00	100.00	Plate, 10½", square, grill		35.00
Bowl, 10", oval vegetable	70.00	80.00	Plate, 10¼", square (crystal only)	26.00	
Butter dish and cover	450.00	1,350.00	Platter, 11¼", oblong	65.00	75.00
Butter dish bottom	75.00	200.00	Salt and pepper, pair	295.00	
Butter dish top	375.00	1,150.00	Saucer	15.00	17.50
Creamer, footed	60.00	95.00	* Sherbet, footed cone	25.00	22.50
Cup	42.00	45.00	Sherbet, 4¼" high	1,500.00	
Hot plate, 5", pointed	895.00	995.00	Sugar	40.00	50.00
Hot plate, 5", round	995.00		Sugar cover	185.00	550.00
Jam dish, 7"		40.00	Tumbler, 4¼", 10 ounce	200.00	135.00
Pitcher, 8½", 80 ounce	3,150.00		Tumbler, 5½", 12 ounce	235.00	165.00
Plate, 5¾", sherbet	35.00	25.00	Tumbler, 5¾", footed, heavy	200.00	135.00
Plate, 7½", salad	40.00		Tumbler, 5½", 10 oz., ftd (Madrid mould)		195.00

*Blue $225.00

"PARTY LINE," "SODA FOUNTAIN," LINE #191, 191½, #192, PADEN CITY GLASS COMPANY, Late 1920s – 1951; CANTON GLASS COMPANY, 1950s

Colors: amber, crystal, green, pink (Cheriglo), red, some turquoise green

Collectors have asked me for years to add this Paden City line in my book. The company touted it in their advertisement as being "the most complete tableware line in America." However, Jerry Barnett reported in his Paden City book that factory workers called this "Soda Fountain," certainly an apt name judging by the abundance of those type pieces made. Actual dinnerware items are not very forthcoming even after having been made into the 1950s.

With so many established Depression glassware patterns vanishing from the collecting market, I'm beginning to see this pattern being gathered by collectors and observant dealers are carrying it to shows. Green is the color most often found and most collected. This would make a great collection for use around decorative bars or soda fountains popular with collectors today. Just yesterday, I found eight green parfaits at an antique fair and my wife spotted six sherbets at a flea mall not long ago. One thing I have noticed, you rarely find "Party Line" one or two pieces at a time, as is the case of most patterns.

If you've been collecting this for years and have insights, other than those multitude of tumblers manufactured are hard to come by, please let me know.

	*All colors			*All colors			*All colors
Banana split, 8½", oval	25.00	Custard, 6 ounce	8.00	Shaker, sugar	155.00
Bottle, 22 ounce, wine w/stopper	50.00	Ice tub & pail	60.00	Sherbet, 3½ or 4½ ounce, footed	10.00
Bottle, 48 ounce, water, no stopper	50.00	Ice tub, 6½", w/tab handle	50.00	Shaker, sugar	155.00
Bowl, 4½", nappy	8.00	Jar w/lid, high, crushed fruit	75.00	Sherbet, 3½ or 4½ ounce, footed	10.00
Bowl, 6½", berry	10.00	Marmalade, w/cover, 12 ounce	35.00	Sherbet, 6 ounce, high foot	12.50
Bowl, 7", mixing	20.00	Mayo, 6", footed	25.00	Stem, 9 ounce	15.00
Bowl, 8", mixing	25.00	Parfait, 5 ounce (2 styles)	12.50	Sugar, 7 ounce	10.00
Bowl, 9", berry	25.00	Pitcher, 30 ounce, jug, w/cover	70.00	Sugar w/id, 10 ounce, hotel	22.50
Bowl, 9", low foot comport, flare	27.50	Pitcher, 32 ounce, grape juice w/lid	100.00	Sundae, 4 or 6 ounce, tulip	15.00
Bowl, 9", mixing	30.00	Pitcher, 36 ounce, measure w/5½"		Sundae, 9 ounce, crimped	20.00
Bowl, 10½", high foot, flare	35.00	reamer	125.00	Syrup, 8 ounce	50.00
Bowl, 11", low foot comport	35.00	Pitcher, 70 ounce, jug w or w/optic,		Syrup w/glass cover, 12 ounce	80.00
Bowl, 11", vegetable, flare	35.00	w/lid	135.00	Tumbler, 1½ oz., footed, cordial	16.00
Butter box, w/cover, round flat lid	60.00	Plate 6"	6.00	Tumbler, 2½ or 3½ oz., ftd, cocktail	12.50
Candy, footed w/cover	35.00	Plate, 8"	10.00	Tumbler, 3 ounce, wine	12.00
Cigarette holder w/cover, footed	45.00	Plate, 10½" cracker, w/covered		Tumbler, 4½ ounce, juice	8.00
Cocktail shaker, 18 ounce, w/lid	65.00	cheese	65.00	Tumbler, 5 ounce, coke	12.00
Cologne, 1½ ounce	60.00	Saucer, 5¾"	3.00	Tumbler, 6 ounce, 3 styles	12.00
Creamer, 7 ounce	10.00	Server, 10", center handle	40.00	Tumbler, 7 ounce, 2 styles	12.00
Cup, 6 ounce	8.00	Shaker, pair	35.00	Tumbler, 8 ounce, 3 styles	14.00
				Tumbler, 9 ounce, barrel	12.00
				Tumbler, 10 ounce, 3 styles	12.00
				Tumbler, 12 ounce, blown	15.00
				Tumbler, 12 ounce, 4 styles	14.00
				Tumbler, 14 ounce, 3 styles	14.00
				Vase, 6", fan	40.00
				Vase, 7", fan	45.00
				Vase, 7", crimped	45.00

*Double the price for red and 50% for crystal.

PATRICIAN, "SPOKE," FEDERAL GLASS COMPANY, 1933 – 1937

Colors: pink, green, crystal, and amber ("Golden Glo")

Amber Patrician was broadly marketed. When I first started learning about Depression glass, Patrician was one of the few patterns I could easily find in my area. Only Madrid was found as frequently. I discovered my mom had stacks of plates stored in the ceiling cabinets (received with the purchase of flour when she first married) and had been giving them away with meals sent home with her daycare help. My dad had been given a set for getting additional subscribers for a newspaper as a boy.

Besides availability to recommend it, Patrician has never been reproduced as has Madrid, et al. Sets of green or pink Patrician can possibly be assembled with fortitude, but at greater cost. The plentiful amber, 10½" "dinner" plates were premiums with 20-pound sacks of flour for use as cake plates. Exhibits of these plates sat on the counter near the cash register, and when you paid for your flour, you were handed one of these as an additional benefit. When I started buying Depression glass over 30 years ago, that was known as a dinner plate.

The jam dish is a butter bottom without the indented ledge for the top as in Federal's "Parrot" and Sharon patterns. It measures 6¾" wide and stands 1¼" deep. This is the same measurement as the butter bottom; however, Patrician cereal bowls are often sold as jam dishes. Cereals are 6" in diameter and 1¾" deep. Prices differ only slightly today; but be aware of which is which. In the past, jam dishes were considered rare, and sold for almost double the price of the cereal. Today, collectors seek only one jam dish and multiples of the cereals that have now attained the price range of the jam. That is another version of how pricing concepts have evolved.

There is more green Patrician offered than either pink or crystal. Even so, green dinner plates are sparse. Completing a set of pink is problematical, but it might not be feasible in crystal since not all pieces have turned up.

Amber pitchers were purportedly made in two styles. One has a moulded handle. If anyone owns an applied handle amber pitcher, let me know as I am beginning to doubt it exists. In crystal and green, the applied handled pitcher is the norm.

In Patrician, mint condition sugar lids, jam dishes, footed tumblers, cookie or butter bottoms, and footed tumblers are harder to find than other pieces. The heavy cookie and butter tops have fared better than the thinner bottoms. Check sugar lids for signs of repair. Many a glass grinder has cut his teeth on those and some cut them badly. This is another pattern where saucers are harder to find than cups.

	Amber, Crystal	Pink	Green
Bowl, 4¾", cream soup	16.00	22.00	22.00
Bowl, 5", berry	14.00	12.00	13.00
Bowl, 6", cereal	25.00	25.00	32.00
Bowl, 8½", large berry	42.00	35.00	40.00
Bowl, 10", oval vegetable	33.00	30.00	35.00
Butter dish and cover	95.00	225.00	140.00
Butter dish bottom	60.00	175.00	80.00
Butter dish top	30.00	50.00	60.00
Cookie jar and cover	85.00		675.00
Creamer, footed	11.00	12.00	15.00
Cup	9.00	15.00	14.00
Jam dish	30.00	30.00	40.00
Pitcher, 8", 75 ounce, moulded handle	135.00	125.00	165.00
Pitcher, 8¼", 75 ounce, applied handle	*110.00	150.00	175.00

	Amber, Crystal	Pink	Green
Plate, 6", sherbet	9.00	8.00	10.00
Plate, 7½", salad	13.00	15.00	20.00
Plate, 9", luncheon	13.00	16.00	16.00
Plate, 10½", dinner	8.00	45.00	45.00
Plate, 10½", grill	14.00	15.00	20.00
Platter, 11½", oval	32.00	25.00	30.00
Salt and pepper, pair	60.00	120.00	80.00
Saucer	9.50	10.00	9.50
Sherbet	12.00	17.00	14.00
Sugar	9.00	9.00	15.00
Sugar cover	60.00	70.00	85.00
Tumbler, 4", 5 ounce	30.00	33.00	33.00
Tumbler, 4¼", 9 ounce	28.00	26.00	30.00
Tumbler, 5½", 14 ounce	45.00	45.00	55.00
Tumbler, 5¼", 8 ounce, footed	60.00		75.00

*Crystal only

"PATRICK," LANCASTER GLASS COMPANY, Early 1930s

Colors: yellow and pink

Luncheon sets of yellow "Patrick" are about the only pieces being found in this pattern, although I did stumble across a center-handled server. I had reports of some crystal being seen, but was unable to confirm this. Look for a piece for me. A few pink "Patrick" luncheon sets are turning up in the St. Louis area but the price has scared away all but enthusiastic collectors even though prices have weakened quite a bit for pink. Very few pieces of pink have come up for sale recently, which could account for that. Pink "Patrick" sugar or creamers had been selling for $75.00 each, but new collectors seem to get sticker shock from that price. "Patrick" was a limited production before anyone ever contemplated the idea of restrictive productions in order to sell merchandise for more money.

The "Patrick" three-footed candy is shaped like the Jubilee one. The bottoms of these candies are not etched with the pattern only being found on the top. "Patrick" serving pieces are rare. The pattern is bold on the 11" console bowl. I recently bought a clever comport that I will have to research a little before listing. That's the tease for the next book! There are serving pieces to be found in other patterns on the same blanks used for "Patrick" and Jubilee. However, comparable pieces sell for less than those with "Patrick" mould etchings and Jubilee cuttings which are higher due to demand and collectibility and not necessarily rarity.

	Pink	Yellow		Pink	Yellow
Bowl, 9", handled fruit	175.00	135.00	Mayonnaise, 3-piece	195.00	150.00
Bowl, 11", console	165.00	145.00	Plate, 7", sherbet	20.00	12.00
Candlesticks, pair	195.00	150.00	Plate, 7½", salad	25.00	20.00
Candy dish, 3-footed	225.00	225.00	Plate, 8", luncheon	35.00	22.00
Cheese & cracker set	135.00	110.00	Saucer	20.00	12.00
Creamer	55.00	35.00	Sherbet, 4¾"	65.00	55.00
Cup	55.00	32.00	Sugar	55.00	35.00
Goblet, 4", cocktail	80.00	80.00	Tray, 11", 2-handled	75.00	60.00
Goblet, 4¾", 6 ounce, juice	70.00	65.00	Tray, 11", center-handled	125.00	100.00
Goblet, 6", 10 ounce, water	70.00	75.00			

"PEACOCK REVERSE," "PHEASANT," "DELILAH BIRD," LINE #411, #412 & #991,
PADEN CITY GLASS COMPANY, 1930s

Colors: cobalt blue, red, amber, yellow, green, pink, black, and crystal

Paden City's Line #412 ("Crow's Foot"), Line #991 ("Penny Line"), and Line #411 (Mrs. "B" — square shapes with the corners cut off) comprise the standard lines on which "Peacock Reverse" has been found. Add to those an octagonal #701 Triumph plate, and no telling what other blank may turn up with this etching. Paden City lines have various etched patterns ascribed to them. When you spot a piece from a distance, you are always wondering what etch will be found.

The #701 eight-sided plate is the only pink plate I have owned in "Peacock Reverse." There are bound to be others. That rich red seems to be the color most encountered. We turned up two colored sugars, but have yet to spot a creamer in over 20 years of searching. Few collectors of cups and saucers have "Peacock Reverse" represented. Like Cupid, cup and saucers may be the rarest pieces in the pattern. A lipped, footed comport which measures 4½" tall and 7⅜" wide has been called a gravy by collectors. You see this red comport regularly without an etching.

There are two styles of candy dishes. Both have patterns only on the lids, as is the standard procedure for Paden City candies. The plain bases can be discovered with lids sporting other etches or even plain. That should make bases easier to find, but it hasn't been the case for me. Prices are not set by color as much as with other patterns. Pieces are so infrequently offered, collectors welcome any piece in any color, including crystal.

You could conceivably find this etch on almost any piece listed under "Crow's Foot" (squared) or "Orchid." I would appreciate being apprised of unlisted pieces or colors you see. I was informed by a Paden City worker that the workers at the plants called all these bird patterns "pheasants." When you look at them closely, we may well be plucking the wrong bird!

Those designs, which show white in the photograph, have been accentuated with chalk so you can see them better.

	All colors		All colors
Bowl, 4⅞", square	50.00	Plate, 5¾", sherbet	25.00
Bowl, 8¾", square	125.00	Plate, 8½", luncheon	60.00
Bowl, 8¾", square with handles	125.00	Plate 10⅜", 2-handled	100.00
Bowl, 11¾", console	150.00	Saucer	40.00
Candlesticks, 5¾", square base, pair	175.00	Sherbet, 4⅝" tall, 3⅜" diameter	75.00
Candy dish, 6½", square	195.00	Sherbet, 4⅞" tall, 3⅝" diameter	75.00
Comport, 3¼" high, 6¼" wide	75.00	Server, center-handled	75.00
Comport, 4¼" high, 7⅜" wide	85.00	Sugar, 2¾", flat	110.00
Creamer, 2¾", flat	110.00	Tumbler, 4", 10 ounce, flat	95.00
Cup	150.00	Vase, 10"	250.00

"PEACOCK & WILD ROSE," "NORA BIRD," "PHEASANT LINE," LINE #300, PADEN CITY GLASS COMPANY, 1929 – 1930s

Colors: pink, green, amber, cobalt blue, black, light blue, crystal, and red

At a photography session where a pattern was being outlined with chalk to make it show in the photograph, my wife made a fascinating discovery about Paden City's "Peacock and Wild Rose" and "Nora Bird." They are the same pattern with "Nora Bird" being a condensed (or sectioned off) version of the larger "Peacock and Wild Rose" etching. Examine a tall vase; you will see the small bird at the bottom of the design that appears on the pieces formerly known separately as "Nora Bird." The bird on each piece can be found in flight or getting ready to take flight. Obviously, the entire larger pattern would not fit on the smaller pieces; so, a condensed portion was used. That is why creamers, sugars, and luncheon pieces have never been found in "Peacock and Wild Rose." These pieces from Line #300 have formerly been attributed to a separate pattern when they are from the same etch. Copious amounts of accessory pieces in "Peacock and Wild Rose" can now be combined with cups, saucers, creamers, sugars, and luncheon plates of "Nora Bird" to give a complete pattern. Cups and saucers are rarely seen, but are, at least, possible.

Pheasant patterns were popular during this era and a reader wrote to tell me that old time Paden City plant workers referred to any of the bird etches as "pheasant line." This agrees with the information I received regarding "Peacock Reverse."

The #300 line, flat, three-part candy dish lid also fits the footed 5¼" candy dish. There is also an octagonal flat candy pictured in an earlier book from the #701 Triumph line. Finding a candy in "Peacock and Wild Rose" should be easier now with three known. The green tray below was listed as a #210 Line refreshment tray. A few pieces of light blue have been found including a rolled edge bowl. That bowl recently sold for nearly $500.00.

There are two styles of creamers and sugars (pointed handles and rounded handles). Both types are also found with "Cupid" etch. There is an individual (smaller) sugar and creamer with rounded handles. One green set resides in Oklahoma. Additionally, a collector in Texas has found two green tumblers that are 2¼", 3 ounces; and 5¼", 10 ounces.

Be sure to check out the 8½", 64 ounce pitcher in *Very Rare Glassware of the Depression Years, Sixth Series.* There are very possibly more pieces in this pattern than I have listed; please let me know if you find something else.

"PEACOCK & WILD ROSE"

	All colors		All colors
Bowl, 8½", flat	135.00	Ice tub, 4¾"	210.00
Bowl, 8½", fruit, oval, footed	225.00	Ice tub, 6"	210.00
Bowl, 8¾", footed	175.00	Mayonnaise and liner	110.00
Bowl, 9½", center-handled	165.00	Pitcher, 5" high	395.00
Bowl, 9½", footed	185.00	Pitcher, 8½", 64 ounce	495.00
Bowl, 10½", center-handled	125.00	Plate, 8"	25.00
Bowl, 10½", footed	195.00	Plate, cake, low foot	150.00
Bowl, 10½", fruit	185.00	Relish, 3-part	125.00
Bowl, 11", console	185.00	Saucer	20.00
Bowl, 14", console	195.00	Sugar, 4½", round handle	65.00
Candlestick, 5" wide, pair	180.00	Sugar, 5", pointed handle	65.00
Candlesticks, octagonal tops, pair	225.00	Tray, rectangular, handled	195.00
Candy dish w/cover, 6½", 3-part	195.00	Tumbler, 2¼", 3 ounce	60.00
Candy dish w/cover, 7"	250.00	Tumbler, 3"	65.00
Candy with lid, footed, 5¼" high	195.00	Tumbler, 4"	85.00
Cheese and cracker set	185.00	Tumbler, 4¾", footed	95.00
Comport, 3¼" tall, 6¼" wide	135.00	Tumbler, 5¼", 10 ounce	95.00
Creamer, 4½", round handle	65.00	Vase, 8¼", elliptical	395.00
Creamer, 5", pointed handle	65.00	Vase, 10", two styles	250.00
Cup	80.00	Vase, 12"	295.00
Ice bucket, 6"	225.00		

"PEBBLED RIM," LINE #707, L. E. SMITH GLASS COMPANY, 1930s

Colors: amber, green, pink

"Pebbled Rim" is an attractive L. E. Smith pattern that was marketed as a 40-piece dinner set. Presently, I know of two large sets being offered for sale for at least two years. Again, these owners are not pricing pieces individually; and therefore, collectors who would buy parts or pieces are ignoring such a large initial outlay for an entire set. In addition, both sets have a premium on them because they are large sets. Perhaps because of age they should be that expensive; but, right now, they are not and only a few collectors are presently seeking it. Demand drives prices. If there is little demand, huge prices are not going to fly.

The large, ruffled edge vegetable and deep salad bowls, as well as the platter appear to be the hardest pieces to locate, although any green is more difficult than pink. This simple pattern blends well with other patterns. In fact, I'm certain that accounts for the scarcity of some pieces. People are using them with other sets.

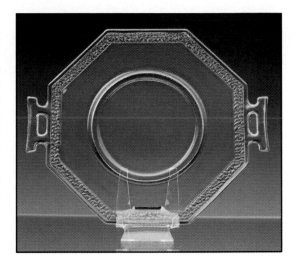

	All colors			All colors
Bowl, 9½", oval	28.00		Plate, 6", bread/butter	4.00
Bowl, berry	8.00		Plate, 7", salad	5.00
Bowl, ruffled edge vegetable, deep	30.00		Plate, 9", dinner	10.00
Bowl, ruffled edge vegetable, shallow	28.00		Plate, 9", two-handle	20.00
Candleholder	20.00		Platter, oval	22.00
Cream	13.00		Saucer	2.00
Cup (two styles)	7.50		Sugar	13.00

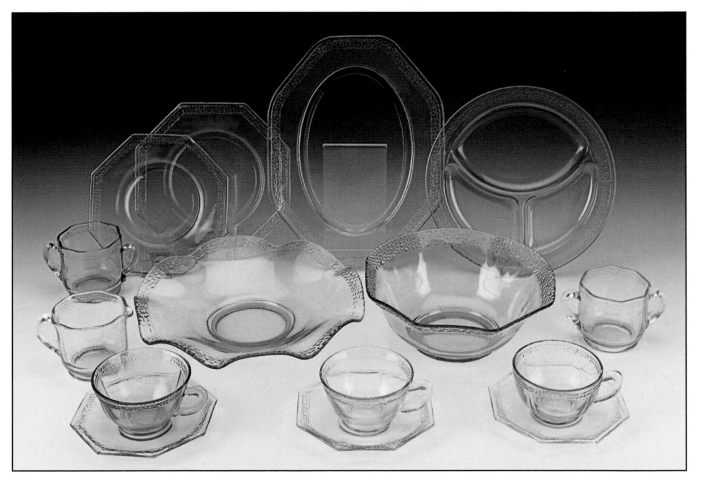

"PENNY LINE," LINE #991, PADEN CITY GLASS COMPANY, c. 1930

Colors: red, green, pink (Cheriglo), amber, primrose (light yellow), black, white, amethyst, royal blue

"Penny Line" is here courtesy of a dealer friend who found it, called to ask if I needed a photo and then packaged a piece of everything and shipped it to the studio. You cannot get service, or friends, any better than that. All collectors owe appreciation to generous people in the trade who assist teaching about glass in any way they can. Since age is beginning to take a toll on my eyes, memory, and energy levels, believe me, I can use all extra help!

Though I have seen it listed six times higher, the cobalt blue goblet price I have listed is more apt in today's market. The Deco age in which this pattern had its beginning was all about form, lines, and shapes. This circular, stacked rings appearance was a definite product of that time and should be appreciated as such by devotees of Depression wares.

Low foot apparently meant goblets with only one wafer and high foot pieces had two. If you have a pitcher, I need ounce sizes, which are not cataloged. The mayo was cataloged with a liner plate, which I assume was the 6" dessert plate also used as a sherbet liner. Notice the unusual handles on the cup. If you find additional pieces, I would appreciate the information.

	*All colors		*All colors
Bowl, finger	15.00	Shaker, pair	38.00
Candle	25.00	Sherbet, low foot	10.00
Creamer	12.50	Stem, 1¼ ounce, cordial	25.00
Cup	10.00	Stem, 3½ ounce, cocktail	12.50
Decanter, 22 ounce w/stopper	45.00	Stem, 3 ounce, wine	15.00
Goblet, low foot, grapefruit	15.00	Stem, 6 ounce, cocktail	12.50
Goblet, low foot, 9 ounce	15.00	Sugar	12.50
Goblet, high foot	17.50	Tray, rectangular, 2 handled, sugar/cream	25.00
Pitcher	55.00	Tumbler, 2½ ounce, wine	12.00
Plate, 6"	5.00	Tumbler, 5 ounce, juice	10.00
Plate, 8", salad	12.50	Tumbler, 9 ounce, table	12.00
Saucer	3.00	Tumbler, 12 ounce, tea	14.00
Server, 10½", center handle	35.00	*Add 50% for royal blue or red	

PETALWARE, MacBETH-EVANS GLASS COMPANY, 1930 – 1950

Colors: Monax, Cremax, pink, crystal, cobalt, and fired-on red, blue, green, and yellow

I have been mentioning red-trimmed Petalware Mountain Flowers decoration on Federal Star pitchers for several books. This time I am showing you both styles (satinized and plain). Enjoy! I had to buy six juice tumblers with the plain pitcher, as the South Carolina lady would not break up the set. I even had to promise to sell it that way after photography — so I did. The frosted pitcher was borrowed from a generous lady in Ohio, so you could see both.

Notice the original boxed set at right. Straight-sided tumblers with matching pastel bands were packed with these sets. Although these tumblers are not Petalware pattern, they were decorated to go with it. These are found in several sizes, all presently selling in the $7.00 to $10.00 range. I can only guarantee the boxed ones on the right are correct, but as long as the colored bands match the dinnerware, that is sufficient for most collectors. Unfortunately, there is no name on the box for what we call "Pastel Bands." Original boxed sets of sherbets unveiled the Mountain Flowers name.

Monax and Ivrene are names given these Petalware colors by MacBeth-Evans. Ivrene refers to the opaque, beige colored Petalware illustrated by the boxed set. Monax is the white shown in all the other pictures. Pastel decorated Ivrene is the design now being pursued. I am continually asked for it at shows. Considering little of it is available, prices are rising.

Collectors are also captivated with various Petalware decorations, which is apparent when those items are put out for sale and are gone before the first two hours pass.

Florette is the second most collected design. It is the pointed petal, red flower decoration without the red edge trim. Soups are seldom seen in Petalware. Therefore, decorated Florette soups are a serious find. One group was located in a garage in Pennsylvania. Since I now own a 1949 company magazine showing a woman painting this Florette design on stacks of plates, it probably should move to the 50s book.

The brightly colored fired-on colors have begun to captivate a few collectors. These seem to be more challenging to find than Anchor Hocking's Rainbow pattern that has been selling briskly. We have tried to show a sample of decorated Petalware focusing on fruits and some florals. We had additional pictures, but I had to limit my choices in order to add new patterns to the book. Look back over the last few editions for additional designs. There are series of fruits, birds, and flowers. Fruit-decorated Petalware (with printed names of fruits) is found in sets of eight. One such set consists of plates showing cherry, apple, orange, plum, strawberry, blueberry, pear, and grape. You may find other sets with different fruits. Some plates have labels, which read "Rainbow Hand Painted." Some have colored bands or 22K gold trim. All series of fruit and bird decorated Petalware sell rapidly.

Pink Petalware has captivated many collectors. This delicate pink is still less costly than most other pink patterns in Depression glass and can be found at markets.

	Crystal	Pink	Cremax, Monax, Plain	Cremax, Monax, Florette, Fired-On Decorations	Red Trim Floral
Bowl, 4½", cream soup	4.50	18.00	12.00	20.00	
Bowl, 5¾", cereal	4.00	15.00	8.00	20.00	42.00
Bowl, 7", soup			65.00	110.00	
*Bowl, 9", large berry	8.50	26.00	20.00	40.00	135.00
Cup	3.00	8.00	5.00	12.00	27.50
**Creamer, footed	3.00	8.00	8.00	15.00	35.00
Lamp shade (many sizes) $8.00 to $15.00					
Mustard with metal cover in cobalt blue only, $10.00					300.00
Pitcher, (Mountain Flowers) juice					
Pitcher, 80 ounce (crystal decorated bands)	35.00				
Plate, 6", sherbet	2.00	2.50	3.00	6.00	22.00
Plate, 8", salad	2.00	7.00	6.00	10.00	25.00
Plate, 9", dinner	4.00	14.00	14.00	20.00	37.50
Plate, 11", salver	4.50	15.00	12.00	30.00	
Plate, 12", salver		15.00	18.00		40.00
Platter, 13", oval	8.50	25.00	15.00	30.00	
Saucer	1.50	2.00	2.00	3.50	10.00
Saucer, cream soup liner			15.00		
Sherbet, 4", low footed			30.00		
**Sherbet, 4½", low footed	3.50	10.00	8.00	22.00	38.00
**Sugar, footed	3.00	9.00	8.00	15.00	35.00
Tidbit servers or Lazy Susans, several styles 12.00 to 17.50					
Tumbler, 3⅝", 6 ounce					50.00
Tumbler, 4⅝", 12 ounce					55.00
***Tumblers (crystal decorated pastel bands) $7.50 to $10.00					

*Also in cobalt at $65.00   **Also in cobalt at $35.00   ***Several sizes

PILLAR OPTIC, "LOGS," "LOG CABIN," ANCHOR HOCKING GLASS COMPANY, 1937 – 1942

Colors: crystal, green, pink, Royal Ruby; amber and iridescent, possible Federal Glass Co.

After adding Pillar Optic to the book, I received letters with two contradictory messages from readers. One was from a collector profusely thanking me for emphasizing that this pattern's pitcher is not Old Café. She had a written agreement that the pink pitcher she had acquired was Old Café and the reputable dealer from whom she bought it had reimbursed her money when she found it was not. About a month later I had one saying I had sabotaged two sales of "Old Café" pitchers with my new book. Pillar Optic pitchers are collectible, just not as Old Café to collectors of that pattern.

The 60-ounce pitcher came in three colors. The two 80-ounce ones are shown here. The panels of the Pillar Optic are evenly spaced (note pretzel jars) and not like Old Cafe's alternating large panel with two smaller ones. Notice that there were two styles of Pillar Optic pitchers manufactured. It is only the ice lip style that is comparable to Old Café.

Hocking promoted a beer and pretzel set (mugs and the pretzel jar) in Pillar Optic, which I first showed in my Kitchenware book. Most collectors call that 130-ounce jar a cookie, but it was not offered as such. The pretzel jar top is hard to find mint. These jars are sometimes found satinized and with hand-painted flowers. On a recent trip my wife and son spotted one of these pretzel jars and were about to purchase it when those younger eagle eyes noticed a chipped spot on the lid; when they declined it, the owner said, "Oh, I can fix that right up in just a minute with something I've got behind the counter!" — which didn't further enhance the piece in their eyes — but which provided quite a bit of merriment in rehashing that startling pronouncement on the remainder of the trip.

Royal Ruby Pillar Optic items are hard to find though those pieces continue to be unearthed as you can see by the photo. It seems that cup, saucer, creamer, and sugar are all rare in red. I have listed seven newly discovered pieces of Royal Ruby. Flat tumblers come in amber and iridescent. However, Federal Glass Company is known to have manufactured like patterned tumblers and its likely amber and iridescent wares may have come from them rather than Anchor Hocking. The amber hue of these tumblers is unlike any Hocking amber I have seen.

Two styles of cups appear illustrated by the rounded cup pictured in green and the flatter red one, which are reminiscent of Colonial styled cups. I finally found a green saucer, but no pink one yet. I have not seen flat green cups or rounded pink ones. The pink sugar and creamer came out of the attic of a former Hocking employee.

Crystal Pillar Optic tumblers have been a staple in Anchor Hocking's restaurant line for years. In fact, in one or their later catalogs, it is shown under the heading "Old Reliable." Many restaurants still use them today.

	Crystal	Amber, Green, Pink	Royal Ruby		Crystal	Amber, Green, Pink	Royal Ruby
Bowl, open vegetable			150.00	Saucer	2.00	4.00	25.00
Bowl, 9", two-handle		65.00	125.00	Sherbet			55.00
Creamer, footed		50.00	85.00	Sugar, footed		50.00	85.00
Cup	10.00	15.00	75.00	Tumbler, 1½ ounce, whiskey	8.00	14.00	
Mug, 12 ounce	12.00	35.00		Tumbler, 3¼", 3 ounce, footed	8.00	15.00	30.00
Pitcher, w/o lip, 60 ounce	25.00	45.00		Tumbler, 4", 5 oz. juice, ftd.	10.00	17.50	35.00
Pitcher, w/lip, 80 ounce	30.00	55.00		Tumbler, 5¼", 10 ounce, ftd.	12.00	25.00	50.00
Pitcher, 80 ounce, tilt	35.00	65.00		Tumbler, 7 ounce, old fashioned	10.00	25.00	
Plate, 6", sherbet	3.00	6.00	25.00	Tumbler, 9 ounce, water	2.50	20.00	
Plate, 8", luncheon	8.00	12.00	30.00	Tumbler, 11 ounce, ftd., cone	12.00	20.00	
Platter, 11" oval			150.00	Tumbler, 13 ounce, tea	4.00	25.00	
Pretzel jar, 130 ounce	85.00	150.00					

PRIMO, "PANELED ASTER," U.S. GLASS COMPANY, Early 1930s

Colors: green and yellow

There are no additional listings in Primo for the first time in ten years. Last time, a grill pate with an indent for a cup made its appearance in green. I have not had any reports for this piece in yellow, but I feel like they will turn up eventually. In 1932, Primo could be purchased as a 14-piece bridge set (with plates, cups, saucers, and sugar and creamer), a 16-piece luncheonette (with grill plates, tumblers, cups, and saucers), an 18-piece occasional set (with plates, tumblers, sugar, creamer, cups, and saucers), a 19-piece hostess set (add a tray), or a 7-piece berry set.

The two-handled hostess tray finally surfaced, so those 19-piece settings may not have been as popular as other assortments. The 11" three-footed console bowl (large berry in old ads) created a furor among Primo collectors when I first pictured it. That bowl is beat up, but I had to buy it for the $20.00 price since "it had to be rare seeing as it wasn't in Gene Florence's book." No one seemed overly excited about the 6¼" sherbet plate not previously listed. I was thrilled enough for everybody when I first spied them in that antique mall. I bought the sherbet plates, but had to buy the sherbets to get them. Finding new pieces for patterns is now my "thrill" rather than the collecting that we did for so many patterns.

A collector wanted to gather Primo and asked me to watch for it, which I have done for almost ten years. From that experience, I found that any bowls, dinner, grill, or cake plates would take some searching. Though I have discovered several new pieces in yellow and green, I have not yet found a green berry bowl to picture.

Frustration in buying Primo comes from excessive mould roughness and inner rim damage on pieces that have rims. These seams are more reminiscent of older pattern glass or of Indiana glassware. I have seen more Primo along the Gulf Coast than any place I have searched, so I suspect it may have been a premium item for someone in that area. I have seen several sets in antique malls between Florida and Texas. However, a preponderance of the pieces were very rough or chipped but had mint pricing; so, I passed on owning them.

The tumbler exactly fits the coaster/ashtray. These coasters have been found in boxed sets with Primo tumblers that were advertised as "Bridge Service Sets." The coasters are also found in pink and black, but no Primo design is found on the coasters. Evidently, U.S. Glass used these with other patterns also.

	Yellow, Green			Yellow, Green
Bowl, 4½"	28.00		Plate, 7½"	15.00
Bowl, 7¾"	45.00		Plate, 10", dinner	30.00
Bowl, 11", 3-footed	75.00		Plate, 10", grill	18.00
Cake plate, 10", 3-footed	50.00		Saucer	3.00
Coaster/ashtray	8.00		Sherbet	14.00
Creamer	12.00		Sugar	12.00
Cup	13.00		Tray, 2-handle hostess	50.00
Plate, 6¼"	15.00		Tumbler, 5¾", 9 ounce	20.00

PRINCESS, HOCKING GLASS COMPANY, 1931 – 1935

Colors: green, Topaz yellow, apricot yellow, pink, and light blue

I reported the different style cup found near Lancaster last year, and even though I pictured it next to the regular cup for comparison, no letters have been forthcoming about additional odd cups. It looks bigger, but is not. It is the one on the left in the picture, shaped differently and with another style handle from the regular cup. There were two of these available; but I suspect there are more awaiting discovery.

All bowls and footed iced tea tumblers are hard to locate in any color of Princess. Green Princess collectors have to search long and hard for the undivided relish and the obscure square-footed pitcher with tumblers to match. Some dealers endorse the undivided Princess relish as a soup bowl. To me, it does not seem deep enough for a soup bowl; but in any case, purchasing more than one will dent your bank account. Admirers of pink Princess have trouble finding coasters, ashtrays, and square-foot pitchers with matching tumblers. The hardest to find yellow pieces include the butter dish, juice pitcher, undivided relish, 10½" handled sandwich plate, coasters, and ashtrays. I found two of the yellow handled plates in a mall. About a year later, a dealer approached me at a show and asked why I had bought those Patrician plates out of his friend's booth last summer. I told him I didn't remember buying Patrician, but I could have. It was later when I figured out what he meant. This plate is just like the handled grill plate without the dividers. You can see one in the background of the photograph at the bottom of this page.

Bowls in all colors of Princess present a problem due to inner rim roughness, "irr" in ads. New collectors are always writing about that "irr" meaning in ads. Stacking the bowls together over the years caused some of this "irr" damage; but the very sharply defined inner rims were themselves ripe for trouble from the moulds. Mint condition bowls are not often found.

There is a distinct color variation in yellow Princess. Topaz is the official color name listed by Hocking, and it is a bright, attractive shade of yellow. However, some yellow turned out looking amber and has been designated apricot by collectors. Most prefer the Topaz, which makes the darker, amber shade challenging to sell. The colors are so mismatched that it is almost as if Hocking meant to have two separate colors. For some reason (probably distribution through premiums) yellow Princess cereal and berry bowls and sherbets flourish in the Detroit area. I pointed that out to a dealer who had a table full of yellow and he said he had never realized that yellow was commonly found there until after he moved from New York to that area. All but one of the known yellow Princess juice pitchers have been found in northern and central Kentucky. Regional distribution "patterns" are noticeable for Depression era wares.

Blue Princess pieces are encountered on rare occasions. The cookie jar, cup, saucer, and dinner plate are finding a ready market. I pictured a three-part relish in my *Very Rare Glassware of the Depression Years, Sixth Edition.* Blue Princess seems too rare to collect a set. Keep looking, though, because you never know these 70 years later what is still waiting to be unearthed. There is some evidence that blue Princess was shipped to Mexico, which could explain its dearth here in the States. There was even an erroneous reproduction report of blue dinner plates, but they turned out to be the real thing.

The grill plate without handles and dinner plate have been corrected to read 9½" in the listing instead of the 9" listed in Hocking catalogs. Measure perpendicularly and not diagonally.

On an annoying level, reproductions in cobalt blue, green, pink, and amber (candy dishes) have been reported. The colors are not close to those original ones. Cobalt or amber was never made originally. The green will not glow under ultraviolet (black) light and the pink has an orange hue. I haven't bought one to compare the actual design yet.

	Green	Pink	Topaz, Apricot		Green	Pink	Topaz, Apricot
Ashtray, 4½"	80.00	95.00	125.00	**Plate, 9½", grill	20.00	20.00	8.00
Bowl, 4½", berry	33.00	33.00	58.00	Plate, 10¼", handled sandwich	16.00	30.00	195.00
Bowl, 5", cereal or oatmeal	42.00	42.00	42.00	Plate, 10½", grill, closed handles	10.00	12.00	5.50
Bowl, 9", octagonal, salad	45.00	60.00	175.00	Platter, 12", closed handles	32.00	32.00	67.50
Bowl, 9½", hat-shaped	50.00	50.00	150.00	Relish, 7½", divided, 4 pint	28.00	30.00	100.00
Bowl, 10", oval vegetable	32.00	28.00	65.00	Relish, 7½", plain	195.00	195.00	250.00
Butter dish and cover	100.00	115.00	850.00	Salt and pepper, 4½" pair	60.00	55.00	85.00
Butter dish bottom	35.00	40.00	250.00	Spice shakers, 5½", pair	40.00		
Butter dish top	65.00	75.00	600.00	***Saucer (same as sherbet plate)	9.00	9.00	3.00
Cake stand, 10"	35.00	35.00		Sherbet, footed	23.00	27.00	35.00
*Candy dish and cover	55.00	95.00		Sugar	10.00	15.00	8.50
Coaster	50.00	85.00	125.00	Sugar cover	25.00	30.00	17.50
**Cookie jar and cover	55.00	70.00		Tumbler, 3", 5 ounce, juice	35.00	35.00	35.00
Creamer, oval	20.00	20.00	20.00	Tumbler, 4", 9 ounce, water	30.00	30.00	25.00
***Cup	11.00	13.00	9.00	Tumbler, 5¼", 13 oz., iced tea	50.00	42.00	32.00
Pitcher 6", 37 ounce	60.00	75.00	895.00	Tumbler, 4¾", 9 oz., sq. ftd	65.00	60.00	
Pitcher, 7⅜", 24 ounce, ftd.	525.00	475.00		Tumbler, 5¼", 10 ounce, ftd.	33.00	28.00	22.00
Pitcher, 8", 60 ounce	60.00	65.00	110.00	Tumbler, 6½", 12½ oz., ftd.	120.00	100.00	175.00
****Plate, 5½" sherbet	9.00	9.00	4.00	Vase, 8"	45.00	60.00	
Plate, 8" salad	20.00	20.00	15.00				
*****Plate, 9½", dinner	30.00	26.00	16.00				

*   Beware reproductions in cobalt blue and amber
**   Blue $995.00
***   Blue $125.00
****   Blue $60.00
*****   Blue $200.00

QUEEN MARY (PRISMATIC LINE), "VERTICAL RIBBED,"
ANCHOR HOCKING GLASS COMPANY, 1936 – 1949

Colors: pink, crystal, and some Royal Ruby

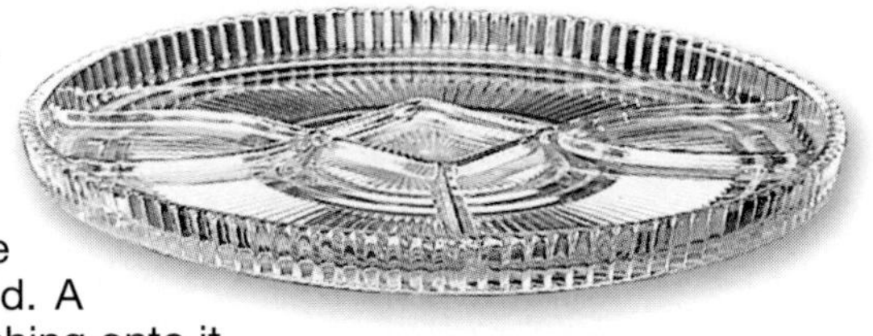

Economics is causing crystal Queen Mary to look more enticing to new collectors than pink. Accessibility and its somewhat modernistic look are other motivations. Nothing is as frustrating as trying to stumble onto pink Queen Mary dinner plates and footed tumblers; and prices for those same items in crystal are engendering upward trends due to new demand. A few pink Queen Mary prices have softened since new collectors are not latching onto it, as they are the crystal. I noticed four dealers with pink Queen Mary dinner plates at a recent show. They were priced from $50.00 to $75.00. I looked at these right before the end of the show. The ones priced at $50.00 and $55.00 were gone except for one and the higher priced ones were still sitting in the dealer's display. A crystal set can still be finished at bearable prices including dinner plates and footed tumblers.

A checkered appearing, cross-veined vase (shaped like Old Cafe with a 400-line number) is pictured along with Queen Mary items in Hocking catalogs. As far as I am concerned, it is only pictured with the pattern; however, my wife thinks there's a chance it should be included in the listing as a Queen Mary item. You decide whether you should fit it with your pattern or not.

The 6" cereal bowl has the same shape as the butter bottom but is smaller in diameter. What we call butter dishes were issued as preserve dishes in Hocking's catalogs. There are two different cups. The smaller rests on the saucer with cup ring. The larger cup rests on the combination saucer/sherbet plate so typical of Hocking's patterns. Lately, the pink smaller cup and saucer have overtaken the larger in price. Some dealers are identifying the 5½" tab-handled bowl as a cream soup. The price on that bowl has gone up rather dramatically due to that homemade description that is not such in catalog listings.

The frosted crystal butter dish with metal band looks somewhat like a crown. These were made about the time of the English Coronation in the mid-1930s. I have seen these priced as high as $150.00 in an Art Deco shop, but I had to consider a while before paying $25.00 for the one pictured previously. A pair of lampshades were found made from frosted candy lids (with metal-banded decorations similar to that butter). Beauty is in the eye of the beholder and these brought tears to my eyes they were so ugly to me. I'm equally certain someone else would go into raptures over them.

I am now confident the little colored shakers pictured previously in amethyst are Hazel Atlas; keep that in mind if they are offered to you as Queen Mary. They, alas, are not.

	Pink	Crystal
Ashtray, 2" x 3¾", oval	5.00	3.00
*Ashtray, 3¼", round		3.00
Ashtray, 4¼", square (#422)		4.00
Bowl, 4", one-handle or none	6.00	3.50
Bowl, 4½", berry	8.00	4.00
Bowl, 5", berry, flared	13.00	6.00
Bowl, 5½", two handle, lug soup	30.00	6.50
Bowl, 6", cereal	25.00	6.00
Bowl, deep, 7½" (#477)	32.00	14.00
Bowl, 8¾", large berry (#478)	25.00	15.00
Butter dish or preserve and cover (#498)	150.00	30.00
Butter dish bottom (#498)	40.00	7.00
Butter dish top (#498)	110.00	25.00
Candy dish and cover, 7¼" (#490)	50.00	22.00
**Candlesticks, 4½", double branch, pair		22.00
Celery or pickle dish, 5" x 10" (#467)	30.00	15.00
Cigarette jar, 2" x 3", oval	7.50	5.50
Coaster, 3½"	6.00	3.00
Coaster/ashtray, 3¼", round (#419)	6.00	5.00
Comport, 5¾"	25.00	15.00

	Pink	Crystal
Creamer, footed	60.00	25.00
Creamer, 5½", oval (#471)	14.00	5.50
Cup, large	9.00	5.50
Cup, small	8.00	8.00
Mayonnaise, 5" x 2¾" h, 6" plate	35.00	20.00
Plate, 6⅝"	6.00	4.00
Plate, 8¾", salad (#438)		5.50
Plate, 9¾", dinner (#426)	55.00	25.00
Plate, 12", sandwich (#450)	30.00	18.00
Plate, 14", serving tray	22.00	12.00
Relish tray, 12", 3-part	18.00	9.00
Relish tray, 14", 4-part	20.00	12.00
Salt and pepper, 2½", pair (#486)		19.00
Saucer/cup ring	5.00	2.50
Sherbet, footed	11.00	5.00
Sugar, footed	60.00	25.00
Sugar, 6", oval (#470)	14.00	4.50
Tumbler, 3½", 5 ounce, juice	15.00	4.00
Tumbler, 4", 9 ounce, water	18.00	6.00
Tumbler, 5", 10 ounce, footed	70.00	38.00
Vase, 6½" (#441)		12.00

*Royal Ruby $5.00; Forest Green $3.00   ** Royal Ruby $125.00

186

RADIANCE, NEW MARTINSVILLE GLASS COMPANY, 1936 – 1939

Colors: red, cobalt and ice blue, amber, crystal, pink, and emerald green

Radiance punch, decanter, and condiment sets continue to be on collectors' want lists. The punch set is arduous to find, but the punch ladle is virtually impossible. The ladle was fashioned by stretching a long handle to a punch cup. If not destroyed through use, collectors and dealers have added to their demise by traveling with them. I have been told several times that the handle detaches from the cup very easily. One dealer has had that misfortune twice. He, personally, has helped elevate the price of red punch ladles.

A cake stand, 11½" x 4" tall, has turned up in red and crystal.

Viking made crystal punch bowls, being found on emerald green and black large plates, after they bought out New Martinsville in the mid 1940s. One such emerald green set was pictured previously. These are found rather frequently — unlike their older counterparts. The punch bowls flair outward rather than inward, like the older "bowling ball" design. Viking's ladle is plain. I have several collectors petitioning me to move Radiance to my Elegant book as it is too fine a glassware to be included in this book. They are probably right. However, Radiance was collected as Depression glass long before my term "Elegant" was ever christened.

Red and ice blue are the most desirable Radiance colors. The most troublesome pieces to find in those colors include the butter dish, pitcher, handled decanter, and the five-piece condiment set. Vases have been made into lamps in several formats. I doubt this was a factory venture, but it could have been.

If you are a collector of Radiance and do not have my *Very Rare Glassware of the Depression Years, Sixth Series,* you need to find a copy. Radiance pictures include an 8" red candlestick with matching bobeches and several odd colored vases. While shopping recently, we saw a pair of vases with decorations of gold, blue, and flowers. I regretted leaving them, but they were so worn, I could not justify the expense. Vases may be found in an array of colors.

Cobalt blue is striking, but few pieces are discovered in that color.

Pink Radiance pieces including creamer, sugar, tray, cup, saucer, vase, and shakers are turning up occasionally. These are selling in the same range as the red since they are scarce at this time. The pieces suggest they were made as luncheon sets, save for the vase, which could have been picked up in a florist grouping.

Price crystal about 50% of amber, but both are difficult to sell. Only crystal pieces that item collectors seek sell well. These include pitchers, butter dishes, decanters, shakers, sugars, creamers, and cordials.

	Ice Blue, Red	Amber		Ice Blue, Red	Amber
Bowl, 5", nut, 2-handle	22.00	12.00	Condiment set, 4-piece w/tray	325.00	175.00
Bowl, 6", bonbon	33.00	17.50	Creamer	25.00	15.00
Bowl, 6", bonbon, footed	35.00	20.00	Cruet, individual	90.00	50.00
Bowl, 6", bonbon w/cover	115.00	55.00	Cup, footed	18.00	12.00
Bowl, 7", relish, 2-part	35.00	20.00	Cup, punch	15.00	7.00
Bowl, 7", pickle	35.00	20.00	** Decanter w/stopper, handle	225.00	125.00
Bowl, 8", relish, 3-part	50.00	35.00	Goblet, 1 ounce cordial	32.00	22.00
* Bowl, 9", punch	225.00	100.00	Honey jar, w/lid	125.00	75.00
Bowl, 10", celery	45.00	22.00	Ladle for punch bowl	150.00	100.00
Bowl, 10", crimped	55.00	30.00	Lamp, 12"	125.00	65.00
Bowl, 10", flared	50.00	25.00	Mayonnaise, 3-piece, set	115.00	65.00
Bowl, 12", crimped	60.00	35.00	*** Pitcher, 64 ounce	325.00	175.00
Bowl, 12", flared	65.00	32.00	Plate, 8", luncheon	16.00	10.00
Butter dish	465.00	210.00	**** Plate, 14", punch bowl liner	85.00	45.00
Candlestick, 6", ruffled, pair	175.00	80.00	Salt & pepper, pair	95.00	50.00
Candlestick, 8", pair	225.00	95.00	Saucer	8.50	5.50
Candlestick, 2-lite, pair	175.00	95.00	Sugar	25.00	15.00
Candy, flat, w/lid	100.00	50.00	Tray, oval	45.00	25.00
Cheese/cracker (11" plate) set	110.00	30.00	***** Tumbler, 9 ounce	32.00	22.00
Comport, 5"	30.00	18.00	****** Vase, 10", flared or crimped	125.00	75.00
Comport, 6"	35.00	22.00	Vase, 12", flared or crimped	175.00	

* Emerald green $125.00   ****Emerald green $25.00

** Cobalt blue $185.00   *****Cobalt blue $28.00

*** Cobalt blue $350.00   ******Cobalt blue $75.00

RAINDROPS, "OPTIC DESIGN," FEDERAL GLASS COMPANY, 1929 – 1933

Colors: green and crystal

Please notice that Raindrops has rounded bumps and not elongated ones. Elongated bumps belong to another pattern usually referred to as "Thumbprint." Almost all Raindrops pieces are embossed on the bottom with Federal's trademark of an F inside a shield. I want to emphasize that that mark is not a Fire-King mark as is being presented to the unknowing in malls.

There are two styles of cups. One is flat bottomed and the other is slightly footed. The flat-bottomed is 2⁵⁄₁₆" high and the footed is 2¹¹⁄₁₆" (reported by an enthusiastic Raindrops collector). I have not measured them myself, but will take the word of someone who adores this pattern. New collectors have pushed up a few prices while others are holding their own at this time. Prices for crystal tumblers run from 50% to 60% less than for green.

Raindrops makes a great little luncheon or bridge set. It even has a few supplementary pieces that other smaller sets do not. You can find three sizes of bowls in Raindrops. The 7½" bowl will be the one you will probably find last. That bowl has always been scarce and with new blood searching for it, the supply has dwindled rapidly. Raindrops will blend well with many other green sets; so, give that a try if you want additional pieces such as dinner sized plates.

That 7½" berry bowl price continues an upward climb and is now the second most expensive piece in Raindrops. It has rushed pass the price of the sugar bowl lid. However, both of these pieces have to take a back seat to the shakers. In actuality, Raindrops sugar lids have turned out to be common in comparison to shakers. Consequently, the price of shakers has launched upward over the last few years. A couple of shaker collectors have told me that these are harder to find than yellow and green Mayfair. Both collectors had at least one of those elusive shakers, but neither one had the Raindrops. I have never seen a Raindrops shaker for sale at any show I have attended in 31 years if that makes any kind of impression on you as to how rare it is. I have owned the one-footed Mayfair shaker and have held two genuine pairs of pink Cherry Blossom shakers. One Raindrops shaker is all I have seen, though I have heard of others. Therefore, there is a possibility of your finding one.

	Green		Green
Bowl, 4½", fruit	6.00	Sugar	7.50
Bowl, 6", cereal	12.50	Sugar cover	42.50
Bowl, 7½", berry	60.00	Tumbler, 3", 4 ounce	5.00
Cup	7.00	Tumbler, 2⅛", 2 ounce	5.00
Creamer	7.50	Tumbler, 3⅞", 5 ounce	6.50
Plate, 6", sherbet	2.50	Tumbler, 4⅛", 9½ ounce	9.00
Plate, 8", luncheon	6.00	Tumbler, 5", 10 ounce	9.00
Salt and pepper, pair	395.00	Tumbler, 5⅜", 14 ounce	14.00
Saucer	2.00	Whiskey, 1⅞", 1 ounce	7.00
Sherbet	8.00		

189

REEDED, WHIRLSPOOL, "SPUN," LINE #701, IMPERIAL GLASS COMPANY, c. 1936 – 1960s

Colors: crystal, cobalt, dark green, amber, tangerine, Midas gold, turquoise, pink, milk, mustard

Reeded was first advertised as beverage sets. Through the years, various other pieces were added to the line, indicative of its enjoying a certain reputation with buyers. I was prompted to put it in the book because Imperial closed, which makes their wares more collectible, and interest has been mounting in the pattern for some time at shows.

Interesting items in the pattern include what they called a console set, usually a rolled edge bowl with candles. In this pattern, the bowl is a bowling-ball shaped rose bowl (see pink one in photo) with small ivy ball vases that have had crystal glass candle inserts (see cobalt one above prices) added to make these candles. Do not pass by any of these if the price is right. The two jars on the top row of the group photo are called Whirlspool and can be found with glass lids as pictured or with metal knobbed lids.

	*All colors
Ashtray, 2¼", cupped	10.00
Bottle, 3 ounce, bitters	38.00
Bowl, 4½", fruit	20.00
Bowl, 7", nappy, straight side	33.00
Bowl, 8" ,nappy	33.00
Bowl, 10", deep salad	45.00
Candle, 2½", ball w/crystal glass insert	45.00
Candy box, footed w/cone lid	50.00
Cigarette holder, wider mouth, 2½" ball	20.00
Cocktail shaker, 36 ounce, w or w/o handles	75.00
Creamer, footed	25.00
Cup	20.00
Ice tub	60.00
Jar, Whirlspool, 4", tall, w/lid or w/metal knob	55.00
Jar, Whirlspool, 5", tall, w/lid or w/metal knob	65.00
Jar, Whirlspool, 6", tall, w/lid or w/metal knob	75.00
Jar, Whirlspool, 7", tall, w/lid or w/metal knob	85.00
Muddler, 4½"	10.00
Perfume w/triangle stop	50.00
Pitcher, 80 ounce, ice lip	75.00
Plate, 8", salad, belled rim	20.00

	*All colors
Plate, 13½", cupped edge	30.00
Plate, 14", server, flat	32.50
Powder jar w/lid	50.00
Saucer	8.00
Sherbet	17.50
Sugar, footed	25.00
Syrup, ball w/chrome spout & handle	60.00
Tumbler, 2 ounce, shot	20.00
Tumbler, 3½ ounce, cocktail	12.50
Tumbler, 5 ounce, juice, straight	12.00
Tumbler, 7 ounce, old fashioned	14.00
Tumbler, 9 ounce	14.00
Tumbler, 12 oz., tea, straight side	15.00
Tumbler, 12 ounce, tea, bulb top	16.00
Vase, 2½", ball	15.00
Vase, 3½", ivy ball, footed	35.00

	*All colors
Vase, ivy ball, 6½", footed	55.00
Vase, 4", ball	17.50
Vase, 5", bud	35.00
Vase, 5", bulbous, tall neck rose	45.00
Vase, 5", rose	40.00
Vase, 6", ball, rose	45.00
Vase, 6", bud	40.00
Vase, 6", slender	40.00
Vase, 8½"	40.00
Vase, 9"	50.00

*Add 50% for red or blue; deduct 25% for crystal

"RIBBON," HAZEL ATLAS GLASS COMPANY, Early 1930s

Colors: green; some black, crystal, and pink

"Ribbon" is one of those hordes of 1930s wares that resonate the era in which they began, filled with unsophisticated lines and clean shapes, which manage to have elegance and movement all at the same time.

"Ribbon" bowls are among the most difficult to find in all of Depression glass and their ever-increasing prices reflect that. They are in even shorter supply than those of its sister pattern, Cloverleaf. The mould shapes are the same. Several "Ribbon" seekers informed me that they coveted the display of both the berry and the cereal in my previous book. In fact, I had a letter from a long-time collector explaining that I was wrong in listing the cereal because it did not exist. (He had an older book.) The cereal and berry are sitting flat in this photo since they looked elliptical when sitting on their sides in the last book. I found four berry bowls and kept one for photography. Sorry, that's all the berry bowls I have ever owned; and you are looking at the only cereal I have seen in the last 20 or more years.

I hardly ever see "Ribbon" for sale at glass shows any more. "Ribbon" is another of the patterns not found in the west according to dealers who travel those areas. Tumblers, sugars, and creamers are not yet as hard to find as bowls, but even they are beginning to disappear. The candy dish prevails as the repeatedly seen piece of "Ribbon." It sells very well as an example piece for beginning collectors.

The panel design on pieces flaring at the top will expand, as seen on the sugar and creamer in the picture. The normally found "Ribbon" design has evenly-spaced small panels. This flared expansion is especially noticeable on a belled rim vegetable bowl you sometimes find in both black and green coloring. I had a letter questioning that the flared bowl was even the "Ribbon" pattern because it looked so different. This flared version has been accepted as "Ribbon" for the 32 years I've been in this business. There is an 8" bowl with straight sides pictured here like the berry and cereal. This bowl is probably the correct one, but the other was accepted as "Ribbon" before I started writing, so it is hard to change tradition.

I have never been convinced that the shakers exist in green. All those purported to be "Ribbon" have always made me wonder if they are. Notice I do not have one pictured.

	Green	Black		Green	Black
Bowl, 4", berry	38.00		Plate, 6¼", sherbet	3.00	
Bowl, 5", cereal	48.00		Plate, 8", luncheon	8.00	14.00
Bowl, 8", large berry, flared	38.00	40.00	*Salt and pepper, pair	30.00	45.00
Bowl, 8", straight side	85.00		Saucer	2.50	
Candy dish and cover	50.00		Sherbet, footed	10.00	
Creamer, footed	15.00		Sugar, footed	15.00	
Cup	5.00		Tumbler, 6", 10 ounce	37.50	

*Pink $35.00

191

RING, "BANDED RINGS," LINE #300, HOCKING GLASS COMPANY, 1927 – 1933

Colors: crystal, crystal w/bands of pink, red, blue, orange, yellow, black, silver, etc.; green, pink, "Mayfair" blue, and Royal Ruby

Ring with colored bands on crystal intrigues more collectors than the ever abundant, ordinary crystal. Crystal with platinum (silver) bands is the next favored form of crystal Ring. Worn trims exasperate collectors, as there is presently no known way to restore them. Colored rings do not seem to suffer from that problem, possibly because the colors did not embellish rims, as did platinum; or perhaps fired-on trims proved more resistant to wear than metal ones.

There is a principal colored Ring arrangement involving black, yellow, red, and orange in that order. Diverse other arrangements drive the meticulous loony. The foot of the crystal cocktail is plain and does not have the normal block/grid design of other footed pieces. Both these styles are also found in Mayfair and Princess, which makes finding one style a problem only when buying by mail or ordering online. Be sure to specify whether you want a plain foot or not.

A reader informed me that ordering a subscription to *Country Gentleman* in the 1930s brought you a green Ring berry bowl set consisting of an 8" berry and six 5" berry bowls. That must not have been too enticing since I have seen few green Ring bowls over the years. You could put a set of green Ring together over time. You will notice that my green accumulation is not building fast, though I now have berry bowls to show in the future.

Pink pitcher and tumbler sets are the only pieces I see regularly in that color. A Wisconsin collector reported that the pink pitchers were bestowed as a dairy premium in her area. The tumblers were packed with cottage cheese and she could not remember what you had to do to receive the pitcher. Pink sets are plentiful in that dairy country.

A few pieces of Ring are discovered intermittently in Royal Ruby and "Mayfair" blue. The luncheon plate and 10-ounce tumbler are fairly common in Royal Ruby, and flat juice tumblers and cups have turned up, albeit in inadequate quantities. I have had no reports of saucers to go with those cups. Let me know if you spot any Royal Ruby or blue Ring saucer/sherbet plates.

You may observe items decorated with Ring-like colors, only to find that these pieces have no actual rings moulded into the design. It is not Ring unless it has the mould indentations. A reader sent me an ad from the mid-30s that described these look-alike wares as Fiesta. Hocking had a number of different striped patterns in ads of this period. I assume the Fiesta was one version of those.

	Crystal	Green, Dec.		Crystal	Green, Dec.
Bowl, 5", berry	4.00	8.00	Plate, 11¼", sandwich	7.00	14.00
Bowl, 7", soup	10.00	15.00	****Salt and pepper, pair, 3"	25.00	50.00
Bowl, 5¼", divided	12.00	40.00	Sandwich server, center handle	16.00	27.50
Bowl, 8", large berry	7.00	14.00	Saucer	1.50	2.00
Butter tub or ice tub	25.00	38.00	Sherbet, low (for 6½" plate)	8.00	15.00
Cocktail shaker	20.00	27.50	Sherbet, 4¾", footed	6.00	11.00
** Cup	6.00	9.00	Sugar, footed	6.00	10.00
Creamer, footed	6.00	10.00	Tumbler, 3", 4 ounce	4.00	12.00
Decanter and stopper	28.00	45.00	Tumbler, 3½", 5 ounce	5.00	12.00
Goblet, 7¼", 9 ounce	12.00	15.00	Tumbler, 4", 8 ounce, old fashioned	15.00	18.00
Goblet, 3¾", 3½ ounce, cocktail	11.00	18.00	Tumbler, 4¼", 9 ounce	4.50	14.00
Goblet, 4½", 3½ ounce, wine	13.00	20.00	Tumbler, 4¾", 10 ounce	7.50	13.00
Ice bucket	20.00	35.00	* Tumbler, 5⅛", 12 ounce	8.00	10.00
Pitcher, 8", 60 ounce	17.50	25.00	Tumbler, 3½" footed, juice	6.00	10.00
* Pitcher, 8½", 80 ounce	22.00	35.00	Tumbler, 5½" footed, water	6.00	12.00
Plate, 6¼", sherbet	2.00	2.50	Tumbler, 6½" footed, iced tea	8.00	15.00
Plate, 6½", off-center ring	5.00	7.00	Vase, 8"	17.50	35.00
***Plate, 8", luncheon	4.00	5.00	Whiskey, 2", 1½ ounce	7.00	15.00

* Also found in pink. Priced as green.   ** Red $65.00 Blue $45.00   *** Red $17.50   **** Green $55.00

ROCK CRYSTAL, "EARLY AMERICAN ROCK CRYSTAL," McKEE GLASS COMPANY,
1920s and 1930s in colors

Colors: four shades of green, aquamarine, Canary yellow, amber, pink and frosted pink, red slag, dark red, red, amberina
red, crystal, frosted crystal, crystal with goofus decoration, crystal with gold decoration, amethyst, milk glass,
blue frosted or "Jap" blue, and cobalt blue

Rock Crystal had one of the longest production runs of patterns in this book. Introduced around 1915 in crystal, it began marked as Prescut, which was McKee's trademarked name for moulded patterns at the end of the cut glass production era. All the major glass companies designed moulded wares to simulate cut glass when most of the experienced cut glass workers left the glass shops for the war and there weren't enough available to handle the production. Rock Crystal is a very attractive, graceful pattern with its design firmly rooted in the past. It may interest you to know that hand-cut wares made for a king's table centuries ago reportedly inspired the design itself. Crystal was made until the early 1940s.

Color production ran from the 1920s until the late1930s.Those long years of production made for a tremendous volume of this glassware with a large variety of pieces produced. Some types of pieces exist that had only been found in pattern glass production or elegant glassware of the time such as salt dips, syrups, cruets, and egg cups. Unfortunately, catalogs showing all the pieces are not available. Colored glassware production years are well authenticated, but unexpected pieces are still showing up. A red syrup pitcher turned up a few years ago, which is a piece from a time when red was presumably not made. Thus, an older syrup pitcher mould was revived and used during the red production. Why only one has been found is the mystery. That gives hope for shakers, cruets, and other pieces not yet seen in red. You can view this syrup in *Very Rare Glassware of the Depression Years, Fourth Series*. We bought a large collection of red Rock Crystal from a former McKee employee in the late 1970s. He had eight or nine flat candy bottoms in this lot, which, he explained, were soup bowls. I assume that may have been a method to get rid of excess stock (McKee's originally, and his at the time we were buying his set).

Red, crystal, and amber sets can be finished with persistence. There are various pieces available; you need to decide what items you want. Instead of buying every tumbler and stem made, you can select a couple of each, choosing a style you favor. Even collectors with limited budgets can start a small crystal or amber set. Red will take a deeper pocket. Red coloration varies and can drive you crazy trying to match colors. It runs from very light to a very deep red that looks almost black. We collected red for about 20 years and many times we passed on a piece we needed because it was too dark or too light a color, something I would not do today because it has become so scarce.

Non-colored Rock Crystal pieces are sometimes acquired by collectors of other patterns to use as complementary items. Vases, cruets, candlesticks, and an abundance of serving pieces are some of the favored items. Serving pieces flourish; enjoy using them.

There are two different sizes of punch bowls. The base for the larger bowl has an opening 5" across, and stands 6¹⁄₁₆" tall. This base fits a punch bowl that is 4³⁄₁₆" across the bottom. The other style base has only a 4³⁄₁₆" opening, but is also 6¹⁄₁₆" tall. The bowl to fit this base is only 3¼" across the bottom.

Egg plates are often found with gold trim; they were probably a promotional item. In central Florida, I see a dozen Lazy Susans a year. They consist of a revolving metal stand with a Rock Crystal relish for a top. I have only found these here; so, they may have been a give-away or premium in this region.

In the 20s and 30s, Tiffin also made a Rock Crystal similar to McKee's. Their wares had one 8- to 11-petaled daisy flower with ruffled rim lines above it, round pedestal feet, and ribbed type handles. In addition, McKee, itself, made a similar pattern to their Rock Crystal, which was called Puritan and was part of their Prescut series as was Rock Crystal. Puritan had two 11-petaled daisy flowers, honeycombed-effect stems, and ribbed handles, but no long, "S" type scrolls surrounding the (five-petal) flower that enhances the Rock Crystal design.

ROCK CRYSTAL

	Crystal	All other colors	Red
* Bonbon, 7½", s.e.	22.00	35.00	60.00
Bowl, 4", s.e.	12.00	22.00	32.00
Bowl, 4½", s.e.	20.00	22.00	32.00
Bowl, 5", s.e.	22.00	24.00	45.00
** Bowl, 5", finger bowl with 7" plate, p.e.	35.00	45.00	95.00
Bowl, 7", pickle or spoon tray	30.00	40.00	75.00
Bowl, 7", salad, s.e.	24.00	37.50	75.00
Bowl, 8", salad, s.e.	27.50	37.50	85.00
Bowl, 8½", center handle			250.00
Bowl, 9", salad, s.e.	45.00	50.00	125.00
Bowl, 10½", salad, s.e.	25.00	50.00	100.00
Bowl, 11½", 2-part relish	38.00	50.00	85.00
Bowl, 12", oblong celery	27.50	45.00	95.00
*** Bowl, 12½", footed center bowl	85.00	125.00	295.00
Bowl, 12½", 5-part relish	45.00		
Bowl, 13", roll tray	45.00	60.00	125.00
Bowl, 14", 6-part relish	50.00	65.00	
Butter dish and cover	335.00		
Butter dish bottom	200.00		
Butter dish top	135.00		
**** Candelabra, 2-lite, pair	50.00	105.00	295.00
Candelabra, 3-lite, pair	65.00	195.00	395.00
Candlestick, flat, stemmed, pair	40.00	65.00	150.00
Candlestick, 5½", low, pair	40.00	65.00	195.00
Candlestick, 8", tall, pair	100.00	165.00	475.00
Candy and cover, footed, 9¼"	75.00	90.00	295.00
Candy and cover, round	75.00	85.00	195.00
Cake stand, 11", 2¾" high, footed	35.00	52.50	125.00
Cheese stand, 2¾"	22.00	30.00	50.00
Comport, 7"	50.00	50.00	95.00
Creamer, flat, s.e.	37.50		
Creamer, 9 ounce, footed	20.00	32.00	67.50
Cruet and stopper, 6 ounce, oil	115.00		
Cup, 7 ounce	15.00	27.50	70.00
Egg plate	38.00		
Goblet, 7½ ounce, 8 ounce, low footed	20.00	27.50	57.50
Goblet, 11 ounce, low footed, iced tea	20.00	30.00	67.50
Ice dish (3 styles)	40.00		
Jelly, 5", footed, s.e.	30.00	27.50	52.50
Lamp, electric	295.00	395.00	695.00
Parfait, 3½ ounce, low footed	20.00	35.00	75.00
Pitcher, quart, s.e.	165.00	225.00	
Pitcher, ½ gallon, 7½" high	135.00	195.00	
Pitcher, 9", large covered	175.00	295.00	895.00
Pitcher, fancy tankard	195.00	695.00	995.00
Plate, 6", bread and butter, s.e.	9.00	9.50	22.00
Plate, 7½", p.e. & s.e.	10.00	12.00	25.00
Plate, 8½", p.e. & s.e.	15.00	12.50	35.00
Plate, 9", s.e.	18.00	22.00	55.00
Plate, 10½", s.e.	25.00	30.00	65.00
Plate, 10½", dinner, s.e. (large center design)	47.50	70.00	195.00
Plate, 11½", s.e.	18.00	25.00	57.50
Punch bowl and stand, 14" (2 styles)	695.00		
Punch bowl stand only (2 styles)	250.00		
Salt and pepper (2 styles), pair	90.00	125.00	
Salt dip	60.00		
Sandwich server, center-handle	30.00	40.00	145.00

* s.e. McKee designation for scalloped edge   ** p.e. McKee designation for plain edge
*** Red Slag $350.00; Cobalt $325.00   **** Cobalt $325.00

	Crystal	All other colors	Red
Saucer	7.50	8.50	18.00
Sherbet or egg, 3½ ounce, footed	20.00	28.00	55.00
Spooner	45.00		
Stemware, 1 ounce footed, cordial	18.00	35.00	55.00
Stemware, 2 ounce, wine	25.00	28.00	50.00
Stemware, 3 ounce, wine	22.00	33.00	55.00
Stemware, 3½ ounce, footed, cocktail	16.00	21.00	45.00
Stemware, 6 ounce, footed, champagne	16.00	23.00	35.00
Stemware, 7 ounce	16.00	25.00	52.50
Stemware, 8 ounce, large footed goblet	22.00	26.00	57.50
Sundae, 6 ounce, low footed	12.00	18.00	38.00
Sugar, 10 ounce, open	15.00	22.00	45.00
Sugar, lid	35.00	50.00	135.00
Syrup with lid	225.00		895.00
Tray, 5⅜" x 7⅜", ⅞" high	65.00		
Tumbler, 2½ ounce, whiskey	20.00	30.00	50.00
Tumbler, 5 ounce, juice	16.00	25.00	57.50
Tumbler, 8 ounce, old fashioned	20.00	30.00	60.00
Tumbler, 9 ounce, concave or straight	22.00	26.00	52.50
Tumbler, 12 ounce, concave or straight	30.00	35.00	75.00
Vase, 6", cupped	90.00		
Vase, cornucopia	125.00	165.00	275.00
Vase, 11", footed	85.00	145.00	225.00

"ROMANESQUE," L. E. SMITH GLASS COMPANY, Early 1930s

Colors: black, amber, crystal, pink, yellow, and green

The jeweled arches of "Romanesque" are fascinating collectors and Internet buyers with their characteristic appeal.

Notice the black 10½" console bowl that is not footed, but comes with a separate base. The bowl rests on that plain, detached base. I imagine these may have been a smidgen wobbly; but a number of companies made bowls during this era, which resided on matched or different colored stands. This one would be difficult to place items in without tipping it unless they were well centered. Usually these type bowls held a glass frog in the center for mounting floral arrangements which would have worked just fine. You may find the bowl separate from the base these days, making it appear something like a turned edge plate. These were originally designed as console sets, having a pair of candles at each side, to be used as centerpieces on the rectangular "sideboards" and buffets which were de rigueur in madam's house. The stands elevated the bowls for visual appeal. Black pieces have the design on the bottoms; thus, the console bowl was turned over so you could see the pattern. I have only seen bowls and cake stands in black.

Pink is the difficult color to find, so notice the footed console in that color.

Green and amber seem to be widespread colors; we have, so far, found plates, candles, ruffled sherbets, and the bowl part of the console in amber. Notice the newly listed two-handled plate in the photo. The yellow is a bright, canary yellow that is often called "vaseline" by collectors.

Snack trays were sold with a sherbet to hold fruit or dessert. An original ad called these a luncheon set which is not what most companies considered their luncheon set. The fan vase is rarely seen as those who buy only fan vases have reported to me.

If you have other information or unlisted pieces in this pattern, please let me know.

	* All colors		* All colors
Bowl, 10", footed, 4¼" high	80.00	Plate, 8", round	10.00
Bowl, 10½"	50.00	Plate, 10", octagonal	25.00
Cake plate, 11½" x 2¾"	45.00	Plate, 10", octagonal, 2-handled	30.00
Candlestick, 2½", pair	30.00	Tray, snack	15.00
Plate, 5½", octagonal	6.00	Sherbet, plain top	10.00
Plate, 7", octagonal	8.00	Sherbet, scalloped top	12.00
Plate, 8", octagonal	12.00	Vase, 7½", fan	60.00

*Black or canary add 30%

ROSE CAMEO, BELMONT TUMBLER COMPANY, 1931

Color: green

Belmont Tumbler Company patented Rose Cameo. It only has seven pieces and it is possible that the actual production was fulfilled at Hazel Atlas. After all, Belmont was essentially a tumbler-making company. Glass cullet has been found in digs at a Hazel Atlas factory site in West Virginia. On the other hand, a yellow Cloverleaf shaker was excavated at the site of Akro Agate's factory in Clarksburg, West Virginia; and we doubt Akro had anything to do with making Cloverleaf. (Did you know some glass collectors apparently engage in archaeological quests for glass?) Actually, as we learn more about how the companies lent out their moulds and/or, contracted glass runs, anything is possible. Rather than lose a contract, a company could make some agreement with another who was running the requested color rather than change over vats to run it themselves. A bonded person transferred the valuable moulds between the plants. A dealer friend talked with a man whose job this was, and he told her he made about three runs per week between factories.

All three Rose Cameo bowls are difficult to find; but the smaller berry is the easiest. Most collectors are not finding the straight-sided 6" bowl at any price. That is the bowl pictured on its side on the far right, although the angle makes it look more like another plate.

Rose Cameo is not confusing new collectors as it once did. Cameo, with its dancing girl, and this cameo-encircled rose were often misidentified in the past when we were all learning. A well educated collecting public rarely makes those mistakes today.

There are two styles of tumblers; one flares and one does not. Some day I will show them together again as I once did.

Bowl, 4½", berry	16.00	Plate, 7", salad	15.00
Bowl, 5", cereal	24.00	Sherbet	15.00
Bowl, 6", straight sides	32.00	Tumbler, 5", footed (2 styles)	28.00

ROSE POINT BAND, "WATER LILY," "CLEMATIS," INDIANA GLASS COMPANY, c. 1915

Color: crystal

This ware was a contemporary of Depression glass and as such, we have included it simply because it's charming and can be found residing alongside Depression wares on flea market shelves. Indeed, I think I recall seeing a piece in the 1928 Sears catalog we have; but I can't put my hand on that right now to verify it. When it was first made, you could buy 240 pounds of it for $13.20 and command a net profit of $5.78! Most items were ten to 15¢, though the pitcher was 25¢! It was advertised to dealers as a "sure repeater and money maker" and was their "peerless common sense assortment" of eight dozen pieces! You got a half dozen of the shown items with the exception of the plate, sauce bowl, and small-footed sugar and creamer. The lot appears to have been shipped to dealers in a barrel. The plate and footed sugar shown in the picture were not included in the catalog listing I have; so, there probably are other items to be found. Let me know what you uncover so I can get it in the listing.

Bowl, sauce	8.00	Creamer, ftd.	12.50
Bowl, 7½", deep berry	15.00	Creamer, flat	12.50
Bowl, 7½", footed salad	15.00	Cruet (vinegar)	47.50
Bowl, 8½", footed fruit	22.50	Pitcher, ½ gal.	55.00
Bowl, 9½", footed, "fancy"	27.50	Plate, 11¾" ped. foot	25.00
Bowl, 10", crimped berry	30.00	Spoon (cupped tumbler for spoons)	25.00
Bowl, 10", orange (flared, straight rim)	30.00	Sugar, ftd.	12.50
Butter, w/cover	45.00	Sugar w/cover	17.50
Compote (footed jelly)	15.00	Tray, 8½", footed (flat compote)	22.00
Compote w/cover, 5½"	25.00	Vase (celery)	35.00

ROSEMARY, "DUTCH ROSE," FEDERAL GLASS COMPANY, 1935 – 1937

Colors: amber, green, pink; some iridized

The Rosemary pattern was a redesign of Federal's delightful Mayfair pattern because of Hocking's earlier patent of the Mayfair name. The story of Rosemary's having been redesigned from Federal's Mayfair pattern can be read on page 129. Rosemary is an appealing pattern particularly in green or pink. I've never heard anybody say they were regretful they chose it to collect — even those still searching for pieces to finish sets.

An amber set can be put together; there are only a few scarce pieces, namely the cereal and tumblers. I cannot remember when I have seen green cream soups, cereals, or tumblers. Pink Rosemary is found in even lesser amounts as you might surmise by the prices. Tumblers and grill plates have vanished into collections. I know it is exasperating to try to collect a color or pattern that is not being found at any price. Take heart. With the letters I get lamenting having *just* given it away, sold it for next to nothing, or plain trashed the Depression glass in their kin's estate, there's quite a bit more out there yet to be made available to the market.

The transitional green cream soups (see Federal Mayfair) could be placed with Rosemary in a pinch and few would be the wiser. An entire set of green Rosemary will probably take some time to gather.

Cereal bowls, cream soups, grill plates, and tumblers are rare in all colors. I noticed several want lists for green Rosemary cream soups on the Internet. I do not have one for photography. New collectors should know that grill plates are the divided plates usually associated with diners or grills (restaurants) of that time. Food was kept from running together by those raised partitions (normally three).

The sugar has no handles and is often identified as a sherbet. There is no sherbet.

There's a trend now to mix colors (and patterns, for that matter) into what are being called rainbow collections. That might serve you here as well if you are as charmed by this design as many are.

	Amber	Green	Pink		Amber	Green	Pink
Bowl, 9", two-handle		65.00	125.00	Plate, 6¾", salad	6.00	8.50	13.00
Bowl, 5", berry	6.00	10.00	15.00	Plate, dinner	10.00	15.00	25.00
Bowl, 5", cream soup	18.00	33.00	48.00	Plate, grill	10.00	20.00	30.00
Bowl, 6", cereal	30.00	40.00	52.00	Platter, 12", oval	16.00	27.00	40.00
Bowl, 10", oval vegetable	18.00	33.00	52.00	Saucer	5.00	5.00	6.00
Creamer, footed	10.00	12.50	25.00	Sugar, footed	10.00	12.50	25.00
Cup	7.50	9.50	12.00	Tumbler, 4¼", 9 ounce	30.00	42.00	78.00

ROULETTE, "MANY WINDOWS," HOCKING GLASS COMPANY, 1935 – 1938

Colors: green, pink, and crystal

This "winning" pattern, as Hocking once publicized Roulette, has six different tumblers. I now know why. These tumblers were used for promotion with pitchers as beverage sets. These were packaged with various tumblers and presented to retailers as product lures to attract customers to their shops. Once there for the "special" (usually a pitcher and six tumblers for around $1.00), they then could expect enthusiasm of the customer to take over and bask in an abundance of sales. Since this appears to have been a widely accepted custom, it evidently worked. Sometimes an entire luncheon set of 14 or 19 pieces was the bait. This pattern was touted for these functions. That may be why there are so few pieces. It may never have been advertised as a pattern by itself.

Roulette is the bona fide name of the pattern which collectors formerly called "Many Windows."

Pink pitchers and tumblers are easier to find than green ones, but pink Roulette was not made in any other pieces but those. Both colors are correspondingly priced. There are five sizes of pink flat tumblers; but I have never heard of a pink-footed tumbler.

Cups, saucers, sherbets, and luncheon plates can be attained in green. The 12" sandwich plate and fruit bowls are not so easily unearthed. Juice tumblers and the old fashioned are most evasive. I have not found a green juice in several years; but thanks to a reader, I was finally able to buy some green whiskeys. Those whiskeys sell very well to the shot-glass collecting group that is making its presence known in collecting spheres. One jovial gentleman told me he'd had a drink from all 114 of the ones he owned and "had enjoyed every one of 'em!" I couldn't decide whether he meant the glass shots, the drinks — or both!

Crystal tumbler and pitcher sets are very seldom found; however, there is limited demand for the few that have surfaced. Some crystal sets are adorned with colored stripes. In fact, this striped effect gives them an Art Deco air that pleases the Deco crowd.

	Crystal	Pink, Green		Crystal	Pink, Green
Bowl, 9", fruit	9.50	28.00	Sherbet	3.50	6.00
Cup	4.00	8.00	Tumbler, 3¼", 5 ounce, juice	7.00	28.00
Pitcher, 8", 65 ounce	32.00	48.00	Tumbler, 3¼", 7½ oz., old fashioned	23.00	50.00
Plate, 6", sherbet	3.50	5.00	Tumbler, 4⅛", 9 ounce, water	13.00	30.00
Plate, 8½", luncheon	5.00	8.00	Tumbler, 5⅛", 12 ounce, iced tea	16.00	38.00
Plate, 12", sandwich	11.00	17.50	Tumbler, 5½", 10 ounce, footed	14.00	38.00
Saucer	1.50	3.50	Whiskey, 2½", 1½ ounce	14.00	18.00

"ROUND ROBIN," ECONOMY GLASS CO., Probably early 1930s

Colors: green, iridescent, and crystal

The Domino tray is the expensive, unexpected piece in this small pattern. Hocking's Cameo is another pattern in Depression glass which offers a sugar cube tray. "Loaf sugar" was trendy, elegant even with tiny silver sugar tongs made especially to serve it. So, having *this* piece in this small pattern is slightly incongruous. If they were more abundant, we'd speculate they were after a premium contract with the sugar company! This tray has, so far, only been found in green "Round Robin." It is shown with the creamer on it in the picture. For new readers, the Domino tray held the creamer in the center ring with sugar cubes surrounding it. A famous sugar company made sugar cubes, and this tray became synonymous with that name. Few of these have ever been displayed at shows and they have been grabbed up for collections of sugar related items or by the few collectors of "Round Robin" who are lucky enough to see one.

Sherbets and berry bowls are the most difficult green pieces to come across outside the Domino tray. I have not even found a green berry bowl to photograph. Sherbets and berry bowls abound in iridescent. Saucers seem to be harder to find than the cups in both colors. Only a few patterns can claim that. The "Round Robin" cup is one of the small number of footed cups available in Depression glass. I have never found an iridescent cup and saucer.

Some crystal "Round Robin" is found today. Crystal was sprayed and baked to accomplish the iridized look. Obviously, not all the crystal was sprayed, since we find it occasionally. In addition, Cathy just found a "Round Robin" creamer that the top half is iridized and bottom half crystal. Their spraying hand, or technique, wasn't too meticulous, either!

A reader sent me word that author James Measell has definitely identified the manufacturer of this pattern as Economy Glass.

	Green	Iridescent
Bowl, 4", berry	12.00	9.00
Cup, footed	7.00	7.00
Creamer, footed	12.50	9.00
Domino tray	125.00	
Plate, 6", sherbet	3.00	2.50
Plate, 8", luncheon	8.00	4.00
Plate, 12", sandwich	14.00	10.00
Saucer	2.00	2.00
Sherbet	9.00	10.00
Sugar	12.50	9.00

ROXANA, HAZEL ATLAS GLASS COMPANY, 1932

Colors: "Golden Topaz," crystal, and some white

I've pictured a plate with its design highlighted in gold in hopes the Roxana pattern would show better in the photograph.

All seven known pieces are pictured below. This small pattern was obviously created strictly as promotional ware for product, thus, its shortage of pieces. Hazel Atlas only chronicled Roxana for one year.

Only the 4½" deep bowl has been found in Platonite; so if you find any other item, please let me know.

Thanks to a couple of Michigan collectors, we now know why Roxana seemed to be more prevalent there. An ad they supplied has been shown in previous editions. If you ate Star Brand Oats, you were able to receive one piece of "Golden Topaz" table glassware in every package. This "Golden Topaz" is what we now call yellow Roxana. That ad may show why the deep 4½" bowl and the 5½" plates are so hard to find. They were not packed as a premium in these oats. Roxana may have been used as a premium for something else, but so far that has not been revealed.

	Yellow	White
Bowl, 4½" x 2⅜"	15.00	20.00
Bowl, 5", berry	16.00	
Bowl, 6", cereal	22.00	
Plate, 5½"	12.00	
Plate, 6", sherbet	10.00	
Sherbet, footed	12.00	
Tumbler, 4¼", 9 ounce	25.00	

ROYAL LACE, HAZEL ATLAS GLASS COMPANY, 1934 – 1941

Colors: cobalt blue, crystal, green, pink; some amethyst (See Reproduction Section.)

Royal Lace collectors searching for green number almost as many as for the lovely cobalt blue. Green is found in quantity in England and many of those finds are being brought back home via Internet and freight shipments from abroad. A wealth of basic "tea" sets are there, i.e. cups, saucers, creamers, and sugars. The straight-sided pitcher must be the prevailing style in England as I bought several from a dealer there. I never bought any other style pitcher and only water tumblers, never other sizes. Shakers with original Hazel Atlas labels declaring, "Made in America" were on several sets I purchased. You have to wonder if Hazel Atlas named this pattern specifically for this "royal" market. It seems likely since this would have been made during the English coronation that so captivated everybody.

Royal Lace in cobalt blue is ever dear to my heart because I took box loads of it to my first Depression glass show in Springfield, Missouri, in 1971, and very nicely enhanced my paultry teaching salary by selling it to dealers and authors alike. I met the pioneer authors, Weatherman and Stout. Weatherman told me that the cobalt color for Royal Lace pattern was something of a fluke according to a factory employee because a cereal contractor didn't want any more Shirley Temple cobalt glassware. Since the factory had all that blue glass left in the vats they decided to make the Royal Lace they were running in that color, too. She also told me that Hocking did not make green cookie jars or yellow Mayfair indented butter dish bottoms, to her knowledge, and was certainly surprised when I pulled examples of each from my "show and tell" bag. I had found two of the butter bottoms in Dayton, Ohio, and selling one paid all my expenses on the trip. Those were the days when we were all learning new things about the glass every other day it seemed.

There were five different pitchers made in Royal Lace: a) 48 ounce, straight side; b) 64 ounce, 8", no ice lip; c) 68 ounce, 8", w/ice lip; d) 86 ounce, 8", no ice lip; e) 96 ounce, 8½", w/ice lip. The 10-ounce difference in the last two listed is caused by the spout on the pitcher without lip dipping below the top edge of the pitcher. This causes the liquid to run out before you get to the top. All spouted pitchers will vary in ounce capacity (up to eight ounces) depending upon how the spout tilts or dips. Always measure ounce capacities until no more liquid can be added without running out. The 68-ounce pitcher with ice lip is rarely found in green and cobalt blue.

The 4⅞", ten ounce tumblers have all been swallowed up into collections; but the number of iced teas and juice tumblers is rapidly diminishing. Some collectors only purchase water tumblers and the straight-sided pitcher for their collections. This style of pitcher with water tumblers is more prolific and, therefore, more inexpensively priced; but demand continues to drive up the price even on those. I should point out that "inexpensive" in cobalt Royal Lace is expensive in most other patterns.

Be aware that the cookie jar, juice, and water tumblers have been reproduced in a very dark cobalt blue which is quite dull-looking in comparison to the real thing. These are also out now in pink and possibly, green.

Both a rolled-edge console bowl and rolled-edge candlesticks have been found in amethyst Royal Lace. The only other amethyst pieces are the sherbets in metal holders and the cookie jar bottom used for toddy sets. There were reports of shakers years ago, but they have never been confirmed.

Like many other patterns we pursue today, Royal Lace could be mail ordered from the Sears catalog.

ROYAL LACE

	Crystal	Pink	Green	Blue
Bowl, 4¾", cream soup	17.50	32.00	38.00	50.00
Bowl, 5", berry	18.00	35.00	38.00	55.00
Bowl, 10", round berry	20.00	40.00	30.00	85.00
Bowl, 10", 3-legged, straight edge	35.00	65.00	75.00	95.00
* Bowl, 10", 3-legged, rolled edge	295.00	135.00	145.00	750.00
Bowl, 10", 3-legged, ruffled edge	55.00	115.00	135.00	850.00
Bowl, 11", oval vegetable	28.00	40.00	45.00	75.00
Butter dish and cover	80.00	195.00	275.00	695.00
Butter dish bottom	50.00	140.00	180.00	495.00
Butter dish top	30.00	55.00	95.00	200.00
Candlestick, straight edge, pair	40.00	75.00	95.00	165.00
** Candlestick, rolled edge, pair	60.00	155.00	175.00	550.00
Candlestick ruffled edge, pair	50.00	150.00	195.00	575.00
Cookie jar and cover	35.00	60.00	100.00	385.00
Cream, footed	16.00	22.00	28.00	60.00
Cup	9.00	22.00	20.00	45.00
Nut bowl	350.00	550.00	550.00	1,695.00
Pitcher, 48 ounce, straight sides	40.00	100.00	135.00	190.00

	Crystal	Pink	Green	Blue
Pitcher, 64 oz., 8", w/o lip	45.00	110.00	120.00	295.00
Pitcher, 8", 68 oz., w/lip	50.00	115.00	225.00	310.00
Pitcher, 8", 86 oz., w/o lip	50.00	135.00	175.00	395.00
Pitcher, 8½", 96 oz., w/lip	75.00	150.00	160.00	495.00
Plate, 6", sherbet	8.00	9.00	12.00	17.00
Plate, 8½", luncheon	8.00	15.00	16.00	43.00
Plate, 9⅞", dinner	18.00	33.00	38.00	48.00
Plate, 9⅞", grill	11.00	22.00	28.00	40.00
Platter, 13", oval	20.00	45.00	42.00	65.00
Salt and pepper, pair	42.00	65.00	140.00	340.00
Saucer	5.00	7.00	10.00	14.00
Sherbet, footed	17.00	20.00	25.00	55.00
*** Sherbet in metal holder	4.00			42.00
Sugar	11.00	20.00	22.00	40.00
Sugar lid	20.00	60.00	60.00	195.00
Tumbler, 3½", 5 ounce	20.00	33.00	40.00	60.00
Tumbler, 4⅛", 9 ounce	16.00	28.00	32.00	50.00
Tumbler, 4⅞", 10 ounce	40.00	85.00	95.00	165.00
Tumbler, 5⅜", 12 ounce	40.00	75.00	75.00	140.00

**** Toddy or cider set includes cookie jar, metal lid, metal tray, 8 roly-poly cups, and ladle   295.00

* Amethyst $900.00   ** Amethyst $900.00   *** Amethyst $40.00   **** Amethyst $195.00

ROYAL RUBY, ANCHOR HOCKING GLASS COMPANY, 1938 – 1940

Color: Ruby red

Anchor Hocking's patented Royal Ruby (red) color was introduced in 1938 using their existing moulds. I am identifying and pricing only pieces of Royal Ruby produced before 1940 in my listing here. Royal Ruby pieces made after 1940 are now in the *Collectible Glassware from the 40s, 50s, 60s....* Remember, only Anchor Hocking's red can rightfully be called Royal Ruby even though many collectors use that term for any red glassware. Oyster and Pearl, Old Cafe, and Coronation were among the patterns used in the original Royal Ruby production. A smattering of pieces in Royal Ruby have been found in other Anchor Hocking lines including Colonial, Ring, Manhattan, Queen Mary, Pillar Optic, and Miss America. These Royal Ruby pieces are generally considered rare in these highly collected patterns and most are of extraordinary quality for Anchor Hocking, having ground bottoms, which are usually not found on the normal mass-produced glassware. There were other designs produced that were numbered lines and never given pattern names. None of those items is priced in the listing below.

I suspect that the name of the color was inspired by our country's fascination with the English coronation of Edward VIII in 1936 and his subsequent renouncing of that royal crown.

Bonbon, 6½"	8.50		Cup, round	6.00
Bowl, 3¾", berry (Old Cafe)	9.00		Goblet, ball stem	12.00
Bowl, 4½", handled (Coronation)	8.00		Jewel box, 4¼", crystal w/Ruby cov.	12.50
Bowl, 4⅞", smooth (Sandwich)	12.50		Lamp (Old Cafe)	150.00
Bowl, 5¼", scalloped (Sandwich)	20.00		Marmalade, 5⅛", crystal w/Ruby cov.	7.50
Bowl, 5½", 1-handled (Oyster & Pearl)	22.00		Plate, 8½", luncheon (Coronation)	10.00
Bowl, 6½", deep-handled (Oyster & Pearl)	30.00		Plate, 9⅛", dinner, round	11.00
Bowl, 6½", handled (Coronation)	20.00		Plate, 13½", sandwich (Oyster & Pearl)	55.00
Bowl, 6½", scalloped (Sandwich)	27.50		Puff box, 4⅝", crystal w/Ruby cov.	9.00
Bowl, 8", handled (Coronation)	20.00		Relish tray insert (Manhattan)	4.00
Bowl, 8¼", scalloped (Sandwich)	50.00		Saucer, round	2.50
Bowl, 10½", deep fruit (Oyster & Pearl)	60.00		Sherbet, low footed (Old Cafe)	16.00
Candle holder, 3½", pair (Oyster & Pearl)	65.00		Sugar, footed	7.50
Candle holder, 4½", pair (Queen Mary)	125.00		Sugar, lid	11.00
Candy dish, 8" mint, low (Old Cafe)	20.00		Tray, 6" x 4½"	12.50
Candy jar, 5½", crystal w/Ruby cov. (Old Cafe)	25.00		Tumbler, 3", juice (Old Cafe)	22.00
Cigarette box/card holder, 6⅛" x 4", crystal w/Ruby top	65.00		Tumbler, 4", water (Old Cafe)	35.00
Creamer, footed	9.00		Vase, 7¼" (Old Cafe)	55.00
Cup (Coronation)	6.50		Vase, 9", two styles	17.50
Cup (Old Cafe)	12.00			

"S" PATTERN, "STIPPLED ROSE BAND," MacBETH-EVANS GLASS COMPANY, 1930 – 1933

Colors: crystal; crystal w/trims of silver, blue, green, amber; pink; some amber, green, fired-on red; ruby, Monax, and light yellow

When collecting Depression glass started in the early '70s, there was real excitement about "S" pattern. It came in various colors and trims, with a couple of styles of pitchers and a huge cake plate like the much-ballyhooed Dogwood one. On a trip to Ohio in 1972, I bought six or seven red "S" pattern luncheon plates like American Sweetheart, but they had never been seen before. They sold for $70.00 each and I kept one for myself. Since then, I had only seen one other priced for $100.00 several years ago. Last fall I ran into a group of five and have been unable to sell them for $40.00, some 30 years later. Times change as do collectors' interests. Early on, color and unusual pieces were highly admired, but today, collectors do not pay big prices for odd colors and unusual pieces unless they are in a major, highly desired pattern. Now, I see this dear, delicate little pattern, which wasn't long in production, being ignored at markets. It would be a great pattern for a beginning collector to latch onto.

"S" Pattern with platinum or pastel bands commands more respect than does plain crystal. Amber, blue, or green-banded crystal was made. Crystal luncheon plates could be striking against a colored charger plate that would emphasize the romanticized fleur de lis pattern occurring as a scrolled rim design.

Amber "S" Pattern sometimes appears more yellow than amber. The color is almost the hue of Hocking's Princess. A dinner plate does occur in amber "S" Pattern and the amber pitcher in this pattern is rare. No crystal (nor crystal with trim) dinner plates have been spotted.

A pink or green pitcher and tumbler set appears occasionally. Years ago, there were a number of pitcher collectors per se; rare pitchers sold fast in the $200.00 – 500.00 range. Now, those same pitchers are commanding four-figure prices, but, alas, not those of "S" pattern.

Finding a pink tumbler that has a moulded blossom design will indicate a Dogwood moulded tumbler and not "S" Pattern. The only pink or green tumblers found in "S" Pattern have an applied, silk-screened "S" design on the glass. However, crystal tumblers come with moulded "S" designs.

This is a sweet pattern which really doesn't deserve to be such a wallflower now, after being the belle of the ball years ago!

	Crystal	Yellow, Amber, Crystal w/Trims		Crystal	Yellow, Amber, Crystal w/Trims
˙Bowl, 5½", cereal	5.00	9.00	Plate, grill	6.50	8.00
Bowl, 8½", large berry	15.00	20.00	Plate, 11¾", heavy cake	50.00	65.00
*Creamer, thick or thin	5.00	7.00	***Plate, 13", heavy cake	70.00	90.00
*Cup, thick or thin	3.50	4.50	Saucer	2.00	2.50
Pitcher, 80 ounce (like "Dogwood"), green or pink $550.00	65.00	160.00	Sherbet, low footed	4.50	7.00
			*Sugar, thick and thin	5.00	6.50
Pitcher, 80 ounce (like "American Sweetheart")	90.00		Tumbler, 3½", 5 ounce	5.00	8.00
Plate, 6", sherbet, Monax 8.00	2.50	3.00	Tumbler, 4", 9 ounce, green or pink $50.00	10.00	12.00
**Plate, 8¼", luncheon	7.00	6.00	Tumbler, 4¾, 10 ounce	11.00	12.00
Plate, 9¼", dinner		10.00	Tumbler, 5", 12 ounce	12.00	15.00

* Fired-on red items will run approximately twice price of amber   **Red $40.00; Monax $10.00   ***Amber $77.50

SANDWICH, INDIANA GLASS COMPANY, 1920s–1980s

Colors: crystal late 1920s – today; teal blue 1950s – 1980s; milk white mid-1950s; amber late 1920s – 1980s; red 1933, 1970s; Smokey Blue 1976 – 1977; pink, green 1920s – early 1930s

Since green Indiana Sandwich was chosen for the cover of my *Pocket Guide to Depression Glass, 12th Edition,* I have received numerous calls and letters from people who think they have old Sandwich, but who actually have Tiara's 1980s version called Chantilly. None of the Tiara green will glow under ultraviolet light. I hasten to add that this is not a general test for age of glass. There is glass made yesterday which will glow under black light. It is a test for this particular green Sandwich vs. Chantilly pattern. Any green piece that has no price listed is presumably new. Indiana also made a lighter pink in recent years.

Amber Sandwich is priced here with crystal. Realize that most all amber found today is from the Tiara issues and is not Depression-era glass. There is no easy way to distinguish old crystal from new as most of the new was made from original moulds.

Only six items in red Sandwich date from 1933, i.e., cups, saucers, luncheon plates, water goblets, creamers, and sugars. In the 1970s, Tiara Home Products marketed red Sandwich. Today, there is no difference in pricing red unless you have some marked 1933 Chicago World's Fair, which will fetch considerably more as guaranteed old and a World's Fair collectible.

	Amber, Crystal	Teal Blue	Red	Pink, Green
Ashtrays (club, spade, heart, diamond shapes, each)	3.00			
Basket, 10" high	30.00			
Bowl, 4¼", berry	3.50			
Bowl, 6"	4.00			
Bowl, 6", hexagonal	5.00	14.00		
Bowl, 8½"	11.00			
Bowl, 9", console	16.00			40.00
Bowl, 11½", console	18.50			50.00
Butter dish and cover, domed	22.00	*155.00		
Butter dish bottom	6.00	42.50		
Butter dish top	16.00	112.50		
Candlesticks, 3½", pair	16.00			45.00
Candlesticks 7", pair	30.00			
Creamer	9.00		45.00	
Celery, 10½"	16.00			
Creamer and sugar on diamond shaped tray	16.00	32.00		
Cruet, 6½ ounce and stopper	26.00	135.00		175.00
Cup	3.50	8.50	27.50	
Decanter and stopper	25.00		80.00	150.00

	Amber, Crystal	Teal Blue	Red	Pink, Green
Goblet, 9 ounce	13.00		45.00	
Mayonnaise, footed	13.00			35.00
Pitcher, 68 ounce	20.00		130.00	
Plate, 6", sherbet	3.00	7.00		
Plate, 7", bread and butter	4.00			
Plate, 8", oval, indent for cup	5.50			15.00
Plate, 8⅜", luncheon	4.75		20.00	
Plate, 10½", dinner	8.00			20.00
Plate, 13", sandwich	12.75	24.00	35.00	25.00
Puff box	16.00			
Salt and pepper, pair	17.50			
Sandwich server, center	18.00		45.00	35.00
Saucer	2.50	4.50	7.50	
Sherbet, 3¼"	5.50	14.00		
Sugar, large	9.00		45.00	
Sugar lid for large size	12.00			
Tumbler, 3 ounce, footed, cocktail	6.00			
Tumbler, 8 ounce, footed, water	8.00			
Tumbler, 12 ounce, footed, iced tea	9.00			
Wine, 3", 4 ounce	5.00		12.50	25.00

*Beware recent vintage sell $22.00

SHARON, "CABBAGE ROSE," FEDERAL GLASS COMPANY, 1935 – 1939

Colors: pink, green, amber; some crystal (See Reproduction Section.)

In the last few books, I have shown an old advertising page where coupons could be exchanged for various items of Federal's "Golden Glow" (amber) glassware. I pointed out that the plain pitcher in that ad (without design), would sell in the $35.00 range. It did *not* occur to me that someone would assume that plain pitcher without design to be Sharon. However, I received an irate e-mail from someone trying to sell one of these plain green pitchers as rare green Sharon on an Internet auction. As with all patterns in this book, if the pattern is not on the piece, it is only moulded like the item and not the pattern itself.

Green Sharon pitchers and tumblers in all sizes are difficult to find. Surprisingly, the green pitcher without ice lip is rarer than the one with an ice lip. You will find thick or thin flat iced teas and waters. The thick tumblers are easier to find in green; and the price reflects that. In amber and pink, the heavy iced teas are more rarely seen than the waters. There are no green soup bowls, only jam dishes.

Prices have softened a bit for common pieces of amber and pink Sharon, which are presently sitting at markets. Footed amber tumblers in Sharon are rare and pitchers with ice lips are twice as difficult to locate as pink. However, there are definitely fewer collectors for them right now, which translates into fewer dollars commanded due to lack of demand.

The decreasing calls for pink Sharon have caused some deflation in those prices. New collectors were timid about starting this extremely popular pink pattern a few years ago due to some reproductions flooding markets. However, once everyone learned how to recognize them (see the reproduction section), demand for this durable, 65-year-old pattern flourished once again. Then the economic problems hit and collecting has slowed. Cathy's grandmother told her she remembered the drummer who came around selling Sharon put the plate on the floor and stood on it to show how sturdy this ware was. The price for a pink Sharon cheese dish has jumped into four figures. The top for the cheese and butter dish is the same piece. The bottoms are different. The butter bottom is a 1½" deep bowl with a sloping, indented ledge while the cheese bottom is a flat salad plate with a raised band of glass on its surface within which the lid rests. The bottom piece is the rare part of this cheese. Amber cheese dishes were made; but none has ever surfaced in green. A collector told me he'd found an old ad showing these were a special promotion item run for some cheese products. It would appear no one much wanted the product, else more of these dishes would have been produced and we wouldn't have such a scarcity of them, today. Other infrequently found pink Sharon items include flat, thick iced teas and jam dishes. The jam dish is like the butter bottom except it has no indentation for the top. It differs from the 1⅞" deep soup bowl by standing only 1½" tall. Occasionally, you can find a jam dish priced as a soup bowl; but that happens rarely in today's world of informed collectors and dealers.

SHARON

	Amber	Pink	Green
Bowl, 5", berry	8.00	12.00	18.00
Bowl, 5", cream soup	28.00	52.00	55.00
Bowl, 6", cereal	22.00	28.00	30.00
Bowl, 7¾", flat soup, 1⅞" deep	55.00	55.00	
Bowl, 8½", large berry	5.00	32.00	38.00
Bowl, 9½", oval vegetable	16.00	30.00	35.00
Bowl, 10½", fruit	22.00	45.00	42.50
Butter dish and cover	50.00	60.00	90.00
Butter dish bottom	25.00	30.00	40.00
Butter dish top	25.00	30.00	50.00
* Cake plate, 11½", footed	27.50	40.00	65.00
Candy jar and cover	45.00	50.00	175.00
Cheese dish and cover	215.00	1,600.00	
Creamer, footed	14.00	20.00	22.50
Cup	10.00	14.00	20.00
Jam dish, 7½"	40.00	285.00	65.00
Pitcher, 80 ounce, w/ice lip	155.00	195.00	450.00
Pitcher, 80 ounce, w/o ice lip	140.00	185.00	475.00
Plate, 6", bread and butter	5.00	8.00	9.00
** Plate, 7½", salad	15.00	22.00	25.00
Plate, 9½", dinner	11.00	18.00	25.00

*Crystal $10.00   **Crystal $50.00   ***Crystal $20.00

	Amber	Pink	Green
Platter, 12½", oval	16.00	30.00	35.00
Salt and pepper, pair	38.00	58.00	70.00
Saucer	5.00	9.00	11.00
Sherbet, footed	12.00	16.00	37.50
Sugar	9.00	12.00	16.00
Sugar lid	22.00	32.00	40.00
Tumbler, 4⅛", 9 ounce, thick	26.00	45.00	80.00
Tumbler, 4⅛", 9 ounce, thin	26.00	42.00	85.00
Tumbler, 5¼", 12 ounce, thin	55.00	55.00	110.00
Tumbler, 5¼", 12 ounce, thick	65.00	100.00	110.00
*** Tumbler, 6½", 15 ounce, footed	90.00	55.00	

"SHIPS" or "SAILBOAT" also known as "SPORTSMAN SERIES,"
HAZEL ATLAS GLASS COMPANY, Late 1930s

Colors: cobalt blue w/white, yellow, and red decoration, crystal w/blue

Regrettably, cobalt Moderntone decorated with white "Ships" is now rarely seen especially in mint condition. Sherbet plates are harder to find than dinner plates, but both have vanished into long-standing collections. There is no Moderntone cup with a "Ships" decoration that fits the saucer, which does have a "Ships" decoration. The cup is just a normal Moderntone cup. Prices below are for mint pieces. Discolored (beige) or worn items should sell for less, but some collectors will only accept mint. When the "Ships" pattern is partly missing, it would be easier to sell if the whole ship had sunk and you only had a cobalt blue piece.

The confusing "Ships" shot glass is the smallest (2½", two-ounce) tumbler, not the heavy bottomed tumbler that holds four-ounces and is 3¼" tall. I have letters from people who purchased this 4-ounce tumbler under the impression (or having been told) it was a shot glass. It was sold as a liquor tumbler with the cocktail shaker, but never as the shot. Shot glasses never hold more than 2-ounces according to some of my drinking friends. You will notice there is a large price difference between the authentic, 2-ounce shot and the 4-ounce tumbler. The price for that 4-ounce tumbler has increased, maybe due to its sale as supposed shot glasses. Do you suppose they made that tumbler heavy bottomed for trembling hands and blurry eyesight?

At least one yellow "Ships" old-fashioned tumbler has surfaced in "raincoat" yellow. Pieces also are found with red and white "Ships" or crystal tumblers with a blue boat.

I enjoy the decorations that have the red boats with white sails. So far, only pitchers and tumblers are found with this patriotic red, white, and blue combination. Have you spotted other items?

I might mention that no red glass pitcher has ever been found to go with the red glass (different design) ships tumblers ($10.00) often found in the markets. I receive several dozen letters a year asking about those.

	Blue, White		Blue, White		Blue, White
Cup (Plain), "Moderntone"	11.00	Plate, 8", salad	30.00	Tumbler, 5 ounce, 3¾", juice	14.00
Cocktail mixer w/stirrer	33.00	Plate, 9", dinner	42.00	Tumbler, 6 ounce, roly poly	12.00
Cocktail shaker	40.00	Saucer	22.00	Tumbler, 8 oz., 3⅜", old fashioned	18.00
Ice bowl	40.00	Tumbler, 2 oz., 2¼", shot glass	235.00	Tumbler, 9 oz., 3¾", straight, water	14.00
Pitcher w/o lip, 82 ounce	65.00	Tumbler, 3½", whiskey	25.00	Tumbler, 9 oz., 4⅝", water	11.00
Pitcher w/lip, 86 ounce	75.00	Tumbler, 4 oz., heavy bottom	25.00	Tumbler, 10½ oz., 4⅞", iced tea	16.00
Plate, 5⅞", sherbet	28.00	Tumbler, 4 oz., 3¼", heavy bottom	25.00	Tumbler, 12 ounce, iced tea	28.00

SIERRA, "PINWHEEL," JEANNETTE GLASS COMPANY, 1931 – 1933

Colors: green, pink, and some Ultra Marine

The word Sierra is of Spanish origin meaning saw or sawtooth, which makes this an excellent name choice for this delightful 1930s Jeannette glassware. Collectors are charmed by it though it is now all but disappearing from the market in both colors. Pink and green pitchers, tumblers, and oval vegetable bowls are safely tucked into collections and few are being offered for sale. I rushed over to check out a vegetable bowl in a mall, recently, only to notice one of the points was missing. A consummate problem with Sierra is finding mint condition items. If pieces were used much, one or more of those points is usually chipped or nicked.

Always closely examine any pink Sierra butter dishes to check for the Adam/Sierra combination lid. That is how I found my first one. Be sure to read about this elusive and pricey butter under Adam. One is pictured in *Very Rare Glassware of the Depression Years, Fifth Series*.

Wrong cups are often placed on Sierra saucers. Any pink cup of nondescript origin can be found atop the saucers. Original cups have the design on the cup without the serrated rim. You would have an excellent dribble cup if it were on the rim. You have to be vigilant when you are out shopping. Saucers are becoming harder to find than cups because of damaged points. The cups, pitchers, and tumblers all have smooth edges instead of the serrated edges of the other pieces and, therefore, do not chip as easily.

Mint sugar bowls are harder to find than lids because of the points on the bowl.

There have been four Sierra Ultra Marine cups found and one is pictured below, but no saucer has been reported. Were these a sample run made at the time Jeannette was making Ultra Marine Doric and Pansy or Swirl? You might even see some fired-on colors of Sierra. They have been reported several times, even though I haven't witnessed any.

	Pink	Green		Pink	Green
Bowl, 5½", cereal	15.00	18.00	Platter, 11", oval	60.00	80.00
Bowl, 8½", large berry	35.00	40.00	Salt and pepper, pair	45.00	45.00
Bowl, 9¼", oval vegetable	85.00	160.00	Saucer	8.00	9.00
Butter dish and cover	75.00	80.00	Serving tray, 10¼", 2 handles	22.50	20.00
Creamer	22.50	25.00	Sugar	25.00	30.00
Cup	13.00	16.00	Sugar cover	18.00	18.00
Pitcher, 6½", 32 ounce	140.00	175.00	Tumbler, 4½", 9 ounce, footed	80.00	100.00
Plate, 9", dinner	25.00	28.00			

SPIRAL, HOCKING GLASS COMPANY, 1928 – 1930

Colors: green, crystal, and pink and fired-on red

Hocking's Spiral is one of many spiraling patterns from the Depression era which have their origin in older, pattern glass lines. Availability of Spiral in crystal and pink is very limited; but green can be collected with some effort. The real difficulty lies in recognizing Hocking's Spiral among the many others produced. Notice shape! Many pieces of Hocking's Spiral, the ice tub, platter, cake plate, creamer, and sugar, are shaped like their popular Cameo and Block Optic patterns. The seldom seen platter has closed or tab handles, as do many made by Hocking. A recent discovery is a Rainbow Spiral vase in red.

A luncheon set can be assembled rather inexpensively in Spiral. However, this is not a pattern often displayed for sale at glass shows. You will have to ask for it.

The Hocking Spiral center-handled server has a solid handle while its Imperial Glass Company counterpart, Twisted Optic (Line #313), has an open handle. The pitcher shown has the rope top treatment like those found in Cameo and Block Optic. There is also a 7⅝", 54-ounce bulbous based one (like shown in Block Optic) available with the Spiral pattern. Notice there are two styles of sugars and creamers found in Spiral, one a flat based, utilitarian style, like the Block Optic flat style, and one footed with a fancier handle, like Cameo. Generally speaking, Spiral swirls go to the left or clockwise while Twisted Optic spirals go to the right or counterclockwise. (Westmoreland's #1710 Spiral line and Duncan's Spiral Flutes have hand-polished bottoms on flat pieces, something not found on Hocking's machine-made Spiral; also the pattern lines have different shapes from the Hocking line; so, there should be no confusion between these and Hocking Spiral.)

I just received a photograph of a footed cake plate with an embossed ad for White Lily flour around the edge. Be on the lookout for another.

A few pieces of Hocking Spiral have turned up in crystal though few collectors care. Green is the Spiral color dear to collectors' hearts. At this stage of collecting, I am beginning to wonder if pink Spiral exists even though listed in an old catalog. Do you own a piece?

	Green		Green
Bowl, 4¾", berry	8.00	Platter, 12"	35.00
Bowl, 7", mixing	15.00	Preserve and cover	35.00
Bowl, 8", large berry	12.50	Salt and pepper, pair	35.00
Cake plate	20.00	Sandwich server, center handle	25.00
Creamer, flat or footed	10.00	Saucer	2.00
Cup	5.00	Sherbet	5.00
Ice or butter tub	32.00	Sugar, flat or footed	10.00
Pitcher, 7⅝", 54 ounce, bulbous	45.00	Tumbler, 3", 5 ounce, juice	4.50
Pitcher, 7⅝", 58 ounce	40.00	Tumbler, 5", 9 ounce, water	10.00
Plate, 6", sherbet	2.50	Tumbler, 5⅞", footed	18.00
Plate, 8", luncheon	3.50	Vase, 5¾", footed	65.00

SPRINGTIME, MONONGAH GLASS COMPANY, c. 1927

Color: crystal w/24-karat gold band decoration

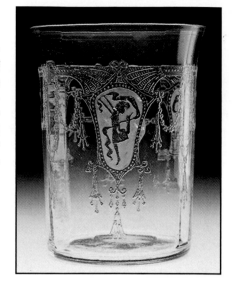

Monongah, who advertised themselves as "pioneers in the manufacture of the automatic machine pressed tumbler," was absorbed by Hocking and this pattern became their basis for the enormously popular Cameo pattern. Springtime was made with a 24-karat gold band trim, which, 75 years later, is mostly absent from pieces you find; and the blanks have an optic rib effect. You find this only occasionally; so I would suggest that you buy whatever crosses your path if you wish to collect this lovely older design. Often the piece is inexpensive since it is mostly unrecognized — and usually a lone tumbler or stem.

Bowl, finger	45.00
Creamer	35.00
Decanter, 26 oz., w/cut facet stop	125.00
Pitcher, 30 oz., juice w/lid	100.00
Pitcher, 50 oz., water, straight rim	125.00
Pitcher, 50 oz., tea w/lid	195.00
Pitcher, 60 oz., water, slope rim	165.00
Plate, 6½"	10.00
Plate, 8½", luncheon	17.50
Stem, ¾ oz., brandy cordial	145.00
Stem, 1½ oz., ftd. almond	35.00
Stem, 2½ oz., wine	45.00
Stem, 2½ oz., cocktail	35.00
Stem, 4 oz., claret	50.00
Stem, 5½ oz., parfait	45.00

Stem, 5½ oz., high sherbet	25.00
Stem, 5½ oz., low sherbet	25.00
Stem, 9 oz., goblet	30.00
Stem, 6" confection stand (compote)	30.00
Sugar, open	35.00
Tumbler, 2½ oz., whiskey	55.00
Tumbler, 5 oz., juice	35.00
Tumbler, 7 oz., ginger ale	35.00
Tumbler, 8 oz., water	30.00
Tumbler, 9 oz., water	30.00
Tumbler, 10 oz., tea	35.00
Tumbler, 13 oz., hdld. ice tea	65.00
Tumbler, 13 oz., tea	50.00

* Deduct 10 – 20% for missing gold trim

SQUARE "HAZEN," LINE #760 et al., IMPERIAL GLASS COMPANY, c. 1930s

Colors: crystal, green, pink, ruby

Square was an interesting small line of Imperial's which was promoted as luncheon sets having 15, 21, or 27 pieces. I was lucky enough to find a large set in an antique mall close to our home. The unusual style handles and the rich, ruby coloring intrigued me.

Although the owner of the set knew only that it was red glass, she had a high evaluation of its worth. Often, it is not easy to buy red, cobalt blue, black, or older canary glass from sellers who do not know what they have for sale. Color is frequently highly priced — and often inflated. As an example, I picked up a piece of Emerald green Cambridge to look for a price at a recent antique fair. The owner informed me that it was an old piece of "vaseline" and he only wanted $125.00 (for that $40.00 item on a good day). I casually mentioned that the company that made it called it Emerald green and he looked at me as if I had sprouted horns. No form of green is "vaseline" no matter what you are told. My experience is that you cannot deal with uninformed sellers who already know more than you do. Just watch for their mistakes in pricing; they will make some!

	Crystal, Pink, Green	Ruby		Crystal, Pink, Green	Ruby
Bowl, 4½", nappy	14.00	18.00	Plate, 8", salad	12.50	17.50
Bowl, 7", square, soup/salad	18.00	25.00	Saucer	5.00	7.50
Creamer, footed	20.00	25.00	Server, 10½", center handled	35.00	50.00
Cup	18.00	25.00	Shaker, square, foot, pair	35.00	50.00
Plate, 6", dessert	7.50	10.00	Sugar, footed	20.00	25.00

STARLIGHT, HAZEL ATLAS GLASS COMPANY, 1938 – 1940

Colors: crystal, pink; some white, cobalt

Starlight is an economically priced pattern; the difficulty lies in locating it. This small pattern has never been assembled by large numbers of collectors, but the ones who do try for a set report shortages of sherbets, cereals, and the large salad bowl and liner/serving plate. One collector told me they used that bowl as a punch bowl. It is not very deep, so maybe her parties are small or the punch is very strong and not much is needed. However, that bowl is the basis for the punch set pictured below. Pink and cobalt blue bowls make nice accessory pieces with the crystal, but only bowls are available in those colors.

Do notice the Starlight punch bowl set pictured which a number of collectors wish was theirs. This set is similar in make up to the Royal Lace toddy set, having a bowl in a metal holder with an extending flat rim to accommodate cups. A metal ladle with a red knob rests in the bowl. I owe this find to a collector who bought it just for me to use in my book, a gesture mightily appreciated. She told me, "I knew the moment they put that up for auction that you would like that for your book."

The 5½" cereal is handled and measures 6" including the handles. Measurements in this book do not include handles, unless specified in the price listing.

I often pondered why Starlight shakers were found with a one hole shaker top. I now know. It was a specially designed top made to keep the salt "moisture proof." Airko shakers with these tops are often seen in southern areas where the humid air caused shaker holes to clog. One of these moisture-proof shakers is pictured here with an original label.

	Crystal, White	Pink		Crystal, White	Pink
Bowl, 5½", cereal, closed handles	8.00	12.00	Plate, 9", dinner	8.00	
* Bowl, 8½", closed handles	12.00	20.00	Plate, 13", sandwich	15.00	18.00
Bowl, 11½", salad	30.00		Relish dish	15.00	
Bowl, 12", 2¾" deep	40.00		Salt and pepper, pair	22.50	
Creamer, oval	8.00		Saucer	2.00	
Cup	5.00		Sherbet	15.00	
Plate, 6", bread and butter	3.00		Sugar, oval	8.00	
Plate, 8½", luncheon	5.00		* Cobalt $32.50		

STRAWBERRY, U.S. GLASS COMPANY, Early 1930s

Colors: pink, green, crystal; some iridized

Most Depression glass patterns that U.S. Glass made are reminiscent of pattern glassware designs of the late 1890s and early 1900s. Both shape, and to some extent the Strawberry pattern itself, is a direct throwback to pattern glass. Since both Strawberry and its sister pattern, Cherryberry, are so popular with today's collectors, this shows a certain ageless, continuity of appreciation, which is nice to see in this age of throw-away-everything. Strawberry is asked for at every show if I do not have any on display.

The crystal and iridescent pitchers are in few collections, but it is not necessarily Strawberry collectors who are plucking them. Carnival collectors cherish iridescent Strawberry pitchers and tumblers more highly than Depression glass collectors do. By cherish more highly, I mean they will shell out more for them. The overriding carnival glass test is that it has to have full, vivid color that does not fade out toward the bottom, as many do. This prejudice holds with Depression glass collectors who want strong color also. Crystal is priced with iridescent because it is, categorically, rare.

Green Strawberry acquires more attention than pink and matching color tones of green seems to be an inconsequential issue unlike other patterns where color is a primary concern. Green or pink Strawberry can be collected as a set; however, there are no cups, saucers, or dinner-sized plates. There is usual mould roughness on the seams. Even pieces that are identified as mint may have extra glass roughness where it came out of the mould.

Strawberry sugar covers and the 6¼", 2" deep bowl are hard to find. Some mistakenly label the sugar with no lid and no handles as a spooner; however, by the Depression era, spooners were passé.

Strawberry has a plain butter dish bottom that is adaptable to other U.S. Glass patterns. Some of those other U.S. Glass pattern butters have been stripped of their bottoms over the years to use with Strawberry tops. Strawberry butter dishes have been desirable to collectors since day one. In fact, in the 35-year-ago "pioneering" days of Depression glass collecting, there was a strong cadre of butter dish collectors. That would be prohibitive today, even if they were available in the markets to the degree they once were.

	Crystal, Iridescent	Pink, Green		Crystal, Iridescent	Pink, Green
Bowl, 4", berry	6.50	14.00	Pickle dish, 8¼", oval	9.00	20.00
Bowl, 6¼", 2" deep	65.00	165.00	Pitcher, 7¾"	175.00	225.00
Bowl, 6½", deep salad	15.00	25.00	Plate, 6", sherbet	5.00	12.00
Butter dish and cover	135.00	195.00	Plate, 7½", salad	12.00	18.00
Butter dish bottom	77.50	100.00	Sherbet	8.00	10.00
Butter dish top	57.50	75.00	Sugar, small, open	12.00	22.00
Comport, 5¾"	18.00	35.00	Sugar, large	22.00	45.00
Creamer, small	12.00	22.00	Sugar cover	45.00	75.00
Creamer, 4⅝", large	22.50	40.00	Tumbler, 3⅝", 8 ounce	22.00	42.00
Olive dish, 5", one-handle	9.00	20.00			

"SUNBURST," "HERRINGBONE," JEANNETTE GLASS COMPANY, Late 1930s

Colors: crystal

I have found no catalog or publication sharing any name for this pattern that I have heard called both "Sunburst" and "Herringbone," but more people use "Sunburst."

"Sunburst" candlesticks are the most frequently seen pieces, while sherbets, dinner plates, and tumblers are the hardest to spot. The tumbler is comparable in style to the flat Iris with a flared top, since it was made from the same shaped moulds as Iris. Perhaps by next book I'll find one to show! Wouldn't one of these type berry bowls and the divided relish have been great additions to the Iris pattern? Inner rims are easily nicked and need to be checked just as in the Iris pattern; and rims should be protectively stacked with paper plates. The large clear areas on plates show wear and scratches if used, so check that out when buying plates. Collectors would probably not have noticed "Sunburst" had it not been for the popular sister pattern, Iris. Several collectors told me they started buying "Sunburst" when they were collecting Iris or shortly after Iris reached those elevated prices that it fetches today.

I am listing only pieces I have found or pieces that have been in photographs sent me over the years. I would not be amazed by additional finds. Let me know what you have in your collection.

Bowl, 4¾", berry	10.00	Plate, 11¾", sandwich	25.00
Bowl, 8½", berry	20.00	Relish, 2-part	15.00
Bowl, 10¾"	27.50	Saucer	4.00
Candlesticks, double, pair	25.00	Sherbet	17.50
Creamer, footed	10.00	Sugar	10.00
Cup	10.00	Tray, small, oval	12.00
Plate, 5½"	9.00	Tumbler, 4", 9 ounce, flat	35.00
Plate, 9¼", dinner	22.00		

SUNFLOWER, JEANNETTE GLASS COMPANY, 1930s

Colors: pink, green, some Delphite; some opaque colors and Ultra Marine

Sunflower, like Cloverleaf, is an easily recognized pattern of Depression glass even by non-collectors. The omnipresent cake plate may help explain that, since they were packed in or given away with 20-pound bags of flour, which sold in huge quantities in the 1930s because home baking was the norm then. Sometimes, displays of the give-away items were near the cash register and you were handed one when you made your purchase. However, I've been told these were packaged in the sacks themselves. You not only got the flour sack from which you made everything from dresses to curtains, but you also got a cake plate on which to display your baking skills. A pink cake plate is pictured. If you look closely, you can see a couple of the legs showing through. A dilemma taking place with the green cake plate is that many are uncovered in a deep, dark green that does not even come close to the shade of other pieces of green Sunflower shown here. No other pieces of green are found in this darker hue. That heavy, round piece in green is a paperweight found in a former Jeannette employee's home.

Judging by the questions I get, there is still some befuddlement over the cake plate and the rarely found Sunflower trivet. Think 7 inches! The 7" trivet has an edge that is slightly upturned and it is three inches smaller than the omnipresent 10" cake plate. The 7" trivet remains the most elusive piece of Sunflower. Dollar signs seem to get in the way of seeing the difference in 10" and 7". Collector demand for the trivet keeps prices accelerating. Green Sunflower pieces are found less often than pink as evidenced by my photo; consequently, prices for green are greater than for those of pink.

Sunflower suffers a lack of saucers in both colors. The last few sets of Sunflower I have seen have had more cups than saucers. Two lots of green had no saucers at all. In total, there were 29 cups and only 13 saucers. Maybe the cups were a premium, which never offered saucers, or the cups were offered longer than the saucers. If you run into a stack of Sunflower saucers, remember that they could be a good deal if the price is cheap because numerous collectors still need them.

The Ultra Marine ashtray pictured is the only piece I have found in that color. Opaque colors show up sporadically, usually creamers and sugars. Only a creamer, plate, 6" tab-handled bowl, cup, and saucer have been documented in Delphite blue. You can see all but the creamer in *Very Rare Glassware of the Depression Years, Fifth Series.*

	Pink	Green
* Ashtray, 5", center design only	9.00	12.00
Cake plate, 10", 3 legs	15.00	15.00
** Creamer, opaque $85.00	28.00	28.00
Cup, opaque $75.00	18.00	20.00
Plate, 8", luncheon	35.00	
Plate, 9", dinner	24.00	26.00

	Pink	Green
Saucer	8.00	10.00
Sugar, opaque $85.00	28.00	28.00
Tumbler, 4¾", 8 ounce, footed	38.00	38.00
Trivet, 7", 3 legs, turned up edge	395.00	395.00
* Found in Ultra Marine $30.00 **Delphite $95.00		

SUNSHINE, LINES #731 – #737, LANCASTER GLASS COMPANY, c. 1932

Colors: pink, green w/crystal

To answer the question I have received the most often after including this in my book two years ago: Yes, Sunshine comes both in satinized and non-satinized. We just kept finding the frosted when we were searching for items to buy. Thanks to several readers, there are some new listings added. Keep that information coming!

This was another of those small lines sold as an assortment of pieces. There appear to have been series of hexagonal blanks used for the pattern. You could buy up to a 36-piece assortment of Sunshine; so there should be more of it available than seems to be showing up. I have never heard of any dinner plates, though they may have been made judging from the other luncheon type pieces we do know were available.

I will warn you, you will seldom find a piece of this line for a small price, not because the dealer has any notion what it is, just because it "looks like better glass." Most of the pieces pictured here were at least $40.00 when we found them for sale.

	Pink, Green		Pink, Green
Bowl, 8", 2-handled, hex edge	55.00	Mayonnaise, liner, 7¼", 2-handled, hex edge	20.00
Bowl, 9", 2-handled, hex edge	65.00	Plate, 10½", 2-handled, hex edge	40.00
Bowl, 10½ x 8", oval, 2 raised sides,		Plate, 14", serving, hex edge	50.00
2-handled, hex edge	75.00	Server, 10", center handled sandwich,	
Bowl, 12", flat rim, hex edge	65.00	hex edge	50.00
Candle, single, hex foot	35.00	Sugar, round, footed	25.00
Creamer, round, footed	25.00	Tray, 10", roll edge, "bun" tray,	
Mayonnaise, 5½", 2-handled, hex edge	35.00	hex edge	55.00

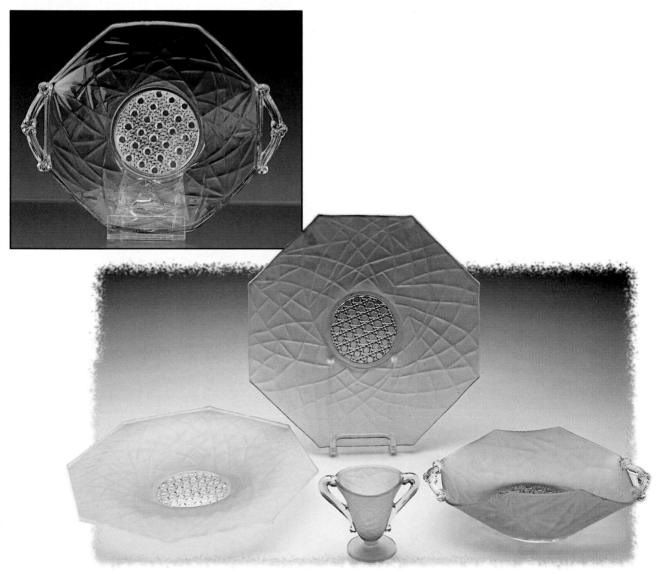

SWANKY SWIGS, 1930s – Early 1940s

"Why, I remember those. We used them when I was growing up!" or "Look, Mommy, those are like I used at Granny's house!" These are the type comments I often hear when Swanky Swigs are spotted. Serious collectors seek all types and sizes; casual collectors like flowers, particularly daffodils, red tulips, violets, and bachelor buttons. See *Collectible Glassware from the 40s, 50s, 60s...* for later made Swanky Swigs and their metal lids, which have become collectible themselves. Check your local grocery as Kraft has issued two new ones in the spring of 2003. One has stars and stripes; the other one hearts and stripes.

Top Row:

Band No.1	Red & black	3⅜"	2.00 – 3.00
	Red & blue	3⅜"	3.00 – 4.00
	Blue	3⅜"	3.50 – 5.00
Band No. 2	Red & black	4¾"	4.00 – 5.00
	Red & black	3⅜"	3.00 – 4.00
Band No. 3	Blue & white	3⅜"	3.00 – 4.00
Circle & Dot:	Blue	4¾"	8.00 – 10.00
	Blue	3½"	5.00 – 6.00
	Red, green	3½"	4.00 – 5.00
	Black	3½"	5.00 – 6.00
	Red	4¾"	8.00 – 10.00
Dot	Black	4¾"	7.00 – 9.00
	Blue	3½"	5.00 – 6.00

2nd Row:

Star	Blue	4¾"	7.00 – 8.00
	Blue, red, green, black	3½"	3.00 – 4.00
	Cobalt w/white stars	4¾"	18.00 – 20.00
Centennials	W.Va., cobalt	4¾"	22.00 – 25.00
	Texas, cobalt	4¾"	35.00 – 40.00

	Texas, blue, black, green	3½"	35.00 – 40.00
Checkerboard	Blue, red	3½"	30.00 – 35.00

3rd Row:

Checkerboard	Green	3½"	30.00 – 35.00
Sailboat	Blue	4½"	12.00 – 15.00
	Blue	3½"	10.00 – 12.00
	Red, green	4½"	12.00 – 15.00
	Green, light green	3½"	12.00 – 15.00
Tulip No. 1	Blue, red	4½"	15.00 – 20.00
	Blue, red	3½"	3.00 – 4.00

4th Row:

Tulip No. 1	Green	4½"	15.00 – 20.00
	Green, black	3½"	3.00 – 4.00
	Green w/label	3½"	12.00 – 15.00
*Tulip No. 2	Red, green, black	3½"	30.00 – 35.00
Carnival	Blue, red	3½"	5.00 – 7.00
	Green, yellow	3½"	5.00 – 7.00
Tulip No. 3	Dark blue, light blue	3¾"	2.50 – 3.50

*West Coast slightly lower price

SWIRL, "PETAL SWIRL," JEANNETTE GLASS COMPANY, 1937 – 1938

Colors: Ultra Marine, pink, Delphite; some amber and "ice" blue

Ultra Marine Swirl can be found with two different borders on most pieces, ruffled and plain. Pink is customarily found with plain borders. This makes a difference if you mail order or shop the Internet for your pattern. You need to specify what style you want, though there should be no difference in price.

Ultra Marine Swirl pitchers (pictured in previous editions) are found with great difficulty. Three have turned up since the first one was found in 1974. So far, none has been forthcoming in pink. Some collectors of Jeannette Swirl mingle this pattern with Jeannette's "Jennyware" kitchenware line that does have a flat, 36-ounce pink pitcher in it. If you find mixing bowls, measuring cups, or reamers, then you have crossed into the kitchenware line and out of Swirl dinnerware. See *Kitchen Glassware of the Depression Years* for "Jennyware" listings and pricing.

Swirl candy and butter dish bottoms are more bountiful than tops. Bear that in mind before you buy only a bottom unless it is very reasonably priced. That deficiency of tops holds true for 90 percent of the butter and candy dishes in Depression glass. Unless you are good at recalling color hues, it might be prudent to take your half piece with you when trying to match this Ultra Marine color. Swirl has some green-tinged pieces as well as the normally found color. This green tint is hard to match, and some collectors shun this shade. Because of this, many times you can buy this green tint at a cheaper price if you are willing to accumulate that shade. This coloration problem occurs with all Jeannette patterns made in Ultra Marine. The smaller, flat tumbler on the bottom row shows this green tint. A boxed console set labeled "One 1500/3 Console Set, Ultra Marine from Jeannette Glass Co., Jeannette, Pa." was bought for my candlestick book. It had the footed console and candles in the green shade, but as luck would have it, the printers did an excellent job of hiding that green in the photo.

Pink candleholders are not considered rare even though they were omitted from some of my earlier editions. Omissions or mistakes on my part do not make a piece rare.

The pink coaster is frequently found inside a small rubber tire and used for ashtrays. These tire advertisements have become collectible. Those with a tire manufacturer's name on the glass insert are more in demand; but those with a non-advertising glass insert (such as this coaster) are collected if the miniature tire is embossed with the name of a tire company. Many of these tires dried up or decayed over the years leaving only the glass inserts as reminders. I certainly see few in Florida, but they are seen frequently in Ohio and Pennsylvania. Rubber in Florida's heat rapidly breaks down. You should see what it does for elastic in clothes.

Swirl was produced in several scarce colors. A smaller set can be assembled in Delphite blue; it would only have basic pieces and a serving dish or two. Vegetable bowls (9") were made in several trial colors. A recent find was a small amethyst berry bowl pictured in *Very Rare Glassware of the Depression Years, Fifth Series.*

	Pink	Ultra Marine	Delphite		Pink	Ultra Marine	Delphite
Bowl, 4⅞" & 5¼", berry	14.00	16.00	14.00	Plate, 6½", sherbet	7.00	8.00	6.00
Bowl, 9", salad	26.00	35.00	30.00	Plate, 7¼"	12.00	15.00	
Bowl, 9", salad, rimmed	30.00	35.00		Plate, 8", salad	10.00	15.00	9.00
Bowl, 10", footed, closed				Plate, 9¼", dinner	18.00	24.00	12.00
handles	40.00	35.00		Plate, 10½"			25.00
Bowl, 10½", footed, console	20.00	32.00		Plate, 12½", sandwich	22.00	32.00	
Butter dish	200.00	295.00		Platter, 12", oval			38.00
Butter dish bottom	35.00	60.00		Salt and pepper, pair		50.00	
Butter dish top	165.00	235.00		Saucer	3.00	4.00	5.00
Candle holders, double				Sherbet, low footed	18.00	25.00	
branch, pair	90.00	60.00		Soup, tab handle (lug)	45.00	55.00	
Candle holders, single				Sugar, footed	10.00	16.00	12.00
branch, pair			125.00	Tray, 10½", 2-handle			27.50
Candy dish, open, 3 legs	15.00	20.00		Tumbler, 4", 9 ounce	22.00	40.00	
Candy dish with cover	120.00	185.00		Tumbler, 4⅝", 9 ounce	20.00		
Coaster, 1" x 3¼"	15.00	16.00		Tumbler, 5⅛", 13 ounce	60.00	135.00	
Creamer, footed	10.00	16.00	12.00	Tumbler, 9 ounce, footed	25.00	50.00	
Cup	11.00	16.00	10.00	Vase, 6½" footed, ruffled	23.00		
Pitcher, 48 ounce, footed		2,000.00		Vase, 8½" footed, two styles		27.50	

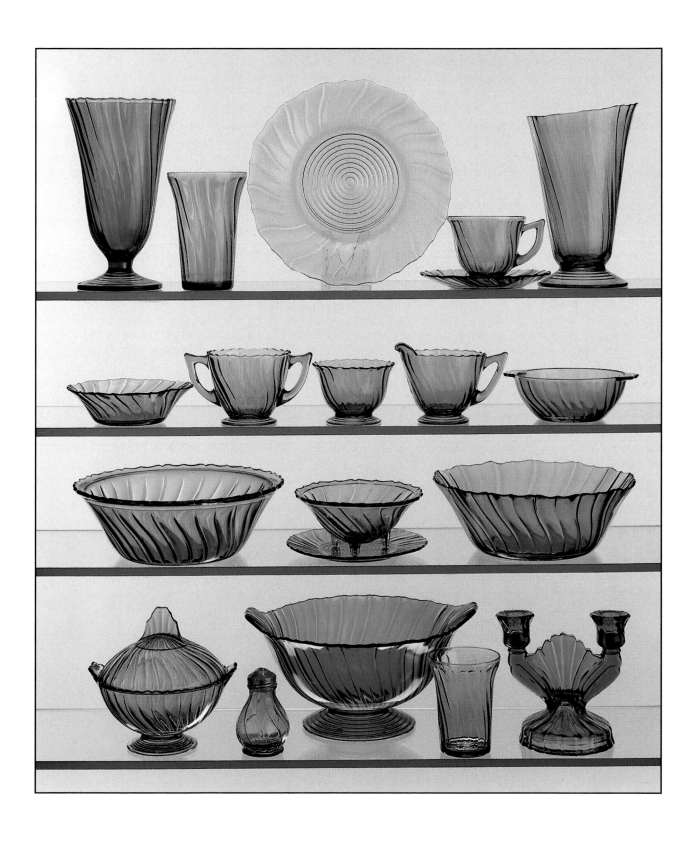

TEA ROOM, INDIANA GLASS COMPANY, 1926 – 1931

Colors: pink, green, amber, and some crystal

Tea Room collecting is expanding. I mentioned that I had been contacted about a 9½" amber ruffled vase in New Zealand in the last book. Now Australia is getting in the game with several smaller 6½" amber Tea Room ruffled vases turning up there. I also bought a green tumbler that is slightly different in color from those we normally find here. The Internet is garnering Depression glass devotees from all over the world.

As the name suggests, the very Deco Tea Room pattern was produced to be used in the tearooms and ice cream parlors of that day. That is the reason you find so many soda fountain items not seen in other patterns. Two styles of banana splits are found with the flat one twice as pricey as the footed one, which affirms the rarity of the flat one. Many times, you can find banana splits priced reasonably, because they are not recognized as being Tea Room.

Tea Room prices are not escalating as they once did due to a lack of available merchandise in the market to encourage buying. This occasionally transpires when newer collectors cannot find enough to launch a set. Rarely found pieces are not coming on the market unless a previously collected set is being broken up. Thus, a predicament in accumulating Tea Room is finding an adequate amount to buy.

The biggest problem is finding mint condition pieces. Check the underneath sides of flat pieces, which are inclined to chip and flake on all the unprotected points. I once witnessed the opening of a factory box of Tea Room that had 32 each cups, saucers, and luncheon plates. There were less than a dozen in mint condition as we define it today. These had never been used; so there was doubtless a mould release problem with Tea Room initially. It is perfectly fine to buy and use flawed pieces; just don't pay mint prices for them.

Green Tea Room is sought more than pink; and some people are starting to search for crystal. Crystal pieces are fetching about 75 to 80 percent of the pink prices listed except for the commonly found 9½" ruffled vase and the rarely found pitcher, priced separately below. That crystal pitcher is even harder to find than the amber one. I have bought and sold four amber pitchers over the years, but only one crystal. Amber pitchers and tumblers are often found in the Atlanta metro area. I was told they were Coca-Cola premiums, but have never been able to confirm that. Creamers and sugars emerge occasionally in amber.

Pink and crystal parfaits are being found, but not the green ones. The flat sugar and marmalade bottoms are the same. However, the marmalade has a notched lid; the sugar lid is not notched. Finding either is not an easy task. The mustard comes with a plain or notched lid, also.

Some interesting lamps are showing up which used frosted Tea Room tumblers in their makeup. We recently photographed a chandelier, which employed a ruffled top vase, but I am having trouble finding a place to use it in my book. The regular lamp is not as plentiful as it once was.

	Green	Pink		Green	Pink
Bowl, finger	70.00	70.00	Salt and pepper, pair	80.00	75.00
Bowl, 7½", banana split, flat	200.00	200.00	* Saucer	30.00	30.00
Bowl, 7½", banana split, footed	100.00	95.00	Sherbet, low, footed	25.00	22.00
Bowl, 8¼", celery	35.00	32.00	Sherbet, low, flared edge	30.00	26.00
Bowl, 8¾", deep salad	100.00	95.00	Sherbet, tall, footed, 4½"	60.00	60.00
Bowl, 9½", oval vegetable	80.00	75.00	Sugar w/lid, 3"	110.00	100.00
Candlestick, low, pair	80.00	85.00	Sugar, 4½", footed, amber $125.00	20.00	20.00
Creamer, 3¼"	27.50	27.50	Sugar, rectangular	25.00	20.00
Creamer, 4½", footed, amber $125.00	20.00	20.00	Sugar, flat with cover	200.00	165.00
Creamer, rectangular	25.00	20.00	Sundae, footed, ruffled top	95.00	75.00
Creamer & sugar on tray, 4"	85.00	85.00	Tray, center-handle	200.00	145.00
* Cup	55.00	60.00	Tray, rectangular sugar & creamer	50.00	40.00
Goblet, 9 ounce	80.00	70.00	Tumbler, 8 ounce, 4³⁄₁₆", flat	110.00	120.00
Ice bucket	65.00	60.00	Tumbler, 6 ounce, footed	35.00	35.00
Lamp, 9", electric	150.00	135.00	Tumbler, 8 ounce, 5¼", high, footed, amber $125.00	35.00	35.00
Marmalade, notched lid	225.00	175.00	Tumbler, 11 ounce, footed	50.00	45.00
Mustard, covered	195.00	160.00	Tumbler, 12 ounce, footed	75.00	70.00
Parfait	100.00	100.00	*** Vase, 6½", ruffled edge	110.00	110.00
** Pitcher, 64 ounce, amber $695.00	175.00	150.00	**** Vase, 9½", ruffled edge	150.00	150.00
Plate, 6½", sherbet	32.00	30.00	Vase, 9½", straight	100.00	95.00
Plate, 8¼", luncheon	35.00	30.00	Vase, 11", ruffled edge	250.00	295.00
Plate, 10½", 2-handle	60.00	45.00	Vase, 11", straight	160.00	165.00
Relish, divided	22.00	18.00			

* Prices for absolutely mint pieces   ** Crystal $400.00   *** Amber $350.00   **** Crystal $16.00

Prices given are for mint items. These prices are high because mint condition items are difficult to obtain. I cannot emphasize that too much. Damaged pieces are often bought to supplement sets until mint items can be found. Not everyone can afford to buy only mint items, and they are willing to accept Tea Room pieces with some minor flaws at lesser prices. New collectors may have to accept some damage on items or do without. The other side of the mint-only coin is if you've sought an item forever and find it damaged slightly, you might want to own the item anyway since this might be your only chance to do so. You have to weigh all factors as they fit you in regards to the glass.

THISTLE, MacBETH-EVANS, 1929 – 1930

Colors: pink, green; some yellow and crystal

Thistle pattern has definitely been the nettle pricking every photographer with whom I have worked. In 1972, we photographed Thistle in black and white and there was enough Bon-Ami used to highlight the pattern to have washed several windows. Photography lights cause Thistle to do a fading act, something all too familiar for Thistle collectors. Our photographer seems to have captured it, but you will never know how many Polaroid test shots were made before both the delicate color and the pattern were captured.

Green Thistle is even more scattered than pink except for the large fruit bowl that is practically an illusion in pink. I have owned the one pictured here for over 25 years, and I have only seen two others.

Thistle pieces have the same mould shapes as the thin Dogwood; however, no Thistle creamer or sugar is known. The Thistle grill plate has the pattern on the edge only. Those plain centers scratched very easily; beware of that should you locate a grill plate. Frankly, they're so scarce anymore, if you find one with a distinguishable pattern, buy it.

If you encounter a thick butter dish, pitcher, tumbler, creamer, sugar, or other heavy moulded pieces with impressed Thistle designs, they are probably newly made. Mosser Glass Company in Cambridge, Ohio, is making these pieces in various colors. They are not a part of this pattern, but designs based on a much older Cambridge pattern glass. Should you encounter the older Cambridge ware, it will probably be embossed with the words "near cut" in its center. If you have a piece of Thistle not in the photograph, then you probably do not have a piece of Depression glass Thistle made by MacBeth-Evans. All seven pieces known in the pattern are shown here. Many companies made thistle designs sometime during their productions.

	Pink	Green
Bowl, 5½", cereal	35.00	38.00
Bowl, 10¼", large fruit	550.00	350.00
Cup, thin	28.00	30.00
Plate, 8", luncheon	22.00	24.00
Plate, 10¼", grill	30.00	35.00
Plate, 13", heavy cake	210.00	235.00
Saucer	12.00	12.00

"TOP NOTCH," "SUNBURST," NEW MARTINSVILLE, c. 1930s

Colors: red, green, cobalt, amber

I have heard several names in use for this pattern. In the Northeast, the name "Top Notch" or "Top Prize" is used; but in the south, "Sunburst" is the label. Most of the pieces I have seen have been in New York although I only get that way once a year. Cathy asked one dealer where her name label came from and she said she "found it in some old magazine a couple of years ago" though she couldn't pinpoint which one. A northern dealer asked us at the last show in New York if we had any of that "Top Notch" pattern, and it took a moment to realize he was speaking of this ware. No matter what it's being called, it is a wonderful design and comes in rich jewel colors. I had a letter from a lady who thought she had some pieces in amethyst, but they were packed away and she would contact me when they were unpacked.

We know these items from a luncheon set were made. I don't remember seeing other type pieces, though I would presume there could well be some. I have, however, run into a second set having these same green items here in Florida. The problem with running into glass in Florida is that who knows where it was before being transplanted to this state. There is a still a lot of excellent collectible glass that was brought here by retirees and much of that is now reaching the market. We acquired the red cup and saucer in Kentucky and I have seen one in blue. A friend with whom I was discussing the pattern believes she's seen amber. That would fit with New Martinsville colors from this period; so, I feel confident in listing that color. Let me hear from you about what you have or find.

	All colors
Cup	22.00
Creamer	28.00
Plate, luncheon	20.00
Plate, serving tray	38.00
Saucer	8.00
Sugar	28.00

TULIP, DELL GLASS COMPANY, Late 1930s – Late 1940s

Color: amethyst, turquoise (blue), crystal, green

Please notice that we now have a photo of that elusive amethyst decanter found with the Tulip stopper that has been pictured in several colors. The decanter bottom is not tulip design, though it does have an optic in the glass itself, rather than being plain glass. Now, you know what to look for at markets. I stumbled onto a blue decanter bottom just this past month, so keep your eye out for these.

There are two styles of candleholders. One style is made from an ivy bowl (not a sherbet as the piece was previously thought to be). That ivy bowl (sherbet) is shown in the 1946 Montgomery Ward catalog with ivy growing in it. We have pictured that ad in past books; for clarification, the violin vase pictured here and in the ad would not be considered part of the pattern, although the neck of the violin is just like the neck on the decanter.

The juice tumbler (cigarette holder in an ad in previous books) is 2¾" tall and holds three ounces while the whiskey is only 1¾" and holds one ounce. The ad for Tulip shows no stippling on the pieces. Early in buying this pattern, I ignored some pieces without stippling; both styles are acceptable to collectors.

I started buying Tulip about 13 years ago when I found nine green sugar bowls for $10.00. I could not turn them down at that price, though I did not know whether there were collectors for this pattern or not. I soon found out! Those sugars are often found in sets of four or more, making me believe they may also have been sold as cream soups. I see about a dozen sugars for every creamer.

In buying Tulip, I have found that the scalloped rims have a tendency to have some damage. Most of the damage occurs under the rim edge; be sure to turn the piece over and check each of the pointed scallops. Many times a scallop or two will be absent and not show from the top side.

I have priced the crystal with the green since you will not see much of it. Crystal may be the rarest "color."

	Amethyst, Blue	Crystal, Green		Amethyst, Blue	Crystal, Green
Bowl, oval, oblong, 13¼"	115.00	95.00	Plate, 6"	11.00	10.00
Candleholder, 3¾" (ivy bowl)	38.00	30.00	Plate, 7¼"	16.00	13.00
Candleholder, 5¼" base, 3" tall	65.00	45.00	Plate, 10"	35.00	32.00
Candy w/lid, footed (6" w/o lid)	225.00	185.00	Saucer	7.00	6.00
Creamer	25.00	22.00	Sherbet, 3¾", flat (ivy bowl)	22.00	20.00
Cup	20.00	16.00	Sugar	22.00	20.00
Decanter w/stopper	495.00		Tumbler, 2¾", juice	33.00	22.00
Ice tub, 4⅞" wide, 3" deep	75.00	65.00	Tumbler, whiskey	35.00	25.00

229

TWISTED OPTIC, LINE #313, IMPERIAL GLASS COMPANY, 1927 – 1930 and onward

Colors: pink, green, amber; some blue and Canary yellow, ruby and iridized crystal

First, you should realize that many glass companies made twisting patterns besides this one from Imperial or Hocking's Spiral, represented by the flat candy shown on this page.

The true, rounded style Twisted Optic candy is shown in the Canary photo on page 231. This color is often mislabeled vaseline. I was able to buy enough pieces from a dealer selling a set to illustrate the color wonderfully. Seeing all the items he had accumulated besides these was breathtaking and I was very tempted to buy it all.

A collector has informed me there is also a Twisted Optic two-handled vase that is bulbous at the top with an inch or so of rim flare, besides the straight edge, fan, and flat-rimmed versions. Aside from those pictured, there is also a footed comport style candy and one like it without the pedestal foot. It looks like a flat, deep comport bowl with a lid. The lids for these are the tall cone, pointed knob style. The covered bowl with the round knob is the powder. There are two console bowls, one footed, 10½" oval with tiny scroll side decorations and 3" matching scroll point candles; and the other is a round, 11½" diameter bowl which originally rested on a black paneled base with the 8½" tall candles towering above it.

	Blue, Canary Yellow	All other colors		Blue, Canary Yellow	All other colors
Basket, 10", tall	95.00	60.00	Plate, 7", salad	8.00	4.00
Bowl, console, scroll tab hdld., oval, ftd.	65.00	50.00	Plate, 7½" x 9", oval with indent	12.00	5.00
Bowl, 4¾", fruit	25.00	15.00	Plate, 8", luncheon	8.00	6.00
Bowl, 5", cereal	16.00	9.00	Plate. 9½", cracker	30.00	18.00
Bowl, 7", crimped	30.00	20.00	Plate, 10", sandwich	20.00	9.00
Bowl, 7", salad	25.00	15.00	Plate, 12"	20.00	15.00
Bowl, 9"	35.00	15.00	Plate, 14", buffet	35.00	25.00
Bowl, 9¼", salad	40.00	25.00	Platter, oval	35.00	25.00
Bowl 10", salad	45.00	30.00	Powder jar w/lid	75.00	45.00
Bowl, 10½", console	45.00	25.00	Preserve (same as candy w/slotted lid)		30.00
Bowl, 11½", 4¼" tall	55.00	30.00	Sandwich server, open center handle	35.00	20.00
Candlesticks, 3", pair (3 styles)	45.00	50.00	Sandwich server, two-handle	18.00	12.00
Candlesticks, 8½", pair	75.00	55.00	Saucer	4.00	2.00
Candy jar w/cover, flat	90.00	50.00	Server, center handle, bowl shape	40.00	20.00
Candy jar w/cover, flat, flange edge	100.00	55.00	Sherbet	12.00	6.00
Candy jar w/cover, ftd., flange edge	100.00	55.00	Sugar	18.00	7.00
Candy jar w/cover, ftd., short, fat	110.00	60.00	Tumbler, 4½", 9 ounce		6.00
Candy jar w/cover, footed, tall	135.00	60.00	Tumbler, 5¼", 12 ounce		8.00
Compote, cheese	20.00	12.00	Vase, 7¼", 2-handle, rolled edge	75.00	45.00
Creamer	18.00	8.00	Vase, 7¼", flat rim	65.00	40.00
Cup	12.00	5.00	Vase, 8", 2-handle, fan	95.00	50.00
Mayonnaise	50.00	30.00	Vase, 8", 2-handle, straight edge	95.00	45.00
Pitcher, 64 ounce		45.00	Vase, 8½", 2-handle, bulbous neck	11.00	65.00
Plate, 6", sherbet	6.00	3.00			

"U.S. SCROLL," "STAR FLOWER," "PINWHEEL," UNITED STATES GLASS COMPANY, c. 1925

Colors: black, green, pink

This ware is octagonal in shape and is generally marked with the intertwined U.S.G. symbol. Black pieces will have to be turned over to see the "scroll" design. Although listed in pink, I don't recall seeing it in that color. It is usually found in small sets rather than a piece at a time. This pattern is most often found in green and should answer those 50 or more letters I receive each year asking about it.

	Black	Green, Pink
Creamer	10.00	7.50
Cup	8.00	6.00
Plate, 7½"	8.00	5.00
Plate, 8½"	12.00	9.00
Saucer	3.00	2.00
Sugar	10.00	7.50

"U.S. SWIRL," U.S. GLASS COMPANY, Late 1920s

Colors: green, some pink, iridescent, and crystal

"U.S. Swirl" is a swirl pattern easily recognized because it has shapes and pieces very similar to the popular Aunt Polly and Strawberry patterns made by U.S. Glass. Pink, iridescent, and crystal items are unearthed very infrequently in "U.S. Swirl." I have only found one pink shaker and a butter dish in all the years I have been hunting. Doubtless, very little pink was manufactured, or perhaps not a complete line, just some special items. In the listings, I separated the colors based on demand for green outweighing that of pink, but not all pink items may exist. Occasionally, I see crystal sherbets. The 5⅜" tall, rarely found comport is pictured behind the sherbet for size comparison. I know some drinkers prefer I call it a martini glass, the fashionable use for comports these days. (That's why Manhattan comport supplies have dried up. Collectors are buying six or more for drinks instead of one for candy.)

Several "U.S. Swirl" iridescent butter dishes have been noticed, but those and sherbets are the only pieces sprouting in that color. The tumbler listing 3⅝" conforms with the only known size of Aunt Polly and Cherryberry/Strawberry tumblers; but the 12 ounce tumbler, pictured, has only been found in "U.S. Swirl."

"U.S. Swirl" has the plain butter bottom that is compatible with other patterns made by U.S. Glass. The butter dish in this pattern is the one that many Strawberry or Cherryberry collectors have purchased over the years to borrow the base for their butter lids. This plundering has reduced the number of butters in "U.S. Swirl" pattern, particularly in scarce pink.

The shallow, 1¾" deep, 8⅜" oval bowl in front of the 2¾" deep, oval bowl is seldom found; it may be rare, as none of the other U.S. Glass patterns has a similar bowl and this is the only one known now. There is a two-handled candy dish in "Swirl" like those found in Aunt Polly. I recently spotted one in Ohio.

	Green	Pink		Green	Pink
Bowl, 4⅜", berry	5.50	6.50	Creamer	20.00	20.00
Bowl, 5½", 1-handle	9.50	10.50	Pitcher, 8", 48 ounce	90.00	90.00
Bowl, 7⅞", large berry	15.00	16.00	Plate, 6⅛", sherbet	2.50	2.50
Bowl, 8¼", oval (2¾" deep)	50.00	45.00	Plate, 7⅞", salad	5.50	6.50
Bowl, 8⅜", oval (1¾" deep)	60.00	55.00	Salt and pepper, pair	65.00	65.00
Butter and cover	120.00	120.00	Sherbet, 3¼"	4.50	5.00
Butter bottom	100.00	100.00	Sugar w/lid	45.00	45.00
Butter top	20.00	20.00	Tumbler, 3⅝", 8 ounce	10.00	10.00
Candy, footed, 2-handled	35.00	30.00	Tumbler, 4¾", 12 ounce	15.00	16.00
Candy w/cover, 2-handled	27.50	32.00	Vase, 6½"	30.00	25.00
Comport	35.00	30.00			

"VICTORY," DIAMOND GLASS-WARE COMPANY, 1929 – 1932

Colors: amber, pink, green; some cobalt blue and black

Amber and black "Victory" is pictured below. That color combination works well together and one new collector told me that photo combination started his looking for "Victory." Intermixing colors is catching on amongst collectors. It gives you more than just one color to buy. Many times, you will spot your pattern for sale only to have it be the wrong color. This does not happen as often if you are buying several colors. The black with gold trim displays better in the photo than the gold-trimmed amber. As with most black glass of this era, the pattern is on the reverse, you have to flip it over to see the piece is "Victory" unless you can recognize it from the indented edges. Collectors of black glass are more prone to own black "Victory" than Depression glass people, though they often bring it to shows for identification since they have no clue it's an actual named pattern.

Diamond used several enhancement techniques besides the 22K gold trim. Floral decorations and even a Deco looking black design on pink and green are found. I have spied more floral decorated console sets (bowl and candlesticks) than anything in this pattern. I suppose that complete sets of gold decorated pink and green can be found while black pieces decorated with gold appear to be available only in luncheon or console sets.

Sets of "Victory" can be accumulated in pink, green, or amber with a great deal of searching. Cobalt blue or black will take more hunting and some good fortune. It can be done even in today's market, but it will be expensive. After I mentioned that cobalt blue "Victory" was being found in the northeast, especially in Maine, I have heard of other sets there, the latest of which was bought in an antique mall. Rarely, do I see blue for sale in my area though I did buy a center-handled server.

Gravy boats with platters are the most sought pieces to own in all colors. I have only found one amber and one green set, but three cobalt blue ones. A green gravy and platter can be seen at the bottom of page 235. The "Victory" goblet, candlestick, cereal, soup, and oval vegetable bowls will keep you looking long and hard no matter what color you desire.

	Black, Amber, Pink, Green	Blue
Bonbon, 7"	11.00	20.00
Bowl, 6½", cereal	14.00	45.00
Bowl, 8½", flat soup	22.00	70.00
Bowl, 9", oval vegetable	35.00	115.00
Bowl, 11", rolled edge	30.00	50.00
Bowl, 12", console	35.00	65.00
Bowl, 12½", flat edge	30.00	70.00
Candlesticks, 3", pair	35.00	135.00
Cheese & cracker set, 12" indented plate & compote	40.00	
Comport, 6" tall, 6¾" diameter	15.00	
Creamer	15.00	50.00
Cup	12.00	30.00
Goblet, 5", 7 ounce	25.00	95.00
Gravy boat and platter	250.00	300.00
Mayonnaise set: 3½" tall, 5½" across, 8½" indented plate, w/ladle	42.00	100.00
Plate, 6", bread and butter	6.00	16.00
Plate, 7", salad	7.00	20.00
Plate, 8", luncheon	7.00	30.00
Plate, 9", dinner	20.00	55.00
Platter, 12"	30.00	95.00
Sandwich server, center handle	29.00	75.00
Saucer	4.00	8.00
Sherbet, footed	14.00	26.00
Sugar	15.00	50.00

235

VITROCK, "FLOWER RIM," HOCKING GLASS COMPANY, 1934 – 1937

Colors: white and white w/fired-on colors, usually red or green

Vitrock was not an actual pattern per se, but a mid-1930s milk white color of Hocking's similar to Hazel Atlas's Platonite. There are many different patterns found on this very robust line, but collectors have embraced the decorated Lake Como (page 110) and the "Flower Rim" dinnerware sets as patterns to collect.

Vitrock was Hocking's impetuous leap into the milk glass market. Today, platters, soup plates, and cream soups are pieces that are nearly impossible to find. If you locate a flat soup, you are usually wishing it had the Lake Como decoration. I finally obtained a regular Vitrock flat soup pictured with label in the bottom row. These are rarer than I previously thought. Also turning out harder to find than they should be are the 9½" vegetable bowls. Several collectors have stated that the fired-on Vitrock is less visible than Rainbow dinnerware. Since I have only found two fired color pieces, I have no doubt that it is.

Vitrock's claim to fame with collectors is its kitchenware line of reamers, measuring cups, and mixing bowls. It was advertised as ware that "will not craze or check," a major flaw in many pottery wares of the time and thus, a good selling point. Those large Vitrock mixing bowls are probably so hard to find today because they cost a quarter, which may have accounted for a half-day's wage for a worker then. At the time, Vitrock competed with Hazel Atlas's Platonite; and from all implications now, Platonite won.

You can see more Vitrock in my book *Kitchen Glassware of the Depression Years*. Some collectors are assembling patterns that cross other fields. This is a prime example of a pattern that fits into both collecting areas. Hazel Atlas did the same with their Platonite. It made wonderful business sense to sell supporting items that matched your everyday dishes.

	White		White
Bowl, 4", berry	4.00	Plate, 7¼", salad	4.00
Bowl, 5½", cream soup	15.00	Plate, 8¾", luncheon	5.00
Bowl, 6", fruit	5.50	Plate, 9", soup	33.00
Bowl, 7½", cereal	9.00	Plate, 10", dinner	10.00
Bowl, 9½", vegetable	15.00	Platter, 11½"	30.00
Creamer, oval	6.00	Saucer	2.50
Cup	6.00	Sugar	6.00

WATERFORD, "WAFFLE," HOCKING GLASS COMPANY, 1938 – 1944

Colors: crystal, pink; some yellow, Vitrock; forest green 1950s

Waterford summons up images of elite, costly cut lead crystal when mentioned to most collectors. Well, this pattern was Hocking's answer to that, a sort of poor man's Waterford. This Waterford sells very well because it is available and priced reasonably. It also looks impressive. Regrettably, pink is rarely observed any longer. Most admirers would be crazy about pink cereal bowls, a pitcher, or a butter dish residing on their table. Of these three pieces, the cereal is the most elusive. It has always been annoying to find, and worse, challenging to find mint. The inside rim is inevitably damaged from stacking or use. A little roughness is predictable; do not let that keep you from owning a hard-to-find piece. Because of the scalloped rim design, Waterford chips or flakes more easily than most other patterns.

There are some scarce crystal pieces. Cereal bowls, pitchers, and even water goblets are waning in number. Those crystal shakers pictured were used by many restaurants through the 1960s, which is why they are regularly seen today. There are two styles of sherbets. One has a scalloped top and base. It is not as commonly found and is not as acknowledged as the regular, plain edged one.

There is a Waterford "imposter" footed cup that is intermittently sold as a Waterford punch cup. These cups, and the larger lamps that are often exhibited as Waterford, are only comparable to Waterford. There is a round, softball sized cologne bottle with a tiny neck and mitered diamonds that belongs to Duncan's Miter line, as well. Waterford has a flattened (not rounded) diamond shape on each section of the design. There is also a large pink pitcher with an indented, circular design in each diamond, which is not Waterford. This pitcher was made by Hocking, but has more of a bull's-eye look. These pink pitchers with circular designs only sell for $40.00 and crystal for $20.00; do not pay Waterford prices for one.

A few pieces of Vitrock Waterford and some Dusty Rose and Springtime Green ashtrays turn up occasionally, and sell near crystal prices. Examples of those rose and green colors can be seen in the Oyster and Pearl pattern (page 166). Forest green Waterford 13¾" plates were made in the 1950s promotion of Forest Green; these are usually found in the $30.00 range. Many of these have white sections sitting around them similar to those found in Manhattan. Some crystal has also been found trimmed in red. There is not enough of the red trim to collect a set one piece at a time.

Advertising ashtrays, such as the "Post Cereals" shown below, are selling for $20.00 to $25.00 depending upon the significance of the advertising on the piece. An advertisement for Anchor Hocking itself will fetch $35.00 to $40.00.

Items listed below with Miss America shape noted in parentheses are Waterford patterned pieces with the same mould shapes as Miss America. Some of these are shown in the seventh edition of this book or the first *Very Rare Glassware of the Depression Years.*

Those yellow and amber goblets shown below are compliments of Anchor Hocking's photographer from items stored in their morgue. I have never seen yellow ones for sale, but amber ones sell for around $25.00 when they can be found.

	Crystal	Pink		Crystal	Pink
* Ashtray, 4"	7.50		Plate, 6", sherbet	4.00	7.00
Bowl, 4¾", berry	7.00	20.00	Plate, 7⅛", salad	7.00	15.00
Bowl, 5½", cereal	18.00	35.00	Plate, 9⅝", dinner	12.00	26.00
Bowl, 8¼", large berry	15.00	28.00	Plate, 10¼", handled cake	12.00	20.00
Butter dish and cover	30.00	225.00	Plate, 13¾", sandwich	13.00	40.00
Butter dish bottom	8.00	30.00	Relish, 13¾", 5-part	20.00	
Butter dish top	22.00	205.00	Salt and pepper, 2 types	10.00	
Coaster, 4"	4.00		Saucer	3.00	6.00
Creamer, oval	6.00	12.00	Sherbet, footed	5.00	20.00
Creamer (Miss America shape)		45.00	Sherbet, footed, scalloped base	6.00	
Cup	6.50	15.00	Sugar	6.00	12.50
Cup (Miss America shape)		50.00	Sugar cover, oval	12.00	32.50
Goblets, 5¼", 5⅝"	16.00		Sugar (Miss America shape)		45.00
Goblet, 5½" (Miss America shape)	40.00	135.00	Tumbler, 3½", 5 oz. juice (Miss America shape)		125.00
Lamp, 4", spherical base	26.00		Tumbler, 4⅞", 10 ounce, footed	15.00	28.00
Pitcher, 42 ounce, tilted, juice	25.00		* With ads $15.00 – 40.00 depending on item popularity		
Pitcher, 80 ounce, tilted, ice lip	42.00	175.00			

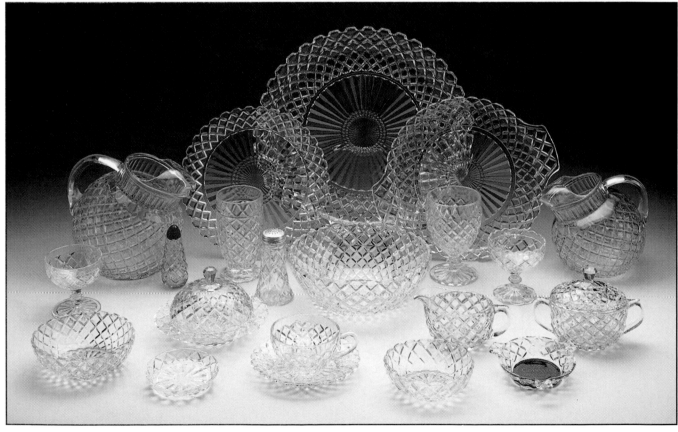

WINDSOR, "WINDSOR DIAMOND," JEANNETTE GLASS COMPANY, 1936 – 1946

Colors: pink, green, crystal; some Delphite, amberina red, and ice blue

Unusual crystal Windsor items continue to be revealed that are not found in pink or green. The one-handled candlestick, 10½" pointed edge tray, and three sizes of footed tumblers come to mind, but there are others if you look at the price list. There are many collectors for colored Windsor, but fewer seek crystal. Color was terminated about 1940, but crystal pieces were cataloged as late as 1946. Redesigned moulds for the Windsor butter, creamer, and sugar were later passed on to the Holiday pattern when that was introduced in 1947. There are two styles of sugars and lids. One is moulded like Holiday and has no lip for the lid to rest upon; the pink sugar below represents the second style with lip. The pink sugar and lid shaped like Holiday are rare and expensive when found.

Square relish trays can be found with or without tabbed (closed) handles. Pictured on page 240 are relish trays with tab handles; the large one holds two sizes of relishes without the tabs. Trays without handles commonly appear in crystal, but pink trays without handles are seldom found. Two styles of sandwich plates were produced. The normally found one is 10¼" and has open handles. The recently discovered tray is 10" and has closed handles.

Green Windsor tumblers are evasive. The water tumbler, commonly found in pink, is scarce. Mould roughness is found on seams of tumblers; and Windsor tumblers have an inclination to chip on the jutted out sides. The diamond pattern protrudes outward, making the sides an easy target for chips and flakes. Check these seams vigilantly before you buy. There are color variations in green; be mindful of that.

The pink 13⅝" plate is often found as an underliner tray for a beverage set with a pitcher and six water tumblers. This set may have been a premium item since so many pitchers and water tumblers are available today. Green sets do not experience this profusion.

The 8" pointed rim bowl is rarely seen in pink, but is pictured on the bottom far right below. The large crystal bowl, along with the comport, make up a punch bowl and stand. The upended comport fits snugly inside the base of the bowl to keep it from sliding off. In recent years, there have been newly made comports in crystal with sprayed colors that have a beaded edge. This recently made version will not work as a punch stand because the beaded edge will not fit inside the base of the bowl.

A different style pink ashtray and a tab-handled berry bowl can be seen in the *Very Rare Glassware of the Depression Years, Second Series.* While looking there, check out the blue Windsor butter dish.

Windsor usually brings a feeling of fulfillment when it comes up on my computer screen since it signals the end of updating information about patterns, now for the sixteenth time. However, I have left the 13 new patterns until last, so the hardest work still lies ahead. My hope is that you will find it worth my effort! Good luck hunting for these treasures!

WINDSOR

	Crystal	Pink	Green
* Ashtray, 5¾"	13.50	38.00	55.00
Bowl, 4¾", berry	4.00	12.00	12.00
Bowl, 5", pointed edge	9.00	33.00	
Bowl, 5", cream soup	7.00	24.00	29.00
Bowls, 5⅛", 5⅜", cereal	8.50	25.00	35.00
Bowl, 7⅛", three legs	9.00	30.00	
Bowl, 8", pointed edge	18.00	60.00	
Bowl, 8½", large berry	10.00	25.00	25.00
Bowl, 9", 2-handle	10.00	22.00	25.00
Bowl, 9½", oval vegetable	8.00	22.00	30.00
Bowl, 10½", salad	15.00		
Bowl, 10½", pointed edge	32.00	165.00	
Bowl, 12½", fruit console	30.00	145.00	
Bowl, 7" x 11¾", boat shape	20.00	40.00	40.00
Butter dish (two styles)	28.00	65.00	110.00
Cake plate, 10¾", footed	8.50	25.00	28.00
Candleholder, one handle	15.00		
Candlesticks, 3", pair	30.00	110.00	
Candy jar and cover	20.00		
Coaster, 3¼"	6.00	15.00	20.00
Comport	10.00		
** Creamer	5.00	14.00	18.00
Creamer (shaped as "Holiday")	7.50		
** Cup	5.00	10.00	12.50
Pitcher, 4½", 16 ounce	27.50	195.00	
*** Pitcher, 6¾", 52 ounce	25.00	35.00	65.00
Plate, 6", sherbet	2.50	5.00	8.00
Plate, 7", salad	4.50	20.00	25.00
** Plate, 9", dinner	10.00	25.00	25.00
Plate, 10", sandwich, closed handle		25.00	
Plate, 10½", pointed edge	10.00		
Plate, 10¼", sandwich, open handle	6.00	18.00	25.00
Plate, 13⅝", chop	15.00	38.00	42.00
Platter, 11½", oval	15.00	25.00	25.00
**** Powder jar	15.00	60.00	
Relish platter, 11½", divided	15.00	250.00	
Salt and pepper, pair	20.00	45.00	55.00
Saucer, ice blue $15.00	2.50	5.00	6.00
Sherbet, footed	3.50	13.00	15.00
Sugar & cover	12.00	30.00	33.00
Sugar & cover (like "Holiday")	15.00	135.00	
Tray, 4", square, w/handle	5.00	10.00	12.00
Tray, 4", square, w/o handle	10.00	50.00	
Tray, 4⅛" x 9", w/handle	4.00	10.00	16.00
Tray, 4⅛" x 9", w/o handle	12.00	60.00	
Tray, 8½" x 9¾", w/handle	6.50	24.00	35.00
Tray, 8½" x 9¾", w/o handle	15.00	95.00	
** Tumbler, 3¼", 5 ounce	12.00	22.00	35.00
** Tumbler, 4", 9 ounce, red 55.00	7.00	18.00	30.00
Tumbler, 5", 12 ounce	10.00	32.00	52.00
Tumbler, 4⅝", 11 ounce	9.00		
Tumbler, 4", footed	8.00		
Tumbler, 5", footed, 11 ounce	11.00		
Tumbler, 7¼", footed	18.00		

* Delphite $45.00   ** Blue $65.00   *** Red $450.00   **** Yellow $175.00; Blue $185.00

"WOOLWORTH," "STIPPLED GRAPE," "OREGON GRAPE," WESTMORELAND GLASS COMPANY, c. 1930s

Colors: crystal, green, pink

This small Westmoreland pattern has attracted many collectors over the years. Internet buyers discovered this embossed fruit design and doubled the prices in a short year. Due to the demand and requests for "Woolworth," I have included it this time. This grape pattern has been called "Woolworth" because it was mainly marketed in that chain of stores. A grape name would seem apropos, but no actual name has been forthcoming.

My measurements are from the pieces pictured. I discovered up to ½" discrepancy on similar pieces due to the amount of flaring and ruffling on each item. These ruffles and flairs were done by hand with a wooden tool. A heavy-handed worker might push down harder making a bowl shallower than one made by a light-handed worker.

Crystal prices approach those of pink or green due to scarcity more than demand. Most collectors I have met buy all colors and not just one. That is a different concept than collecting most other patterns.

	Crystal	Green, Pink
Basket, 5½", hdld.	20.00	25.00
Bowl, 5½", hdld.	18.00	20.00
Bowl, 5⅞", square nappy	22.00	28.00
Bowl, 6⅜", round, 2¼" deep nappy	15.00	20.00
Bowl, 6¾", round, 2¼" deep nappy	17.50	22.50
Bowl, 7⅜", round, 2" shallow nappy	20.00	25.00

	Crystal	Green, Pink
Bowl, 7⅝", round, 1⅞" shallow nappy	20.00	25.00
Creamer	15.00	18.00
Plate, 8½", scalloped rim	20.00	25.00
Plate, 8⅝", plain rim	22.00	28.00
Sugar	15.00	18.00

REPRODUCTIONS

NEW "ADAM," PRIVATELY PRODUCED OUT OF KOREA THROUGH ST. LOUIS IMPORTING COMPANY
ONLY THE ADAM BUTTER DISH HAS BEEN REPRODUCED.

The reproduction Adam butter dish is finally off the market as far as I can determine. Identification of the reproduction is easy. Do not use any of the following information for any piece of Adam save the butter dish.

Top: Notice the veins in the leaves.

New: Large leaf veins do not join or touch in center of leaf.

Old: Large leaf veins all touch or join the center vein.

A further note about the original Adam butter dish: the veins of all the leaves at the center of the design are very clear cut and precisely moulded; in the new, these center leaf veins are very indistinct and almost invisible in one leaf of the center design.

Bottom: Place butter dish bottom upside down for observation. Square it, flat side, to your body.

New: Four arrowhead-like points line up in northwest, northeast, southeast, and southwest directions of compass. These points head in the wrong directions from old. There are very bad mould lines and a very glossy light pink color on the butter dishes I examined.

Old: Four arrowhead-like points line up in north, east, south, and west directions of compass.

NEW "AVOCADO," INDIANA GLASS COMPANY Tiara Exclusives Line, 1974 – 1980s
Colors: pink, green, and fifteen additional colors never made originally

In 1979, a green Avocado pitcher was reproduced. It was darker than the original green and was a limited hostess gift item. Yellow pieces are all recently made. Yellow was never made originally.

The old pink color Indiana made was a delicate, attractive pink. The first reproduced pink pitcher appeared in 1973. The newer, tends to be more orange than the original color. The other colors shown pose little threat since none of those colors was made originally.

I understand that Tiara sales counselors told potential customers that their newly made glass was collectible because it was made from old moulds. I do not share this view. I feel it's like saying that since you were married in your grandmother's wedding dress, you will have the same happy marriage for the 57 years she did. All you can truly say is that you were married in her dress. I think all you can say about the new Avocado is that it was made from the old moulds. Time, scarcity, and people's whims determine collectibility as far as I'm able to determine it. It has taken nearly 50 years or more for people to turn to collecting Depression glass — and that's done, in part, because of what we call the "nostalgia factor" — everyone remembers it; they had some in their home at one time or another; it has universal appeal. Who is to say what will be collectible in the next 50 years? If we knew, we could all get rich! Now, that Tiara is out of business, perhaps some of their wares will become collectible. Unhappily, there are many collectors who were taken in by some of this glass being represented as old, and most of them have long enough memories to avoid it during their generation.

If you like Tiara products then of course buy them; but don't do so depending upon their being collectible. You have an equal chance, I feel, of going to Las Vegas and depending upon getting rich at the blackjack table.

NEW "CAMEO"
Colors: green, pink, cobalt blue (shakers); yellow, green, and pink (children's dishes)

I hope you can still see how very weak the pattern is on this reproduction shaker. It was originally made by Mosser Glass Company in Ohio, but is now being made overseas. In addition, you can see how much glass remains in the bottom of the shaker; and, of course, the new tops all make this easy to spot at the market. These were to be bought wholesale at around $6.00 but did not sell well. An importer made shakers in pink, cobalt blue, and a terrible green color. These, too, are weakly patterned. They were never originally made in the blue, but beware of pink.

Children's dishes in Cameo (called "Jennifer" by the manufacturer) pose no problem to collectors since they were never made originally. These, also made by Mosser, are scale models of the larger size. This type of production I have no quarrel with since they are not made to dupe anyone.

There are over 50 of these smaller pieces; thus, if you have a piece of glass that looks like a miniature (child's) version of a larger piece of Cameo, then you probably have a newly manufactured item.

REPRODUCTIONS

NEW "CHERRY BLOSSOM"

Colors: pink, green, blue, Delphite, cobalt, red, and iridized colors

Use information provided only for the piece described. Do not apply the information on the tumbler for the pitcher, etc. Realize that with various importers now reproducing glass, there are more modifications than I can possibly scrutinize for you. Know your dealer and *hope* he knows what he is doing.

Due to all the altered reproductions of the same pieces over and over, please understand this is only a guide as to what you should look for when buying. We've now seen some reproductions of those reproductions. All the items pictured on the next page are easy to spot as reproductions once you know what to look for with the possible exception of the 13" divided platter pictured in the center. It's too heavy, weighing 2¾ pounds, and has a thick ⅜" of glass in the bottom; but the design isn't too bad. The edges of the leaves aren't smooth; but neither are they serrated like old leaves.

There are many differences between old and new scalloped bottom, AOP Cherry pitchers. The easiest way to tell the difference is to turn the pitcher over. The branch crossing the bottom of my old Cherry pitchers looks like a branch. It's knobby and gnarled and has several leaves and cherry stems directly attached to it. One variation of the new pitcher just has a bald strip of glass cutting the bottom of the pitcher in half. Further, the old Cherry pitchers have a plain glass background for the cherries and leaves in the bottom of the pitcher. In the new pitchers, there's a rough, filled in, straw-like background. You see no plain glass.

As for the new tumblers, look at the ring dividing the patterned portion of the glass from the plain glass lip. The old tumblers have three indented rings dividing the pattern from the plain glass rim. The new has only one. Again, the pattern at the bottom of the new tumblers is brief and practically nonexistent in the center curve of the glass bottom. The pattern, when there is one, mostly hugs the center of the foot.

two-handled tray — old: 1⅞ lb.; ³⁄₁₆" glass in bottom; leaves and cherries east/west from north/south handles (some older trays were rotated so this is not always true); leaves have real spine and serrated edges; cherry stems end in triangle of glass. **new:** 2⅛ lb.; ¼" glass in bottom; leaves and cherries north/south with the handles; canal type leaves (but uneven edges; cherry stem ends before canal shaped line).

cake plate — new: color too light pink; leaves have too many parallel veins that give them a feathery look; arches at plate edge don't line up with lines on inside of the rim to which the feet are attached.

8½" bowl — new: crude leaves with smooth edges; veins in parallel lines.

cereal bowl — new: wrong shape, looks like 8½" bowl, small 2" center. **old:** large center; 2½" inside ring; nearly 3½" if you count the outer rim before the sides turn up.

dinner plate — new: smooth-edged leaves, fish spine type center leaf portion; weighs one pound plus; feels thicker at edge with mould offset lines clearly visible. **old:** center leaves look like real leaves with spines, veins, and serrated edges; weighs ¾ pound; clean edges; no mould offset (a slight step effect at the edge).

cup — new: area in bottom left free of design; canal centered leaves; smooth, thick top to cup handle (old has triangle grasp point).

saucer — new: offset mould line edge; canal leaf center.

The Cherry child's cup (with a slightly lopsided handle) having the cherries hanging upside-down when the cup was held in the right hand appeared in 1973. After I reported this error, it was quickly corrected by re-inverting the inverted mould. These later cups were thus improved in design but slightly off color. The saucers tended to have slightly off center designs, too. Next came the child's butter dish that was never made by Jeannette. It was essentially the child's cup without a handle turned upside-down over the saucer and having a little glob of glass added as a knob for lifting purposes.

Pictured are some of the colors of butter dishes made so far. Shaker reproductions were introduced in 1977 and some were dated '77 on the bottom. Shortly afterward, the non-dated variety appeared. How can you tell new shakers from old — should you get the one in a million chance to do so?

First, look at the tops. New tops could indicate new shakers. Next, notice the protruding edges beneath the tops. In the new they are squared off juts rather than the nicely rounded scallops on the old. The design on the newer shakers is often weak in spots. Finally, notice how far up inside the shakers the solid glass (next to the foot) remains. The newer shakers have almost twice as much glass in that area. They appear to be ¼ full of glass before you ever add the salt.

In 1989, a new distributor began making reproduction glass in the Far East. He made shakers in cobalt blue, pink, and a hideous green, that is no problem to spot. These shakers are similar in quality to those made before. However, the present pink color is good; yet the quality and design of each batch could vary greatly. Realize that only two original pairs of pink Cherry shakers have ever been found and those were discovered before any reproductions were made in 1977.

Butter dishes are naturally more deceptive in pink and green since those were the only original colors. The major flaw in the new butter is that there is one band encircling the bottom edge of the butter top; there are two bands very close together along the skirt of the old top.

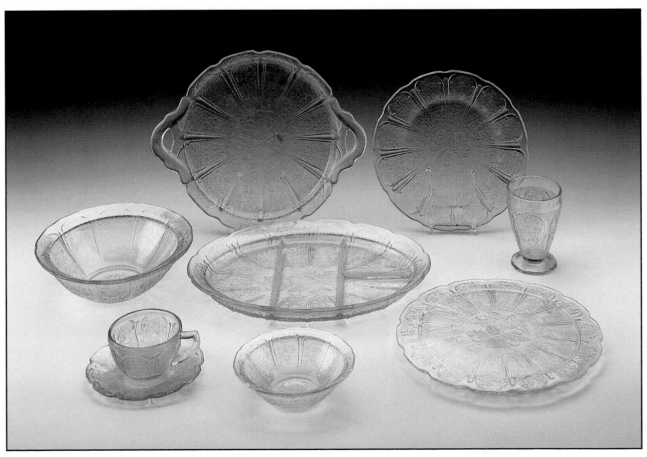

REPRODUCTIONS

NEW "FLORAL," IMPORTING COMPANY OUT OF GEORGIA

Reproduction Floral shakers can now be found in pink, red, cobalt blue, and a dark green color. Cobalt blue, red, and the dark green Floral shakers are of little concern since they were never made in those colors originally. The green is darker than the original green, but not as deep as forest green. The pink shakers are not only a very good pink, but they are also a very good copy. There are many minor variations in design and leaf detail to someone who knows glassware well; but the easy way to tell the Floral reproductions is to take off the top and look at the threads where the lid screws onto the shaker. On the old, there is a pair of parallel threads on each side or a least a pair on one side, which end right before the mold seams down each side. The new Floral has one continuous line thread that starts at one side and continues around the shaker until it ends above the beginning line on the other side. There is approximately one inch of overlapped thread making two lines for that inch; but the whole thread is one continuous line and not two separate ones as on the old. No other Floral reproductions have been made as of May 2003.

NEW "FLORENTINE" NO. 1, IMPORTING COMPANY OUT OF GEORGIA

Although a picture of a reproduction shaker is not shown, I would like you to know it exists.
Florentine No. 1 shakers have been reproduced in pink, red, and cobalt blue. There may be other colors to follow. No red or cobalt blue Florentine No. 1 shakers have ever been found, so those colors are no problem. I have only examined one reproduction shaker, and it is difficult to know if all shakers will be as badly molded as this is. There is little or no design on the bottom. I compared the pink shaker to several old pairs. The old shakers have a major open flower on each side. There is a top circle on this blossom with three smaller circles down each side. The seven circles form the outside of the blossom. The new blossom looks more like a strawberry with no circles forming the outside of the blossom. This repro blossom looks like a poor drawing. Do not use the Floral thread test for the Florentine No. 1 shakers, however. It won't work for Florentine although the same importing company out of Georgia makes these.

NEW "FLORENTINE" NO. 2, IMPORTING COMPANY OUT OF GEORGIA

A reproduced footed Florentine No. 2 pitcher and footed juice tumbler appeared in 1996. First to surface was a cobalt blue set that alerted knowledgeable collectors that something was strange. Next, sets of red, dark green, and two shades of pink began to be seen at the local flea markets. All these colors were dead giveaways since the footed Florentine No. 2 pitcher was never made in any of those shades.

The new pitchers are approximately ¼" shorter than the original and have a flatter foot as opposed to the domed foot of the old. The mold line on the lip of the newer pitcher extends ½" below the lip while only ⅜" below on the original. All of the measurements could vary over time with the reproductions and may even vary on the older ones. The easiest way to tell the old from the new, besides color, is by the handles. The new handles are ⅞" wide, but the older ones were only ¾" wide. That ⅛" seems even bigger than that when you set them side by side as shown below.

The juice tumbler differences are not as apparent; but there are two. The old juice stands 4" tall and the diameter of the base is 2⅛". The reproduction is only 3¹⁵⁄₁₆" tall and 2" in base diameter.

REPRODUCTIONS

NEW "IRIS," IMPORTING COMPANY

New Iris iced tea tumblers have two distinct differences. First, turn these upside down and feel the rays on the foot. New rays are very sharp and will almost cut your finger if you press on them hard. Old tumbler rays are rounded and feel smooth in comparison. The paneled design on the new tumbler gets very weak in several places as you rotate it in you hand. Old tumbler paneled designs stay bold around the entire tumbler.

New dinner plates have two characteristics. The extreme edge of the pattern on the new dinners is pointed outward (upside down V). Old dinner plate designs usually end looking like a stack of the letter V, though optical illusions sometimes distort that a bit. In addition, the inside rim of the new dinner slopes inward toward the center of the plate, whereas original inside rims are almost perpendicular and steeper sided against the center portion of the plate.

New flat tumblers do not have herringbone in the bottom pattern design. There are other differences, especially the crystal, clear color of the new ones; however, missing herringbone is the easiest to observe.

In the fall of 2000, several large lots of Iris coasters appeared on an Internet auction site. All of these coasters had origins in Ohio and were like the tumblers and dinner plates in one major respect. The crystal color was too good. If you take any old piece of Iris and place it on a white background, it will have a gray or yellow tint to it. If you place the new dinner plates or iced tea tumblers on white, they have no tinted hue of any sort. The coasters are the same — no tint. The other sure-fire way to tell these newer coasters is to look from the side across the coaster edge. New ones look half-full of glass or slightly over. The older ones are only a quarter-full of glass. You can keep up with current reproductions through a website where I have posted pictures. Go to www.glassshow.com and then the Reading Room. Click on Reproductions for the latest information available.

Iris 6½" footed ice tea tumblers (new on left).

New flat tumblers (left) do not have herringbone in the pattern. There are many other minor differences, but that is the easiest to observe.

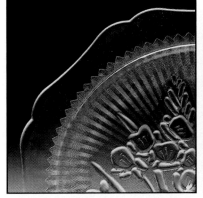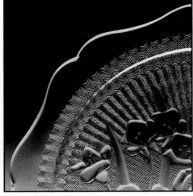

Iris dinner plate (new on left).

247

Iris coasters (new on right).

REPRODUCTIONS

NEW "MADRID" CALLED "RECOLLECTION," RECENTLY BEING MADE

I hope you have already read about Recollection Madrid on page 124. Indiana Glass made Madrid in teal after making it in blue, pink, and crystal. This light teal color was never made originally, so there is no problem of it being confused with old. The teal was sold through all kinds of outlets ranging from better department stores to discount catalogs. In the past couple of years, we have received several ads stating that this is genuine Depression glass made from old moulds. None of this is made from old glass moulds unless you consider 1976 old. Most of the pieces are from moulds never made originally.

The light blue was a big seller for Indiana according to reports I am receiving around the country. It is a brighter, more fluorescent looking blue than the soft, original color. More and more of it is turning up in antique malls. Buy it if you like it; just don't pay antique prices for it.

Look at the picture below. Only the cup, saucer, and oval vegetable were ever made in old Madrid. The new grill plate has one division splitting the plate in half, but the old had three sections. A goblet or vase was never made. The vase is sold with a candle making it a hurricane lamp. The heavy tumbler was placed on top of a candlestick to make this a vase/hurricane lamp. That candlestick gets a workout. It was attached to a plate to make a pedestal cake stand and to a butter dish to make a preserve stand. That's a clever idea, actually. You would not believe the mail spawned by those last two, newly manufactured pieces.

The shakers are short and heavy and you can see an original style pictured on page 124. The latest item I have seen is a heavy 11-ounce flat tumbler being sold in a set of four or six called "On the Rocks." The biggest giveaway to this newer pink glass is the pale, washed out color.

The only concerns in new pink Madrid pieces are the cups, saucers, and oval vegetable bowl. These three pieces were made in pink in the 1930s. None of the others shown were ever made in the 1930s in pink; so realize that when you see the butter dish, dinner plate, soup bowl, or sugar and creamer. These are new items. Once you have learned what this washed-out pink looks like by seeing these items for sale, the color will be a clue when you see other pieces.

The least difficult piece for new collectors to tell new from old is the candlestick. The new ones all have three raised ridges inside to hold the candle more firmly. Old ones do not have any inside ridges. You may even find new candlesticks in black.

REPRODUCTIONS

NEW "MAYFAIR," IMPORTING COMPANY

Colors: pink, green, blue, cobalt (shot glasses), 1977; pink, green, amethyst, cobalt blue, red (cookie jars), 1982; cobalt blue, pink, amethyst, red, and green (odd shade), shakers 1988; green, cobalt, pink, juice pitchers, 1993

Only the pink shot glass need cause any concern for collectors because that glass was not made in any other color originally. At first glance, the color of the newer shots is often too light pink or too orange. Dead giveaway is the stem of the flower design, however. In the old that stem branched to form an "A" shape at the bottom; in the new, you have a single stem. Further, in the new design, the leaf is hollow with the veins moulded in. In the old, the leaf is moulded in and the veining is left hollow. In the center of the flower on the old, dots (anther) cluster entirely to one side and are rather distinct. Nothing like that occurs in the new design.

As for the cookie jars, at cursory glance the base of the cookie has a very indistinct design. It will feel smooth to the touch, because it's so faint. In the old cookie jars, there's a distinct pattern that feels like raised embossing to the touch. Next, turn the bottom upside-down. The new bottom is perfectly smooth. The old bottom contains a 1¾" mould circle rim that is raised enough to catch your fingernail in it. There are other distinctions as well; but that is the quickest and easiest way to tell old from new.

In the Mayfair cookie lid, the new design (parallel to the straight side of the lid) at the edge curves gracefully toward the center "V" shape (rather like bird wings in flight); in the old, that edge is a flat straight line going into the "V" (like airplane wings sticking straight out from the side of the plane as you face it head on).

The green color of the cookie, as you can see from the picture, is not the pretty, yellow/green color of true green Mayfair. It also doesn't glow under black light as the old green does; so, that is a simple test for green.

The corner ridges on the old Mayfair shaker rise half way to the top and then smooth out. The new shaker corner ridges rise to the top and are quite pronounced. The measurement differences are listed below, but the diameter of the opening is the critical and easiest way to tell old from new.

	OLD	NEW
Diameter of opening	¾"	⅝"
Diameter of lid	⅞"	¾"
Height	4¹⁄₁₆"	4"

OLD   **NEW**

Mayfair juice pitchers were reproduced in 1993. The old pitchers have a distinct mould circle on the bottom that is missing on the newly made ones. This and the oddly applied handles on the repros make these easily spotted. The blue pitcher is the old one in the photos.

OLD   **NEW**

REPRODUCTIONS

NEW "MISS AMERICA"

Colors: crystal, green, pink, ice blue, red amberina, cobalt blue

Miss America reproduction creamers and sugars are smaller than the originals; Miss America was not made in cobalt, but other colors have followed. These creamer and sugars are poorly made. There are many bubbles in the glass of the ones I have seen.

The reproduction butter dish in the Miss America design is probably the best of the newer products; yet there are three differences to be found between the original butter top and the newly made ones. The obvious thing is how the top knob sticks up away from the butter caused by a longer than usual stem at the knob.

Pick up the top of the new dish and feel up inside it. If the butter top knob is filled with glass so that it is convex (curved outward), the dish is new; the old inside knob area is concave (curved inward).

Finally, from the underside, look through the top toward the knob. In the original butter dish, you would see a perfectly formed multi-sided star; in the newer version, you see distorted rays with no visible points.

Miss America shakers have been made in green, pink, cobalt blue, and crystal. The latest copies of shakers are becoming more difficult to distinguish from the old. The measurements given below for shakers do not hold true for all the latest reproductions. It is impossible to know which generation of shaker reproductions that you will encounter, so you have to be careful on these.

New shakers most likely will have new tops; but since some old shakers have been given new tops, that isn't conclusive at all. Unscrew the lid. Old shakers have a very neatly formed ridge of glass on which to screw the lid. It overlaps a little and has rounded off ends. Old shakers stand 3⅜" tall without the lid. Most new ones stand 3¼" tall. Old shakers have almost a forefinger's depth inside (female finger) or a fraction short of 2½". Most new shakers have an inside depth of 2", about the second digit bend of a female's finger. (I'm doing finger depths since most of you will carry those with you to the flea market, rather than a tape measure.) In men, the old shaker's depth covers my knuckle; the new shaker leaves my knuckle exposed. Most new shakers simply have more glass on the inside of the shaker — something you can spot from 12 feet away. The hobs are more rounded on the newer shaker, particularly near the stem and seams; in the old shaker, these areas remained pointedly sharp.

New Miss America tumblers have ½" of glass in the bottom, have a smooth edge on the bottom of the glass with no mould rim, and show only two distinct mould marks on the sides of the glass. Old tumblers have only ¼" of glass in the bottom, have a distinct mould line rimming the bottom of the tumbler, and have four distinct mould marks up the sides of the tumbler.

New Miss America pitchers (without ice lip only) are all perfectly smooth rimmed at the top edge above the handle. All old pitchers that I have seen have a hump in the top rim of the glass above the handle area, rather like a camel's hump. The very bottom diamonds next to the foot in the new pitchers squash into elongated diamonds. In the old pitchers, these get noticeably smaller, but they retain their diamond shape.

NEW "ROYAL LACE," IMPORTING COMPANY

Colors: Cobalt blue

The first thing you notice about the reproduced pieces of Royal Lace is the harsh, extra dark, vivid cobalt blue color or the orange cast to the pink. It is not the soft cobalt blue originally made by Hazel Atlas. So far, only the cookie jar, juice, and water tumblers have been made as of May 2003.

The original cookie jar lid has a mould seam that bisects (cuts in half) the center of the pattern on one side, and runs across the knob and bisects the pattern on the opposite side. There is no mould line at all on the reproduction.

There are a multitude of bubbles and imperfections on the bottom of the new cookie jar that I am examining. The bottom is poorly moulded and the pattern is extremely weak. Original bottoms are plentiful anyway; learn to distinguish the top and it will save you money.

As for tumblers, the first reproduction tumblers had plain bottoms without the four-pointed design. The new juice tumbler has a bottom design, but it is as large as the one on the water tumbler and covers the entire bottom of the glass. Originally, this design was very small and did not encompass the whole bottom, as does this reproduction. Additionally, there are design flaws on both size tumblers that stand out. The four ribs between each of the four designs on the side of the repro tumblers protrude far enough to catch your fingernail. The original tumblers

have a very smooth, flowing design that you can only feel. The other distinct flaw is a semi-circular design on the rim of the glass above those four ribs. Originally, these were very tiny on both tumblers with five oval leaves in each. There are three complete diamond-shaped designs in the new tumblers with two being doubled diamonds (diamond shapes within diamonds); and the semi-circular design almost touches the top rim. There's at least an ⅛" of glass above the older fan.

Also, on the bottom of the tumblers, the four flower petal center designs in the old is open-ended leaving ⅛" of open glass at the tip of each petal. In the new version, these ends are closed, causing the petals to be pointed on the end.

NEW "SHARON," PRIVATELY PRODUCED 1976...(continued page 253)

Colors: blue, dark green, light green, pink, cobalt blue, opalescent blue, red, burnt umber

A blue Sharon butter turned up in 1976 and turned my phone line to liquid fire. The color was Mayfair blue — a fluke and dead giveaway as far as real Sharon is concerned. The original mastermind of reproductions did not know his patterns very well and mixed up Mayfair and Sharon. (He admitted that when I talked to him.)

When Sharon butters are found in colors similar to the old pink and green, you can immediately tell that the new version has more glass in the top where it changes from pattern to clear glass. It is a thick, defined ring of glass as opposed to a thin, barely defined ring of glass in the old. The knob of the new dish tends to stick up more. In the old butter dish, there is barely room to fit your finger to grasp the knob. The new butter dish has a sharply defined ridge of glass in the bottom around which the top sits. The old butter has such a slight rim that the top easily scoots off the bottom.

In 1977 a cheese dish appeared having the same top as the butter and having all the flaws inherent in that top which were discussed in detail above. However, the bottom of this dish was wrong. It was about half way between a flat plate and a butter dish bottom — bowl shaped; and it was very thick, giving it an awkward appearance. The real cheese bottom was a salad plate (not bowl) with a rim of glass for holding the top inside that rim. These round bottomed cheese dishes are but a parody of the old and are easily spotted.

REPRODUCTIONS

NEW "SHARON" (continued)

Some of the latest reproductions in Sharon are a too-light-pink creamer and sugar with lid. They are pictured with the "Made in Taiwan" label. These retail for around $15.00 for the pair and are easy to spot as reproductions. I'll just mention the most obvious differences. Turn the creamer so you are looking directly at the spout. In the old creamer, the mould line runs dead center of that spout; in the new, the mould line runs decidedly to the left of center spout.

On the sugar, the leaves and roses are "off" but not enough to describe it to new collectors. Therefore, look at the center design, both sides, at the stars located at the very bottom of the motif. A thin leaf stem should run directly from that center star upward on both sides. In this new sugar, the stem only runs from one; it stops way short of the star on one side; or look inside the sugar bowl at where the handle attaches to the bottom of the bowl; in the new bowl, this attachment looks like a perfect circle; in the old, its an upside down "v"-shaped teardrop.

As for the sugar lid, the knob of the new lid is perfectly smooth as you grasp its edges. The old knob has a mould seam running mid circumference (equator). You could tell these two lids apart blindfolded.

While there is a slight difference between the height, mouth-opening diameter, and inside depth of the old Sharon shakers and those newly produced, I will not attempt to upset you with those sixteenths and thirty-seconds of an inch of difference. It is safe to say that in physical appearance, they are very close. However, when documenting design on the shaker, they are miles apart.

The old shakers have true appearing roses. The flowers really look like roses. On the new shakers, the roses appear as poorly drawn circles with wobbly concentric rings. The leaves are not as clearly defined on the new shakers as the old are. However, forgetting all that, in the old shakers, the first design you see below the lid is a rose bud. It is angled like a rocket shooting off into outer space with three leaves at the base of the bud (where the rocket fuel would burn out). In the new shakers, this bud has become four paddles of a windmill. It is the difference between this ✼ and this ✺.

New "Sharon" candy dishes have been made in pink, green, cobalt blue, red, and opaque blue that goes to opalescent. These candy jars are among the easiest items to discern old from new. Pick up the lid and look from the bottom side. On the old there is a 2" circle ring platform below the knob; on the new, that ring of glass below the knob is only ½". This shows from the top also but it is difficult to measure with the knob in the center. There are other major differences, but this one will not be easily corrected. The bottoms are also simple to distinguish. The base diameter of the old bottom is 3¼" and the new is only 3". On the example I have, quality of the new is rough, poorly shaped and moulded; but I do not know if that will hold true for all reproductions of the candy. I hope so.

OTHER BOOKS BY GENE FLORENCE

Collectible GLASSWARE from the 40s, 50s, and 60s, 7th Edition *Gene Florence*

Gene Florence, the foremost authority on glassware, has produced a revamped edition of *Collectible Glassware from the 40s, 50s, and 60s.* Covering collectible glassware made after the Depression era, this is the only book available that deals exclusively with the handmade and mass-produced glassware from this period. It is completely updated, featuring many original company catalog pages and 19 new patterns — making a total of 121 patterns from Anniversary to Yorktown, with many of the most popular Fire-King patterns in between. Each pattern is alphabetically listed, all known pieces in each pattern are described and priced, and gorgeous color photographs showcase both common and very rare pieces. Florence's descriptive text offers insights into and evaluations of each pattern's history, popularity, and value on today's exciting collectibles market. 2004 values.

Item #6325 • ISBN: 1-57432-351-2 • 8½ x 11 • 256 Pgs. • HB • $19.95

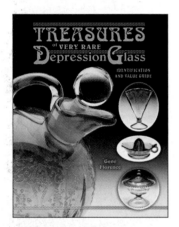

Treasures of VERY RARE DEPRESSION GLASS *Gene Florence*

Our *Very Rare Glassware of the Depression Years* books have been bestsellers for many years, helping collectors spot those rare and valuable pieces of Depression glass that may come around once in a lifetime. Rarity can be determined by an unusual color or pattern; many pieces here are one of a kind or can be found only in limited quantities. This new book features over 1,000 rare examples of Depression items, as well as elegant and kitchen items. It features many famous glass companies, including Duncan & Miller, Federal, Fostoria, Fenton, A.H. Heisey, Hocking, Imperial, Jeannette, Paden City, Tiffin, and more. Values are given for these rare items. The essential information and experience that Florence provides in his books will help you know what to look for in your glass searches and teach you to be an informed collector. 2003 values.

Item #6241• ISBN: 1-57432-336-9 • 8½ x 11 • 368 Pgs. • HB • $39.95

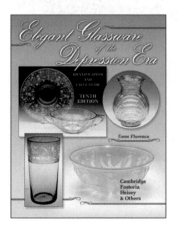

ELEGANT GLASSWARE of the Depression Era, 10th Edition *Gene Florence*

This new edition holds hundreds of new photographs, listings, and updated values. This book features the handmade and acid-etched glassware that was sold in department and jewelry stores from the Depression era through the 1950s, not the dimestore and give-away glass known as Depression glass. As always, glassware authority Gene Florence has added many new discoveries, 10 additional patterns, and re-photographed many items from the previous books. Large group settings are included for each of the more than 100 patterns, as well as close-ups to show pattern details. The famous glassmakers presented include Fenton, Cambridge, Heisey, Tiffin, Imperial, Duncan & Miller, U.S. Glass, and Paden City. Florence provides a list of all known pieces, with colors and measurements, along with 2003 values.

Item #6125 • ISBN: 1-57432-298-2 • 8½ x 11 • 240 Pgs. • HB • $24.95

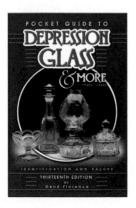

Pocket Guide to DEPRESSION GLASS & More, 13th Edition *Gene Florence*

Gene Florence has completely revised his *Pocket Guide to Depression Glass* with over 4,000 values updated to reflect the ever-changing market. Many of the photographs have been reshot to improve the quality and add new finds. There are a total of 119 new photos for this edition, including 29 additional patterns that have not appeared in previous editions. These gorgeous photographs show great detail, and the listings of the patterns and their available pieces make identification simple. There is even a section on re-issues and the numerous fakes flooding the market. This is the perfect book to take with you on your searches through shops and flea markets and is the ideal companion to Florence's comprehensive *Collector's Encyclopedia of Depression Glass.* 2003 values.

Item #6136 • ISBN: 1-57432-309-1 • 5½ x 8½ • 224 Pgs. • PB • $12.95

Anchor Hocking's FIRE-KING & More, 2nd Edition
Gene Florence

From the 1940s to the 1970s Anchor Hocking Glass Corp. of Lancaster, Ohio, produced an extensive line of glassware called Fire-King. Their lines included not only dinnerware but also a plethora of glass kitchen items — reamers, measuring cups, mixing bowls, mugs, and more. This is the essential collectors' reference to this massive line of glassware. Loaded with hundreds of new full-color photos, vintage catalog pages, company materials, facts, information, and values, this book has everything collectors expect from Gene Florence. 2002 values.

Item #5602 • ISBN: 1-57432-164-1 • 8½ x 11 • 224 Pgs. • HB • $24.95

Glass CANDLESTICKS of the Depression Era
Gene Florence

Florence has compiled this book to help identify the candlestick patterns made during the Depression era. More than 500 different candlesticks are shown in full-color photographs. The book is arranged according to color: amber, black, blue, crystal, green, iridescent, multicolor, pink, purple, red, smoke, white, and yellow. Many famous glassmakers are represented, such as Heisey, Cambridge, Fostoria, and Tiffin. The descriptive text for each candleholder includes pattern, maker, color, height, and current collector value. A helpful index and bibliography are also provided. 2000 values.

Item #5354 • ISBN: 1-57432-136-6 • 8½ x 11 • 176 Pgs. • HB • $24.95

KITCHEN GLASSWARE of the Depression Years, 6th Edition
Gene Florence

This exciting new edition of our bestselling *Kitchen Glassware of the Depression Years* is undeniably the definitive reference on the subject. More than 5,000 items are showcased in beautiful professional color photographs with descriptions and values. Many new finds and exceptionally rare pieces have been added. The highly collectible glass from the Depression era through the 1960s fills its pages, in addition to the ever-popular Fire-King and Pyrex glassware. This comprehensive encyclopedia provides an easy-to-use format, showing items by color, shape, or pattern. The collector will enjoy the pages of glass, from colorful juice reamers, shakers, and rare and unusual glass knives to the mixing bowls and baking dishes we still find in our kitchen cupboards. 2003 values.

Item #5827 • ISBN: 1-57432-220-6 • 8½ x 11 • 272 Pgs. • HB • $24.95

Florence's Glassware
PATTERN IDENTIFICATION Guide
Gene Florence

Florence's Glassware Pattern Identification Guides are great companions for his other glassware books. Volume I includes patterns featured in his *Collector's Encyclopedia of Depression Glass, Collectible Glassware from the 40s, 50s, and 60s,* and *Collector's Encyclopedia of Elegant Glassware,* as well as many more — nearly 400 patterns in all. Volume II holds nearly 500 patterns, with no repeats from Volume I. Volume III also showcases nearly 500 patterns with no repeats from the previous volumes. Carefully planned close-up photographs of representative pieces for every pattern show great detail to make identification easy. With every pattern, Florence provides the names, the companies which made the glass, dates of production, and even colors available. These guides are ideal references for novice and seasoned glass collectors and dealers, and great resources for years to come. No values.

Vol. I • Item #5042 • ISBN: 1-57432-045-9 • 8½ x 11 • 176 Pgs. • PB • $18.95
Vol. II • Item #5615 • ISBN: 1-57432-177-3 • 8½ x 11 • 208 Pgs. • PB • $19.95
Vol. III • Item #6142 • ISBN: 1-57432-315-6 • 8½ x 11 • 272 Pgs. • PB • $19.95

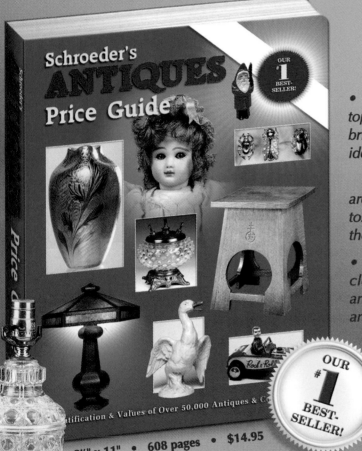